ASIAN DEVELOPMENT
OUTLOOK

APRIL 2024

ASIAN DEVELOPMENT BANK

© 2024 Asian Development Bank
6 ADB Avenue, Mandaluyong City, 1550 Metro Manila, Philippines
Tel +63 2 8632 4444; Fax +63 2 8636 2444
www.adb.org

Some rights reserved. Published in 2024.

ISBN 978-92-9270-657-9 (print); 978-92-9270-658-6 (PDF); 978-92-9270-659-3 (ebook)
ISSN 0117-0481 (print), 1996-725X (PDF)
Publication Stock No. FLS240221-3
DOI: http://dx.doi.org/10.22617/FLS240221-3

Notes:
In this publication, "$" refers to US dollars.
ADB recognizes "Hong Kong" as Hong Kong, China; "China" as the People's Republic of China; "Korea" and "South Korea" as the Republic of Korea; "Russia" as the Russian Federation; and "Vietnam" as Viet Nam.

Cover design by Anthony Victoria.

Cover artwork rendered by Samantha Ty licensed exclusively to ADB © 2024 "Collision" Samantha Ty.

CONTENTS

PART 3

Statistical Appendix   269

FOREWORD

Prospects for Asia and the Pacific remain strong as the post-pandemic recovery continues, with growth projected at 4.9% in both 2024 and 2025. Despite a property-driven slowdown in the People's Republic of China, healthy domestic demand in many economies—including in South and Southeast Asia—will drive the region's expansion. At the same time, challenges remain.

This year's *Asian Development Outlook* highlights the region's vulnerability to escalating geopolitical tensions and conflict, which could disrupt supply chains and reignite inflationary pressures. The report also documents how public debt has stabilized in many economies following pandemic-related stimulus, but debt levels remain higher than before the pandemic. Elevated interest rates and slow revenue growth continue to pose a challenge to public finances throughout the region.

Policies aimed at boosting the region's resilience to external shocks will be key. Governments in the region must calibrate and coordinate fiscal and monetary policies. With development partners, they must continue to support regional cooperation on trade and investment to strengthen supply chains. They must also strengthen social safety nets for the most vulnerable populations and bolster energy and food security.

Moreover, policymakers in the region should ensure that reduced fiscal space does not lead to further delays in supporting priority areas. This includes infrastructure projects needed to support growth and substantial green investments to decarbonize economies and adapt to climate change. Policymakers must mobilize revenues and reorient spending toward these priorities, including by reducing fossil fuel subsidies, which remain significant in some regional economies. To help meet these investment requirements, policymakers must also focus on mobilizing the private sector.

I am confident that *Asian Development Outlook April 2024* will offer valuable insights for the region's policymakers as they navigate the road ahead. The Asian Development Bank remains committed to supporting these efforts as we build a more prosperous, inclusive, resilient, and sustainable Asia and the Pacific.

MASATSUGU ASAKAWA
President
Asian Development Bank

ACKNOWLEDGMENTS

Asian Development Outlook (ADO) April 2024 was prepared by staff of the regional departments and resident missions of the Asian Development Bank (ADB) under the guidance of the Economic Research and Development Impact Department (ERDI). Representatives of these departments met regularly as the Regional Economic Outlook Task Force to coordinate and develop consistent forecasts for the region.

Abdul Abiad, director of the Macroeconomics Research Division led the production of this report, assisted by Priscille Villanueva and Edith Laviña. Jerome Abesamis, Emmanuel Alano, Shiela Camingue-Romance, David Keith De Padua, Nedelyn Magtibay-Ramos, Jesson Pagaduan, Homer Pagkalinawan, Melanie Quintos, Pilipinas Quising, Mia Andrea Soriano, Dennis Sorino, Michael Timbang, and Mai Lin Villaruel provided technical and research support. Economic editorial advisors Robert Boumphrey, Eric Clifton, Joshua Greene, and Reza Vaez-Zadeh made substantial contributions to the chapters of Part 2.

The support and guidance of ADB Chief Economist Albert Park, Deputy Chief Economist Joseph E. Zveglich Jr., and Deputy Director General Chia-Hsin Hu are gratefully acknowledged.

Authors who contributed the sections are bylined in each chapter. The subregional coordinators were Lilia Aleksanyan, Kenji Takamiya, and Rene Cris Rivera for the Caucasus and Central Asia; Akiko Terada-Hagiwara and Dorothea Ramizo for East Asia; Rana Hasan for South Asia; James Villafuerte and Dulce Zara for Southeast Asia; and Kaukab Naqvi and Cara Tinio for the Pacific.

Peter Fredenburg and Guy Daniel Sacerdoti edited *ADO April 2024*. Prince Nicdao and Glenda Cortez did the typesetting and graphics. Art direction for the cover was by Anthony Victoria, with artwork from Samantha Ty. Kevin Nellies designed the landing page for ADO. Heili Ann Bravo, Dyann Buenazedacruz, Fermirelyn Cruz, and Elenita Pura provided administrative and logistical support. A team from the Department of Communications and Knowledge Management, led by David Kruger and Terje Langeland, planned and coordinated the dissemination of *ADO April 2024*.

DEFINITIONS AND ASSUMPTIONS

The economies discussed in *Asian Development Outlook April 2024* are classified by major analytic or geographic group. For the purposes of this report, the following apply:

- **Association of Southeast Asian Nations** (ASEAN) comprises Brunei Darussalam, Cambodia, Indonesia, the Lao People's Democratic Republic, Malaysia, Myanmar, the Philippines, Singapore, Thailand, and Viet Nam. ASEAN 4 are Indonesia, Malaysia, the Philippines, and Thailand.

- **Developing Asia** comprises the 46 members of the Asian Development Bank listed below by geographic group.

- **Caucasus and Central Asia** comprises Armenia, Azerbaijan, Georgia, Kazakhstan, the Kyrgyz Republic, Tajikistan, Turkmenistan, and Uzbekistan.

- **East Asia** comprises Hong Kong, China; Mongolia; the People's Republic of China; the Republic of Korea; and Taipei,China.

- **South Asia** comprises Afghanistan, Bangladesh, Bhutan, India, Maldives, Nepal, Pakistan, and Sri Lanka.

- **Southeast Asia** comprises Brunei Darussalam, Cambodia, Indonesia, the Lao People's Democratic Republic, Malaysia, Myanmar, the Philippines, Singapore, Thailand, Timor-Leste, and Viet Nam.

- **The Pacific** comprises the Cook Islands, the Federated States of Micronesia, Fiji, Kiribati, the Marshall Islands, Nauru, Niue, Palau, Papua New Guinea, Samoa, Solomon Islands, Tonga, Tuvalu, and Vanuatu.

Unless otherwise specified, the symbol "$" and the word "dollar" refer to US dollars.

A number of assumptions have been made for the projections in *Asian Development Outlook April 2024*. The policies of domestic authorities are maintained. Real effective exchange rates remain constant at their average from 1 February–31 March 2024. The average price of oil is $82/barrel in 2024 and $79/barrel in 2025. The 6-month London interbank offered rate for US dollar deposits averages 5.2% in 2023 and 4.2% in 2024, the European Central Bank refinancing rate averages 4.2% in 2024 and 3.1% in 2025, and the Bank of Japan's overnight call rate averages 0.0% in 2024 and 0.1% in 2025.

All data in *Asian Development Outlook April 2024* were accessed from 1 February–31 March 2024.

ABBREVIATIONS

ADB	Asian Development Bank
ADO	Asian Development Outlook
AI	artificial intelligence
AIS	Automatic Identification System
ASEAN	Association of Southeast Asian Nations
BDI	Baltic Dry Index
BNM	Bank Negara Malaysia
bp	basis point
COFA	Compact of Free Association
CDF	Constituency Development Fund
COVID-19	coronavirus disease
CPI	consumer price index
DOC	Department of Customs
DRM	domestic resource mobilization
DSR	debt-to-service ratio
ECB	European Central Bank
EU	European Union
FDI	foreign direct investment
FOMC	Federal Open Market Committee
FSC	Financial Services Commission
FY	fiscal year
FSM	Federated States of Micronesia
GBA	Greater Bay Area
GDP	gross domestic product
GEDS	Green Economy Development Strategy
GFT	garments, footwear, and travel goods
GST	goods and services tax
GVC	global value chain
H	half
HKG	Hong Kong, China
IMF	International Monetary Fund
JKN	National Health Insurance (Indonesia)
Lao PDR	Lao People's Democratic Republic
LDC	least-developed country
LNG	liquefied natural gas
LGFV	local government financing vehicle
M2	broad money supply
NFRK	National Fund for the Republic of Kazakhstan
NDVI	Normalized Difference Vegetation Index
OPEC	Organization of the Petroleum Exporting Countries

mb/d	million barrels a day
MSMEs	micro, small, and medium-sized enterprises
NDC	nationally determined contribution
PMI	purchasing managers' index
pp	percentage point
PPP	public–private partnership
PRC	People's Republic of China
Q	quarter
qoq	quarter on quarter
ROK	Republic of Korea
RPC	Regional Processing Centre (Nauru)
saar	seasonally adjusted annualized rate
SBV	State Bank of Viet Nam
SDR	special drawing right
US	United States of America
VAT	value-added tax
WCI	World Container Index
WTO	World Trade Organization
yoy	year on year
ytd	year to date

ADO APRIL 2024
HIGHLIGHTS

Growth in developing Asia will remain robust this year, in spite of uncertainty in the external environment. The end of interest rate hiking cycles in most economies as well as continued recovery in goods exports from an upturn in the semiconductor cycle will support growth. India's investment-driven growth will underpin South Asia's outlook this year. For the region, the outlook is broadly positive, with developing Asia forecast to grow by 4.9% in 2024 and 2025. Inflation will moderate to 3.2% in 2024 and 3.0% in 2025. Policymakers, however, should monitor several downside risks.

Escalating conflict and geopolitical tensions could disrupt supply chains and amplify commodity price volatility. Risks related to the path of United States monetary policy, property market stress in the People's Republic of China, and the effects of adverse weather-related events are other pressure points for the region. Policymakers should step up efforts to promote resilience by continuing to enhance trade, cross-border investment, and commodity supply networks.

Albert F. Park
Chief Economist
Asian Development Bank

Robust Growth amid Uncertain External Prospects

- **Developing Asia's growth momentum continued during 2023, driven by domestic demand.** Strong consumption and investment which accelerated during the second half of the year supported economic activity. Growth varied across subregions, however. In East Asia, growth rebounded to 4.7% in 2023 from 2.9% in 2022, as the People's Republic of China (PRC) removed all pandemic-related mobility restrictions early in the year. By contrast, economic contractions in Pakistan and Sri Lanka moderated growth in South Asia from 6.6% in 2022 to 6.4% last year. Growth in Southeast Asia also slowed to 4.1%. Growth fell by more than half in the Pacific as the contraction in Papua New Guinea's resource sector more than offset the tourism-related recovery in the subregion's island economies. Meanwhile, growth in the Caucasus and Central Asia increased marginally to 5.3% from 5.2% in 2022.

- **External demand remained fragile last year as goods exports bottomed out before semiconductors turned the corner in the fourth quarter.** Export growth for high-income technology exporters turned positive in the last quarter of 2023, rising by 5.4% as demand for semiconductors and electronics began to gain traction. The Republic of Korea and Hong Kong, China recorded the strongest gains, while the PRC also performed well.

- **Tourism revenues increased further, while remittances largely stabilized. International tourism continued to recover, reaching 73% of pre-pandemic levels by the end of 2023.** Both travel receipts and international arrivals rose. Tourism-dependent economies drove the recovery across the region, with some economies—Armenia, Maldives, Fiji, and Samoa—surpassing pre-pandemic levels. Remittances to South Asia, Southeast Asia, and the Pacific increased marginally, while money transfers to the Caucasus and Central Asia were volatile given the uncertainty over the evolving Russian invasion of Ukraine.

- **Financial markets performed well, overcoming spikes in global risk aversion.** Equity markets across developing Asia climbed gradually during 2023. Better-than-expected economic growth and the gradual end of monetary tightening cycles contributed to easing financial conditions. Higher global risk aversion in September over persistent US inflation concerns led to some tightening in the region, but financial conditions eased again when the US Federal Reserve signaled a pause in rate hikes from November. Reflecting positive market sentiment in the region, sovereign bond yields declined, risk premia narrowed, currencies stabilized, and net portfolio investment flows were positive in 2023. The pattern has continued into 2024, despite some uncertainty on the timing of the US Federal Reserve's expected monetary policy easing.

- **Inflation continued to moderate, but for the region excluding the PRC, both headline and core inflation remain elevated relative to pre-pandemic levels.** Monetary policy tightening in 2022–2023 and the further easing of some supply-side pressures helped to gradually stabilize prices. Excluding the PRC, however, regional food inflation remains high, contributing 2.7 percentage points to overall inflation in 2023—just over double its pre-pandemic contribution. In particular, rice prices have risen due to adverse weather conditions and export restrictions, which has increased food inflation in some economies. The PRC ended 2023 in deflationary territory, primarily driven by lower food prices.

- **Growth in developing Asia will remain healthy at 4.9% in 2024 and 2025, despite a slowdown in the PRC**. While growth in the PRC will decline from 5.2% in 2023 to 4.8% this year and 4.5% next year, it will accelerate in the rest of developing Asia—from 4.8% in 2023 to 5.0% this year and 5.3% in 2025. The slowdown in the PRC will be driven by the weak property market and amplified by fading domestic consumption growth after last year's reopening. In the rest of developing Asia, faster growth will be driven by domestic demand and some improvement in semiconductor and services exports, including tourism.

- **Stronger growth in South Asia and Southeast Asia will offset lower growth in other subregions.** India is expected to affirm its position as a major growth engine within Asia, driven by strong investment, recovering consumption, and gains in electronics and services exports. Macroeconomic stabilization in Pakistan and Sri Lanka will bring positive growth this year, accelerating in 2025. In Southeast Asia, domestic demand and the remaining post-pandemic tourism rebound will support growth. In the Caucasus and Central Asia, however, growth will normalize after the record-high 2022–2023 levels driven by spillovers from the Russian invasion of Ukraine. And in the Pacific, gains in Papua New Guinea due to the reopening of its main gold mine will be offset by more normal tourism growth in Fiji and some other Pacific island economies, following last year's sharp rebound.

- **Inflation is forecast to drop further as monetary policies remain relatively tight despite some easing.** Developing Asia's inflation is projected to fall from 3.3% in 2023 to 3.2% in 2024 and 3.0% in 2025. In most subregions, the decline will come from lower global inflationary pressures and more stable fuel prices. While most central bank hiking cycles are complete and some have started to ease, policy rates remain high. As a result, real interest rates have increased due to the drop in forecast inflation. The lagged effects of tight monetary policy and higher agricultural production will also mitigate inflation dynamics in South Asia, Southeast Asia, and the Caucasus and Central Asia.

- **Public debt relative to GDP has stabilized across much of developing Asia, but it remains high compared to pre-pandemic levels and vulnerable to higher-for-longer interest rates.** Improved growth has helped lower debt ratios. In addition, stabilization policies and reforms under International Monetary Fund programs have alleviated debt distress risks in crisis-affected economies such as Sri Lanka and Pakistan, although challenges remain in sustaining reforms given the substantial debt servicing costs. Conditions are improving in two other high-risk economies, Maldives and Mongolia, but have deteriorated in the Lao People's Democratic Republic due to the significant depreciation of the kip. High global interest rates will remain a significant concern for economies in the region given high debt levels.

- **An escalation in conflict and geopolitical tensions would worsen regional prospects.** Trade and shipping routes have been disrupted since October due to ongoing conflicts in the Middle East. Attacks on vessels transiting through the Red Sea have led to supply chain disruptions and the re-routing of cargo ships to avoid the area, a key trading route connecting Europe and Asia. Shipping costs have more than doubled, affecting trade and boosting price pressures, although the current spikes are just half of those seen during the 2021–2022 supply disruptions. Analysis in this report suggests that the recent spike in shipping costs could add half a percentage point to inflation in developing Asia this year. Further escalation could rekindle inflation and potentially weigh on the region's growth outlook through tighter monetary and financial conditions.

■ **The path of US monetary policy poses risks.** While the Federal Reserve is expected to start loosening its monetary policy stance in mid-2024, uncertainty remains. Slower-than-expected disinflation in the US could delay easing. While the risk tilts toward delayed easing, faster-than-expected disinflation could trigger loosening earlier, thus supporting the growth outlook. Analysis in this report indicates that higher-for-longer rates and tighter global financial conditions would marginally affect prices in developing Asia via imported inflation, whereas the impact on regional growth would be more muted.

■ **Intensified property market stress in the PRC could affect the region's outlook.** A worse-than-expected deterioration in the PRC's property market would further dampen consumer sentiment and domestic demand. A protracted and severe downturn would negatively affect the growth outlook, with potential spillovers to trading partners.

■ **Adverse weather and climatic conditions could threaten the outlook.** The average global surface temperature in January 2024 was the highest on record for the month. Temperatures were above average across most of Asia as well, exacerbated by El Niño. These climatic changes lead to more frequent and extreme weather events that can threaten agriculture and other sectors. The consequences could be particularly severe in low-income economies, where agriculture usually accounts for a significant share of the economy, and where food insecurity is more acute.

Asia's Artificial Intelligence-Driven Semiconductors Revival

■ **The artificial intelligence (AI) boom is driving the rebound in Asia's semiconductor industry, with some variation across economies depending on their specialization.** A *Special Topic* in this report assesses recent developments. The Republic of Korea is seeing rapidly growing AI-related demand for memory chips, for which it is a leading global manufacturer and which accounted for around 50% of its total semiconductor exports in 2023. Taipei,China, another key global semiconductor manufacturer, has so far been less affected by AI-driven shifts in demand given its specialization in more diverse semiconductor applications. Other East Asian economies are aiming to boost production of advanced microchips, while Southeast Asia may also profit from the AI boom through increased demand for testing and packaging.

GDP Growth Rate and Inflation, % per year

	GDP Growth				Inflation			
	2022	2023	2024	2025	2022	2023	2024	2025
Developing Asia	**4.3**	**5.0**	**4.9**	**4.9**	**4.4**	**3.3**	**3.2**	**3.0**
Developing Asia excluding the PRC	**5.5**	**4.8**	**5.0**	**5.3**	**6.8**	**6.3**	**5.1**	**4.4**
Caucasus and Central Asia	**5.2**	**5.3**	**4.3**	**5.0**	**12.9**	**10.5**	**7.9**	**7.0**
Armenia	12.6	8.7	5.7	6.0	8.6	2.0	3.0	3.5
Azerbaijan	4.6	1.1	1.2	1.6	13.9	8.8	5.5	6.5
Georgia	10.4	7.0	5.0	5.5	11.9	2.5	3.5	4.0
Kazakhstan	3.2	5.1	3.8	5.3	15.0	14.5	8.7	6.3
Kyrgyz Republic	9.0	6.2	5.0	4.5	13.9	10.8	7.0	6.5
Tajikistan	8.0	8.3	6.5	6.5	4.2	3.8	5.5	6.5
Turkmenistan	6.2	6.3	6.5	6.0	11.2	5.9	8.0	8.0
Uzbekistan	5.7	6.0	5.5	5.6	11.4	10.0	10.0	9.5
East Asia	**2.9**	**4.7**	**4.5**	**4.2**	**2.3**	**0.6**	**1.3**	**1.6**
Hong Kong, China	–3.7	3.2	2.8	3.0	1.9	2.1	2.3	2.3
Mongolia	5.0	7.0	4.1	6.0	15.2	10.4	7.0	6.8
People's Republic of China	3.0	5.2	4.8	4.5	2.0	0.2	1.1	1.5
Republic of Korea	2.6	1.4	2.2	2.3	5.1	3.6	2.5	2.0
Taipei,China	2.6	1.3	3.0	2.7	2.9	2.5	2.3	2.0
South Asia	**6.6**	**6.4**	**6.3**	**6.6**	**8.0**	**8.4**	**7.0**	**5.8**
Afghanistan	–20.7	–6.2	...	...	7.8	10.8	...	...
Bangladesh	7.1	5.8	6.1	6.6	6.2	9.0	8.4	7.0
Bhutan	5.2	4.0	4.4	7.0	5.6	4.2	4.5	4.2
India	7.0	7.6	7.0	7.2	6.7	5.5	4.6	4.5
Maldives	13.9	4.4	5.4	6.0	2.3	2.9	3.2	2.5
Nepal	5.6	1.9	3.6	4.8	6.3	7.7	6.5	6.0
Pakistan	6.2	–0.2	1.9	2.8	12.2	29.2	25.0	15.0
Sri Lanka	–7.3	–2.3	1.9	2.5	46.4	17.4	7.5	5.5
Southeast Asia	**5.7**	**4.1**	**4.6**	**4.7**	**5.3**	**4.1**	**3.2**	**3.0**
Brunei Darussalam	–1.6	1.4	3.7	2.8	3.7	0.4	1.1	1.0
Cambodia	5.2	5.0	5.8	6.0	5.3	2.1	2.0	2.0
Indonesia	5.3	5.0	5.0	5.0	4.1	3.7	2.8	2.8
Lao People's Democratic Republic	2.5	3.7	4.0	4.0	23.0	31.2	20.0	7.0
Malaysia	8.7	3.7	4.5	4.6	3.4	2.5	2.6	2.6
Myanmar	2.4	0.8	1.2	2.2	27.2	22.0	15.5	10.2
Philippines	7.6	5.6	6.0	6.2	5.8	6.0	3.8	3.4
Singapore	3.8	1.1	2.4	2.6	6.1	4.8	3.0	2.2
Thailand	2.5	1.9	2.6	3.0	6.1	1.2	1.0	1.5
Timor-Leste	4.0	1.9	3.4	4.1	7.0	8.4	3.5	2.9
Viet Nam	8.0	5.0	6.0	6.2	3.2	3.3	4.0	4.0
The Pacific	**7.9**	**3.5**	**3.3**	**4.0**	**5.2**	**3.0**	**4.3**	**4.1**
Cook Islands	10.5	13.3	9.1	5.2	3.6	13.2	2.3	2.3
Federated States of Micronesia	–0.6	2.6	3.1	2.8	5.0	5.3	4.1	3.5
Fiji	20.0	7.8	3.0	2.7	4.3	2.4	3.7	2.6
Kiribati	3.9	4.2	5.3	3.5	5.3	9.7	4.0	3.0
Marshall Islands	–0.7	2.5	2.7	1.7	3.2	6.5	5.5	3.7
Nauru	2.8	1.6	1.8	2.0	1.5	5.2	10.3	3.5
Niue	...	...	...	...	3.1	8.6	...	...
Palau	–1.7	–0.2	6.5	8.0	13.2	12.4	5.5	1.0
Papua New Guinea	5.2	2.0	3.3	4.6	5.3	2.3	4.5	4.8
Samoa	–5.3	8.0	4.2	4.0	8.8	12.0	4.5	4.3
Solomon Islands	–4.2	2.5	2.2	2.2	5.4	4.6	3.2	2.7
Tonga	–2.2	2.8	2.6	2.3	8.2	9.7	4.5	4.2
Tuvalu	0.7	3.9	3.5	2.4	12.2	7.2	3.0	3.0
Vanuatu	2.0	1.0	3.1	3.6	6.7	13.5	4.8	2.9

... = not available, GDP = gross domestic product, PRC = People's Republic of China.

Notes: The current uncertain situation permits no forecasts for Afghanistan. ADB placed on hold its regular assistance in Afghanistan effective 15 August 2021. Effective 1 February 2021, ADB placed a temporary hold on sovereign project disbursements and new contracts in Myanmar.

Source: *Asian Development Outlook* database.

1

ROBUST GROWTH AMID UNCERTAIN EXTERNAL PROSPECTS

ROBUST GROWTH AMID UNCERTAIN EXTERNAL PROSPECTS

Growth in developing Asia remained strong in 2023, driven by robust consumption and investment, which helped act as a buffer against subdued global demand. _High-income technology exporters performed well toward the end of 2023 as the global cycle for semiconductors turned upwards. Financial conditions eased by the end of the year, following a bout of tightening from August to November as disinflation stalled in the United States (US). As investor sentiment improved, the region attracted net portfolio inflows in 2023. Meanwhile, inflation continued to moderate._

Developing Asia's growth outlook remains resilient this year despite an uncertain external environment. _With central banks pausing or reversing interest rate hikes in most economies, growth in the region will be supported by robust domestic demand. A continued recovery in goods exports and tourism is expected. Stronger growth in South Asia and Southeast Asia will offset slower expansion in other parts of the region this year and next, with India's investment-led growth driving South Asia. Developing Asia is forecast to grow by 4.9% in 2024 and 2025. Inflation will continue to gradually moderate, falling from 3.3% last year to 3.2% in 2024 and 3.0% in 2025._

Policymakers in developing Asia should remain vigilant with several downside risks to the outlook. _Conflicts and geopolitical tensions could escalate, leading to disruptions in supply chains and greater commodity price volatility. Uncertainty over the path of US monetary policy, intensified property market weakness in the People's Republic of China, and the effects of extreme weather events could also hamper the regional outlook._

This section was written by Abdul Abiad, John Beirne (lead), Shiela Camingue-Romance, David Keith De Padua, Jaqueson K. Galimberti, Jules Hugot, Matteo Lanzafame (colead), Nedelyn Magtibay-Ramos, Yuho Myoda, Homer Pagkalinawan, Pilipinas Quising, Shu Tian, and Mai Lin Villaruel of the Economic Research and Development Impact Department, ADB, Manila.

Growth Momentum Continues as Inflation Eases

Developing Asia's economy expanded by 5.0% in 2023 from 4.3% in 2022, but growth was uneven across subregions. Growth in East Asia rebounded to 4.7% in 2023, thanks to the lifting of pandemic-related domestic mobility restrictions in the People's Republic of China (PRC) in early 2023. By contrast, growth moderated from 6.6% in 2022 to 6.4% last year in South Asia as Pakistan and Sri Lanka contracted. Southeast Asia's expansion also slowed, from 5.7% to 4.1%, as weaker external demand contributed to slower growth in nine of the subregion's 11 economies. For the Pacific, growth more than halved to 3.5% last year as a weak resource sector in Papua New Guinea outweighed tourism-related recoveries in the subregion's island economies. Meanwhile, growth in the Caucasus and Central Asia increased marginally to 5.3% last year from 5.2% in 2022.

Strong domestic demand shielded many economies from external challenges (Figure 1.1.1A). Consumption remained strong in the second half of 2023 as consumer confidence improved. Investment was resilient overall, with strengthening investment activity in India; Indonesia; and Hong Kong, China offsetting weaknesses in the Republic of Korea (ROK); Singapore; Taipei,China; and Thailand. There are also signs that external demand is turning the corner. In particular, the contribution of net exports to growth in the ROK and Taipei,China turned from negative in the first half of 2023 to positive in the second half, as demand for semiconductors started to gain traction.

Industry rebounded in 2023, while services slightly moderated in the second half of the year (Figure 1.1.1B). Gradually strengthening manufacturing activity boosted industrial production in most economies. In the PRC, increased manufacturing of electrical devices contributed significantly to industrial growth. Notably, the production of electrical machinery such as solar cells grew robustly. After a lackluster performance in the first half, industrial

output rebounded in the ROK and was less negative in Singapore and Taipei,China, buoyed by rising global demand for electronics. Mining and construction improved in Indonesia and the Philippines, while larger declines in petrochemicals and other manufactures dented industrial activity in Thailand and Malaysia. Meanwhile, services slowed in the second half of the year, except in Hong Kong, China and Taipei,China, which benefited from improved tourism and retail trade.

Industrial production picked up considerably among high-income technology exporters. Some high-income technology exporters—with significant global shares in the production of semiconductor devices and electronic integrated circuits—benefited from the upward shift in the global semiconductor cycle (Figure 1.1.2). Industrial production in Indonesia, Malaysia, the Philippines, and Viet Nam saw modest growth in 2023. In Thailand, where export-oriented industries account for more than 60% of total production, output declined throughout the year. Industrial production among high-income technology exporters was also reflected in manufacturing purchasing managers' indexes (PMIs) (Table 1.1.1). Singapore's manufacturing PMI signaled increased activity in February 2024 for the sixth consecutive month. The ROK's PMI remained above the 50 threshold in both January and February, suggesting manufacturing had finally turned the corner after 16 months of below-50 readings ending October 2023. Overall, PMI readings for the first 2 months of 2024 were consistent with manufacturing gains across economies, with the exception of Malaysia; Thailand; and Taipei,China—which only partly benefited from the upturn in the semiconductor cycle (see *Special Topic on Asia's Rebounding Semiconductor Sector and the Role of Artificial Intelligence*). Available services PMIs are also improving, particularly in India and Sri Lanka, driven by continued expansion in personal services, hotel and accommodation, and financial services.

Figure 1.1.1 Contributions to Growth, Developing Asia, 2023

A. Demand-Side

Consumption and investment supported growth in 2023.

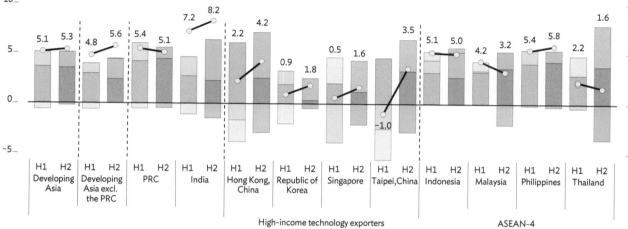

B. Supply-Side

Industry gained in most economies, led by India and the PRC.

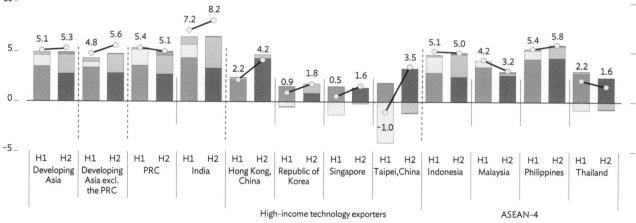

ASEAN = Association of Southeast Asian Nations, PRC = People's Republic of China, H = half.
Notes: Panel A excludes statistical discrepancies. Panel B excludes taxes and subsidies on imports. Developing Asia weighted using GDP (purchasing price parity).
Source: Haver Analytics.

Figure 1.1.2 Industrial Production

Industrial production picked up in part as electronic exports increased.

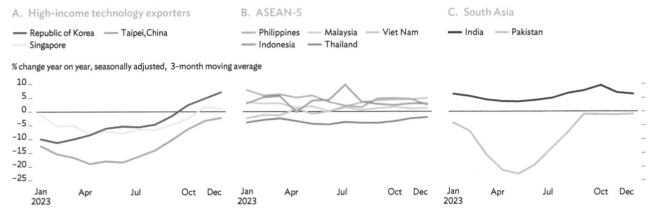

Note: Index refers to manufacturing production, except in India and Viet Nam where it includes mining.
Source: CEIC Data Company.

Table 1.1.1 Purchasing Managers' Index

Manufacturing activity is strengthening across economies, while services remains solid.

Manufacturing PMI, seasonally adjusted

| Economy | 2023 | | | | | | | | | | | | 2024 | |
| | Q1 | | | Q2 | | | Q3 | | | Q4 | | | Q1 | |
	Jan	Feb	Mar	Apr	May	Jun	Jul	Aug	Sep	Oct	Nov	Dec	Jan	Feb
India	55.4	55.3	56.4	57.2	58.7	57.8	57.7	58.6	57.5	55.5	56.0	54.9	56.5	56.9
Indonesia	51.3	51.2	51.9	52.7	50.3	52.5	53.3	53.9	52.3	51.5	51.7	52.2	52.9	52.7
Philippines	53.5	52.7	52.5	51.4	52.2	50.9	51.9	49.7	50.6	52.4	52.7	51.5	50.9	51.0
PRC	49.2	51.6	50.0	49.5	50.9	50.5	49.2	51.0	50.6	49.5	50.7	50.8	50.8	50.9
Republic of Korea	48.5	48.5	47.6	48.1	48.4	47.8	49.4	48.9	49.9	49.8	50.0	49.9	51.2	50.7
Singapore, *nsa*	49.8	50.0	49.9	49.7	49.5	49.7	49.8	49.9	50.1	50.2	50.3	50.5	50.7	50.6
Viet Nam	47.4	51.2	47.7	46.7	45.3	46.2	48.7	50.5	49.7	49.6	47.3	48.9	50.3	50.4
Malaysia	46.5	48.4	48.8	48.8	47.8	47.7	47.8	47.8	46.8	46.8	47.9	47.9	49.0	49.5
Taipei,China	44.3	49.0	48.6	47.1	44.3	44.8	44.1	44.3	46.4	47.6	48.3	47.1	48.8	48.6
Thailand	54.5	54.8	53.1	60.4	58.2	53.2	50.7	48.9	47.8	47.5	47.6	45.1	46.7	45.3

Services PMI, seasonally adjusted

India	57.2	59.4	57.8	62.0	61.2	58.5	62.3	60.1	61.0	58.4	56.9	59.0	61.8	60.6
PRC	52.9	55.0	57.8	56.4	57.1	53.9	54.1	51.8	50.2	50.4	51.5	52.9	52.7	52.5
Sri Lanka, *nsa*	50.2	48.7	55.1	49.6	53.5	56.7	59.5	57.6	54.7	56.2	59.4	58.9	60.1	...
Philippines, *nsa*	53.7	54.9	53.4	56.9	54.0	53.0	48.8	53.0	53.2	50.1	50.0	56.2	...	...

... = not available, nsa = not seasonally adjusted, PMI = purchasing managers' index, PRC = People's Republic of China, Q = quarter.

Notes: Pink to red indicates deterioration (<50) and white to green indicates improvement (>50). The series for Singapore, Sri Lanka, and the Philippines are not seasonally adjusted.

Source: CEIC Data Company.

Inflation continued to moderate, but for the region excluding the PRC both headline and core inflation remain elevated relative to pre-pandemic levels (Figure 1.1.3). Headline inflation in developing Asia continued to converge toward its pre-pandemic average, as the lagged impact of monetary policy tightening and easing of some supply-side pressures helped to stabilize prices gradually. Global energy and food prices (excluding rice) stabilized, leading to lower inflation for the energy and food components of the consumer price index (CPI). Excluding the PRC, however, regional food inflation remained relatively high, contributing 2.7 percentage points to overall inflation in 2023—just over double its pre-pandemic contribution. The effects of adverse weather on crop production, as well as food export restrictions in the region, drove domestic food prices higher in many economies. This happened across all subregions, except in the Pacific where domestic prices climbed more due to lower agricultural production. The PRC ended 2023 in deflationary territory, primarily due to lower food prices. Meanwhile, core inflation remained high in the region, driven largely by services, though with signs of easing in most economies.

Rising international rice prices pushed up food inflation, especially in import-reliant economies. On average, food accounts for around 33% of the overall CPI basket across the region, and rice alone for about 4.2% of the total. Thus, global food inflation strongly affects headline inflation in the region. For instance, the 15-year high surge in benchmark Thai rice prices in August 2023 subsequently led to large domestic rice price increases in economies where the share of rice in the overall consumption basket is high (Box 1.1.1).

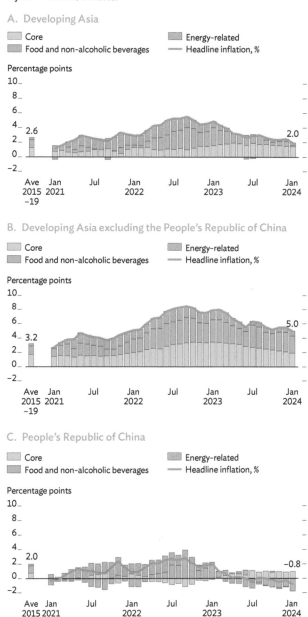

Figure 1.1.3 Contributions to Inflation by Food, Energy, and Core Price Basket, Developing Asia

Headline inflation in the region continues to moderate, but core inflation remains elevated.

A. Developing Asia

Notes: Core inflation excludes food and energy. Subregional averages are weighted using GDP purchasing price parity. Central Asia includes Armenia, Georgia, and Kazakhstan; East Asia includes Hong Kong, China; Mongolia; the People's Republic of China; the Republic of Korea; Taipei,China; South Asia includes India, Pakistan, Maldives, Nepal, and Sri Lanka; Southeast Asia includes Cambodia, Indonesia, the Lao People's Democratic Republic, Malaysia, the Philippines, Singapore, and Thailand; the Pacific includes Fiji and Tonga.

Sources: Haver Analytics; CEIC Data Company; official sources.

Box 1.1.1 The Challenges of High Rice Prices

Global rice prices started to surge in 2023.
Benchmark Thai rice prices soared from an average of $467/metric ton (mt) in December 2022 to $660/mt by January 2024, a substantial 41.3% increase (box figure 1). The last time the average monthly rice price exceeded this level was in September 2008. Despite a drop to $613/mt in March, prices remain 29% higher than in March 2023. The spike in 2008 was fueled by many factors, including export restrictions by key rice-exporting economies like India and Viet Nam, as well as panic buying by importing economies like the Philippines (ADB 2012). Similar factors are shaping current rice price dynamics.

1 Global Rice Prices

Rice prices have soared to their highest levels in 15 years.

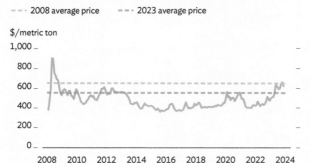

Notes: Data refer to average monthly price of Thai rice, 5%. 2024 data is up to March.
Source: World Bank Commodity Pink Sheet.

Export restrictions, weather abnormalities, and stockpiling contributed to the surge. India, the world's largest rice exporter, plays an important role in shaping the rice market. In July 2023, the Indian government banned non-basmati white rice exports to stabilize domestic food prices by ensuring adequate domestic supply. This had far-reaching implications for the world's rice trade, with India accounting for more than 40% of global rice exports. In addition, adverse weather affected rice production in various regions, further pushing up prices. Temperatures in Asia were the second highest on record in 2023, and the unusually dry weather in South and Southeast Asia affected agricultural productivity (NCEI 2024; FAO 2023, 2024). In the Philippines, for example, the National Disaster Risk Reduction and Management Council

in its 11 March 2024 report indicated that El Niño had already cost ₱1.2 billion ($22 million) in crop damage across much of the country.[a] Similarly, the Office of Agricultural Economics of Thailand, in its 4–10 March 2024 Production and Market Situation Report, highlighted the decline in cultivated land area attributed to El Niño. The shortage of rain and water led farmers in specific regions to abandon their fields and restrict rice cultivation to just once a year. Insufficient rainfall also hampered seedling germination and growth, and triggered outbreaks of disease and pests. Fears over the protracted El Niño effect on domestic food security also contributed to the global price increase as importers stockpiled rice.

As global rice prices increased, domestic rice prices followed suit. In some economies, government policies helped mitigate the pass-through effect of global rice price increases to domestic rice prices. However, the effectiveness of these policies can be limited, especially in the face of significant exchange rate fluctuations or other domestic factors affecting production and supply. For instance, between December 2022 and December 2023, benchmark Thai rice prices rose by 37.9%, but domestic retail prices skyrocketed by more than 80% in Myanmar, 70% in Pakistan, and close to 50% in the Lao People's Democratic Republic. Wholesale rice prices also increased by around 50% in Viet Nam and Cambodia. The Philippines, Indonesia, India, and Timor-Leste also saw double-digit increases over the same period (box table).

Importing economies where rice holds a large share of the CPI food basket were particularly exposed (box figure 2). Rice is fundamental to many Asian diets, accounting for up to 70% of the daily caloric intake and as much as 36% of the food price basket in certain economies. Low-income households typically spend more on rice and are thus more vulnerable to high rice prices, while rice shortages can severely impact food security, leading to malnutrition

---

[a]   El Niño is a climate pattern associated with rising surface temperatures in the central and eastern tropical Pacific Ocean (NOAA 2023). El Niño's opposite is La Niña, which is associated with cooler-than-average ocean surface temperatures. Both have the potential to significantly affect weather patterns, ocean conditions, and marine fisheries worldwide.

Box 1.1.1 *Continued*

Rice Inflation, Selected Developing Asian Economies, % year on year

Rice inflation increased in many economies, doubling in some since August 2023.

	Bangladesh	Brunei Darussalam	Cambodia	Hong Kong, China	India	Indonesia	Lao PDR	Malaysia	Myanmar	Pakistan	Papua New Guinea	Philippines	Republic of Korea	Singapore	Sri Lanka	Thailand	Timor-Leste	Viet Nam
Jan 2023	3.5	0.5	2.2	-1.2	10.4	8.5	53.7	0.7	58.9	61.3		2.7	-9.5	1.0	33.2	5.2	8.3	16.7
Feb	5.0	0.6	5.6	-3.1	11.2	11.0	54.1	0.9	59.4	70.8	9.2	2.2	-8.3	0.5	22.7	3.1	7.3	15.9
Mar	3.4	0.4	11.1	-3.2	11.5	12.7	54.6	1.3	57.4	74.1		2.5	-7.9	1.8	16.4	4.5	12.5	13.2
Apr	5.7	0.4	...	-1.2	11.4	13.5	51.2	1.0	...	77.3		2.9	-6.8	0.8	-5.7	4.6	9.9	19.5
May	5.0	0.7	...	-1.0	11.5	14.4	52.0	1.4	...	77.4	7.8	3.4	-4.8	5.0	-11.8	2.6	9.3	22.3
Jun	2.7	0.5	11.1	-1.1	12.0	15.1	46.0	1.4	78.8	80.4		3.6	-3.2	2.0	-19.4	1.9	10.3	23.7
Jul	-1.0	0.4	11.1	0.7	13.1	15.2	40.5	2.4	96.0	85.3		4.2	-0.8	1.7	-26.2	0.6	11.2	31.7
Aug	-4.6	0.5	22.2	-0.1	12.5	14.9	40.3	3.0	90.6	87.1	8.3	8.7	5.7	3.2	-20.1	2.1	15.1	62.4
Sep	-5.6	0.6	36.6	-0.1	11.9	17.7	38.9	5.0	71.4	87.9		17.8	11.2	4.8	-7.4	5.0	24.2	53.7
Oct	-4.4	0.3	36.9	0.0	11.6	19.8	38.8	5.3	60.8	85.5		13.2	15.3	5.4	-5.5	5.3	26.6	52.2
Nov	-4.5	0.6	...	-0.9	11.8	19.7	36.8	4.7	63.8	78.4	8.1	15.9	8.9	4.9	-1.5	5.7	27.9	49.2
Dec	-6.0	0.1	47.5	2.1	12.3	16.6	46.5	4.6	80.7	69.5		19.6	9.1	4.8	0.4	4.8	27.7	51.1
Jan 2024	...	-0.1	55.0	2.1	12.9	15.8	36.3	4.7	72.9	39.8	...	22.6	10.4	4.3	0.4	3.9	...	48.9
Feb	...	...	50.0	...	12.8	...	...	...	76.5	29.8	...	23.7	8.5	...	5.7	5.2	...	29.8

Color legend: ▢ < than 2%, ▢ between 2% and 5%, ▢ between 5% and 25%, ▣ > than 25%.

... = not available, Lao PDR = Lao People's Democratic Republic.

Notes: Rice inflation is based on rice consumer price indices, except for the following economies where it is proxied by the average retail prices of certain rice varieties or available data for major cities or provinces: Dhaka rice for Bangladesh, traditional rice for Indonesia, Colombo white rice for Sri Lanka, two rice varieties for Lao PDR, Yangon Emata rice for Myanmar, and the average price in Karachi for Pakistan. For Cambodia, rice inflation is estimated using the average wholesale price in Phnom Penh, and for Viet Nam, using different rice varieties in three provinces.

Sources: Staff calculations using data from official sources; Haver Analytics; Food and Agriculture Organization of the United Nations, Food Price Monitoring and Analysis Tool.

2 Cereals and Related Products, Percent Share of Food Price Basket, Selected Developing Asian Economies

Rice holds a substantial share of the food price basket in some economies.

■ Rice   ■ Wheat and other grains   ○ Cereals and related products

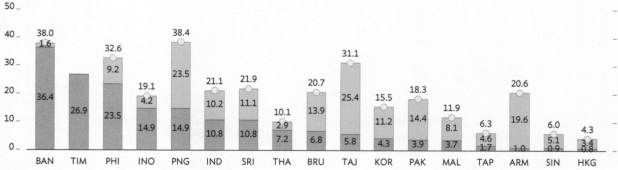

% of food CPI basket

ARM = Armenia; BAN = Bangladesh; BRU = Brunei Darussalam; CPI = consumer price index; HKG = Hong Kong, China; IND = India; INO = Indonesia; KOR = Republic of Korea; MAL = Malaysia; PAK = Pakistan; PHI = Philippines; PNG = Papua New Guinea; ROK = Republic of Korea; SIN = Singapore; SRI = Sri Lanka; TAP = Taipei,China; TAJ = Tajikistan; THA = Thailand; TIM = Timor-Leste.

Note: For Timor Leste, CPI weight data for wheat and other grains is not available.

Sources: Haver Analytics; official sources.

Box 1.1.1 *Continued*

and other health complications (Ludher and Teng 2023, Rosegrant et al. 2010). In Indonesia, the Philippines, and Timor Leste—three rice importers—the contribution of rice inflation to headline inflation increased, prompting governments to reassess their food security policies and interventions (box figure 3).

Several factors could keep rice prices high in 2024. The US National Oceanic and Atmospheric Administration forecasts El Niño will persist until the second quarter of this year, potentially transitioning into La Niña later in the year (Figure 1.3.2). This will likely add upward pressure on rice prices given rice's susceptibility to changes in temperature and precipitation and high risk of crop losses during El Niño (Cao et al. 2023). The dry conditions and insufficient monsoon rains are expected to reduce rice production for the 2023–2024 crop year, particularly in India, the PRC, and Thailand (box figure 4). To minimize the impact on crop yields, some economies reduced land available for rice cultivation. In Thailand, farmers were urged to plant less rice to conserve water amid low rainfall, while in Indonesia and the Philippines, some farmers delayed

planting to minimize crop losses. India's continuing ban and related restrictions on rice exports, as well as the geographic concentration of rice production and exports in Asia will also likely keep upward pressure on rice prices.

To manage surging rice prices, governments can implement both short- and medium-term measures (ADB 2024a, 2024b). In the short term, targeted subsidies for vulnerable populations can be used to ensure affordable rice access, along with enhancing market transparency and monitoring to prevent price manipulation and hoarding. In the medium term, establishing strategic rice reserves can stabilize prices during periods of volatility. Promoting integrated sustainable rice production, encouraging crop diversification, and investing in modern and innovative agricultural technology and infrastructure can raise productivity while fostering long-term price stability and food security. Collaborating with international organizations and neighboring economies can bolster regional cooperation in managing rice prices and their impact.

3 Contribution of Rice Inflation to Headline Inflation, Selected Developing Asian Economies

The contribution of rice inflation to overall inflation increased in 2023, particularly for rice importers.

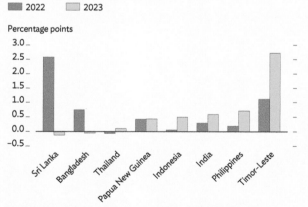

Notes: For India, rice refers to non-subsidized rice. For Bangladesh, rice inflation is proxied by retail prices of Dhaka rice; Indonesia, traditional rice; and Sri Lanka, white rice. Data for India are for calendar years.
Sources: Haver Analytics; official sources.

4 Change in Rice Production and Exports, 2023–2024 crop year vs. 2022–2023 crop year, Selected Developing Asian Economies

The strong El Niño in 2023 will likely reduce rice production and exports among the region's top rice producers and exporters.

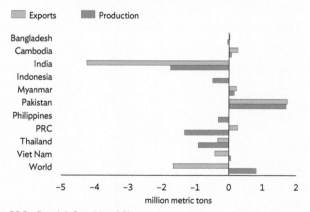

PRC = People's Republic of China
Source: US Department of Agriculture. Foreign Agricultural Service. Production, Supply and Distribution online database. PSD Online.

Box 1.1.1 *Continued*

References:
ADB (Asian Development Bank). 2024a. Emerging Food Security in Rice Markets and ADB's Responses. AFNR Sector Office Briefing Note.
——. 2024b. $500 Million ADB Loan to Support Philippine Agriculture Sector Reforms.
——. 2012. Enhancing ASEAN's Resiliency to Extreme Rice Price Volatility.
Cao, J., Z. Zhang, F. Tao, Y. Chen, X. Luo, and J. Xie. 2023. Forecasting Global Crop Yields Based on El Niño Southern Oscillation Early Signals. *Agricultural Systems*. 205, 103564.
FAO (Food and Agriculture Organization). 2023. AMIS Market Monitor. December.
——. 2024. AMIS Market Monitor. March.

Ludher, E. and P. Teng. 2023. Rice Production and Food Security in Southeast Asia under Threat from El Niño. *Yusof Ishak Institute Perspective*. Issue 2023, Number 53. July.
NCEI (National Centers for Environmental Information). 2024. Annual 2023 Global Climate Report.
NOAA (National Oceanic and Atmospheric Administration). 2023. Understanding El Niño.
Rosegrant, M. W., H. Bhandari, S. Pandey, and T. Sulser. 2010. Rice Price Crisis: Causes, Impacts, and Solutions. *Asian Journal of Agriculture and Development*. 7(2), 1–15.

This box was written by Pilipinas Quising and Shiela C. Romance of the Economic Research and Development Impact Department, ADB, Manila.

External Sector Regaining Momentum

Exports of goods bottomed out in 2023. After an initial spike following the PRC's reopening, developing Asia's growth in goods exports hit a new low in June, contracting by 13.7% relative to June 2022 (Figure 1.1.4). The sharp decline was partly due to strong base effects from the export peak in mid-2022 when the region experienced strong demand for work-from-home equipment. Also, a shift from goods to services spending as pandemic-related restrictions were lifted contributed to lower demand for goods exports. Despite the subdued external demand, exports slowly regained momentum in late 2023 and increased by an annual rate of 1.9% in November and 2.5% in December.

High-income technology exporters are leading the recovery. After a year in negative territory, export growth among high-income technology exporters turned positive during the last quarter of 2023, rising to 5.4%. A rebound in electronics drove much of the turnaround. High-income technology exporters added 1.5 percentage points to developing Asia's export growth, with Hong Kong, China and the ROK recording the strongest gains. The PRC also performed better toward the end of the year, as exports increased by 2.4% in December relative to December 2022. Similarly, export growth from the rest of developing Asia is trending upwards, but has yet to break into positive territory.

Early signs of a turnaround in electronics are strengthening. Electronics is the largest contributor to export revenues in the region, with its share fluctuating around 30% of total exports. While the electronics contraction since November 2022 dragged down export growth, the decline has been narrowing steadily since June 2023 (Figure 1.1.5, panel A). In November, electronics exports registered the first positive growth in more than a year, increasing by 3.2% over November 2022. This suggests that the global downturn in semiconductor demand may be over (see *Special Topic* on Asia's Rebounding Semiconductor Sector and the Role of Artificial Intelligence).

Figure 1.1.4 Nominal Goods Export Growth in Developing Asia

Goods exports growth is gradually recovering.

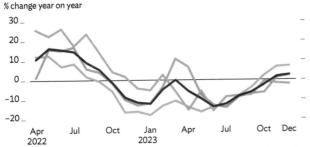

% change year on year

Notes: High-income technology exporters include Hong Kong, China; the Republic of Korea; Singapore; and Taipei,China.
Source: CEIC Data Company.

Figure 1.1.5 Sector Contributions to Nominal Goods Export Growth in Developing Asia

A. Developing Asia

The recovery in export growth is driven by electronics.

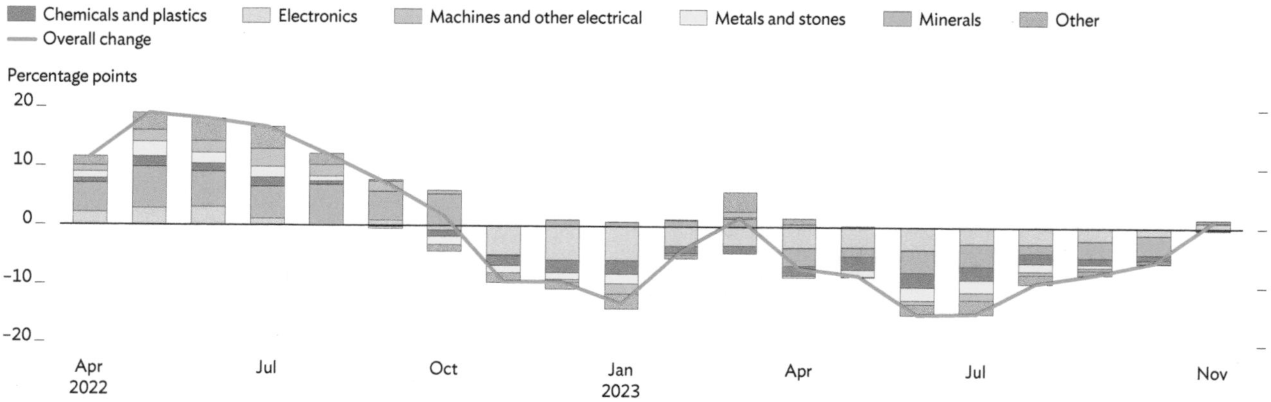
Chemicals and plastics
Electronics
Machines and other electrical
Metals and stones
Minerals
Other
Overall change
Percentage points
20
10
0
-10
-20
Apr
2022
Jul
Oct
Jan
2023
Apr
Jul
Nov

B. Caucasus and Central Asia

Lower oil prices reduced export revenues.

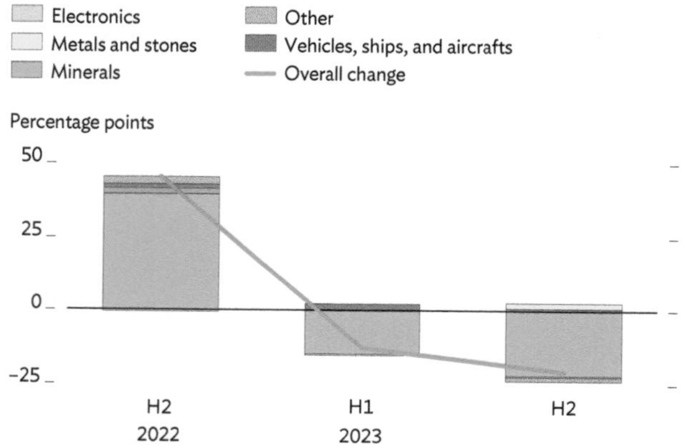
Electronics
Metals and stones
Minerals
Other
Vehicles, ships, and aircrafts
Overall change
Percentage points
50
25
0
-25
H2
2022
H1
2023
H2

C. East Asia

Electronics exports bottomed out.

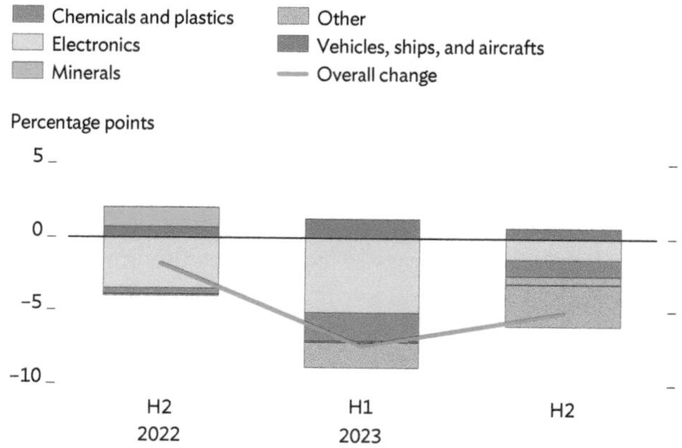
Chemicals and plastics
Electronics
Minerals
Other
Vehicles, ships, and aircrafts
Overall change
Percentage points
5
0
-5
-10
H2
2022
H1
2023
H2

D. South Asia

Exports of metals and precious stones picking up.

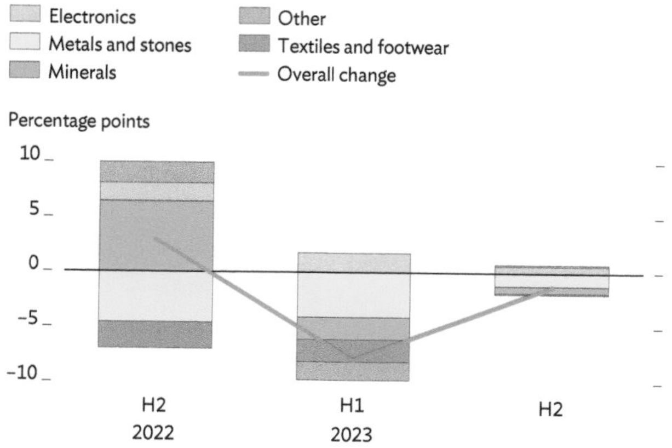
Electronics
Metals and stones
Minerals
Other
Textiles and footwear
Overall change
Percentage points
10
5
0
-5
-10
H2
2022
H1
2023
H2

E. Southeast Asia

Broad-based recovery in electronics lags.

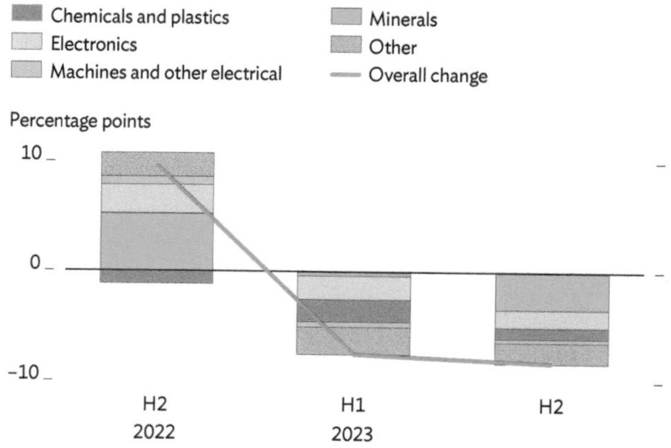
Chemicals and plastics
Electronics
Machines and other electrical
Minerals
Other
Overall change
Percentage points
10
0
-10
H2
2022
H1
2023
H2

H = half.

Notes: Growth rates are relative to the same period in the previous year. Caucasus and Central Asia include Armenia, Azerbaijan, Georgia, and Uzbekistan; East Asia includes Hong Kong, China; Mongolia; the People's Republic of China; Republic of Korea; and Taipei,China; South Asia includes India (Pakistan is not included due to a data lag); Southeast Asia includes Indonesia, Malaysia, the Philippines, Singapore, and Thailand; developing Asia is the aggregate of these economies (covering about 90% of the region's exports). H2 2023 growth rates are through November except for East Asia.

Sources: UN Comtrade; International Trade Center.

East Asia is driving the upturn in electronics exports, while Southeast Asia lags behind.
East Asia's exports of electronics bottomed out in the first half of 2023. The contribution of electronics to the subregion's export growth remained negative last year, but narrowed from –5.1 percentage points in the first half to –1.4 percentage points in the second half (Figure 1.1.5, panel C). The improvement was underpinned by increased sales of electronic integrated circuits from Hong Kong, China; the ROK; and the PRC. For Taipei,China, the upturn was driven by renewed downstream demand for computers and laptops, while smartphone exports from the PRC also rose. By contrast, Southeast Asia's exports of electronics contracted by 7.5% in 2023 (up to November) after a strong 19.1% expansion in 2022 (Figure 1.1.5, panel E). With the exception of Singapore, the subregion has been less involved in producing the AI and automotive chips driving the upturn in the semiconductor demand cycle. Southeast Asia still relies on a more broad-based recovery in electronic devices and appliances.

Lower oil prices significantly affected export revenues in the region. Following strong mineral exports in 2022, lower coal and oil prices reduced export revenues in the region by 3.2% in October 2023 compared with October 2022 (Figure 1.1.5, panel A). International Brent crude prices declined by 18.2% between 2022 and 2023 on average, while Newcastle/Port Kembla coal prices declined by 49.9%. These lower mineral prices strongly affected export values for the Caucasus and Central Asia. They also lowered nominal export values from Southeast Asia, especially for Indonesia where coal accounts for about 15% of goods exports (Figure 1.1.5, panels B and E). As the strong base price effects from 2022 subsided, mineral exports began to stabilize. In November, mineral exports in developing Asia increased by 4% relative to November 2022.

Metals and precious stone exports are picking up in South Asia. The contraction in exports of metals and precious stones was the biggest drag on India's exports in 2023, reducing total exports by 4.6 percentage points in the second half of 2022 and 4.1 percentage points in the first half of 2023 (Figure 1.1.5, panel D). For metals, steel exports have been limited by shifting production to meet domestic demand, where prices are higher due to import duties. Exports of diamonds

and jewelry also declined due to lower global demand—diamonds also faced supply constraints. These trends reversed in the second half of 2023, while other exports such as textiles and footwear gained traction, helping to mitigate the decline in South Asia's overall exports. Available data on exports from Pakistan also suggest garment exports may have bottomed out. In July, Pakistan's textiles and footwear exports had grown 10.3% relative to the February 2023 trough. South Asia's electronics exports are also expanding as economies in the subregion seek to further integrate into the global supply chain for electrical components.

Green product exports are trending upwards, but from a low overall share. Electric and hybrid cars are the fastest-growing product exports from developing Asia (Figure 1.1.6). The sector has been boosted by increased efforts to curb carbon emissions and by the falling costs of solar and wind energy and battery production, which also raised demand for rechargeable batteries and solar panels. Although around 60% of 2022 global electric vehicle sales were in the PRC, demand from Europe and the US—which account for 25% and 8% of global sales, respectively—remains high according to a 2023 report of the International Energy Agency. Exports of electric and hybrid cars rose by 68.0%, rechargeable batteries by 22.9%, and solar panels by 12.6% in the first 9 months of 2023.

Figure 1.1.6 Best and Worst Performing Goods Exports in Developing Asia

Electric and hybrid cars are leading the upturn in export growth.

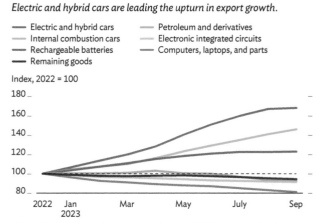

Notes: 12-month moving average relative to 2022 average. Goods at Harmonized System (HS) 4-digit classification were selected on the basis of their contribution to the aggregate export growth of the following economies: Armenia; Azerbaijan; Hong Kong, China; Fiji; Georgia; India; the Kyrgyz Republic; Malaysia; the People's Republic of China; the Philippines; and Uzbekistan.

Source: UN Comtrade.

Their combined share of exports, however, increased from just 2.4% in 2022 to a still rather low 3.2% in 2023 (up to September), not enough to prevent a contraction in overall goods exports. In the first 9 months of 2023, electric and hybrid car exports contributed 0.3 percentage points to growth, rechargeable batteries also contributed 0.3 percentage points, and solar panels 0.1 percentage points.

Weak global demand softened intraregional trade.
Lower demand from advanced economies together with a short-lived boost from the PRC's reopening kept growth of goods exports in developing Asia subdued throughout most of 2023 (Figure 1.1.7). In the first 3 quarters of 2023, exports to the US declined by 12.2%, the euro area by 6.0%, and the PRC by 8.7%. The softening of global demand had a knock-on lagged effect on intraregional trade, which declined by 14.7% in the second and third quarters of 2023. The drop in exports to Emerging and Developing Asia dragged down growth in the second quarter by 3.0 percentage points and in the third quarter by 2.4 percentage points. Nevertheless, demand from the US and the

PRC appears to be recovering, with its lagged effects on developing Asia's exports likely this year. This is despite trade disruptions in the Red Sea and Panama Canal since the end of 2023, which have affected cargo ship transit times on key shipping routes for Asian exports to the US and euro area (Box 1.1.2).

After a surge in 2021–2022, growth in services exports slowed in 2023, related to lower shipping revenues. Services exports account for about 16% of developing Asia's total exports. From a high of 34.2% in the third quarter of 2021, services export growth in developing Asia declined until it turned mildly negative in the third quarter of 2023, due to a contraction in transport services (Figure 1.1.8, panel A). In turn, the decline in transport services exports was driven by a plunge in shipping prices, as supply chains normalized following the sharp increase in prices caused by pandemic-related supply chain disruptions in 2021 and 2022. This had a significant impact on services exports from the PRC, ROK, and Singapore (Figure 1.1.8, panels B and D).

Figure 1.1.7 Contributions to Nominal Goods Export Growth in Developing Asia by Destination

The slowdown in advanced economies spilled over to intraregional trade.

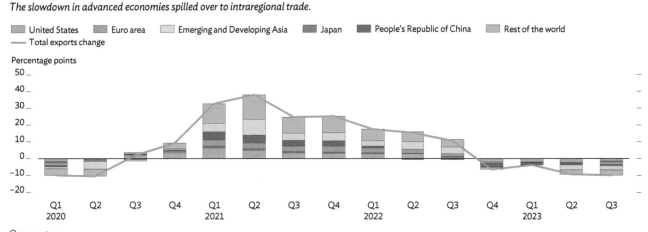

Q = quarter.
Note: Emerging & Developing Asia consists of 29 economies, excluding the People's Republic of China, as classified by the International Monetary Fund. All 29 economies are ADB developing members.
Source: CEIC Data Company.

A strong recovery in travel and recreation contributed to services export growth. Travel and recreation services were severely affected by COVID-19 pandemic lockdowns. Before the pandemic, the sector accounted for 25% of services exports in developing Asia. When restrictions began easing, the sector started to recover in 2021, moving from contraction to an export growth of 43.3% in the second quarter of 2021. Growth in travel and recreation services exports surged to 163.3% in the first quarter of 2023, before moderating to 60.5% in the third quarter. Although the share of travel and recreation in services exports has not fully recovered (a 14% share in 2023), its contribution to growth from the fourth quarter of 2022 to the third quarter in 2023 was larger than those of other service sectors combined. This helped to prevent export

services growth from contracting for the region as a whole, despite exports of travel and recreation from the PRC remaining subdued following its reopening in early 2023.

India retains its strong position in exports of information technology services. India's services exports, which account for 47% of the region total, continued to expand last year, albeit at a gradually slower pace (Figure 1.1.8, panel C). Growth was driven by telecom and information technology services on the back of booming global demand for digital services related to the work-from-home shift. India is well-positioned with a strengthening software development industry as well as growth in consulting and other business services.

Figure 1.1.8 Sectoral Contributions to Nominal Services Export Growth in Developing Asia

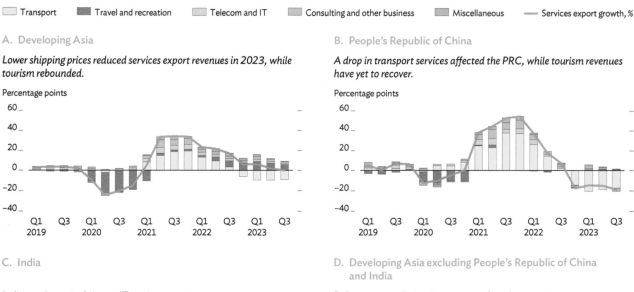

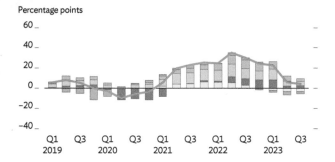

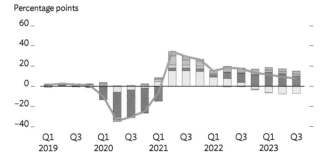

IT = information technology, PRC = People's Republic of China, Q = quarter.
Note: Miscellaneous includes intellectual property, construction, finance, government, insurance and pension, maintenance and repair, and manufacturing services. Growth rate is year on year.
Source: CEIC Data Company.

Box 1.1.2 Using Automatic Identification System Data to Track Shipping Disruptions from Asia

The Automatic Identification System (AIS) is used by vessels to communicate during navigation. It was originally designed to prevent collisions. When in motion, vessels with AIS equipment send near real-time radio messages on their location, speed, destination, and voyage details every 2 to 10 seconds. The granularity and real-time aspects of AIS data allow for tracking vessel movements and examining specific trade routes. The AIS is thus a useful tool for monitoring any disruptions in global maritime trade.

Global Movements Data (GMD), developed by the Asian Development Bank (2023), can be used to document the recent trade disruptions caused by the Panama Canal drought and attacks in the Red Sea (ADB 2023). GMD is produced by aggregating raw AIS signals of vessel movements tagged with port information based on the World Port Index database. The daily count of transit indicators for major passageways—the Panama Canal, Suez Canal, and the Bab El-Mandeb Strait—and the transit time of select major trade routes (from Shanghai, People's Republic of China to Los Angeles, United States; and Shanghai to Rotterdam, the Netherlands) can be calculated based on GMD.

Transit through Major Shipping Chokepoints

The Panama Canal is an important channel for international maritime trade, connecting the Atlantic and Pacific oceans. It was the primary route for 57.5% of all cargo transported in container ships from Asia to the US east coast in 2022 (Panama Canal Authority 2023a). The canal has suffered severe drought since the beginning of 2023 due to the El Niño phenomenon, with October 2023 the driest October since records began in 1950—41% less rainfall than usual (Panama Canal Authority 2023b). The drought has been a significant threat to the canal's daily operations (box figure 1). The daily number of transits through the Panama Canal have been trending downwards from early 2023 and fell to a 5-year low in December 2023. Shipping companies have diverted vessels to a much longer route around South America's Magellan Strait.

1 Automatic Identification System-Based Daily Transits along Major Passageways

Daily transits via the Bab El-Mandeb Strait and Suez Canal dropped significantly since recent attacks on ships, and daily transits via the Panama Canal have trended downwards since the drought in early 2023.

A. Suez Canal

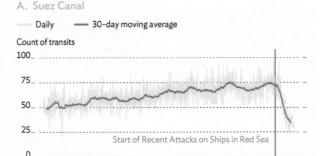

B. Bab El-Mandeb Strait

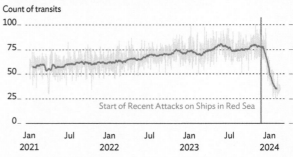

C. Panama Canal

Note: Data is up to 13 March 2024.
Source: Asian Development Bank calculations using United Nations Global Platform for Official Statistics. 2024. AIS Data.

Box 1.1.2 *Continued*

Meanwhile, the recent attacks on cargo ships caused shipping companies to divert vessels away from the Red Sea. In normal times, ships passing through the Suez Canal to or from the Indian Ocean must pass the Bab El-Mandeb Strait and the Red Sea. There has been a sharp decrease in the number of daily transits via both the Bab El-Mandeb Strait and Suez Canal since October 2023, suggesting that shipping routes have been disrupted.

Effect on Transit Time

Recent shipping disruptions have increased transit times from Asia to Europe, although freight cost rises have been more broad-based. The impact of recent disruptions on trade in Asia can also be seen by examining the median transit time and freight costs of the Shanghai–Los Angeles and Shanghai-Rotterdam trade routes (box figure 2) (Freightender 2024). The transit time of vessels

on the Shanghai-Los Angeles route seems to have remained stable recently as trade from Asia to the US east coast has not faced any major disruptions. However, the transit time of vessels from Shanghai to Rotterdam has increased substantially in recent months. This could be attributed to the fact that vessels traveling from Shanghai to Rotterdam are avoiding the Suez Canal and rerouting around the Cape of Good Hope further south, which substantially lengthens total transit time. While sharp spikes in the transit time of vessels have moved largely in line with freight cost fluctuations based on the World Container Index (WCI) over time, notably during global supply chain disruptions during 2021–22, the correlation is less evident in the recent period.[a] Moreover, rises in freight costs during the Red Sea attacks are almost equivalent for both the Shanghai–Rotterdam and Shanghai–Los Angeles routes, suggesting that factors other than vessel transit times are affecting freight costs.

2 Median Transit Time and World Container Index for Shanghai–Los Angeles and Shanghai–Rotterdam Routes

Transit time remained stable on the Shanghai-Los Angeles route but increased sharply on the Shanghai-Rotterdam route, partially coinciding with the pickup in costs.

A. Shanghai to Los Angeles

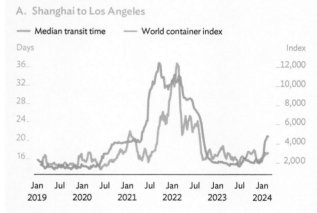

B. Shanghai to Rotterdam

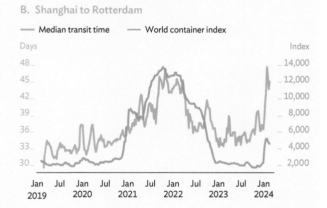

Note: Data is up to 13 March 2024.
Sources: Asian Development Bank calculations using United Nations Global Platform for Official Statistics. 2024. AIS Data; Bloomberg.

References:
ADB (Asian Development Bank). 2023. Methodological Framework for Unlocking Maritime Insights Using Automatic Identification System Data: A Special Supplement of Key Indicators for Asia and the Pacific 2023.
Freightender. 2024. World Container Index: An Overview of Drewry's Composite of Container Freight Rates.
Panama Canal Authority. 2023a. Weekly update on transits through the Panama Canal.
———. 2023b. The driest month of October since 1950.

[a]   The World Container Index (WCI) is a measure of global freight rates for containers on vessels across eight major trade routes, but its interpretation can be limited since it only tracks spot rates and may not take into account other factors that can affect shipping rates.

This box was written by Mahinthan Mariasingham of the Economic Research and Development Impact Department (ERDI), ADB, Ed Kieran Reyes, Cherryl Chico, and Zhaowen Wang, ERDI consultants.

Recovery in Tourism Continues, while Personal Transfers Remain Healthy

Tourism continues to recover but still has some way to go. The tourism recovery is gaining ground across the region. Between 2022 and 2023, available data for 15 developing Asia economies show increases in both travel receipts and number of tourist arrivals (Figure 1.1.9). The upturn in tourist arrivals is broadly associated with a proportional increase in travel receipts. Armenia leads these two indicators compared with 2019, while Taipei,China lags behind. Although the tourism recovery is progressing well, tourist arrivals and receipts remain below pre-pandemic levels in most economies.

Travelers from most economies have returned, except from the PRC. Tourist destinations in developing Asia differ by source economies of international arrivals (Figure 1.1.10). For example, visitors from Australia and New Zealand led the tourism recovery in Fiji, with an increase of 15.3% relative to pre-pandemic levels. Tourists from Europe continue to come to Maldives, with their share averaging 57.5% over the past 5 years. Arrivals from Europe are also

Figure 1.1.9 Tourist Arrivals and Travel Receipts in Developing Asian Economies, 2022 and 2023 Year to Date

Travel receipts are increasing as tourist arrivals rise.

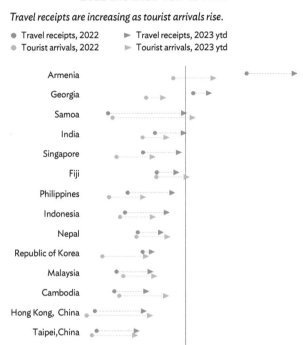

Source: CEIC Data Company.

Figure 1.1.10 Visitor Arrivals in Selected Developing Asian Economies by Origin

Major tourism markets differ across economies.

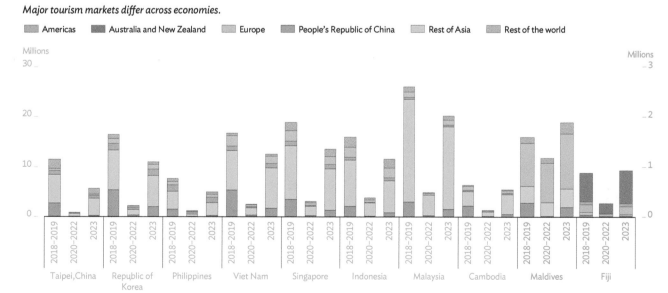

Notes: The Philippines excludes visiting overseas Filipinos. Taipei,China 2023 data is until November. For Fiji, Americas includes the United States and Canada only. Rest of Asia is South Asia, Southeast Asia, and East Asia.
Source: CEIC Data Company.

prominent in economies like Fiji, Viet Nam, Singapore, and Indonesia. Intraregional travelers hold the largest share in many economies, except for Fiji and Maldives. Among the eight East and Southeast Asian economies in the figure, Malaysia recorded the largest share (89.6%) of intraregional visitors in 2023, while the Philippines had the lowest (56%). The main source economies for tourists from within the region vary—for example, Japan and the ROK for Taipei,China; Japan and the PRC for the ROK; PRC and the ROK for Viet Nam; Indonesia and the PRC for Singapore; Malaysia and Singapore for Indonesia; Singapore and Indonesia for Malaysia; Thailand and Viet Nam for Cambodia. While the number of visitors from the Americas and Europe are almost back to pre-pandemic levels, those from the PRC have not yet recovered.

Personal transfers remain above pre-pandemic levels. Of the 13 economies with available data, 11 exceeded their 2019 personal transfer levels from 2021 to 2023 (Figure 1.1.11). The exceptions are Sri Lanka, which missed that target in all 3 years, and the Kyrgyz Republic, where personal transfers fell below pre-pandemic levels in 2022 and 2023. Tajikistan had the highest remittances relative to GDP in 2022 at 50.9%. Remittances in the Philippines account for 2.2% of GDP, Bangladesh 4.7%, Cambodia 8.9%, Fiji 9.2%, Georgia 15.6%, and Nepal 22.8%. The Philippines received the most personal transfers by value among the 13 economies, receiving $21.8 billion in the first 3 quarters of 2023.

Figure 1.1.11 Personal Transfers

For most, personal transfers have grown above pre-pandemic levels.

■ 2021 ■ 2022 ■ 2023 ytd

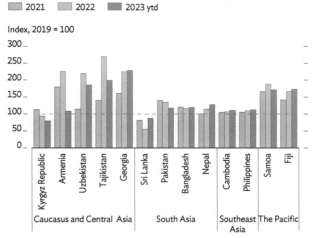

ytd = year to date.
Sources: CEIC Data Company; official sources.

Robust Financial Market Conditions, Equities Perform Well

Financial markets in developing Asia performed well during 2023, overcoming a period of tightening in financial conditions late in the year due to increased concerns over US inflation. By the end of 2023, financial conditions in the region eased on the back of a less hawkish Fed. Equity markets rose, sovereign bond yields declined and bond spreads narrowed, currencies mildly depreciated but largely stabilized, and net portfolio inflows into the region increased. The momentum has continued into 2024 thus far, despite some uncertainty on the timing and the magnitude of the Fed's expected rate cuts this year.

Most equity markets in the region have climbed since November amid expectations of less hawkish US monetary policy. Equity markets across the region rose gradually since March last year but lost steam in September, due to persistent US inflation and the anticipation that the Fed would keep interest rates higher for longer. Nonetheless, by the end of the year, Asian equity markets had performed well, recording a weighted-average return of 11.5% in 2023 (Figure 1.1.12). This was supported by looser financial conditions, following the Fed's decision to keep policy rates steady in November and hints of possible rate cuts in 2024 during the Federal Open Market Committee (FOMC) December meeting. In January 2024, Asian stock markets declined slightly after a rally as the Fed left rates unchanged for the fourth

Figure 1.1.12 Developing Asia Equity Market Performance

Regional equity markets rallied since November, after the Fed signaled a less hawkish monetary policy stance.

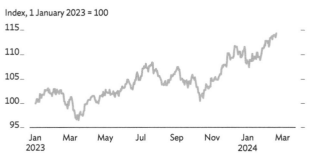

Note: Equity markets in the region are aggregated using market capitalization shares as weights. Data is as of 12 March 2024.
Source: Bloomberg.

straight FOMC meeting. In addition, some East Asian markets, particularly, Hong Kong, China and the PRC, faced renewed concerns about the property sector and overall economic conditions. However, equity markets in the region rallied in February, led by Hong Kong, China and the PRC where investor sentiment improved following policy support to stabilize the economy.

Most currencies in the region broadly stabilized, mildly depreciating since the second half of 2023.
Continued tightness in US monetary policy led to a marginal weakening of many regional currencies relative to the US dollar. Across developing Asia, GDP-weighted currencies depreciated by 2.3% against the US dollar in 2023, while currencies in South Asia and the Pacific fell by slightly more than the regional average (Figure 1.1.13). During the last quarter of 2023, most regional currencies strengthened following the Fed's signal of an end to its monetary policy tightening cycle. This trend was not long-lasting, however. Signs of persistent US inflation and amplified market uncertainty over the timing of expected US monetary easing at the start of the year led to a mild depreciation of GDP-weighted average of currencies for developing Asia in Q1 2024.

Government bond yields declined and the average risk premium on sovereign bonds continued to narrow. The 10-year government bond yields

of selected Asian economies remained stable in the first half of 2023. Reflecting the more hawkish stance of the Fed and resultant net capital outflows from the region, some sovereign bond yields rose in August, before reverting downward by the end of the year (Figure 1.1.14). Most bond yields in the region continued to fall until March this year amid signals of the Fed easing in 2024, slowing inflation, and stable economic growth. Meanwhile, the average bond spread for the region has narrowed by about 35 basis points (bps) so far this year as financial market conditions improved. South Asia's average bond spread dropped by 125 bps and the Caucasus and Central Asia's narrowed by 30 bps, while spreads remained relatively stable in East Asia and Southeast Asia (Figure 1.1.15).

There were positive net portfolio inflows in 2023, benefitting from improved investor sentiment.
The region had net portfolio inflows of $53.1 billion in 2023, driven by the positive investor outlook on regional growth and gradual easing in global risk aversion (Figure 1.1.16). While the region experienced outflows from August to October, due to escalating property market stress in the PRC and the prospect of higher-for-longer interest rates in the US, portfolio inflows resumed in November and December following the Fed's less hawkish monetary policy stance. In the first quarter of 2024, momentum continued as the region registered net portfolio inflows of $29.3 billion.

Figure 1.1.13 Exchange Rate Movement Against the US Dollar, by Subregion

After a slight appreciation at the end of 2023, currencies in the region began to depreciate in first quarter of 2024, especially in East Asia and Southeast Asia.

— Caucasus and Central Asia   — Southeast Asia
— East Asia   — The Pacific
— South Asia

Index, 1 January 2023 = 100

Note: Subregional exchange rate indexes are aggregated using gross domestic product purchasing power parity shares as weights. Data is as of 12 March 2024.
Source: Bloomberg.

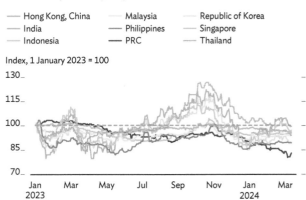

Figure 1.1.14 10-Year Sovereign Bond Yield

Long-term government bond yields broadly declined in 2023 and continued to fall in the first quarter 2024.

— Hong Kong, China   — Malaysia   — Republic of Korea
— India   — Philippines   — Singapore
— Indonesia   — PRC   — Thailand

Index, 1 January 2023 = 100

PRC = People's Republic of China.
Note: Data is as of 12 March 2024.
Source: Bloomberg.

Figure 1.1.15 JP Morgan EMBI Stripped Spreads, by Subregion

Risk premiums in most regional markets narrowed in 2023 on improved financial market conditions.

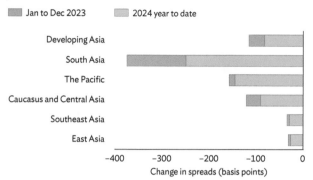

Notes: Caucasus and Central Asia includes Armenia, Azerbaijan, Kazakhstan, Tajikistan. East Asia includes Mongolia, the People's Republic of China, and Republic of Korea. South Asia includes India, Pakistan, and Sri Lanka. Southeast Asia includes Indonesia, Malaysia, the Philippines, and Viet Nam. Pacific includes Papua New Guinea. Subregional bond spreads are aggregated using gross domestic product purchasing power parity shares as weights. 2024 year to date is from 1 January to 12 March 2024.

Source: Bloomberg.

Figure 1.1.16 Portfolio Flows in the Region

The region saw a turnaround in portfolio inflows since November, after a period of outflows.

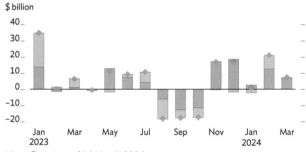

Note: Data is as of 14 March 2024.

Source: Institute of International Finance.

In the PRC, however, uncertainty over the outlook contributed to portfolio outflows from November to January, but these were significantly less than in the preceding months as the effects of stimulus measures to support the property sector and the economy began to take hold. In February, the PRC recorded net inflows for the first time since July 2023, following the government's announcement of further policy measures.

Foreign direct investment (FDI) inflows to developing Asia declined in 2023. FDI growth was strong in 2021 and continued in 2022, albeit at a more moderate pace—peaking in the first quarter of 2022 and slowing down afterwards. The latest available data show a continued deceleration up to the third quarter of 2023. This was mainly due to a reduction in flows to the PRC, which usually accounts for a large share of FDI in the region (Figure 1.1.17). In the third quarter, FDI into the PRC declined significantly, by $11.8 billion, as foreign firms' profits fell and many companies paused new investments due to economic uncertainty and geopolitical risks.

Figure 1.1.17 Foreign Direct Investment

FDI inflows to the region continued to moderate since the first quarter of 2022, driven by declining flows to the PRC.

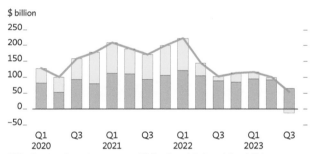

FDI = foreign direct investment, PRC = People's Republic of China, Q = quarter.

Note: Developing Asia includes Armenia; Azerbaijan; Bangladesh; Cambodia; the People's Republic of China; Georgia; Hong Kong, China; India; Indonesia; Kazakhstan; Malaysia, Nepal; Pakistan; the Philippines; the Republic of Korea; Singapore; Tajikistan; Thailand; Timor-Leste; and Uzbekistan.

Source: Haver Analytics.

Rate Hiking Cycles Largely Done with Debt Stable but High in a Few Economies

Most central bank hiking cycles have run their course. The region continued to see some policy rate hikes last year, notably in Pakistan where the central bank increased rates four times for a total of 600 basis points to combat persistent double-digit inflation. Elsewhere in the region, tightening paused with roughly two-thirds of decisions leaving rates unchanged as inflationary pressures started to wane (Figure 1.1.18).

Figure 1.1.18 Policy Rate Decisions

Most hiking cycles are done, with some gradually shifting to easing.

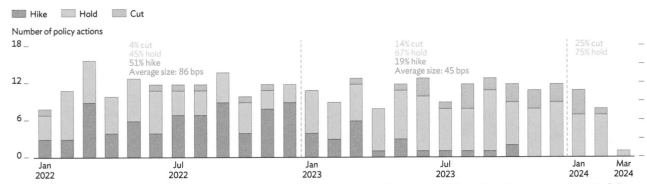

Note: The figure covers Armenia; Azerbaijan; Georgia; Hong Kong, China; India; Indonesia; Kazakhstan; the Kyrgyz Republic; Malaysia; Mongolia; Pakistan; the Philippines; the People's Republic of China; the Republic of Korea; Sri Lanka; Tajikistan; Taipei,China; Thailand; and Uzbekistan.
Source: Trading economics.

Figure 1.1.19 Change in Real Interest Rates from 2023 to 2024

Real interest rates increased, driven by lower expected inflation and still-high policy rates in 2023.

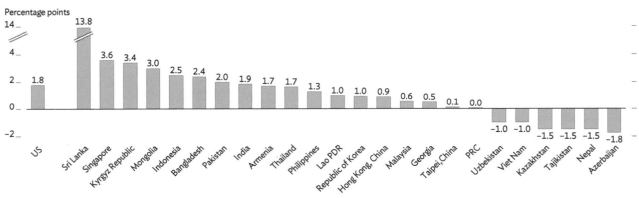

Lao PDR = Lao People's Democratic Republic, PRC = People's Republic of China, US = United States.
Notes: Real interest rates are the difference between policy rates and forecast inflation. The change is the difference between 2023 and 2024 real interest rates.
Source: CEIC Data Company

However, only a few central banks have begun easing. Monetary policy authorities in the region remain cautious, safeguarding against any reacceleration in inflation and monitoring global financial conditions.

Disinflation and still-elevated policy rates have driven real interest rates higher (Figure 1.1.19).
For example, Sri Lanka's central bank cut rates four times for a total of 650 basis points, but that was outpaced by the decline in inflation, which fell sharply from 53.2% in January 2023 to 4.2% in December. As a result, Sri Lanka's real interest rate is now nearly 14 percentage points higher than last year. Real rates increased across most of the region, with the notable exception of the PRC where real interest rates remain unchanged, and some economies in the Caucasus and Central Asia, which saw real rates decline. And with inflation forecast to slow further across the region through 2025, the overall tighter monetary stances suggest there is room for central banks to ease rates to support growth if necessary. Conversely, higher real interest rates could weigh on economic activity if central banks continue to hold policy rates steady even as inflation slows further.

Public debt relative to GDP stabilized but remains elevated in some economies. Most economies continue to face substantially higher public debt compared to pre-pandemic levels (Figure 1.1.20). In particular, debt remains above 100% of GDP in Bhutan, Lao PDR, Sri Lanka, and Maldives. However, sustained growth and high inflation helped reduce debt-to-GDP ratios by an average of 0.2 percentage points in the region last year.

Fiscal positions improved in most of developing Asia and debt is expected to remain stable in 2024 and 2025. Better fiscal positions helped mitigate debt risks, with most economies narrowing deficits in 2023 (Figure 1.1.21). Stabilization policies and reforms under International Monetary Fund programs improved fiscal balances in the crisis-affected economies of Sri Lanka and Pakistan. However, roughly three-fourths of the economies in the region still face deficits which

Figure 1.1.20 Public Debt

Public debt relative to GDP rose substantially after the pandemic but edged down in 2023.

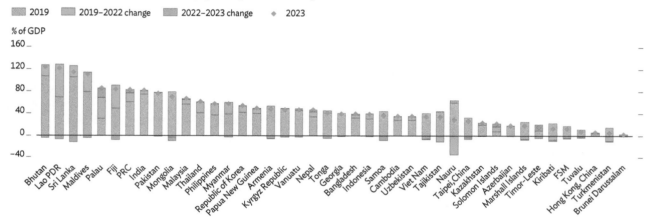

FSM = Federated States of Micronesia, GDP = gross domestic product, Lao PDR = Lao People's Democratic Republic, PRC = People's Republic of China.
Source: IMF World Economic Outlook.

Figure 1.1.21 Fiscal Balances

Fiscal positions improved for most economies but deficits remain sizeable in some.

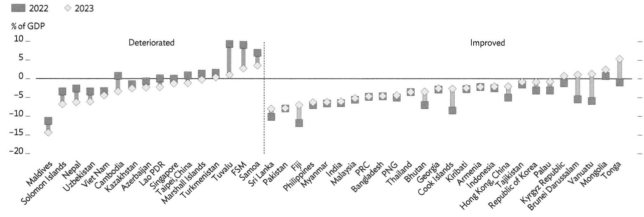

FSM = Federated States of Micronesia, GDP = gross domestic product, Lao PDR = Lao People's Democratic Republic, PNG = Papua New Guinea, PRC = People's Republic of China.
Source: Asian Development Outlook database.

are expected to persist through 2024 and 2025, exerting upward pressure on public debt levels. Still, public debt ratios are expected to remain flat, in large part due to GDP growth offsetting higher primary deficits (Figure 1.1.22). There is some variation across subregions. Notably, in East Asia increases in primary balances will drive public debt ratios 1 percentage point higher on average. In contrast, strong growth in South Asia will drive debt lower by an average of 0.8 percentage points.

Figure 1.1.22 Drivers of Public Debt to GDP Ratios 2024–2025 Average

Resilient GDP growth will offset upward pressure on public debt ratios from primary deficits.

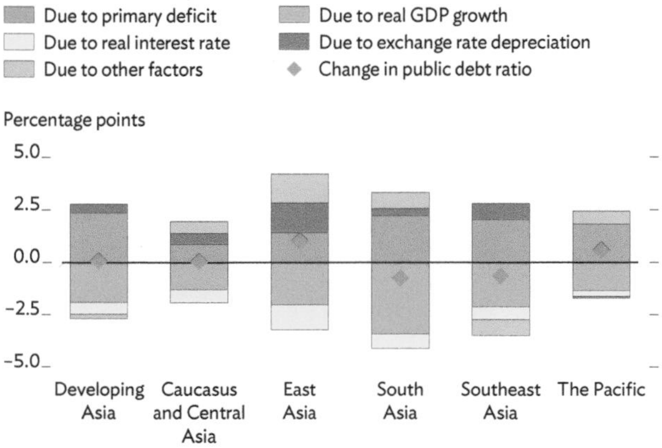

- Due to primary deficit
- Due to real interest rate
- Due to other factors
- Due to real GDP growth
- Due to exchange rate depreciation
- ◆ Change in public debt ratio

GDP = gross domestic product.
Source: Asian Development Bank. 2024. *Asian Sovereign Debt Monitor.* Manila.

Despite improvements, the debt structures of some economies suggest that vulnerabilities remain. In the Maldives, the primary deficit is expected to decline substantially in 2024, which will help reduce public debt. External debt and gross financing needs are also expected to decline as the fiscal deficit narrows. In Mongolia, lower public and external debt are expected, with solid economic growth and relatively high inflation effectively lowering debt-service costs. In Pakistan and Sri Lanka, challenges remain in sustaining reforms given the substantial debt servicing costs. In Pakistan, fiscal revenues remain weak with rising interest payments expected to consume 63% of budget revenues (compared to 39.5% in 2022). Sri Lanka could face external debt above 70% of GDP even after relief. Complex coordination efforts are underway, but the terms of restructuring remain unclear. Meanwhile, the situation has deteriorated in Lao PDR, where the depreciation of the kip has inflated foreign currency-denominated public debt, now roughly 60% of total debt. The narrow tax base, with revenues at only 15% of GDP, will also come under further pressure as high interest payments consume nearly a quarter of total budget revenues.

Regional Outlook Remains Resilient Even with Growth Decelerating in the PRC

Growth will slow and diverge across major advanced economies in 2024, weakened by lagged effects of high interest rates and softening trade.
In the US, growth is forecast to decline to 1.9% in 2024 and 1.7% in 2025 on softer labor market conditions and moderating consumption growth. In the euro area, growth will accelerate to 0.7% in 2024 and 1.4% in 2025, supported by gradual pickup in domestic demand. However, this could be offset by a less supportive external environment due to weaker growth in the US and the PRC. And in Japan, growth is forecast to slow to 0.6% in 2024 before rising slightly to 0.8% in 2025, down from last year's 1.9%, as exports and investment remain subdued and the post-pandemic recovery fades. Overall, growth in major advanced economies is projected to slow down from 1.7% in 2023 to 1.3% in 2024, before picking up to 1.5% in 2025 (Table 1.5.1).

Declining inflation is expected to prompt monetary easing that will support growth in 2025. Monetary policy is forecast to begin easing by mid-2024 as disinflation progresses in the US and euro area (Figure 1.2.1). US average inflation will drop from 4.1% in 2023 to 2.6% this year and 2.2% in 2025. Disinflation is also well underway in the euro area, where headline inflation is forecast to decline to 2.4% in 2024 and 2.0% in 2025, from 5.4% in 2023. Month-on-month headline and core inflation in the euro area have been close to or below zero since the end of 2023. In Japan, inflation is projected to decline to 1.9% in 2024 and 1.3% in 2025 due to falling energy prices—which pushed headline inflation lower in January this year—and slowing core inflation. However, the 5.9% wage hike agreed to by leading industrial corporations on 13 March—the biggest in 33 years—suggests that wage increases could lead to higher demand-side inflationary pressures.

Table 1.5.1 Baseline Assumptions on the International Economy

	2023	2024	2025
	Estimate	*Forecast*	
GDP growth, %			
Major advanced economies	1.7	1.3	1.5
United States	2.5	1.9	1.7
Euro area	0.5	0.7	1.4
Japan	1.9	0.6	0.8
Inflation, %			
Major advanced economies	4.5	2.4	2.0
United States	4.1	2.6	2.2
Euro area	5.4	2.4	2.0
Japan	3.3	1.9	1.3

GDP = gross domestic product.
Sources: Bloomberg; CEIC Data Company; Haver Analytics; IMF World Economic Outlook; Asian Development Bank estimates.

Figure 1.2.1 Policy Rates in the Euro Area and United States

Monetary policy will start easing by mid-2024.

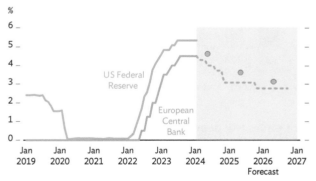

US = United States.
Note: Data as of 25 March 2024.
Sources: European Central Bank; US Federal Reserve.

Sluggish demand is expected to keep oil prices relatively stable despite lower production. The announcement of additional voluntary supply cuts in November for the first quarter of 2024 by several OPEC+ countries did little to raise oil prices. Moreover, attacks on shipping vessels in the Red Sea since early January only marginally affected Brent crude oil prices, which rose from about $75/barrel in early January to $83/barrel as of 8 March (Annex). Meanwhile, the drought in the Panama Canal is restricting transit and raising oil export costs from the Gulf of Mexico to Asia. Still, the Brent crude oil price was $12/barrel lower on 8 March than its 19 September peak price for 2023, suggesting that global supply and demand conditions play a much larger role than these disruptions in determining oil prices. While an escalation of tensions in the Red Sea could exert upward pressure, the US Energy Information Administration's February report forecasts Brent crude oil prices to average $82/barrel in 2024 and $79/barrel in 2025 (Figure 1.2.2).

Figure 1.2.2 Average Annual Brent Crude Oil Price and Forecast

Oil prices will remain around $80/barrel unless major geopolitical turmoil disrupts the market.

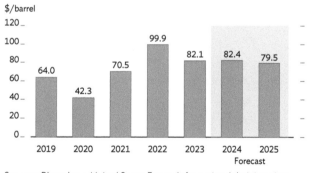

$/barrel

- 2019: 64.0
- 2020: 42.3
- 2021: 70.5
- 2022: 99.9
- 2023: 82.1
- 2024: 82.4
- 2025: 79.5

Forecast

Sources: Bloomberg, United States Energy Information Administration.

Rice prices will depend on several factors. Among these is the ongoing El Niño weather phenomenon that will persist until the second quarter of the year, as forecast by the US National Oceanic and Atmospheric Administration. El Niño events result in drier weather, heightening the risk of losses for water-intensive crops, including rice. India's ongoing ban on rice exports and the geographic concentration of production and exports in Asia are also expected to keep rice prices elevated (Figure 1.2.3). The current El Niño, however, has the potential to transition into La Niña, which may result in

greater rainfall than normal, boosting rice crops and thus reducing prices. Among developing Asian economies, Bangladesh, Timor-Leste, and the Philippines are most at risk of rice price increases boosting headline inflation, as rice and rice products account for at least 20% of their respective food price baskets (Box 1.1.1).

Figure 1.2.3 Rice Price

Rice prices have trended upward since April 2023.

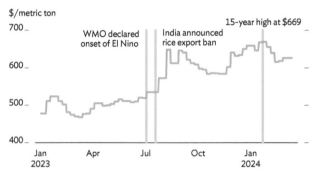

$/metric ton

WMO declared onset of El Nino

India announced rice export ban

15-year high at $669

WMO = World Meteorological Organization.
Note: Rice price refers to 5% broken, white rice, milled from Thailand.
Source: Bloomberg.

South Asia and Southeast Asia Will Drive Growth, with Slowdowns Elsewhere

Regional growth is forecast at 4.9% for both 2024 and 2025, fractionally weaker than the 5.0% recorded in 2023 (Table 1.2.2). The slowdown in the PRC—driven by the property sector correction and the fading post-pandemic rebound in services—will be offset by sustained growth in South Asia and Southeast Asia where domestic demand remains strong. The pickup in the semiconductor cycle, driven by increasing global demand for artificial intelligence (AI) microchips, will propel growth for the region's high technology exporters (see *Special Topic* on Asia's Rebounding Semiconductor Sector and the Role of Artificial Intelligence). Growth in the Caucasus and Central Asia will decline as last year's boost in services wears off, while growth in the Pacific will slightly decline as a slower tourism recovery outweighs higher gold production.

Growth in the PRC will moderate to 4.8% in 2024 and 4.5% in 2025 amid continued property sector weakness. Growth in services will moderate as the effect of the post-pandemic reopening fades. Domestic and external demand for low-carbon technologies will remain strong, including electric vehicles, batteries, and renewables. Policy support will likely continue in 2024 for technology industries such as semiconductors and AI. Infrastructure investment and public projects will underpin construction and support private investment. Private consumption should continue recovering in 2024 as the labor market and household income improve. However, real estate investment will continue to slow with sluggish housing demand and financing constraints for developers. This continues despite government efforts to stabilize the property market by easing access to financing and supporting affordable housing. Continued accommodative monetary policy and further fiscal stimulus could marginally raise growth.

South Asia remains the fastest growing subregion as domestic demand improves on moderating inflation in most economies. Growth in the subregion will continue to exceed the regional average, reaching 6.3% in 2024 and 6.6% in 2025. In India, growth is forecast to remain strong at 7.0% for fiscal year (FY) 2024 (ending on 31 March 2025), albeit slower than the 7.6% growth in FY2023, and is expected to accelerate to 7.2% in FY2025 as rising consumption complements continued investment growth. Services will remain the growth mainstay, with manufacturing expected to play a strong supporting role. In Bangladesh, garment exports will push growth up to 6.1% in FY2024 (ending on 30 June 2024) and 6.6% in FY2025. Private consumption is expected to rise as inflation eases, while public investment will increase due to large infrastructure projects in energy and railways. This will counter subdued public consumption from lower subsidy spending and continued austerity measures. Hydropower investment and the commissioning of a major hydropower plant will drive growth in Bhutan. In Maldives, tourism and construction will boost growth in 2024 and 2025. Growth in Nepal will pick up in FY2024 (ending in mid-July 2024) and FY2025 on rising domestic demand and hydroelectric output, and a continued recovery in tourism.

Pakistan and Sri Lanka should recover from last year's contractions. In Pakistan, growth is forecast to rise 1.9% in FY2024 (ending on 30 June 2024)

and 2.8% in FY2025, up from the 0.2% contraction last fiscal year. The shift back to positive growth will come from a recovery in both agriculture and industry. However, domestic demand will remain constrained by the surge in living costs and tight macroeconomic policies. In Sri Lanka, growth will rebound to 1.9% in 2024 and 2.5% in 2025 from the 2.3% contraction in 2023. This will be driven by rising output in services, resumption in industrial projects, and continuous reform aimed at improving the business climate. Still, tax increases will dampen the recovery in private consumption and investment.

High-income technology exporters are expected to benefit from the rebound in semiconductors. Growth in the ROK is forecast at 2.2% in 2024 and 2.3% in 2025, up from 1.4% in 2023. It will be fueled by exports, driven by sustained demand for semiconductors globally and supported by expanding AI services and cloud-server business. The recovery, however, will be uneven as domestic demand will remain fragile amid the high interest rate environment. Rising demand for specialized AI semiconductor chips will drive growth in Taipei,China to 3.0% in 2024 and 2.7% in 2025, from 1.3% in 2023. In Singapore, manufacturing and trade-related sectors are also expected to drive growth alongside the global turnaround in electronics. Growth will accelerate to 2.4% in 2024 and 2.6% in 2025 from 1.1% in 2023. In contrast, growth in Hong Kong, China will decelerate from 3.2% in 2023 to 2.8% this year and to 3.0% in 2025, mostly due to slowing growth in the PRC.

Growth in Southeast Asia should rise, driven by robust domestic demand and a continued recovery in tourism. The subregion is forecast to grow by 4.6% in 2024 and 4.7% in 2025, up from 4.1% in 2023. Indonesia is poised to maintain 5.0% growth in the next 2 years, supported by robust private consumption, public infrastructure spending, and gradually improving investment during the forecast horizon. On top of strong domestic demand, a turnaround in merchandise exports starting in mid-2024 will drive growth in Thailand (2.6% in 2024 and 3.0% in 2025), Viet Nam (6.0% in 2024 and 6.2% in 2025), the Philippines (6.0% in 2024 and 6.2% in 2025), and Malaysia (4.5% in 2024 and 4.6% in 2025). Tourism will support services growth, while industrial output will move in line with a recovery in exports and easing monetary policy.

Table 1.2.2 GDP Growth in Developing Asia, %

Growth remains healthy in 2024 and 2025.

	2022	2023e	2024f	2025f
Developing Asia	**4.3**	**5.0**	**4.9**	**4.9**
Developing Asia excluding the People's Republic of China	**5.5**	**4.8**	**5.0**	**5.3**
Caucasus and Central Asia	**5.2**	**5.3**	**4.3**	**5.0**
Armenia	12.6	8.7	5.7	6.0
Azerbaijan	4.6	1.1	1.2	1.6
Georgia	10.4	7.0	5.0	5.5
Kazakhstan	3.2	5.1	3.8	5.3
Kyrgyz Republic	9.0	6.2	5.0	4.5
Tajikistan	8.0	8.3	6.5	6.5
Turkmenistan	6.2	6.3	6.5	6.0
Uzbekistan	5.7	6.0	5.5	5.6
East Asia	**2.9**	**4.7**	**4.5**	**4.2**
Hong Kong, China	−3.7	3.2	2.8	3.0
Mongolia	5.0	7.0	4.1	6.0
People's Republic of China	3.0	5.2	4.8	4.5
Republic of Korea	2.6	1.4	2.2	2.3
Taipei,China	2.6	1.3	3.0	2.7
South Asia	**6.6**	**6.4**	**6.3**	**6.6**
Afghanistan	−20.7	−6.2	...	...
Bangladesh	7.1	5.8	6.1	6.6
Bhutan	5.2	4.0	4.4	7.0
India	7.0	7.6	7.0	7.2
Maldives	13.9	4.4	5.4	6.0
Nepal	5.6	1.9	3.6	4.8
Pakistan	6.2	−0.2	1.9	2.8
Sri Lanka	−7.3	−2.3	1.9	2.5
Southeast Asia	**5.7**	**4.1**	**4.6**	**4.7**
Brunei Darussalam	−1.6	1.4	3.7	2.8
Cambodia	5.2	5.0	5.8	6.0
Indonesia	5.3	5.0	5.0	5.0
Lao People's Democratic Republic	2.5	3.7	4.0	4.0
Malaysia	8.7	3.7	4.5	4.6
Myanmar	2.4	0.8	1.2	2.2
Philippines	7.6	5.6	6.0	6.2
Singapore	3.8	1.1	2.4	2.6
Thailand	2.5	1.9	2.6	3.0
Timor-Leste	4.0	1.9	3.4	4.1
Viet Nam	8.0	5.0	6.0	6.2
The Pacific	**7.9**	**3.5**	**3.3**	**4.0**
Cook Islands	10.5	13.3	9.1	5.2
Federated States of Micronesia	−0.6	2.6	3.1	2.8
Fiji	20.0	7.8	3.0	2.7
Kiribati	3.9	4.2	5.3	3.5
Marshall Islands	−0.7	2.5	2.7	1.7
Nauru	2.8	1.6	1.8	2.0
Niue	...	...	...	...
Palau	−1.7	−0.2	6.5	8.0
Papua New Guinea	5.2	2.0	3.3	4.6
Samoa	−5.3	8.0	4.2	4.0
Solomon Islands	−4.2	2.5	2.2	2.2
Tonga	−2.2	2.8	2.6	2.3
Tuvalu	0.7	3.9	3.5	2.4
Vanuatu	2.0	1.0	3.1	3.6

... = not available, e = estimate, f = forecast, GDP = gross domestic product.

Source: *Asian Development Outlook* database.

Caucasus and Central Asia economies will slow after the boost from re-exports and Russian migrant inflows. Growth in the subregion is forecast to fall to 4.3% in 2024, down from 5.3% in 2023, bouncing back to 5.0% in 2025. In Kazakhstan, growth is expected to slow to 3.8% in 2024 as healthy consumption will be balanced by moderation in services and industry. The completion of the Tengiz oil field expansion next year will drive the acceleration to 5.3% growth in 2025. In Uzbekistan, growth is forecast to moderate to 5.5% in 2024 and 5.6% in 2025 from 6.0% in 2023, as services, agriculture, and domestic demand cool on persistent inflation and slower growth in household income. Growth in Armenia and Georgia will also moderate as the windfall impact from the Russian invasion of Ukraine fades. In Azerbaijan, growth will be 1.2% in 2024 and 1.6% in 2025 as services offset declining oil output and revenue.

Growth in the Pacific will slightly decline in 2024 and pick up in 2025. The subregion's economy is projected to expand by 3.3% in 2024 before rising to 4.0% in 2025. In Papua New Guinea, the subregion's largest economy, growth is projected to accelerate to 3.3% in 2024 and 4.6% in 2025, driven by increased

mining activity with the reopening and rising output of major gold mines. This will offset slowing expansion in Fiji, the second-largest economy, from the fading tourism recovery. In the rest of the subregion, growth will be sustained by tourism and stimulus from public infrastructure projects.

Inflation Is Expected to Moderate Further

Regional inflation will cool further. Inflation in developing Asia will moderate to 3.2% in 2024 and 3.0% in 2025, down from 3.3% in 2023 (Figure 1.2.4). Tight monetary policy in most economies will help combat inflation, supported by moderating global food and energy prices. In contrast, inflation in East Asia is expected to pick up from last year as food prices normalize in the PRC.

The PRC is expected to recover from food deflation, with headline inflation forecast at 1.1% in 2024 and 1.5% in 2025 (Table 1.2.3). Pork prices are expected to begin rising again after their sharp decline

Figure 1.2.4 Inflation Forecasts for 2024 for Selected Economies in Developing Asia

Inflation remains elevated in Pakistan, the Lao People's Democratic Republic, and Myanmar.

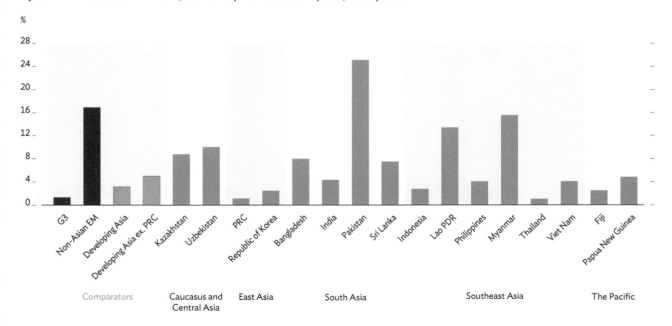

EM = emerging markets; G3 = euro area, Japan, United States; Lao PDR = Lao People's Democratic Republic; PRC = People's Republic of China.
Source: *Asian Development Outlook* database.

Table 1.2.3 Inflation in Developing Asia, %

Regional inflation will ease in 2024 and 2025.

	2022	2023e	2024f	2025f
Developing Asia	**4.4**	**3.3**	**3.2**	**3.0**
Developing Asia excluding the People's Republic of China	**6.8**	**6.3**	**5.1**	**4.4**
Caucasus and Central Asia	**12.9**	**10.5**	**7.9**	**7.0**
Armenia	8.6	2.0	3.0	3.5
Azerbaijan	13.9	8.8	5.5	6.5
Georgia	11.9	2.5	3.5	4.0
Kazakhstan	15.0	14.5	8.7	6.3
Kyrgyz Republic	13.9	10.8	7.0	6.5
Tajikistan	4.2	3.8	5.5	6.5
Turkmenistan	11.2	5.9	8.0	8.0
Uzbekistan	11.4	10.0	10.0	9.5
East Asia	**2.3**	**0.6**	**1.3**	**1.6**
Hong Kong, China	1.9	2.1	2.3	2.3
Mongolia	15.2	10.4	7.0	6.8
People's Republic of China	2.0	0.2	1.1	1.5
Republic of Korea	5.1	3.6	2.5	2.0
Taipei,China	2.9	2.5	2.3	2.0
South Asia	**8.0**	**8.4**	**7.0**	**5.8**
Afghanistan	7.8	10.8	..	..
Bangladesh	6.2	9.0	8.4	7.0
Bhutan	5.6	4.2	4.5	4.2
India	6.7	5.5	4.6	4.5
Maldives	2.3	2.9	3.2	2.5
Nepal	6.3	7.7	6.5	6.0
Pakistan	12.2	29.2	25.0	15.0
Sri Lanka	46.4	17.4	7.5	5.5
Southeast Asia	**5.3**	**4.1**	**3.2**	**3.0**
Brunei Darussalam	3.7	0.4	1.1	1.0
Cambodia	5.3	2.1	2.0	2.0
Indonesia	4.1	3.7	2.8	2.8
Lao People's Democratic Republic	23.0	31.2	20.0	7.0
Malaysia	3.4	2.5	2.6	2.6
Myanmar	27.2	22.0	15.5	10.2
Philippines	5.8	6.0	3.8	3.4
Singapore	6.1	4.8	3.0	2.2
Thailand	6.1	1.2	1.0	1.5
Timor-Leste	7.0	8.4	3.5	2.9
Viet Nam	3.2	3.3	4.0	4.0
The Pacific	**5.2**	**3.0**	**4.3**	**4.1**
Cook Islands	3.6	13.2	2.3	2.3
Federated States of Micronesia	5.0	5.3	4.1	3.5
Fiji	4.3	2.4	3.7	2.6
Kiribati	5.3	9.7	4.0	3.0
Marshall Islands	3.2	6.5	5.5	3.7
Nauru	1.5	5.2	10.3	3.5
Niue	3.1	8.6	..	..
Palau	13.2	12.4	5.5	1.0
Papua New Guinea	5.3	2.3	4.5	4.8
Samoa	8.8	12.0	4.5	4.3
Solomon Islands	5.4	4.6	3.2	2.7
Tonga	8.2	9.7	4.5	4.2
Tuvalu	12.2	7.2	3.0	3.0
Vanuatu	6.7	13.5	4.8	2.9

... = not available, e = estimate, f = forecast.

Source: *Asian Development Outlook* database.

last year as output recovered following the swine fever episode in 2018–2021. Slightly rising energy prices will also sustain positive inflation. However, continued weakness in domestic and external demand, and industrial profits will put downward pressure on producer prices and core inflation. This could be aggravated by the lingering effects of excess capacity in certain manufacturing sectors.

Inflation for the region's high-income technology exporters will continue moderating. Headline inflation in the ROK is projected to average 2.5% in 2024 and 2.0% in 2025 due to easing global oil prices. Its central bank signaled it will maintain tight policy until inflation reverts to its 2% target. Tighter monetary policy in Taipei,China should cool inflation to 2.3% in 2024 and 2.0% in 2025. In Singapore, headline inflation will moderate to 3.0% in 2024 and ease further to 2.2% in 2025. A stronger nominal effective exchange rate will also help contain Singapore's imported inflation. Slightly higher inflation in Hong Kong, China, at 2.3% in both 2024 and 2025, will be due to upward pressure from recovering consumption.

Inflation in South Asia is projected to decline, driven by lower domestic food prices. Inflation in India is forecast to decelerate to 4.6% in FY2024 and 4.5% in FY2025 as food prices moderate from normalized agricultural production after a weak harvest last year. Core inflation will dampen further, helped by lowered inflation expectations. The decline in commodity prices will also moderate inflation in Bangladesh to 8.4% in FY2024 and 7.0% in FY2025, together with still-tight monetary policy and a more favorable crop outlook. Sri Lanka will return to single-digit inflation at 7.5% in 2024 and 5.5% in 2025 after 2 years of high inflation. In Pakistan, rising administered energy prices will keep inflation high at 25.0% in FY2024 and 15.0% in FY2025.

Southeast Asia's inflation will continue to ease. In the near term, moderation in price growth toward central bank targets is expected. However, lower agriculture yield, elevated food prices, and currency depreciation could lead to upward pressure on inflation. Inflation will remain in double digits in the Lao PDR, as the kip depreciates, and in Myanmar, due to conflicts hindering food production.

Lower price pressures are expected in the Caucasus and Central Asia as food production increases and monetary policy remains tight. Continuing tight monetary policy in some economies will pull inflation down to 7.9% in 2024 and 7.0% in 2025, from 10.5% in 2023. Stable exchange rates are expected to temper inflation as well. Inflation will slow further as food production picks up and state subsidies for farmers help to bring down food prices.

Inflation in the Pacific will rise. Prices are forecast to grow by 4.3% in 2024 and 4.1% in 2025, due mainly to higher inflation in the two largest economies, Papua New Guinea and Fiji. In Papua New Guinea, inflation is expected to accelerate to 4.5% in 2024 and 4.8% in 2025, driven by exchange rate depreciation and power supply disruptions. In Fiji, inflation is projected to rise to 3.7% in 2024, mainly caused by the higher value-added tax rate. Nevertheless, for most of the subregion, inflation is expected to slow down due to lower global commodity prices.

Several Downside Risks Could Weigh on the Regional Outlook

While developing Asia's growth prospects are favorable and inflation continues to moderate, risks remain. The end of interest rate hiking cycles in many economies in the region, strong domestic demand, and signs of a gradual recovery in external demand drive the overall positive regional outlook. However, policy makers need to be cognizant of several risks. These include worsening conflict and geopolitical tensions, higher-for-longer global interest rates, spillovers due to amplified PRC property market stress, and more damaging weather-related events than expected.

Escalating conflict and geopolitical tensions could lead to renewed supply chain disruptions, higher commodity prices, and increased global economic uncertainty. Attacks on commercial cargo vessels in the Red Sea since the end of 2023 disrupted specific shipping routes and lengthened transit times, impairing global supply chains. In the week of 9 February, there were just 13 port calls through the Suez Canal—a stark contrast to the peak of 272 port calls at the end of November 2023. Average weekly port calls during the first 2 months of 2024 declined by 82% compared to the same period last year. Longer voyages led shipping companies to raise freight prices, particularly on Europe-Asia routes, resulting in shipping costs more than doubling on some routes compared to a year ago. These additional costs could potentially add inflationary pressures (Box 1.3.1). Despite longer shipping times, acute shortages have not yet materialized due to ample stocks and subdued demand. However, this could change if conditions worsen. Also, concerns persist over the impact of shipping disruptions on energy supply. Although a combination of offsetting factors has kept crude oil prices below $100/barrel, any escalation of the conflict to major oil producers could spike energy prices. This would affect other commodity prices, exacerbate economic uncertainty, dampen investment and thus hamper the outlook.

US monetary policy poses risks. While the Fed is expected to start loosening its monetary policy stance at the end of the second quarter of 2024, uncertainty remains. Slower-than-expected US disinflation could delay easing. Higher-for-longer rates and tighter global financial conditions could transmit to developing Asia through aggregate demand and investor sentiment. Global interest rate differentials relative to developing Asian economies in a higher-for-longer environment and the resulting impact on the region's exchange rates could affect the growth and inflation outlook. While the risk is tilted toward delayed easing, implying higher-for-longer interest rates, faster-than-expected disinflation could accelerate easing, supporting the growth outlook.

Model-based analysis indicates that higher-for-longer global interest rates would marginally affect developing Asia's inflation outlook, with a more muted impact on the region's growth outlook. A scenario is examined using model-based simulations whereby interest rates in the US and euro area are held constant throughout 2024 (Figure 1.3.1). The higher-for-longer scenario could occur if inflation moderates in the US and euro area more slowly than expected, for instance, due to tighter labor market conditions that amplify wage inflation and spill over into core inflation. The results show that higher-for-longer interest rates in the US and euro area compared to the baseline would marginally impact developing Asia's inflation outlook, while the growth outlook would be less affected. The relative appreciation of the US dollar and euro in a higher-for-longer environment would result in higher imported inflation in developing Asia due to weaker regional currencies. This would add around 0.15 percentage points to inflation in high-income technology exporters and other developing Asian economies relative to the baseline in 2024 and 2025. The effect would subside by 2026. The impact would be more pronounced and persistent for India, given the higher sensitivity of this country's inflation to exchange

Box 1.3.1 Potential Impact of Rising Shipping Costs on Inflation

Ongoing conflicts in the Middle East have disrupted shipping routes and raised concerns over the potential impact of rising shipping costs on inflation. Since October 2023, conflict has escalated in Gaza and the wider Middle East, including in the Red Sea where cargo ships entering the Suez Canal have been attacked. Egypt's Suez Canal is a key trade route connecting Europe and Asia, with an estimated 12% of global trade passing through the canal each day.

The Red Sea crisis has led to a re-routing of commercial vessels around South Africa, both a longer and costlier route. Consequently, shipping costs have gone up. The Baltic Dry Index (BDI), a freight-cost index for dry bulk materials transiting more than 20 oceanic shipping routes, has been quite volatile since the attack (box figure 1). Between September and December of 2023, the monthly average index increased by 82.1%, while daily fluctuations have been even sharper. Although the BDI softened in January, it has been spiking again since mid-February. The increase in shipping costs can affect consumer prices globally through its impact on prices of imported goods and local producers' intermediate inputs.

Empirical evidence indicates that higher shipping costs raise global inflation. For a sample of Organisation for Economic Co-operation and Development economies, Guilloux-Nefussi and Rusticelli (2021) estimated that a 50% rise in shipping costs leads to a 0.2 percentage points rise

in consumer price inflation after 4 quarters. Carriere-Swallow et al. (2023) estimated the impact of global shipping costs on consumer price indexes in 143 economies. Inflation generally tends to increase following spikes in shipping costs with the effects peaking around 12 months after the shock. Analysis also showed some dispersion in the effects across regions. In particular, they are more pronounced in small island economies, which tend to be located farther from trading partners.

Under certain assumptions, the inflationary effects of the current spike in shipping costs can be estimated. Assuming the BDI remains at its January 2024 level, the impact of the rise in shipping costs between September 2023 and January 2024 on inflation can be estimated over the forecast period (box figure 2). The assumption of a stable BDI provides conservative estimates, considering the renewed pressures since February. The estimates also assume no changes to other factors such as global and country-specific economic activity, global oil

2 Estimated Impact of the Recent Rise in Shipping Costs on Inflation for Asian, Island, and Landlocked Economies

The impact on inflation in Asia is estimated to peak in 13 months.

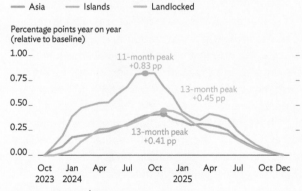

pp = percentage points.

Notes: Impact on year on year consumer prices inflation rates. The scenario is based on the actual dynamics of the Baltic Dry Index from September 2023 to January 2024 plus the assumption that BDI stays at its January 2024 level over the forecast horizon. Estimated impact on headline inflation is based on smoothed estimates from Carriere-Swallow et al. (2023, Figure 5.B), also extending the impact coefficients beyond 18 months following longer range estimates discussed in Guilloux-Nefussi and Rusticelli (2021).

Source: Asian Development Bank calculations.

1 Baltic Dry Index

Conflicts in the Middle East led to a spike in shipping costs.

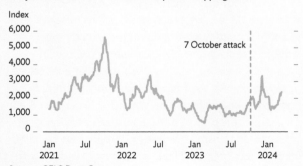

Source: CEIC Data Company.

Box 1.3.1 *Continued*

prices, and global food prices. Thus, the estimated effects can be seen as the additional potential impact of rising shipping costs on top of any effects other factors may have on inflation.

The rise in shipping costs has a persistent effect on consumer price inflation. The effect peaks 13 months after the start of the shocks and is estimated to add 0.41 percentage points to inflation in Asian economies. The effect is slightly larger for landlocked economies, which have no direct access to ocean ports. The impact on small island economies is larger, adding 0.83 percentage points to inflation at its peak 11 months after the start of the shocks. These estimates can be translated into subregional figures by weighting the predictions for each economy, which vary depending on whether it is a landlocked or an island territory, using gross domestic product purchasing power parity weights (box table). The Caucasus and Central Asia is mostly composed by landlocked economies, the only exception being Georgia; the potential impact on inflation rates in the subregion is just 0.04 percentage points higher than East Asia, South Asia, and Southeast Asia, which have fewer landlocked economies. The Pacific is the most exposed to inflationary risks

Estimated Impact of Rising Shipping Costs on Inflation by Subregion

Caucasus and Central Asia	East Asia	South Asia	Southeast Asia	The Pacific
+0.45 p.p.	+0.41 p.p.	+0.41 p.p.	+0.41 p.p.	+0.55 p.p.

p.p. = percentage point.
Notes: Estimates are the peak impact based on assumptions in box figure 2 aggregated to the subregional level using gross domestic product purchasing power parity weights.
Source: Asian Development Bank calculations.

coming from shipping disruptions. By September 2024, year-on-year inflation rates in the Pacific can increase by 0.55 percentage points because of rising shipping costs.

References:
Carriere-Swallow, Y., P. Deb, D. Furceri, D. Jimenez, and J. D. Ostry. 2023. Shipping costs and inflation. *Journal of International Money and Finance* 130 (102771).
Guilloux-Nefussi, S. and E. Rusticelli. How will rising shipping cost affect inflation in OECD countries? OECD ECOSCOPE.

This box was written by Jaqueson K. Galimberti of the Economic Research and Development Impact Department, ADB, Manila.

rate fluctuations and its greater reliance on imported goods. Meanwhile, gains in competitiveness due to the exchange rate effects in a higher-for-longer scenario are estimated to add around 0.05 percentage points to growth relative to the 2024 baseline for high-income technology exporters, India, and the rest of developing Asia. These positive growth effects turn negative in 2025 and 2026 as the impact of monetary policy easing in the US and euro area gradually takes effect, reverting any exchange rate gains from the previous year.

Increased property market stress, and possible deflation, in the PRC could worsen the outlook. A worse-than-expected deterioration in the PRC's property market could dampen consumer sentiment and domestic demand. Property-related industries, such as construction and real estate, would suffer, lowering overall economic activity in the PRC. Lower PRC consumption and investment could also reduce

global trade flows, harming export-oriented economies. Analysis in Asian Development Outlook September 2023 suggests that, under a moderate PRC policy response scenario, negative spillovers to the GDP of developing Asia (excluding the PRC) would be negligible, with GDP declining by about 0.04 percentage points relative to the baseline. Nonetheless, a more protracted and severe downturn than expected in the PRC property market could worsen its slowdown. In the absence of sufficient policy action, this in turn could trigger a rise in global risk aversion and capital flight, with potentially negative repercussions for other economies in developing Asia as financial conditions tighten. In addition, an escalation in deflationary concerns in the PRC could spill over to trading partners, as lower export prices could transmit disinflation abroad. This could hurt investor sentiment and lead to a potential widening of interest rate differentials, triggering capital outflows and worsening the growth outlook.

Figure 1.3.1 Model-Based Simulations of Higher-for-Longer Interest Rates

Monetary policy in the US and euro area: Baseline vs Higher-for-longer scenario.

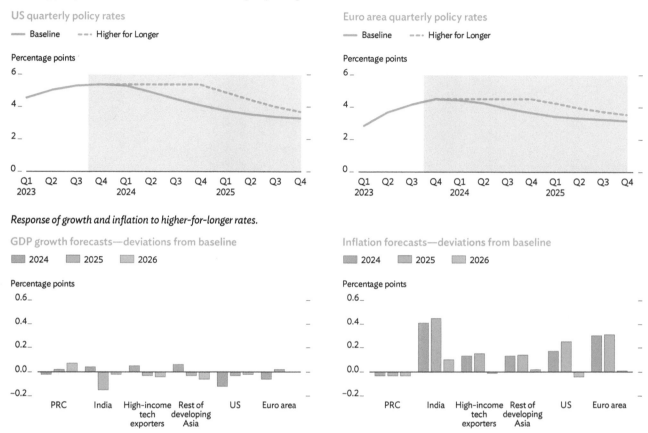

Response of growth and inflation to higher-for-longer rates.

GDP = gross domestic product, PRC = People's Republic of China, Q = quarter, US = United States.

Note: Results based on the Global Projection Model (Asian Development Bank version). Fed rates remain constant in 2024 and ease beginning only in the first quarter of 2025. The results factor in the same assumed monetary policy path for the euro area. More specifically, the scenario includes (i) +50 basis points shock to United States (US) and euro area core consumer price index every quarter in 2024; (ii) interest rates in US and euro area kept constant throughout 2024; (iii) some tightening to bank lending conditions in US, euro area and Japan. Emerging Asia includes Indonesia, Malaysia, the Philippines, and Thailand. High-income tech exporters include the Republic of Korea; Hong Kong, China; Singapore; and Taipei,China.

Source: Asian Development Bank calculations.

Adverse weather conditions associated with El Niño and La Niña could raise commodity prices and exacerbate food insecurity. According to the February 2024 climate forecast from the International Research Institute for Climate and Society (IRICS), several countries in Southeast Asia, including Myanmar, the Philippines, Thailand, and Viet Nam, are forecast to have higher probabilities of below-normal precipitation from March to May 2024 (Figure 1.3.2). Conversely, above-normal precipitation is forecast across various parts of Kazakhstan, Mongolia, and the PRC during the same period. A gradual shift toward above-normal precipitation is expected from April–June 2024, extending until the end of August 2024, covering the Maritime Continent (Indonesia,

Papua New Guinea, and the Philippines) and mainland Southeast Asia. During May-July and June-August 2024, the forecast indicates moderate probabilities of above-normal precipitation across different countries in South Asia. These predicted precipitation patterns align closely with historical La Niña events, typically following a strong El Niño, which is projected to begin in June-August 2024. Weather conditions from March to August are critical as they mark the planting or growing season for wheat, corn, and rice. While some disruptions can be expected based on the IRICS forecast, potentially lowering agricultural production and increasing concerns over commodity prices and food security, worse-than-expected weather conditions would magnify these effects.

Figure 1.3.2 Forecast Precipitation April–June 2024

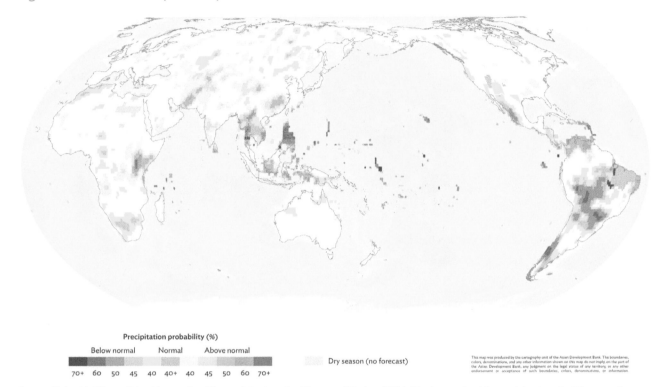

Precipitation probability (%)

Below normal   Normal   Above normal

70+ 60 50 45 40 40+ 40 45 50 60 70+

Dry season (no forecast)

This map was produced by the cartography unit of the Asian Development Bank. The boundaries, colors, denominations, and any other information shown on this map do not imply, on the part of the Asian Development Bank, any judgment on the legal status of any territory, or any other endorsement or acceptance of such boundaries, colors, denominations, or information

Source: Columbia Climate School International Research Institute for Climate and Society. 2024. IRI – International Research Institute for Climate and Society | Seasonal Climate Forecasts (columbia.edu). March.

Climate change continues to be a key medium-term challenge facing the region. Without effective policy action, climate change can lead to more frequent and extreme weather events, threatening production, especially in agriculture. The consequences are particularly critical for low-income nations, where agriculture usually accounts for a significant share of the economy. These countries are particularly susceptible to harsh weather conditions and lack the technologies to mitigate the harm done.

Other medium-term challenges relate to economic fragmentation, public finances, and demographic change. Economic fragmentation can make trade and investment less efficient. Related to this, reconfiguring global supply chains to reduce concentration risks and support diversification can take time, increasing uncertainty in trade and investment. On public finance, while debt levels in the region have stabilized, improving fiscal conditions and creating fiscal space will require greater efforts on generating tax revenue and mobilizing domestic financial resources. Demographic change and population aging in the region also strain public finances, hindering productivity growth and potential output.

Asia's Rebounding Semiconductor Sector and the Role of Artificial Intelligence

High-income and developing economies in East Asia and Southeast Asia together account for more than 80% of global semiconductor manufacturing. This makes the world dependent on the region's semiconductor exports, and the region's economic prospects dependent on the health of global semiconductor demand. Semiconductors are the fundamental building block of modern electronics. Their property to act as either conductors or insulators makes them indispensable in regulating electronic flow and enables them to perform logic operations. Thus, semiconductors are integral not only to consumer electronics but also to technologies like artificial intelligence (AI), 5G telecommunications, and electric and autonomous vehicles, among others.

Semiconductor exports from Asia are rising, driven by increasing global demand for microprocessors and memory chips. After contracting sharply at the end of 2022, exports from Asia's main semiconductor-manufacturing economies picked up over 2023 and were about 15% higher in the last quarter of the year relative to the first quarter (Figure 1.4.1, black line). This increase was comparable to that of exports of other electrical machinery equipment (Figure 1.4.1, blue line). However, while in nominal terms exports of semiconductors ended 2023 not far off the mid-2022 record highs, those of other electrical machinery remained significantly lower than the peaks reached during the COVID-19 pandemic. The pickup in semiconductor exports was primarily driven by increasing demand for a specific subset of semiconductors—microprocessors and memory chips. Their share in overall semiconductor exports from Asia's main producers rose almost five percentage points over 2023 (Figure 1.4.1, orange bars). Putting it differently, exports of microprocessors

Figure 1.4.1 Exports of Electrical Machinery Equipment and Parts, Selected Asian Economies

Exports gradually picked up over 2023, after contracting sharply at the end of 2022.

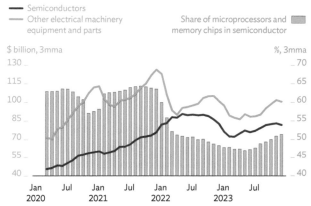

3mma = 3-month moving average.

Notes: Electrical machinery equipment and parts refer to Harmonized System (HS) Code 85. Semiconductors refer to the sum of HS Code 8541 (semiconductor devices) and HS Code 8542 (electronic integrated circuits). Other electrical machinery equipment and parts refer to HS Code 85 less "semiconductors". Microprocessors and memory chips respectively refer to HS Codes 8542.31 (electronic integrated circuits; processors and controllers, whether or not combined with memories, converters, logic circuits, amplifiers, clock and timing circuits, or other circuits) and 8542.32 (electronic integrated circuits; and memory chips). Data cover Hong Kong, China; Japan; Malaysia; the People's Republic of China; the Philippines; Republic of Korea; Singapore; and Taipei,China.

Sources: United Nations COMTRADE Database; International Trade Center Trade Map; Philippine Statistics Authority, OpenStat; Korea Customs Service, Trade Statistics.

and memory chips grew by almost 25% from the first to the last quarter of 2023, while exports of all other semiconductors were up by only around 5%.

The AI boom is fueling demand for advanced microprocessors and memory chips. Advanced microprocessors, including graphics processing units (GPUs) and central processing units (CPUs), execute

This chapter was written by Gabriele Ciminelli, Pilipinas Quising, and Shiela Romance of the Economic Research and Development Impact Department, ADB, Manila.

the complex algorithms and computations required for AI training, where vast amounts of data are processed to learn patterns, make predictions, or generate responses. Memory chips, including high bandwidth memory (HBM) and graphics double data rate 6 (GDDR6), store the vast datasets that AI algorithms need to access and hold the instructions and data to be processed.[1] The launch in November 2022 of ChatGPT, a free-to-use AI language model, ushered in a global race to develop new AI models, which has significantly increased demand for these microchips. This has boosted profits and equity valuations of companies in the upstream semiconductor value chain—like NVIDIA and Advanced Micro Devices, which design these products (Figure 1.4.2, black and red lines)—and increased shipments from Asia to varying degrees. A comparison between Taipei,China and the Republic of Korea (ROK) is instructive.

Figure 1.4.2 Equity Prices of Semiconductor-Related Companies

Market valuations of companies designing microprocessors vastly outperformed the broader semiconductor sector since early 2023.

— Advance Micro Devices   — Samsung
— NVIDIA   — TSMC
— SK Hynix   — VanEck Semiconductor ETF

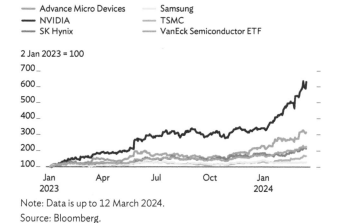

2 Jan 2023 = 100

Note: Data is up to 12 March 2024.
Source: Bloomberg.

Taipei,China is the global leader in semiconductor manufacturing, but its products are used in applications well beyond AI. Headquartered in Taipei,China, TSMC, the world's largest semiconductor manufacturer, is a good example. While an important supplier for NVIDIA, TSMC has a much broader customer base. In the first quarter of 2023, about 80% of its revenues came from the end-market for

smartphones and personal computers (Kim, 2023). The low exposure of TSMC to AI-driven shifts in demand for specific microchips can be seen by comparing its subdued stock market value relative to more AI-exposed semiconductor-related companies (Figure 1.4.2). Other semiconductor manufacturers in Taipei,China serve similar customers, so that overall memory chips and microprocessors accounted for just about 20% of Taipei,China's semiconductor exports in 2023 (Figure 1.4.3, blue and yellow bars). In contrast, other electronic integrated circuits (EICs)—including, among others, power management EICs and EICs integrating multiple components of a computer onto a single chip—made up nearly all the remaining 80%. As a result, Taipei,China's overall semiconductor exports grew only about 12% from the first to last quarter of 2023 (Figure 1.4.4, yellow dots), despite microprocessor exports surging almost 40% and memory chip exports rising almost 15% over the same period.

The Republic of Korea (ROK) is highly specialized in microprocessor and memory chip manufacturing, allowing its semiconductor sector to rebound strongly over 2023. Samsung and Sk Hynix, both headquartered in the ROK, are the world's two largest manufacturers of memory chips, making the country the global leader in producing these specific components (International Trade Administration, 2023). Although Samsung has a larger market share than Sk Hynix for memory chips, its product line is much broader, as it includes smartphones, monitors and televisions, among others. By contrast, Sk Hynix is highly specialized in producing memory chips. This asymmetry can be seen in the divergent stock market prices of the two companies. Sk Hynix's price more than doubled in the 14 months since January 2023 (Figure 1.4.2, purple line) on increasing memory chip orders driven by the AI boom, while Samsung's grew much more modestly. Overall, microprocessors and memory chips made up more than 80% of semiconductor exports from the ROK to the rest of the world in 2023 (Figure 1.4.3, blue and yellow bars). As these microchips are essential for the development of AI models, the ROK is directly benefitting from the current AI boom. This is reflected in the almost 35% growth of overall exports of semiconductors over 2023 (Figure 1.4.4, yellow dots).

---

[1]   See Khan et al. (2021) for a review of the role played by advanced microprocessors and memory chips in AI.

Figure 1.4.3 Shares of Semiconductor Devices and Electronic Integrated Circuits in Overall Exports, Selected Asian Economies, 2023

Asian economies are heterogenous by degree of specialization in producing different types of semiconductors.

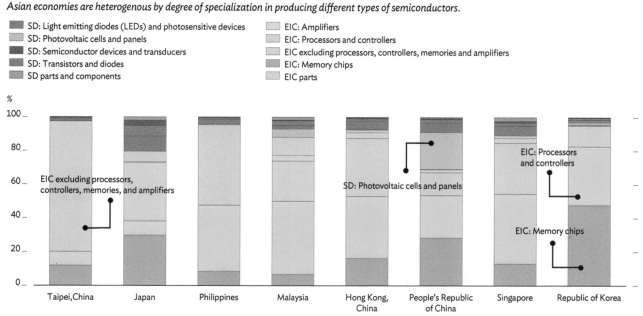

SD = semiconductor devices, EIC = electronic integrated circuits.

Notes: Semiconductors are decomposed into semiconductor devices, Harmonized System (HS) code 8541, and electronic integrated circuits, HS code 8542. Semiconductor devices are further decomposed into photovoltaic cells and panels (HS codes 854143 and 854142); transistors and diodes (HS codes 854129, 854121, 854110 and 854130); light emitting diodes (LEDs) and photosensitive devices (HS codes 854141, 854149 and 854140); semiconductor devices and transducers (HS codes 854159, 854150, 854151 and 854160); parts and components of semiconductor devices (HS codes 854190). Electronic integrated circuits are further decomposed into processors and controllers (HS code 854231); memory chips (HS code 854232); amplifiers (HS code 854233); electronic integrated circuits excluding processors, controllers, memories, and amplifiers (HS code 854239); and parts of electronic integrated circuits (HS code 854290).

Sources: United Nations COMTRADE Database; International Trade Center Trade Map; Philippine Statistics Authority, OpenStat; Korea Customs Service, Trade Statistics.

Other economies in East Asia and Southeast Asia are trying to increase their share in the global semiconductor value chain. PRC exports of semiconductors grew only modestly in 2023 due to a steep drop in demand for photovoltaic cells, for which it is the global leader. Going forward, the PRC plans to refine and scale up production of advanced microchips, including microprocessors and memory chips. But the recent embargo on exports of sophisticated chip-making equipment from the US and other economies to the PRC (Cash, 2024) may constrain its ability to manufacture advanced microchips. Japan's share in the global semiconductor industry fell from over 50% in 1988 to about 10% in 2019 (Tochibayashi and Kutty, 2023). Currently, it is not as specialized in microprocessors and memory chips as other economies, instead being the main supplier of manufacturing equipment and materials for the broader semiconductor industry, but the government is trying to boost domestic production through subsidies and public-private partnerships (Tochibayashi and Kutty, 2023). The share of memory chips and microprocessors directly manufactured in Malaysia, the Philippines, Thailand, and Viet Nam is small. However, these economies may still benefit from the AI-driven demand for specific microchips, given their specialization in downstream services such as assembly, testing, and packaging (Tieying, 2021), critical to the global semiconductor value chain. For example, semiconductor imports into the US from Malaysia were about 20% of overall US semiconductor imports in 2023 (Ruehl, 2024). Singapore manufactures advanced microchips (Tieying, 2021) and—together with Hong Kong, China—also imports and re-exports semiconductor components to other economies after sorting and repackaging.

Figure 1.4.4 Contributions of Semiconductor Devices and Electronic Integrated Circuits to Semiconductor Export Growth, Fourth Quarter 2023 vs First Quarter 2023, Selected Asian Economies

Microprocessors and memory chips contributed the most to overall semiconductor export growth in most economies in 2023.

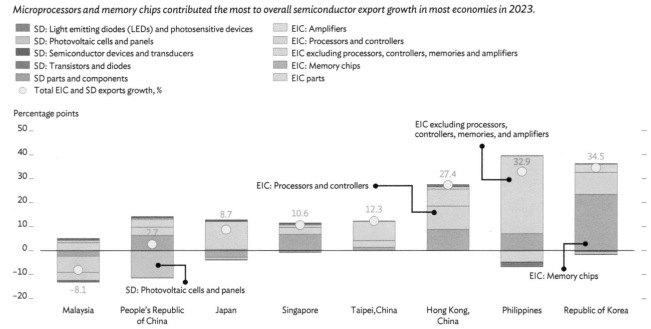

EIC = electronic integrated circuits, SD = semiconductor devices.

Notes: Semiconductors are decomposed into semiconductor devices, Harmonized System (HS) code 8541, and electronic integrated circuits, HS code 8542. Semiconductor devices are further decomposed into photovoltaic cells and panels (HS codes 854143 and 854142); transistors and diodes (HS codes 854129, 854121, 854110 and 854130); light emitting diodes (LEDs) and photosensitive devices (HS codes 854141, 854149 and 854140); semiconductor devices and transducers (HS codes 854159, 854150, 854151 and 854160); parts and components of semiconductor devices (HS codes 854190). Electronic integrated circuits are further decomposed into processors and controllers (HS code 854231); memory chips (HS code 854232); amplifiers (HS code 854233); electronic integrated circuits excluding processors, controllers, memories, and amplifiers (HS code 854239); and parts of electronic integrated circuits (HS code 854290).

Sources: United Nations COMTRADE Database; International Trade Center Trade Map; Philippine Statistics Authority, OpenStat; Korea Customs Service, Trade Statistics.

The prospects for Asia's semiconductor industry depend on the trends in global demand as well as domestic and foreign industrial policies. Despite the short-term ups and downs of the semiconductor cycle, demand for microprocessors and memory chips is expected to continue growing over the medium- to long-term (Mordor Intelligence, 2024). Semiconductor manufacturers could also benefit from a recovery in demand for computers, mobile phones and electric vehicles, which has recently moderated. The COVID-19 pandemic illustrated the vulnerabilities of relying on concentrated production centers, as supply was severely hit when factories were temporarily shut down. In addition, rising geopolitical tensions in East Asia and the desire to counterbalance the PRC's growing market share are pushing economies outside Asia to devise incentives to reshore, nearshore, or at least friendshore production

(Citigroup, 2024). The ROK and Taipei,China risk losing the most from this, while Southeast Asia's economies may gain (Tieying, 2021). Southeast Asia's economies provide younger, more abundant, and lower wage workers that can attract investments from large semiconductor manufacturers in East Asia as they diversify their production base. Anectodical evidence suggests that this is already taking place, with the state of Penang in Malaysia attracting almost $13 billion in semiconductor-related foreign direct investment in 2023, more than the total from 2013 to 2020 combined (Ruehl, 2024). To keep harnessing this potential, governments in the region should continue devising policies that attract foreign direct investment, increase spending on research and development, and invest in human capital development, as semiconductor manufacturing requires highly skilled labor.

References

Cash, J. 2024. China raises concerns with US over chip-making export controls, sanctions. Reuters.

Citigroup. 2024. The U.S.–China Chip War: Who Dares to Win?.

International Trade Administration. 2023. South Korea semiconductors market intelligence.

Khan, FH., M. A. Pasha, and S. Masud. 2021. Advancements in Microprocessor Architecture for Ubiquitous AI-An Overview on History, Evolution, and Upcoming Challenges in AI Implementation. *Micromachines* (Basel). 12(6):665.

Kim, T. 2023. *Barron's Technology Street Notes.* 2 June.

Mordor Intelligence. 2024. Semiconductor Industry Size & Share Analysis - Growth Trends & Forecasts.

Ruehl, M. 2024. Malaysia: the surprise winner from US-[People's Republic of China] chip wars.

Tieying, M. 2021. ASEAN's potential in semiconductor manufacturing. *Development Bank of Singapore Economics and Strategy.*

Tochibayashi, N. and N. Kutty. 2023. How Japan's semiconductor industry is leaping into the future. *World Economic Forum.*

Global Growth Slows Slightly as Inflation Tamed

Growth in the major advanced economies of the United States (US), the euro area, and Japan is expected to slow in 2024, followed by a gradual recovery in 2025, albeit with diverging trajectories. Domestic demand will be tempered this year by the lagged effects of tight monetary policy, and external demand by the ongoing global trade slowdown. As disinflation allows for monetary policy easing starting later this year, growth is expected to gradually improve in 2025 as lower inflation and interest rates bolster domestic demand and investment, and trade benefits from a more stable global environment. In aggregate, growth in the major advanced economies is expected to slow from 1.7% in 2023 to 1.3% in 2024 and pick up to 1.5% in 2025 (Table A.1).

Table A.1 Baseline Assumptions on the International Economy

	2022	2023	2024	2025
	Actual	Estimate	Forecast	
GDP growth, %				
Major advanced economies[a]	2.4	1.7	1.3	1.5
United States	1.9	2.5	1.9	1.7
Euro area	3.4	0.5	0.7	1.4
Japan	1.0	1.9	0.6	0.8
Inflation, %				
Major advanced economies[a]	7.5	4.5	2.4	2.0
United States	8.0	4.1	2.6	2.2
Euro area	8.4	5.4	2.4	2.0
Japan	2.5	3.3	1.9	1.3
Brent crude spot prices, average, $/barrel	100.0	83.0	82.0	79.0
Interest rates				
United States federal funds rate, average, %	1.7	5.0	5.2	4.2
European Central Bank refinancing rate, average, %	0.7	3.9	4.2	3.1
Bank of Japan overnight call rate, average, %	0.0	0.0	0.0	0.1
$ Libor,[b] %	2.1	5.1	5.2	4.2

GDP = gross domestic product.

[a] Average growth rates are weighted by GDP purchasing power parity.

[b] Average London interbank offered rate quotations on 1-month loans.

Sources: Bloomberg; CEIC Data Company; Haver Analytics; International Monetary Fund. World Economic Outlook; Asian Development Bank estimates.

This annex was written by John Beirne, Gabriele Ciminelli, Jules Hugot, Matteo Lanzafame, Pilipinas Quising, Arief Ramayandi, and Dennis Sorino of the Economic Research and Development Impact Department (ERDI), ADB, Manila, and Emmanuel Alano, Michael Timbang, and Jesson Pagaduan, ERDI consultants.

Recent Developments in the Major Advanced Economies

United States

Gross domestic product (GDP) grew by 2.5% in 2023, surpassing expectations and driven by robust consumer and government spending. The latter half of 2023 showcased the resilience of the economy, with GDP surging by 4.9% in the third quarter (Q3) and maintaining a 3.3% growth in Q4 (Figure A.1). Despite a series of interest rate increases that began in 2022 and continued into 2023, consumption remained the key economic driver, expanding by 2.2% on the back of robust growth in employment and real income. Government spending also rose significantly, rising by 4.0% in 2023 after declining by 0.9% in 2022, boosted by a substantial increase in gross investment and compensation of government employees. However, private investment and exports were challenged by weaker global demand. Investment declined by 1.2% in 2023 and export growth decelerated to 2.7% from 7.0% in 2022. Imports also declined by 1.7% as goods imports from the People's Republic of China (PRC) continued to fall.

Figure A.1 Demand-Side Contributions to Growth, United States

Economic expansion continued in 2023, driven by strong consumption.

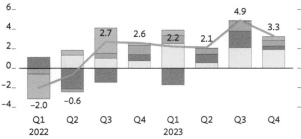

Q = quarter, qoq = quarter on quarter.
Sources: Department of Commerce. Bureau of Economic Analysis; Haver Analytics.

Consumption is projected to remain strong, but the investment outlook is rather bleak. Consumption was strong with the index of consumer confidence improving from 104.5 in December 2023 to 107.3 in January of this year and retail sales remaining stable. The trend of softer inflation and wage growth—backed by resilience in the labor market—is expected to continue to support consumption in 2024. Unemployment has remained at 3.7% since November 2023 despite some signs of slower economic activity. The ISM non-manufacturing activity index indicated robust demand for services. A strong rebound in new orders led to a surge in the services purchasing managers' index (PMI) from 50.5 in December 2023 to 53.4 in January of this year (reading > 50 signals expansion in activity) and led to an increase in the composite PMI from 50.1 in December to 52.9 in January. However, although the manufacturing PMI picked up in January, it has remained in contraction territory since Q4 2022 after the continued increase in interest rates that year (Figure A.2). This reading suggests a cautious outlook for investment, particularly in manufacturing.

Figure A.2 Business Activity, United States

Leading indicators improved in January 2024.

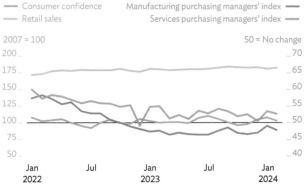

Note: A purchasing managers' index reading < 50 signals deterioration, >50 improvement.
Source: Haver Analytics.

The rapid disinflation since mid-2022 slowed beginning mid-2023, as the job market remains robust. After declining from 9.1% in June 2022 to 3.0% in June 2023, headline inflation has not decreased much since, coming in at 3.1% in January 2024 (Figure A.3). Core inflation has also remained relatively high at 3.9% in January. The Federal Reserve continued to hold its policy rate steady at its January meeting and has emphasized a data-dependent approach in guiding

Figure A.3 Inflation, Federal Funds Rate, and Unemployment Rate, United States

Fed rate stays unchanged as core inflation remains stubborn and employment grows.

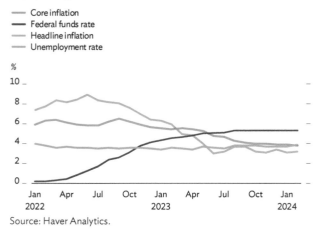

— Core inflation
— Federal funds rate
— Headline inflation
— Unemployment rate

Source: Haver Analytics.

any interest rate changes. The Fed is now expected to start cutting its policy rate only in late Q2. The labor market remained robust with the unemployment rate at 3.9% in February and with continued expansion in job opportunities—February saw an increase of 275,000 jobs in non-farm employment.

Growth is expected to slow to 1.9% in 2024 and 1.7% in 2025. Growth will slow this year amid weaker global demand and the lagged effect of monetary tightening in 2022–2023. Domestic demand will continue supporting growth, but external demand will be less favorable given the ongoing slowdown in global trade. More stable global demand will support growth in 2025, but a softer labor market and a cooling consumption growth should moderate growth in 2025 to 1.7%. Average inflation is expected to soften further from 4.1% in 2023 to 2.6% this year and 2.2% in 2025.

Risks to the forecast are tilted to the downside.
Tighter labor market conditions may put upward pressure on inflation during the forecast horizon, which could delay the Fed from lowering interest rates. While the risk is tilted toward higher-for-longer interest rates, a faster-than-expected acceleration in disinflation could lead to earlier easing of monetary policy. In addition, uncertainties from the upcoming elections will affect the economy beyond 2024 with fiscal and trade policy possibly undergoing substantial changes, which could have either a positive or negative impact on growth forecasts depending on the direction these changes take.

Euro area

Growth in the euro area slowed substantially to 0.5% in 2023 from 3.4% in 2022, hit by both still-high, if declining, energy prices and rising interest rates. The pass through from higher global energy prices to household and firms' energy bills and the broader consumption basket continued in the first half (H1) of 2023, denting consumer spending and weighing on investment. The tightening of monetary policy by the European Central Bank (ECB), which started in Q3 2022 and only ended in Q4 2023, significantly reduced loan demand throughout 2023 (Figure A.4), further contributing to the economic slowdown. Germany dragged down growth with its economy contracting by 0.3% in 2023 on the back of falling industrial production due to high energy prices and weak external demand. Italy and France expanded modestly, by 0.9%, while growth was robust in tourism-dependent economies, including Spain (2.5%), Portugal (2.3%) and Greece (2.0%).

Figure A.4 Changes in Demand for Loans to Firms and Contributing Factors, Euro Area

High interest rates and declining fixed investments reduced firms' loan demand in 2023.

▨ Fixed investment
▨ General level of interest rates
▨ Inventories and working capital
▨ Other financing needs
— Overall demand

Q = quarter.
Note: Overall demand refers to the difference between the percentage of banks reporting an increase in demand for loans and those reporting a decrease relative to the previous quarter. Contributing factors report the difference between the percentages of banks reporting that the given factor contributed to increasing and decreasing demand.
Sources: Haver Analytics; European Central Bank.

The labor market remains resilient and leading indicators point to a tentative pickup in activity in 2024. The unemployment rate continued trending downward in 2023, reaching a historic low in Q4 2023. Wage growth rose to more than 5% year-on-year in Q3 2023. Coupled with rapidly declining inflation rates and still-high pandemic savings, this may bolster household consumer spending in 2024. Although still in contraction territory, the February 2024 key manufacturing PMI stayed close to January's 11-month high, while the economic sentiment indicator remained close to the 10-month high reached in December 2023 and the services PMI moved back into expansion after declining steeply in Q2–Q3 2023 (Figure A.5). The decline in energy prices, if sustained, will support the nascent pickup in activity.

Figure A.5 Economic Sentiment and Purchasing Managers' Index, Euro Area

Leading indicators improved in Q4 2023 after declining steeply in Q2 2023.

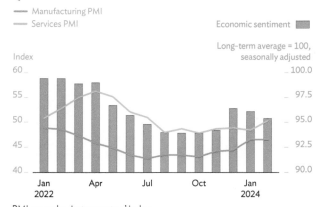

PMI = purchasing managers' index.
Note: A PMI reading <50 signals deterioration, >50 improvement.
Sources: CEIC Data Company; Haver Analytics.

Headline inflation is forecast to soften from 5.4% in 2023 to 2.4% in 2024 and reach 2.0% in 2025. In month-on-month terms, headline and core inflation have been close to zero since the end of 2023, indicating that disinflation is well underway (Figure A.6). With consumer inflation expectations declining robustly and the ECB expected to keep policy rates around current levels at least until mid-2024, before starting to cautiously loosen the monetary stance, domestic demand is unlikely to reverse the trend-decline of core inflation, which reached 3.1% in February 2024 in year-on-year terms. However, supply-

Figure A.6 Realized and Expected Inflation, Euro Area

Headline and core inflation declined rapidly in 2023.

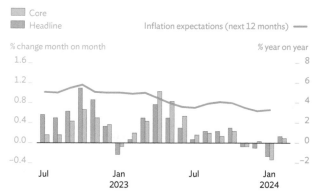

Note: Headline and core inflation are 3-month moving averages. Inflation expectation is the median expectation for euro area inflation for the next 12 months.
Sources: Haver Analytics; European Central Bank.

side disruptions in global energy and shipping markets may still put upward pressure on euro area inflation rates in 2024–2025.

GDP growth is forecast at 0.7% for 2024 and 1.4% for 2025. Activity will pick up only gradually after the near stagnation of H2 2023, amid significant headwinds. While domestic demand should contribute positively, the external environment will be less supportive, with an ongoing global trade slowdown and the expected softening in the US and the PRC. Moreover, credit conditions are likely to remain tight throughout 2024, thus putting the brakes on the recovery of domestic demand. Fiscal policy will be mildly supportive over 2024–2025, owing to rising public investment partly financed through the Recovery and Resilience Facility of the European Union. Growth is expected to increase more robustly from the second half of 2024 and into 2025 as lower inflation and declining interest rates boost domestic demand and investment, and the external environment improves. If successful, ongoing structural reforms may lift medium-term potential growth among the weaker euro area members.

Growth forecasts face downside risks. A spike in ongoing geopolitical tensions may renew supply disruptions and push inflation upwards, as energy and transport costs increase. Rising inflationary pressures may then complicate the expected ECB monetary policy easing. A new flare-up in trade tensions, such as between the European Union and the PRC, and banking stress due to losses in the commercial property sector are other downside risks. Faster-than-expected public investment spending is an upside risk.

Japan

The Japanese economy grew by 1.9% in 2023, up from 1.0% in 2022. Strong performance in H1 2023 compensated for the weak performance in the last two quarters of the year. Revised government data showed GDP expanded by 0.4% quarter-on-quarter (qoq) seasonally adjusted annualized rate (saar) in Q4 2023, after a 3.2% slump in Q3 (Figure A.7). Gross capital investment, which increased by 1.8% (qoq saar), supported the upward revision. Notably, investment in other machinery and equipment jumped by 13.7% following contractions in Q2 and Q3. Additionally, in Q4, exports grew faster than imports, resulting in a net trade contribution of 0.7% points to Q4 growth, compared to a subtraction of 0.1% points in the previous quarter. By contrast, private consumption, which accounts for more than half of GDP, fell for the third consecutive quarter in Q4, dampened by high inflation.

Inflation averaged 3.3% in 2023. This marked the highest inflation rate in nearly a decade for the country. Goods inflation averaged 4.6%, down from an average of 5.5% in 2022. Much of the persistence in goods inflation came from high food prices, which averaged 8.1% in 2023. The yen's depreciation further fueled inflation as firms passed on the higher cost of imported raw materials to consumers. Inflation excluding food and energy jumped to 2.6% from an average of 0.1% in 2022 as services inflation turned positive in 2023 (Figure A.8). The main driver for services inflation was recreational services, particularly hotel charges which spiked 17.3% in 2023 following the recovery of Japan's tourism since May. Recent inflation developments prompted the Bank of Japan on 19 March 2024 to end its negative interest rate policy, moving to a zero to +0.1% range from the previous −0.1% to zero range. The central bank also terminated its yield curve control policy, which had capped Japanese government bond yields at around zero, although purchases of Japanese government bonds can still take place to avert spikes in yields. To help the market function better, flexibility had been introduced during 2023 on yield curve control by widening the band around the target, with a 1% level regarded as a reference rate. While negative interest rates and yield curve control have been abandoned, the Bank of Japan's monetary policy stance remains accommodative.

Figure A.7 Demand-Side Contributions to Growth, Japan

GDP contracted in the last 2 quarters of 2023 after strong performance in the 1st half.

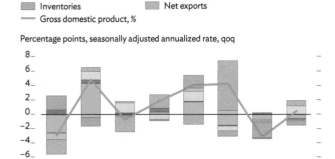

Percentage points, seasonally adjusted annualized rate, qoq

GDP = gross domestic product, Q = quarter, qoq = quarter on quarter.
Source: CEIC Data Company.

Figure A.8 Inflation, Japan

Inflation gradually declined but remains above the Bank of Japan target.

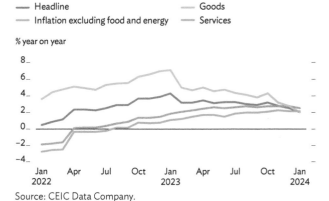

% year on year

Source: CEIC Data Company.

GDP growth is expected to slow to 0.6% in 2024 before picking up to 0.8% in 2025. Exports, which had grown by double digits since 2021, increased by 2.8% in 2023. A broad-based depreciation of the yen in 2023 of around 8% helped to support external demand. The primary driver for export growth in 2023 was a 36.6% increase in motor vehicle shipments, a significant share of which was accounted for by pent-up demand in the US. Net exports in services, buoyed by tourism, also contributed positively. The extent of these factors is likely to dissipate in subsequent years. The 2024 outlook remains fragile, with the Jibun Bank Japan Manufacturing PMI declining again to 47.2 in February after rising fractionally to 48.0 in January. Growth is expected to improve in 2025 as global financial conditions ease and domestic demand rises.

Inflation is projected to decline to 1.9% in 2024 and 1.3% in 2025. Inflation declined for the third consecutive month to 2.2% in January driven largely by the decline in energy prices. Inflation excluding food and energy saw a slight decline to 2.6% after holding steady at 2.8% for the final 3 months of 2023. Headline inflation is expected to rise again in February due to base effects stemming from last year's energy subsidies. Thereafter, inflation is expected to decline as the effects of previous increases in import costs fade.

An important consideration for the inflation outlook will be the ramifications of wage negotiations agreed upon in March 2024. For firms with 30 or more employees, nominal cash earnings in 2023 rose on average by 1.8% (1.7% for firms with more than 5 employees). This was below the average inflation rate in 2023, implying that real wages fell (Figure A.9). Nominal wage increases of 5.9% were agreed to by Japan's large firms on 13 March 2024, the largest increase in 33 years. Given that supply-side drivers of inflation should dissipate, meeting the Bank of Japan's 2% inflation target sustainably over the medium-term will require generating inflation from domestic demand, supported by wage growth. Recent wage hikes agreed to by large firms are a positive sign, but a key consideration will be on whether small and medium sized enterprises can follow suit, given that they account for the majority of the labor force.

Domestic and external factors pose risks to growth in the near term. While inflation is expected to fall during the second half of 2024, generating a virtuous

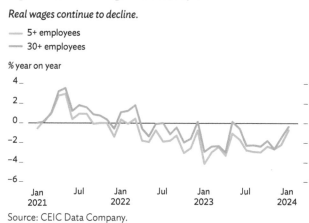

Figure A.9 Real Wage Growth, Japan

Real wages continue to decline.

— 5+ employees
— 30+ employees

Source: CEIC Data Company.

cycle of income and consumption growth, healthy domestic demand will hinge upon the impact of recent wage increases. Externally, increased global economic uncertainty and geo-economic fragmentation could harm growth prospects. In addition, a sharper-than-expected narrowing of interest rate differentials between Japan and the US, and resultant yen appreciation, could be a downside risk to growth via net exports.

Recent Developments and Outlook in Nearby Economies

Russian Federation

The economy remains resilient amid the impact of international sanctions after its invasion of Ukraine. The Federal State Statistics Service stated that economic activity grew by 4.8% on average in October and November 2023, suggesting GDP growth remained strong in Q4, although down from 5.5% in Q3. Soaring public spending supported the economy in Q4 amid a massive increase in defense expenditure (Figure A.10). The government is directing 29% of its national budget in 2024 to the military, from 14% in 2021. Despite sanctions, 23% of 2023 revenue came from energy resources, only a slight decline from 26% in 2021. This was made possible by redirecting oil exports from the European Union to India and the PRC (Figure A.11). Moreover, consumer spending remained upbeat despite rising prices and tighter interest rates in the second half of 2023.

Figure A.10 Monthly Federal Budget, Russian Federation

Government spending rose, supported by increased revenue from oil and gas exports.

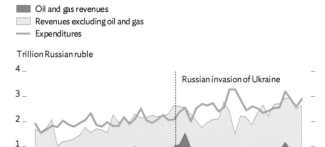

Source: Haver Analytics.

Figure A.11 Monthly Deliveries of Russian Oil by Region

Oil exports have been successfully redirected from the EU to India and the PRC.

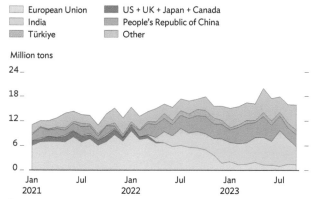

EU = European Union, PRC = People's Republic of China, UK = United Kingdom, US = United States.
Source: Bruegel. Russian Crude Oil Tracker. 8 February 2024.

Inflation remained elevated mainly due to capacity constraints in domestic production. Inflation remained at 7.4% in December, slightly easing from 7.5% in November. This was a significant jump from 6.7% in October. The rise is broad-based as prices for food, non-food goods, and services all picked up mid-way through Q4. Domestic demand will likely continue to rise faster than capacity this year. Coupled with labor shortages, fiscal expansion, sustained international sanctions, and a weak ruble, this will keep prices high this year. In this context, the Central Bank raised its policy rate to 16.0% on 15 December 2023—its fifth consecutive hike since July last year.

GDP growth will soften this year and in 2025 as geopolitical uncertainties continue to cast doubt on the outlook. Domestic demand will suffer from elevated inflation, tighter borrowing costs, a weakening currency, and lingering international sanctions. On the other hand, with no end to the invasion in sight, economic activity will continue to be supported by military spending, including war-related spending in hardware, expenditure in the occupied territories, and payments to military personal in Ukraine and the families of deceased soldiers. Geopolitical developments remain a key risk to the outlook. As of 8 March 2024, Consensus Forecasts had GDP growing by 2.0% in 2024 and expanding by 1.3% in 2025.

Australia

Economic growth slowed to a seasonally adjusted 2.1% last year from 3.8% in 2022, dragged down by higher interest rates. Household consumption expenditure edged down to 1.1% in 2023 from 6.6% in 2022, with household budgets burdened by higher mortgage rates and cost of living (Figure A.12). Growth in government spending also slowed to 1.7%. In contrast, fixed investment rose by 5.4%. Public and private investment both supported growth last year, led by new investments on large-scale transport, health, and education projects, and expansion in major public corporation projects. On the external front, exports

Figure A.12 Demand-Side Contributions to Growth, Australia

Economic growth slowed in 2023, dampened by higher interest rates.

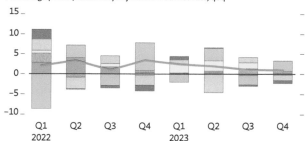

Q = quarter, qoq = quarter on quarter.
Source: CEIC Data Company.

grew by 6.8% with both goods and services contributing positively, driven by mining and coal production, as well as education and personal travel. On the other hand, import growth slowed to 3.3%, primarily led by the fall in imports of consumption and capital goods in Q4. Leading indicators point to diverging economic activity at the beginning of 2024. The services PMI increased to 53.1 in February, as the renewed rise in new orders boosted business activity. By contrast, the manufacturing PMI deteriorated to 47.8 in February, as high inflation, elevated interest rates, and challenging external conditions dampened demand.

Growth will remain subdued over the forecast horizon, as tight monetary policy continues to constrain demand. As prices for goods decreased, headline inflation fell to a lower-than-expected 4.1% in December but remains above the Reserve Bank of Australia's 2%-3% target. As such, the central bank held the policy rate at a 12-year high of 4.35% in March 2024. Weak demand for new housing, elevated construction costs, and ongoing capacity constraints will continue to weigh on new building approvals and housing investment. Household spending will remain soft, but growth will benefit from a continued recovery in tourism, supportive global commodity demand, buoyant private and public investment, and robust services exports. On 8 March 2024, Consensus Forecasts had GDP growing by 1.4% in 2024 and 2.3% in 2025. Inflation was seen at 3.3% this year and 2.8% next year.

New Zealand

GDP growth weakened to a seasonally adjusted 0.6% in 2023 from 2.3% in 2022, dented by high inflation and interest rates. Tight financial conditions reduced domestic demand (Figure A.13). Household spending growth fell to 0.3% last year from 3.2% in 2022, while fixed investment contracted by 1.0%, dragged by declines in plant, machinery, and equipment, and in construction. Public consumption also dropped by 1.1%. On the upside, exports expanded by 9.6% in 2023, on stronger trade in meat and other food and beverage products, coal, crude petroleum, and minerals. On the supply side, manufacturing dropped by 5.2%, while wholesale trade declined by 2.0%, and retail trade and accommodation fell by 3.5%. Leading indicators showed some improvement at the beginning of 2024.

Figure A.13 Demand-Side Contributions to Growth, New Zealand

Growth contracted in Q3 on tight financial conditions and weak external trade.

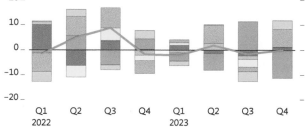

Percentage points, seasonally adjusted annualized rate, qoq

Q = quarter, qoq = quarter on quarter.
Source: CEIC Data Company.

Albeit still in contractionary territory, the seasonally adjusted BusinessNZ Performance of Manufacturing Index edged up to 49.3 in March from 47.5 in January, signaling a gradual turnaround in the sector.

Growth will recover this year and next, fueled by tourism, declining inflation and interest rates. The Reserve Bank of New Zealand held the official cash rate at 5.5% for the fourth consecutive meeting in November and is seen easing its stance this year. Headline inflation remains above the central bank's 1%-3% target, but dropped to 4.7% in Q4 2023 from 5.6% in Q3. High base effects and the lagged impact of monetary policy tightening should continue to reduce inflation. On the downside, slower growth in the PRC, a key trading partner, and fragile external demand will likely dent export growth and constrain the expansion. As of 5 February 2024, Consensus Forecasts had GDP growing by 1.2% in 2024 and 2.4% in 2024. Inflation is seen at 3.2% this year and 2.1% next year.

Oil Prices

Brent crude oil prices averaged $83/barrel in 2023, significantly lower than the 2022 average of $100/barrel, despite an increase in geopolitical conflict. Oil prices were relatively stable in the first half of 2023, at around $80/barrel (Figure A.14).

Figure A.14 Brent Crude Oil Prices

Oil prices were much lower in 2023 than in 2022, despite increased geopolitical tensions.

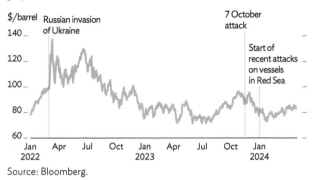

Source: Bloomberg.

A combination of supply cuts and higher global demand pushed prices to a peak of $95/barrel on 19 September. Thereafter, until end-2023, Brent crude oil prices trended downwards amid concerns about the global economic outlook, as well as higher-than-expected supply from non-OPEC+ producers. Geopolitical conflict in the Middle East had a relatively muted effect on oil prices and Brent crude ended 2023 at $77/barrel, $19/barrel less than its September high.

Brent crude oil prices fluctuated in early 2024.
In February, the Brent crude oil spot price averaged $83/barrel, up $3/barrel from January. The increase was partly due to ongoing uncertainty and heightened risks related to attacks on commercial ships in the Red Sea. Additionally, expectations of an extension to voluntary OPEC+ production cuts, officially announced on 4 March, contributed to the price rise. These cuts, initially announced on 30 November 2023, have been extended through the second quarter of 2024, with the Russian Federation also implementing an additional voluntary production cut. Brent crude oil prices hovered around $84/barrel during the first week of March.

Global oil supply and demand is expected to be relatively balanced over the next 2 years (Figure A.15). In its February report, the US Energy Information Administration forecast global crude oil production growth to be lower in 2024 due to both OPEC+ production curbs and slowing non-OPEC growth, particularly in the US. Although growth in US crude oil production will likely continue over the next 2 years due to greater well efficiency, it will be slower due to fewer active drilling rigs as producers have not prioritized capital spending in recent years. Higher crude oil production growth is expected in 2025 as OPEC+ production limits expire, although some voluntary production cuts from members are projected to continue through 2025 to offset forecast production growth from outside the group. Global oil demand growth is forecast to decelerate over the next 2 years due to slower GDP growth in the PRC, the end to pandemic recovery-related growth in 2023, continuous transition to low-carbon energy, and increased fuel efficiency. Oil prices are projected to remain at around $80 per barrel, barring any major geopolitical turmoil or extreme weather events. The Energy Information Administration forecasts Brent crude oil prices to average $82.42 per barrel in 2024 and $79.48 per barrel in 2025.

Figure A.15 World Liquid Fuels Production and Consumption Balance

A comfortable oil balance is forecast for the next 2 years.

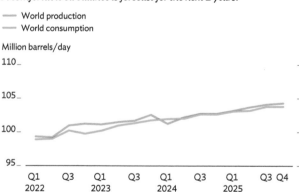

Q = quarter.
Note: Supply includes production of crude oil and other liquids (natural gas plant liquids, biofuels, other liquids, and refinery processing gains). Crude oil accounts for more than 80% of total production.
Source: US Energy Information Administration. *Short-Term Energy Outlook, February 2024.*

2

ECONOMIC TRENDS AND PROSPECTS IN DEVELOPING ASIA

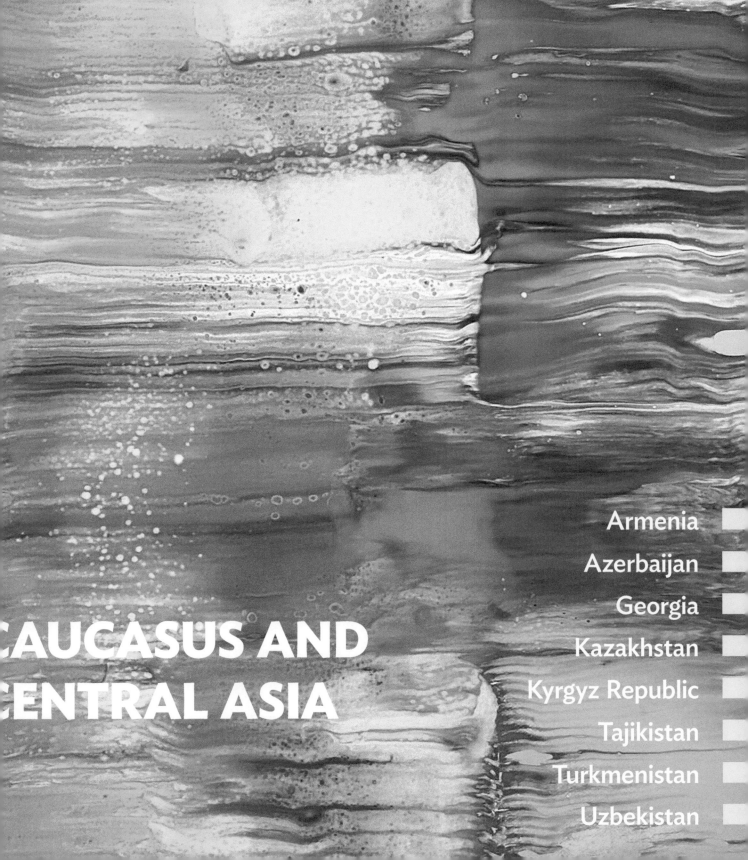

CAUCASUS AND CENTRAL ASIA

Armenia

Azerbaijan

Georgia

Kazakhstan

Kyrgyz Republic

Tajikistan

Turkmenistan

Uzbekistan

ARMENIA

As diminished monetary inflow from the Russian Federation slowed growth in consumption, economic expansion moderated from double digits in 2022 but remained robust. Easing global commodity prices, a stable currency, and cautious monetary policy sharply cut inflation. Growth is expected to moderate further in 2024 as external demand softens before rising in 2025 on higher investment. Inflation is projected to accelerate slightly on more accommodative monetary policy. Reforming health care is essential to improve health outcomes.

Economic Performance

Growth moderated from 12.6% in 2022 to 8.7% in 2023 as decreased monetary inflow slowed growth in private consumption. Total consumption grew by 6.0% on solid employment growth and low inflation. Public consumption increased sharply from 6.7% in 2022 to 17.5%, reflecting salary and pension increases and higher social transfers. However, the growth rate of private consumption was halved from 8.1% in 2022 to 3.9% as remittances declined. Expansion in gross fixed capital formation accelerated from 8.0% in 2022 to 9.7%, reflecting higher private investment and a continuing rise in government spending for infrastructure. With a sharp rise in service inflows, a net deficit in exports of goods and services narrowed further as total export growth outpaced that of imports.

On the supply side, all sectors—services, industry, and agriculture—recorded growth, though at a slower pace than in 2022 (Figure 2.1.1). Growth in services moderated from 17.8% in 2022 to 12.1% in 2023. This reflected smaller gains in most subsectors apart from trade, information and communication technologies, public administration, recreation, and education and health services. Expansion in industry excluding construction moderated from 6.0% in 2022 to 1.7% as a 6.6% decline in mining partly offset increases in manufacturing and utilities. Construction growth slowed from 18.8% but remained high at 15.7%, driven

Figure 2.1.1 Supply-Side Growth

Growth remained strong but moderated across all sectors.

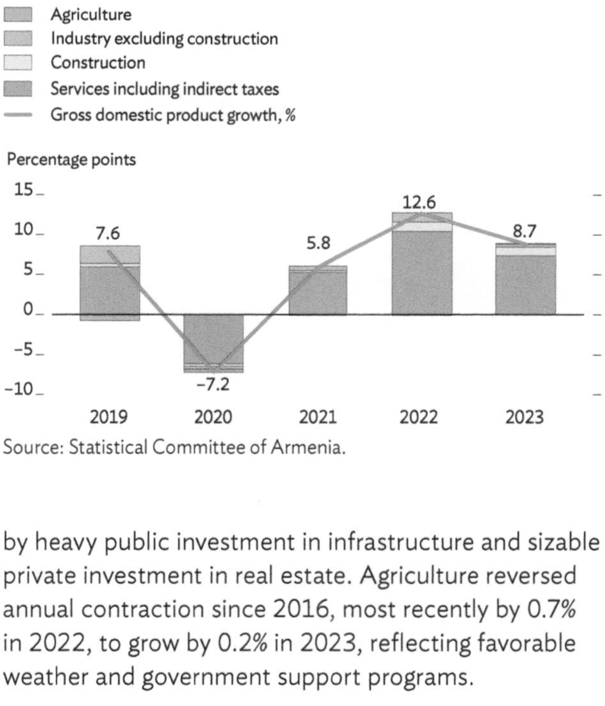

- Agriculture
- Industry excluding construction
- Construction
- Services including indirect taxes
- — Gross domestic product growth, %

Percentage points

2019	2020	2021	2022	2023
7.6	-7.2	5.8	12.6	8.7

Source: Statistical Committee of Armenia.

by heavy public investment in infrastructure and sizable private investment in real estate. Agriculture reversed annual contraction since 2016, most recently by 0.7% in 2022, to grow by 0.2% in 2023, reflecting favorable weather and government support programs.

Inflation dropped sharply despite robust demand. Average annual inflation plunged from 8.6% in 2022 to 2.0% in 2023, reflecting moderating global commodity prices, a stable currency, and cautious monetary

This chapter was written by Grigor Gyurjyan of the Armenia Resident Mission, ADB, Yerevan.

policy (Figure 2.1.2). It slowed from 12.5% to 0.4% for food, from 7.0% to 1.7% for other goods, and from 5.2% to 4.5% for services. Month-on-month deflation by 0.6% was recorded in December 2023, well below the lower bound of the Central Bank of Armenia's target band of 2.5%–5.5%. With low inflationary pressure, the central bank reduced its refinancing rate by a cumulative 225 basis points to 8.5% in several steps from June 2023 to March 2024.

Broad money grew by 17.4% to reach 54.5% of GDP (Figure 2.1.3). Credit to the economy grew by 18.5%, mainly for higher consumer and mortgage lending. Net foreign assets remained virtually unchanged, compared to a 13.5% increase in 2022, as a decline in the net foreign assets of the central bank was offset by higher net foreign assets at depository organizations. With greater exchange rate stability, local currency deposits increased by 22.3% in 2023, while foreign currency deposits increased by 1.5%. The nonperforming loan ratio decreased from 2.8% of all loans at the end of 2022 to 2.4% a year later.

The fiscal deficit remained virtually unchanged at 2.0% of GDP in 2023 versus 2.1% in 2022. Revenue rose by 14.3% to the equivalent of 24.8% of GDP on strong economic growth and further improvements in tax administration and as tax collections surpassed expectations (Figure 2.1.4). Expenditure increased by 13.6% to 26.8% of GDP, reflecting higher social spending and public investment. Capital outlays expanded especially sharply, rising by 24.2% in 2023 following 75.5% growth in 2022 to reach 5.0% of GDP, in line with government plans to gradually increase capital outlays to 6.5% by 2026.

Public debt rose from 49.2% of GDP at the end of 2022 to 49.4% of GDP a year later (Figure 2.1.5). This was comfortably below the official threshold of 60.0%. External public debt, including central bank's external liabilities, increased by 1.0% to $6.5 billion, equal to 27.7% of GDP. Meanwhile, domestic public debt grew by 27.5% to $5.3 billion, raising the share of domestic debt by another 5.7 percentage points to reach 45.1%, in line with the government's strategy to move borrowing to domestic sources.

The estimated current account balance turned negative on a wider merchandise trade deficit and lower personal transfers. This reversed a surplus

Figure 2.1.2 Inflation

Inflation fell sharply across the board.

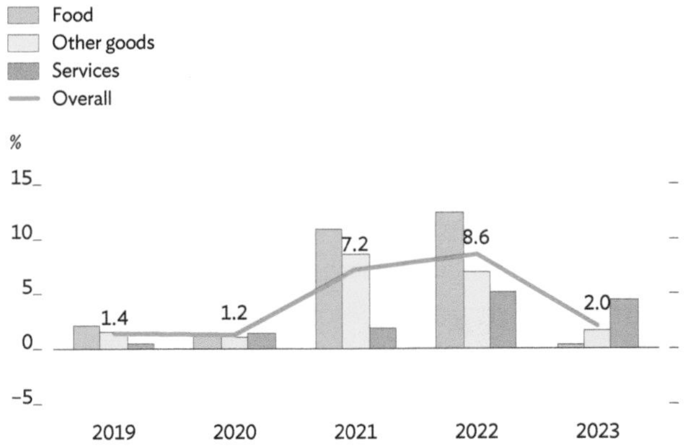

- Food
- Other goods
- Services
- Overall

Source: Statistical Committee of Armenia.

Figure 2.1.3 Broad Money Growth

A rise in domestic credit boosted broad money growth in 2023.

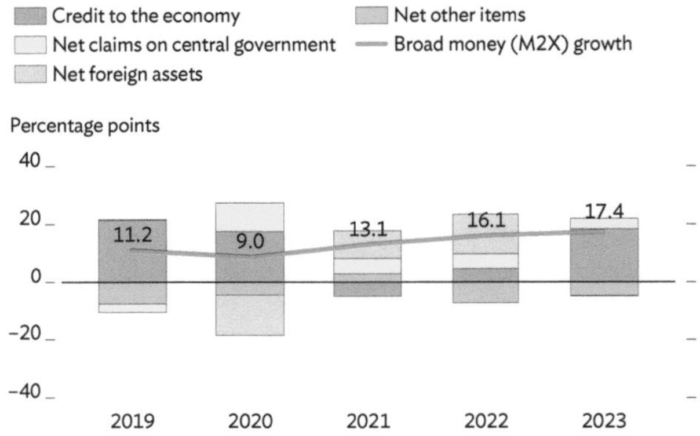

- Credit to the economy
- Net claims on central government
- Net foreign assets
- Net other items
- Broad money (M2X) growth

M2X = sum of dram broad money (M2) and foreign currency deposits and accounts of residents in the real sector.
Source: Central Bank of Armenia.

Figure 2.1.4 Fiscal Balance

The fiscal deficit remained virtually unchanged, with increases in both revenues and expenditures.

- Revenue
- Expenditure
- Balance

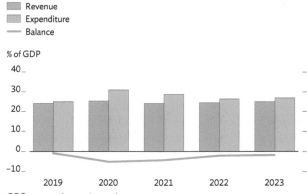

GDP = gross domestic product.
Sources: Ministry of Finance of Armenia; Statistical Committee of Armenia.

Figure 2.1.5 Public Debt

Public debt remained sustainable and manageable.

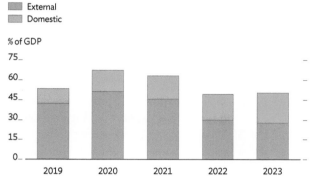

GDP = gross domestic product.

Sources: Ministry of Finance of Armenia; Statistical Committee of Armenia.

of 0.8% of GDP in 2022 to a deficit estimated at 1.7% as the merchandise trade deficit widened from 9.5% of GDP in 2022 to 10.2% (Figure 2.1.6). While merchandise export growth supported by transit trade outpaced that of imports in nominal terms, imports were 1.3 times the value of exports. The surplus in services grew by an estimated 38% in 2023, following fourfold growth in 2022 and reflecting further gains in travel and tourism services. The income deficit widened as a decline in investment income outpaced a rise in employee compensation from abroad. Net money transfer inflows by individuals through banks declined by 36.0% to $1.7 billion in 2023. The current account deficit was largely financed by net financial account inflows and reserves. Gross international reserves declined by 12.4% to $3.6 billion from their all-time high of $4.1 billion at the end of 2022 (Figure 2.1.7).

Figure 2.1.6 Current Account Components

The current account balance reversed from surplus to deficit.

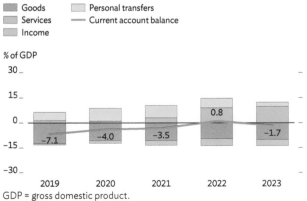

GDP = gross domestic product.

Sources: Central Bank of Armenia; Statistical Committee of Armenia.

Figure 2.1.7 Gross International Reserves and Exchange Rate

Gross international reserves declined from their record high in 2022.

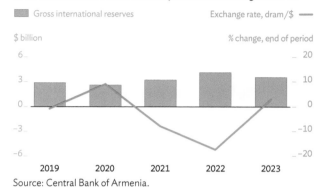

Source: Central Bank of Armenia.

Economic Prospects

Growth is projected to moderate further to 5.7% in 2024, as external demand will likely ease slightly. It will then accelerate to 6.0% in 2025 as the government's expanded investment programs for infrastructure and housing take hold (Table 2.1.1 and Figure 2.1.8). Exports and imports will moderate gradually from record highs in 2022 and 2023. Growth in investment will accelerate to 15.9% in 2024 and 18.5% in 2025, reflecting continuing increases in capital outlays for infrastructure and social investments and further expansion of private investment. Growth in private consumption is projected at 4.0% in 2024 and 4.1% in 2025 as moderate growth in remittances limits the expansion in household income and demand cools further. Public consumption is projected to grow by 12.2% in 2024 with higher transfer payments before moderating to 11.1% in 2025 as the increases taper off.

Table 2.1.1 Selected Economic Indicators, %

Growth will moderate in 2024 before rising in 2025, while inflation will rise but remain low.

	2022	2023	2024	2025
GDP growth	12.6	8.7	5.7	6.0
Inflation	8.6	2.0	3.0	3.5

GDP = gross domestic product.

Sources: Statistical Committee of Armenia; Asian Development Bank estimates.

Figure 2.1.8 Gross Domestic Product Growth

Growth is projected to moderate in 2024 before accelerating further.

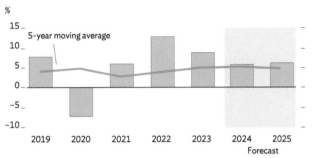

Sources: Statistical Committee of Armenia; Asian Development Bank estimates.

Despite slower growth overall, expansion in construction and consumer services will remain robust. Services are projected to grow by 9.3% in 2024 and 9.4% in 2025, supported by higher tourism inflows and reflecting strong but moderating gains in finance, recreation, retail trade, transport, and information and communication. Industry including construction is projected to expand by 6.2% in 2024 and 7.4% in 2025 with strong growth in construction from higher public investment and in utilities. Manufacturing is projected to expand further, benefiting from higher output of processed foods, textiles, and other nonmetal products. Growth in mining and quarrying will depend on developments in global commodity prices and the opening of new mining sites. Growth in construction is projected to rise to 16.3% in 2024 and 18.1% in 2025, in line with the government's plans to further increase capital outlays and make substantial public investments in roads and social infrastructure. Persistent and complex long-term issues in agriculture will likely limit growth to 0.9% in 2024 and 1.9% in 2025, or less if weather is adverse.

Inflation will accelerate somewhat but likely remain low over the forecast period. With monetary easing, average inflation is projected to increase to 3.0% in 2024 and accelerate further to 3.5% in 2025. By the end of 2024, inflation is forecast to be within the central bank's confidence band of 2.5%–5.5%. The central bank is likely to maintain an accommodative monetary stance to support economic growth, assuming external price pressures remain mild.

Fiscal policy will become more expansionary, with increased allocations for social transfers and capital outlays. The 2024 budget projects a deficit equal to 4.6% of GDP, with revenue forecast at 24.9% of GDP, in line with the government's target of reaching a tax-to-GDP ratio of 25.0% by 2026, through improved tax administration and further enhancements in tax legislation. The implementation of a universal income declaration system for 2024 will also raise government revenue. Expenditure is forecast to reach the equivalent of 30.5% of GDP with plans to increase allocations for social assistance programs and for capital outlays, which are projected to reach 6.6% in 2024. Barring sharp depreciation of the Armenian dram, public debt is expected to increase slightly but remain below 55% of GDP at the end of 2024.

The current account deficit is forecast to widen as trade and income deficits expand. It is expected to equal 2.4% of GDP in 2024 and 2.7% in 2025 (Figure 2.1.9). Growth in merchandise exports and imports is projected to slow in line with moderating aggregate demand and as transit trade diminishes further. However, imports of construction materials and machinery and equipment should be strong as investment in large infrastructure projects picks up. The surplus in services should widen on further expansion of tourism and financial services. Smaller money transfers will deepen the income deficit.

Figure 2.1.9 Current Account Balance

The current account deficit will widen moderately over the next 2 years.

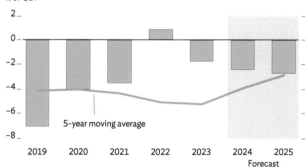

GDP = gross domestic product.

Sources: Central Bank of Armenia; Asian Development Bank estimates.

Policy Challenge—Reforming Health Care for Better Health Outcomes

Armenia's health-care sector faces several challenges that affect the quality of care and access to services. Despite health-care improvements in recent years, out-of-pocket expenditures constituted about 78% of health spending in 2020, and primary health-care visits still fall below average in Europe, as defined by the World Health Organization. This is partly attributed to problems involving the quality of care, with a high percentage of individuals opting for self-treatment instead of seeking professional medical assistance. Addressing these challenges requires a multifaceted approach to improve overall health-care delivery and ensure better health outcomes.

A modern electronic information system as part of an e-health strategy can improve the quality of care. Integrating electronic systems and improving data collection and analysis capabilities will lead to more informed decision-making, better coordination of care, improved diagnosis and treatment outcomes, and an enhancement of the quality and efficiency of medical services. A well-functioning e-health system will also help deliver safer, more effective, and patient-centered care, aligning with the overall goal of improving health-care quality.

Continuous quality improvement and performance monitoring are essential for a well-functioning health-care system. Enhancing the quality of care and ensuring effective health-care delivery require implementation of the quality improvement strategy aligned with national priorities. This includes establishing standards through licensing and accreditation, developing quality improvement programs, reviewing the licensing of medical institutions, adopting clinical guidelines, and promoting a culture of quality through training and education. These measures will improve the quality of care, patient safety, and health outcomes, ensuring that health-care services meet evolving patient needs and maintain high standards.

Insufficient health financing limits equitable access to high-quality health-care services. The government's strategy for health-care reforms in 2023–2026 envisages a sustained increase in public health expenditure to a minimum of 10% of the budget and 2.5% of GDP by 2026. The introduction of a universal health insurance system in 2026 is seen as essential for stabilizing health-care financing, lowering out-of-pocket costs, promoting access to high-quality care, and improving financial protection for the population.

The government has initiated comprehensive health sector reforms to address challenges in health care. Key policy documents—such as the Government Program, 2021–2026; Health Sector Strategy, 2023–2026; the Quality of Care Strategy; and Concept Note for Universal Health Insurance—highlight priorities such as improving the quality of care and implementing universal health insurance for financial risk protection. These reforms aim to increase health sector spending, enhance service readiness, and improve the overall quality of health care. Implementing these reforms will enhance accessibility, affordability, and the quality of health-care services. Thus, improving service readiness, strengthening institutional capacity, creating quality-management practices, and increasing health sector financing will be essential for building a responsive health-care system that meets the needs of the population.

AZERBAIJAN

Growth declined in 2023 with lower oil production and transshipment, which dragged down transport services. Monetary tightening cut annual inflation to single digits. Growth will rise in 2024 and 2025 with higher public spending and transport gains from revived transshipments of Kazakh oil. Inflation should decline in 2024 in line with lower inflation of trade partners before rising in 2025 as fiscal expansion boosts demand. Strengthening public finance management is essential to address climate change and achieve decarbonization targets.

Economic Performance

Growth slowed in 2023, reflecting lower oil production and deceleration in services. Following a strong rebound from the pandemic, growth moderated from 4.6% in 2022 to 1.1% in 2023 because of weak performance in the hydrocarbon economy and a notable slowdown in transshipment services and total transport (Figure 2.2.1). Industry contracted by 1.1% following 1.6% decline in 2022 as technical problems constrained petroleum output. Mining stalled as a 4.2% rise in gas production only partly offset a 7.6% decline in oil output. However, industry aside from petroleum grew by 3.7% on higher production of machinery, furniture, and construction materials. Construction expanded by 13.3%, marginally below 13.4% in 2022, on higher public investment. Growth in services, representing nearly 38.0% of GDP, plunged from 9.7% in 2022 to 2.2% because of a sharp decline in transport. Credit-support programs and subsidies for inputs helped growth in agriculture reach 3.0%, slightly below 3.4% in 2022, with livestock and crop production rising by 3.2% and 2.7%, respectively.

On the demand side, private consumption was a major driver of growth. Expansion in private consumption accelerated from 4.4% in 2022 to 5.5% in 2023, reflecting a sharp rise of 12.8% in household incomes. Growth in investment rose from 8.2% in 2022 to about 11% due to increased spending in

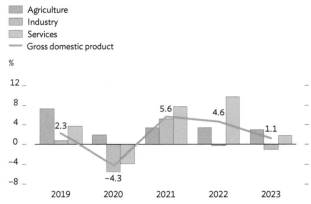

Figure 2.2.1 Supply-Side Growth

Growth slowed in 2023 as oil production declined and expansion in services diminished.

Source: State Statistics Committee of the Republic of Azerbaijan.

public infrastructure investment, while growth in private investment slowed. Declining oil output cut net exports.

Inflation fell with monetary tightening, slower inflation in trade partners, lower global commodity prices, and a return to pre-pandemic prices for major services. Average annual inflation slowed from 13.9% in 2022 to 8.8% in 2023 as price increases slowed from 19.5% to 9.6% for food, from 8.6% to 8.4% for other goods, and from 10.4% to 8.2% for services (Figure 2.2.2).

This chapter was written by Nail Valiyev and Elvin Imanov of the Azerbaijan Resident Mission, ADB, Baku.

Figure 2.2.2 Monthly Inflation

Inflation slowed in 2023, reflecting declines in all components.

— Overall
— Food
— Nonfood
— Services

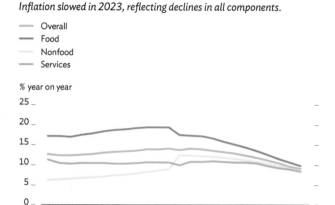

Source: State Statistics Committee of the Republic of Azerbaijan.

Figure 2.2.3 Fiscal Indicators

The budget deficit narrowed from 1.0% of GDP in 2022 to 0.7% in 2023 as revenue picked up.

Expenditure
Revenue
— Fiscal balance

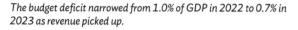
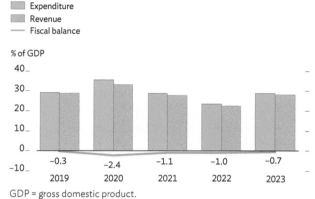

GDP = gross domestic product.
Source: The Ministry of Finance of the Republic of Azerbaijan.

The continued peg between the Azerbaijan manat and the US dollar helped curb pressure from imported inflation. To May 2023, the Central Bank of Azerbaijan raised its policy rate in three steps from 8.25% to 9.00%, before lowering it to 8.00% in two steps from October to December, and then to 7.75% in February 2024 as inflation decreased.

Revenue rose from 22.9% of GDP in 2022 to 28.9% of GDP. This reflecting higher tax collections and increased transfers from the State Oil Fund of Azerbaijan, the sovereign wealth fund, which provided one-third of all revenue (Figure 2.2.3). Total expenditure grew by 13.7% to an estimated 29.6% of GDP in 2023, reflecting increased public investment. Converting part of the government's contingent liabilities into public and publicly guaranteed debt caused total public debt to double, from 11.6% of GDP at the end of 2022 to 21.8% a year later.

The finance sector remained sound. Broad money growth plunged from 23.6% in 2022 to 5.3% in 2023 as net foreign assets expanded very little despite a rise in credit growth from a revised 14.0% in 2022 to 18.8%, driven by consumer lending (Figure 2.2.4). Strict prudential control and strengthened risk management practices at commercial banks helped reduce the share of impaired loans from 2.9% at the end of 2022 to 1.8% a year later. Banks' profitability rose by 7.5% in 2023 on higher lending and timely repayments. Total bank deposits rose by 8.1%.

Figure 2.2.4 Contributions to Broad Money Growth

Broad money growth fell as net foreign assets showed little change.

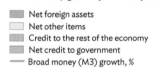

Net foreign assets
Net other items
Credit to the rest of the economy
Net credit to government
— Broad money (M3) growth, %

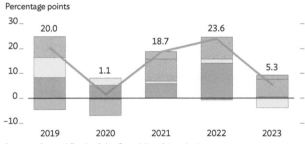

Source: Central Bank of the Republic of Azerbaijan

Declining oil prices and output slashed the current account surplus. The current account surplus fell by half from 25.7% of GDP in 2022 to an estimated 12.5% in 2023 as hydrocarbon export earnings declined. Lower oil earnings cut the trade surplus by more than half, from $17.8 billion in the first 3 quarters of 2022 to an estimated $7.6 billion in the same period of 2023. Hydrocarbons remained the main source of export earnings, though diversification efforts marginally increased the share of other exports. Higher domestic demand boosted merchandise imports by 24.3% in the first 9 months of 2023, slightly above the 23.7% rise a year earlier. In the same period, net secondary income inflows fell from $2.3 billion to $1.9 billion as remittances fell by more than half, from $2.7 billion to $1.2 billion, with smaller inward money transfers from the Russian Federation. Net foreign direct investment in the period slowed by 4.3% to $4.4 billion, with 79.2% reflecting cuts in oil sector investment. Combined central bank and sovereign wealth fund reserves reached $67.6 billion, or 94% of GDP (Figure 2.2.5).

Figure 2.2.5 International Reserves

Total international reserves grew in 2023 as sovereign wealth fund assets increased.

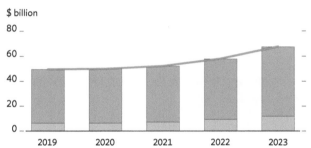

Sources: Central Bank of the Republic of Azerbaijan; State Oil Fund of the Republic of Azerbaijan.

Economic Prospects

Growth is projected to edge up to 1.2% in 2024 and 1.6% in 2025 with higher public spending and gains in services (Figure 2.2.6 and Table 2.2.1). Led by expected increases in retail trade and transportation, expansion in services is projected to rise to 2.3% in 2024 and 3.0% in 2025. Gains in transport will come from an agreement between KazMunaiGas of Kazakhstan and the State Oil Company of Azerbaijan to increase the transit of Kazakh oil via Azerbaijan. Contraction in industry is forecast to ease to 1.6% in 2024 because of slowing performance at oil platforms and further to 1.0% in 2025 as gas production becomes more important. Food processing and the manufacturing of construction materials and petrochemical products will limit the decline in the broader industry sector. The next phase of agriculture support programs will help sustain growth in crop and livestock production.

Private consumption and net exports will drive demand-side growth. Growth in private consumption is forecast to accelerate as economic expansion and

Figure 2.2.6 Gross Domestic Product Growth

Growth is projected to rise in 2024 and accelerate further in 2025.

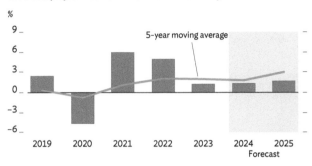

Source: Asian Development Bank estimates.

Table 2.2.1 Selected Economic Indicators, %

Growth will rise slightly in 2024 and further in 2025 as transportation expands, with moderating inflation.

	2022	2023	2024	2025
GDP growth	4.6	1.1	1.2	1.6
Inflation	13.9	8.8	5.5	6.5

GDP = gross domestic product.
Sources: Bureau of National Statistics; Central Bank of Azerbaijan; Asian Development Bank estimates.

a further slowing of inflation boost real household incomes. Higher civil service wages will boost public consumption. Public investment will remain a driver of total investment in the forecast period, though declining oil production and weakening oil prices pose a risk to planned spending. Net exports will rise as export earnings outpace more slowly growing imports.

Inflation should remain in check as the authorities monitor prices over the forecast period. Declining inflation in trade partners is projected to slow inflation to 5.5% in 2024 before it rises to 6.5% in 2025 with faster economic growth (Figure 2.2.7). Continued exchange rate stability will moderate the impact of imported inflation. The central bank is expected to maintain its policy rate at least to mid-2024 and to observe price movements and consumer sentiment before making changes.

Fiscal policy will remain mildly expansionary, with the budget highly dependent on petroleum earnings. The state budget deficit is expected to be around 2.0% of GDP in 2024 and expand to 2.3% in 2025 as

Figure 2.2.7 Inflation

Inflation is projected to diminish in 2024 before rising somewhat in 2025.

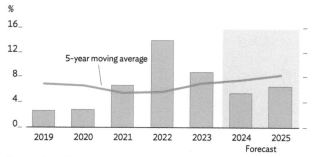

Source: Asian Development Bank estimates.

regional development expenditure increases. Revenue is projected to remain high in 2024 at 27.5% of GDP and reach 28.2% in 2025 as tax administration measures boost tax revenue from the non-oil sector. Expenditure is forecast rising to 29.5% of GDP in 2024 and 30.5% in 2025 to support higher social and capital expenditure. The sovereign wealth fund will remain an important source of budget financing, with its share of revenues rising to nearly 49% in both years to ensure adequate resources to implement a regional development strategy. The deficit excluding sovereign wealth fund transfers will equal 12.0% of GDP during the forecast period. The hosting of the United Nations' 29th Climate Conference might trigger midyear budget revision, raising expenditure during the second half of 2024.

The external position will remain robust but depend heavily on oil prices. The current account is projected to remain in surplus during the forecast period, despite a decline in oil prices, as gas exports increase and the share of non-oil exports rises (Figure 2.2.8). However,

Figure 2.2.8 Current Account Balance

The current account surplus will widen in 2024 and narrow somewhat in 2025.

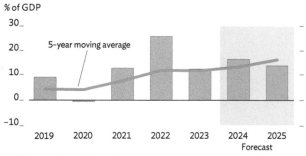

GDP = gross domestic product.
Source: Asian Development Bank estimates.

rising aggregate demand from higher growth will increase imports, narrowing the trade surplus. Higher earnings from transport and tourism will further narrow the deficit in services with a possibility of a wider deficit from reconstruction.

Policy Challenge—Strengthening Public Finance Management to Attain Climate Policy Objectives

Azerbaijan's economy remains heavily dependent on hydrocarbons. During the past 2 decades, petroleum has accounted on average for 40% of GDP and 90% of total export earnings. Limited skilled labor, constraints on market competition, and a heavy presence of state-owned enterprises have constrained growth for the many private firms outside of the petroleum sector. Hydrocarbon revenue has funded expansion of the rest of the economy, making economic growth highly dependent on volatile energy prices. Fossil fuel production poses climate risks. Given COP29 in 2024, the government is taking certain measures on its decarbonization goals to reduce carbon emissions. During 2020–2040, average temperatures in Azerbaijan are expected to be 0.5°C–1.5°C above those during 1971–2000, while precipitation will be 10%–20% less mainly in the mountains and foothills and on the Absheron Peninsula.

Azerbaijan signed and ratified the Paris Agreement without committing to a net-zero target. The latest nationally determined contributions (NDCs) set decarbonization targets of 35% in 2030 and 40% in 2040, which will be hard to achive under current policies. Transport emissions tripled from 2000 to 2019. Electricity generation is the second-largest source of emissions, with methane providing nearly 30% of total emissions. In 2024, the government has joined the Global Methane Pledge.

Strong fiscal policies are a key part of the government's integrated strategies to combat climate change. These policies should be aligned with country's NDCs, and climate dimensions of its sustainable development goals should be reflected in government strategies and budget allocations. The fiscal framework must be inclusive and climate-responsive. The green agenda and its concerns should be considered at an early stage of budget planning.

Medium-term macrofiscal analyses and forecasts and sector strategic plans should include green priorities and indicators. The strategic framework should reflect the government's green plan, financing needs, source of financing, carbon goals and targets, and related items. Green priorities should also be included in fiscal sustanability analyses, along with assessments of the climate implications of budget practices. Reviewing climate concerns during impact assessment and cost and benefit analyses would be useful.

The government should assess the financing gap for green programs and develop a road map for green financing. Soon after strategic planning under the medium-term fiscal framework is completed, it should develop green finance instruments and frameworks for green loans, debt swaps, a carbon market, green bonds, and insurance products. Doing so will expand the scale of green projects and focus public finance more on green outlays. By raising funds with sovereign green bonds, for example, the government can ensure that public investment supports projects with environmental benefits and progress toward achieving carbon targets.

Climate budget tagging is an effective tool to highlight the climate dimension in resource allocation. It involves tagging expenditure items and monitoring their implementation during a reporting year to assess the efficiency of green objectives. The process should continue during budget execution. Moreover, this approach allows tagging other environmental objectives. The process should not be limited to the annual budget cycle but instead govern the whole medium-term expendure framework, given the long-term vision of strategic planning.

Implementing a green fiscal policy will require a number of measures. These include adopting green fiscal risk management practicies and green public procurement principles, implementing climate-sensitive public investment management and assessment, establishing practicies for internal and external control, and promoting fiscal transparency. Clear institutional mechanisms should be established, since the process entails multiagency integration and collaboration. Harnessing the capacity of government institutions will be crucial to successfully implementing a green fiscal policy. The absence of a well-defined public finance management legal framework will be the main challenge to starting the process.

GEORGIA

While moderating in 2023 as tepid global demand reined in manufacturing and mining, growth remained strong with gains in construction and services. Inflation fell sharply as global prices eased and the Georgian lari appreciated. Weak external demand is projected to moderate growth further in 2024 before stronger tourism revives it in 2025. Inflation should accelerate slightly, reflecting somewhat higher commodity prices and some relaxation of monetary policy. Taking greater account of population aging is needed for more inclusive growth.

Economic Performance

Growth moderated from 10.4% in 2022 to an estimated 7.0% in 2023 with slower expansion in industry but remained strong and broadly based.
On the supply side, growth in industry dropped from 15.2% in 2022 to 3.4%, reflecting slower expansion in manufacturing and mining, although growth in construction continued to soar from 15.0% to 16.2% from higher investment (Figure 2.3.1). Expansion in agriculture increased slightly from 0.5% in 2022 to 0.8% with higher fruit production. Growth in services slowed from 9.7% in 2022 to 8.8%, as expansion moderated to 9.9% in wholesale and retail trade and 7.7% in accommodation and food services, despite continued growth in tourism and rapid gains in information and communication at 18.0% and education at 16.9%.

Growth on the demand side reflected higher investment and slower gains in consumption.
Growth in private investment accelerated from 11.6% in 2022 to 12.7% in 2023 as investments in residential and retail construction and other sectors increased. Expansion in private consumption slowed from 5.1% in 2022 to 4.5% in 2023, reflecting the departure of some Russian migrants who had arrived immediately following the Russian invasion of Ukraine. Public consumption also expanded by 4.5%. Growth in net exports declined from 23.0% in 2022 to 5.7% as a stronger Georgian lari supported import growth.

Figure 2.3.1 Supply-Side Growth

Growth moderated but remained robust in 2023, with strong expansion in services.

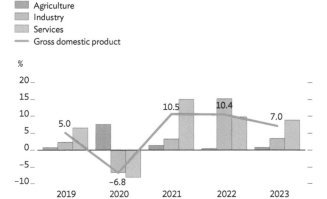

Source: National Statistics Office of Georgia.

Inflation plunged from 11.9% in 2022 to 2.5% in 2023 as global prices moderated and the lari appreciated. The sharp decline below the central bank's target of 3.0% reflected drops in inflation from 17.9% to 3.9% for food, from 8.9% to 4.0% for other goods, and from 6.8% to 0.5% for services (Figure 2.3.2). Core inflation—excluding volatile food, energy, and transport prices—fell from 6.3% in 2022 to 3.9%. The lari appreciated, both in nominal terms by 23.6% and in real effective terms by 11.8%, on sizeable

This chapter was written by George Luarsabishvili of the Georgia Resident Mission, ADB, Tbilisi.

Figure 2.3.2 Monthly Inflation

Rapid declines in inflation for food and services brought headline inflation below 3% in 2023.

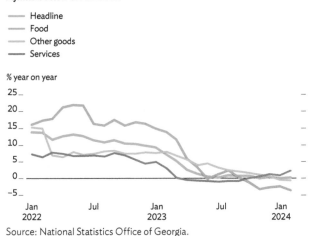

Source: National Statistics Office of Georgia.

foreign inflows, tempering inflation (Figure 2.3.3). As core service and commodity prices flattened, the National Bank of Georgia, the central bank, cut the policy rate by a cumulative 150 basis points to 9.5% in 2023.

Improved revenue performance trimmed the fiscal deficit from 2.6% in 2022 to 2.4% in 2023. This occurred despite higher outlays for civil servant salaries and sustained capital spending. High import tax collections helped increase total revenue by 14.2% in 2023, from 26.8% of GDP in 2022 to 27.7% (Figure 2.3.4). Total expenditure grew by 12.9%, rising from 29.4% of GDP in 2022 to 30.1%, reflecting a 10% increase in the public sector wage bill and continued rapid growth in capital expenditure, which reached 7.0% of GDP. Prudent fiscal policy and currency appreciation reduced public debt from 39.6% of GDP at the end of 2022 to 38.3% a year later (Figure 2.3.5).

The central bank pursued price stability as falling inflation justified a cut in the policy rate. Expansion in broad money supply accelerated from 11.6% in 2022 to 14.5%, with faster credit growth (Figure 2.3.6). Deposit dollarization declined from 53.0% in 2022 to 47.0%, while credit dollarization remained little changed at 44.1% (Figure 2.3.7). The average interest rate on all deposits decreased slightly to 7.6%, and lending rates averaged 12.9%, little changed from 2022. Banks reported high capitalization rates and ample liquidity, for significant loss-absorption capacity, and strong

Figure 2.3.3 Exchange Rates

The Georgian lari appreciated in 2023 on continued foreign inflows.

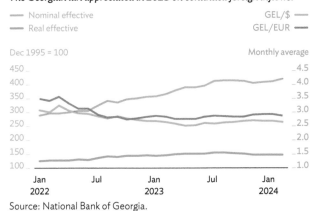

Source: National Bank of Georgia.

Figure 2.3.4 Fiscal Indicators

Strong revenue growth trimmed the fiscal deficit in 2023.

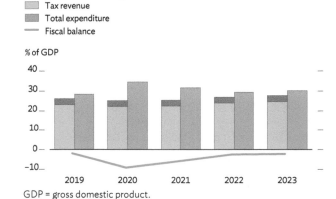

GDP = gross domestic product.
Sources: International Monetary Fund; Ministry of Finance of Georgia.

Figure 2.3.5 Government Gross Debt

Public debt continued to decline as a percentage of gross domestic product.

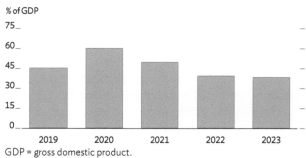

GDP = gross domestic product.
Sources: International Monetary Fund; Ministry of Finance of Georgia.

profitability with returns on assets at 4.2% and on equity at 26.5%—both figures above those reported in 2022. The share of nonperforming loans in total loans remained low at 1.5%.

Figure 2.3.6 Contributions to M3 Broad Money Growth

Credit growth accelerated with a lower policy interest rate.

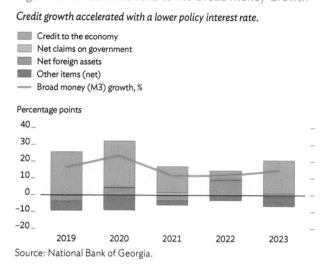

Source: National Bank of Georgia.

Figure 2.3.7 Dollarization in the Banking System

The percentage of deposits and loans in foreign currency declined but remains substantial.

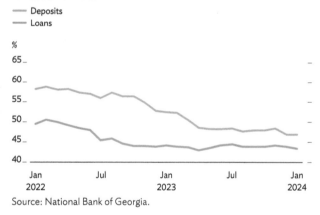

Source: National Bank of Georgia.

The current account deficit narrowed from 4.5% of GDP in 2022 to 4.1% in 2023 on strong foreign inflows and service surpluses (Figure 2.3.8). Strong domestic demand and an appreciating lari helped boost merchandise imports by 13.5%, while merchandise exports expanded by 12.8% as higher exports to the subregion offset much lower exports of ferroalloys, ores, and concentrates to the People's Republic of China. In addition, the reexport of vehicles doubled, reaching 34.9% of all exports and raising vehicle exports and imports alike. Strong revenue from tourism and information technology helped boost service exports by 33.3%, with tourism revenue rising by 17.3% to a record $4.1 billion in 2023 and information-related services nearly doubling. The annual inflow of money

Figure 2.3.8 Current Account Components

The current account deficit narrowed further in 2023.

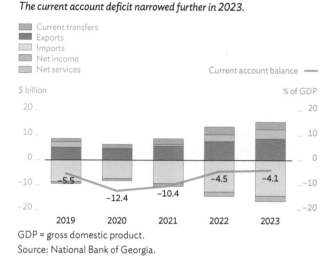

GDP = gross domestic product.
Source: National Bank of Georgia.

transfers decreased by 5.0% to $4.1 billion from an all-time high in 2022. Gross international reserves rose from $4.9 billion at the end of 2022 to more than $5.0 billion a year later, or cover for 5.4 months of imports. Foreign direct investment decreased by 24.0% to $1.6 billion in 2023.

Economic Prospects

Growth is projected to moderate further to 5.0% in 2024 with slowing external demand and decreased expansion of services. It will then recover to 5.5% in 2025 on continued gains in tourism and investment (Figure 2.3.9 and Table 2.3.1). On the supply side, growth in services is projected to slow to 5.5% in 2024 because of geopolitical tensions in the region before rising to 6.3% in 2025 on further growth in tourism. Expansion in industry is projected to accelerate to 4.2% in 2024 and 4.9% in 2025, reflecting higher output of ferroalloys. Growth in agriculture is projected to slow to 0.5% in 2024 because of continued weakness in supply chains, before rising to 1.1% with higher government support for agricultural credit and insurance and expanded investment in new technologies. The European Union's December 2023 decision to make Georgia a candidate for membership should help galvanize reforms supported by EU-funded investments.

On the demand side, growth in private consumption and investment is projected to slow while remaining the main source of expansion. Private consumption

Figure 2.3.9 Gross Domestic Product Growth

Growth will slow to more typical levels during 2024–2025.

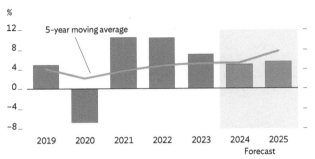

Sources: National Statistics Office of Georgia; Asian Development Bank estimates.

Table 2.3.1 Selected Economic Indicators, %

Growth is projected to slow in 2024 and recover somewhat in 2025, with inflation rising slightly in both years.

	2022	2023	2024	2025
GDP growth	10.4	7.0	5.0	5.5
Inflation	11.9	2.5	3.5	4.0

GDP = gross domestic product.
Source: Asian Development Bank estimates.

should expand at a slower rate of 3.5% in 2024 because of declining money transfers, even as continuing wage increases support domestic demand. Then it should rise somewhat in 2025, by 3.8%, as growth and income accelerate. Spending on goods and services by the remaining Russian migrants will support consumption throughout 2024, but the outlook for this spending in 2025 is less certain. Growth in investment is projected to slow as public capital spending moderates with the slowing economy but still reach 8.5% in 2024 and 10.1% in 2025, as credit expansion boosts private capital accumulation. Net exports are forecast to fall by about 1% in each year as limited export capacity starts to bind.

Inflation is projected to accelerate slightly to 3.5% in 2024 with an expected relaxation of monetary policy. It will accelerate further to 4.0% in 2025 as commodity prices rise moderately (Figure 2.3.10). Broad money growth is projected to decline slightly to 14.0% in 2024 and then rise to 15.0% in 2025 as credit growth accelerates. The 2023 appreciation of the lari should lower inflationary expectations and offset upward pressure on prices from domestic demand spurred by tight labor market conditions that support wage growth.

Figure 2.3.10 Inflation

Inflation will accelerate during 2024–2025 but remain relatively low.

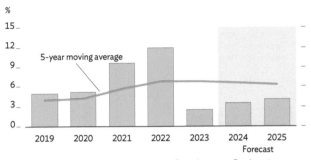

Sources: National Bank of Georgia; Asian Development Bank estimates.

Fiscal policy is expected to show little change over the next 2 years. The fiscal deficit is projected to satisfy the government's fiscal rule by remaining below 3% of GDP in each year, reflecting further improvements in revenue administration, rationalization of tax expenditures, and sound management of public debt. Increased tax collections are projected to raise total revenue to 28.0% of GDP in 2024 and 28.5% in 2025. Total expenditure is forecast to rise slightly, to 30.5% of GDP in 2024 and 31.0% in 2025, as capital spending is maintained and infrastructure outlays remain at about 7.0% of GDP.

The current account deficit is projected to widen in 2024 and 2025. Moderating external demand will trim export growth and widen the merchandise trade deficit despite slower growth in imports. Growth in merchandise exports is projected slowing to 5.7% in 2024, as further growth deceleration in the People's Republic of China and the euro area likely curbs external demand, and then grow by 10.4% in 2025 as advanced economies relax macroeconomic policies to foster growth. Imports are also expected to expand at a slower rate, by 6.1% in 2024, with slower domestic growth and as vehicle reexports moderate, before rising by 11.1% in 2025 with higher growth. Services should rise, albeit more slowly by 3.6% in 2024 and 6.6% in 2025, with continued but more moderate growth in tourism, transit trade, and transportation services. Money transfers are forecast to stabilize at around $3 billion over the next 2 years as external inflows associated with Russian migrants fade and reverse, which could put downward pressure on the lari. Gross reserves are projected to decline to $4.5 billion in 2024 because of the wider current account deficit before rebounding to $5.0 billion in 2025 on higher foreign inflows (Figure 2.3.11). With

Figure 2.3.11 Gross International Reserves

Reserves will decline in 2024 before rebounding in 2025.

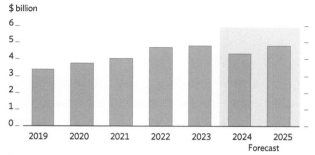

Sources: National Bank of Georgia; International Monetary Fund.

Figure 2.3.12 Government External Debt

External public debt will continue to decline as a percentage of gross domestic product.

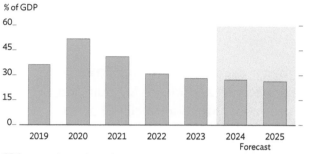

GDP = gross domestic product.
Sources: International Monetary Fund; Ministry of Finance of Georgia.

continued modest fiscal deficits, external public debt is forecast to decline to 26.5% of GDP in 2024 and 25.5% in 2025, barring significant lari depreciation (Figure 2.3.12).

Risks are skewed to the downside. Absent an armistice in Ukraine, further economic dislocations may ensue, negatively affecting the speed of global recovery and possibly contributing to inflationary risks, requiring a retightening of monetary policy by major global actors that would weaken consumer confidence and business sentiment. Otherwise, a strong economic upturn among key trading partners and increased transit trade and investment would lead to stronger growth.

Policy Challenge—Mainstreaming Aging in Development Planning

Georgia's population is aging because of below-replacement fertility, improving life expectancy, and outmigration of working-age people. Data from the United Nations Economic and Social Commission for Asia and the Pacific project show the share of Georgians aged 60 years and older expected to rise from 20.7% in 2020 to 28.1% in 2050. This would more than double Georgia's old-age dependency ratio from the current 25.9% and undermine the sustainability of public finances because of higher outlays for pensions and social welfare, health care, and training programs for elderly workers. Addressing population aging could thus reduce a looming burden on public finances.

The government has already taken some steps to address the welfare costs associated with aging. It has introduced a new, multi-pillar pension system and implemented various social programs to assist the poor and vulnerable, including subsistence farmers. The government has supported agriculture and pursued policies to diversify the economy. Further, it has supported flexible retirement polices enabling senior citizens to continue working beyond normal retirement age and promoted active aging programs that encourage seniors to remain active and engaged in their communities, thereby promoting their physical and mental health and well-being. However, more is needed to address the challenges associated with population aging.

The government needs to promote social inclusion of the elderly. While strengthening social protection programs, the government can facilitate creating new employment opportunities in the formal sector of the economy for those elderly interested and able to work. It can also enhance worker productivity through skill development and greater use of technology. Despite persistent labor shortages, a large gap remains between the labor force participation rates of men and women. Thus, introducing policies to encourage women to enter the labor force is critical. Exploring public–private partnerships in health care should also be prioritized. Ensuring the financial inclusion of the elderly, including their access to diversified financial instruments and capital markets, may also help. Rapid urbanization should not neglect accessible public infrastructure and services to accommodate the needs of the elderly. Finally, the authorities may consider expanding training for social workers and others who address the social needs of the elderly.

KAZAKHSTAN

Growth accelerated in 2023 on higher oil production and expanding construction. Rising real incomes supported consumption, and expansionary fiscal policy boosted infrastructure investment. Inflation declined as the currency appreciated and external inflationary pressure dissipated. Growth will slow in 2024, mostly because of stagnating oil production, before recovering in 2025 with gains in mining and investment. Assuming tight monetary policy and a stable exchange rate, inflation will subside. State-subsidized lending programs distort the credit market and impede monetary policy transmission, requiring reform.

Economic Performance

Higher oil production and investment accelerated growth from 3.2% in 2022 to 5.1% in 2023. On the supply side, mining expanded by 4.6% in 2023, reversing 0.9% decline in 2022, as production rose by 6.8% for oil and 10.5% for gas (Figure 2.4.1). Oil export routes faced no major interruptions, with the Druzhba pipeline becoming a new transport route to Germany. Growth in manufacturing increased from 3.6% in 2022 to 4.2% as investment remained robust. Expansion in services also accelerated, from 2.5% to 5.7%, supported by gains of 11.3% in trade, 7.1% in communication, and 7.1% in transport and warehousing. Growth in construction accelerated from 10.2% in 2022 to 13.3% as the state budget financed the modernization of decaying infrastructure. Drought and adverse weather reversed 9.1% expansion in agriculture during 2022 with 7.7% contraction.

Gains in consumption and investment supported growth on the demand side. Data on the demand side, available for only the first 9 months of 2023, show consumption growing at a post-pandemic high of 8.0% and reversing a decline of 1.5% in the comparable period of 2022. Private consumption rose by 8.1% as real incomes continued to grow and inflation slowed. Growth in investment jumped from 1.0% in 2022 to

Figure 2.4.1 Supply-Side Contributions to Growth

Growth accelerated in 2023 due to large expansions in services and industry.

- Services
- Construction
- Industry
- Agriculture
- —— Gross domestic product growth, %

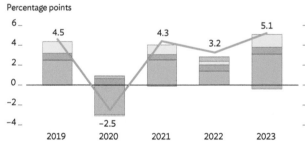

Percentage points

Source: Republic of Kazakhstan, Agency for Strategic Planning and Reforms, Bureau of National Statistics.

23.4% as strong credit growth and higher infrastructure spending boosted fixed capital formation by 23.6%. Net exports declined as higher consumption and investment raised imports of goods and services by 22.6%, while exports increased by only 3.0% as commodity prices stagnated.

This chapter was written by Genadiy Rau of the Kazakhstan Resident Mission, ADB, Astana. Nargiz Zhakupova, intern and Nazarbayev University student, assisted with data collection and analysis for the policy challenge section.

Average annual inflation slowed marginally from 15.0% in 2022 to 14.5% in 2023. Food price inflation fell from 19% in 2022 to 15.2% because of the high base for some items, although supply constraints and rising demand boosted prices by 41.8% for rice and 19.9% for eggs. Inflation for other goods increased from 14.0% in 2022 to 14.8% on rising demand and import prices, while inflation in services rose from 10.3% to 13.2% as rents increased by 19.4% and entertainment prices by 15.2% (Figure 2.4.2). The National Bank of Kazakhstan, the central bank, kept its key policy rate unchanged at 16.75% in the first half of 2023, adjusting in July its medium-term inflation target to 5% from the previous 3%–4% range. With inflation slowing but still above the target, the policy rate was gradually reduced by 100 basis points to 15.75% from August to November 2023 (Figure 2.4.3). The Kazakh

Figure 2.4.2 Average Inflation

Average inflation subsided in 2023, with tight monetary policy and a stable exchange rate.

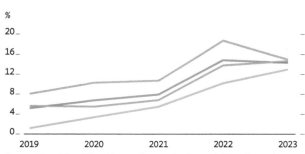

Source: Republic of Kazakhstan, Agency for Strategic Planning and Reforms, Bureau of National Statistics.

Figure 2.4.3 Policy Rate

The policy rate was gradually reduced during the second half of 2023 as inflation slowed.

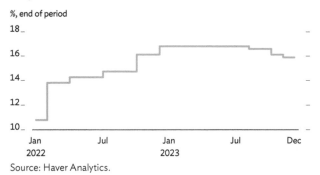

Source: Haver Analytics.

tenge remained stable against the dollar over the year but appreciated by 7.1% in real effective terms, driven largely by a 21.8% appreciation against the Russian ruble.

Lending grew despite a historically elevated policy interest rate. Bank lending rose by 20.3% in 2023 as lending rates averaged 18% for both firms and individuals. Consumer lending grew by 34.2%, and mortgage lending by 14.2%, as the government extended a subsidized lending program. Lending to firms increased by 13.1% in 2023 as loans to small enterprises rose by 25.2%. The share of nonperforming loans decreased from 3.4% at the end of 2022 to a historic low of 3.2% a year later. The share of foreign currency deposits declined from 30.3% at the end of 2022 to 22.9%, and of foreign currency loans from 10.7% to 9.9%. Growth in broad money (M3) slowed from 13.9% in 2022 to 11.7%, with bank deposits rising by 16.6% (Figure 2.4.4). The central bank halved the stock of its own short-term securities, while government-issued domestic securities rose by 24.4% to finance a budget deficit.

Figure 2.4.4 Broad Money Growth

Broad money growth slowed in 2023.

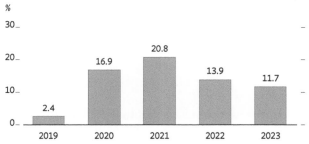

Source: Republic of Kazakhstan, Agency for Strategic Planning and Reforms, Bureau of National Statistics.

Expansionary fiscal policy financed rising social and infrastructure spending. Expenditure increased from the equivalent of 21.6% of GDP in 2022 to 23.2% in 2023 as outlays for state infrastructure modernization jumped by 46.9% from a low base (Figure 2.4.5). Outlays for social services, representing more than half of total expenditure, rose by 22.1% with increases of 28.4% for education, 18.5% for health care, and 17.5% for social assistance. In March 2023, the government raised public expenditure $5 billion for the year, financed mainly through additional transfers from the National Fund of the Republic

Figure 2.4.5 Fiscal Indicators

The fiscal deficit increased marginally in 2023 as expenditure grew more than revenue.

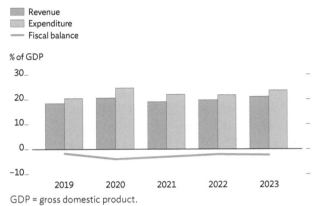

GDP = gross domestic product.
Source: Republic of Kazakhstan, Agency for Strategic Planning and Reforms, Bureau of National Statistics.

of Kazakhstan (NFRK), the sovereign wealth fund. Nevertheless, total transfers were 12.8% lower than in 2022, dropping to 16.1% of budget revenue. The budget received additional support equal to 1.1% of GDP from the NFRK, which purchased national oil company shares from the government. Total budget revenue increased to 20.9% of GDP in 2023 as tax revenue increased by 27.4%, with value-added tax revenue up by 34.3% and corporate tax revenue by 27.3%. The state budget deficit widened from 2.1% of GDP in 2022 to 2.3%, while the non-oil structural deficit shrank from 8.2% of GDP to 6.8%. Government and government-guaranteed debt remained at 22.3% of GDP at the end of 2023.

The current account reverted to deficit as the merchandise trade surplus fell by half. Preliminary estimates show a current account deficit equal to 3.8% of GDP in 2023, reversing a 3.1% surplus in 2022. Lower oil prices cut merchandise exports by 6.6% despite higher output, while higher consumption and investment due in part to tenge appreciation in real terms boosted imports by 20.1%. The deficit in services widened by 43.2% as imports grew by 26.3%, reflecting pent-up demand for personal and business travel after the pandemic, outpacing 23.0% growth in service exports. Profit repatriation stagnated with lower export earnings, while higher outward money transfers further widened the secondary income account deficit. The financial account also moved into deficit, reflecting a sharp decline in foreign direct investment and rise in portfolio investment outflows.

Despite lower exports and budget transfers from the sovereign wealth fund, the central bank reported growth in foreign exchange reserves. NFRK assets rose by 7.7%, surpassing $60 billion (Figure 2.4.6). The central bank sold $9.5 billion in NFRK assets on the foreign exchange market to finance budget transfers and the purchase of national oil company shares. However, the central bank did not sell reserves to support the currency, and gross international reserves rose by 2.5% to $35.9 billion at the end of 2023, providing cover for 5.9 months of imports. By the third quarter of 2023, external debt, 56.9% of it private intercompany debt, had fallen to 64.8% of GDP from 74.0% at the end of 2022, as foreign subsidiaries repaid intracompany loans.

Figure 2.4.6 Foreign Currency Reserves and Sovereign Wealth Fund Assets

Both gross international reserves and sovereign wealth fund assets grew in 2023.

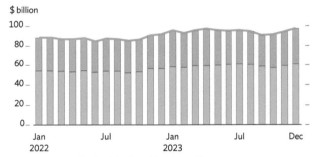

Source: National Bank of the Republic of Kazakhstan.

Economic Prospects

GDP growth is expected to moderate in 2024 but rebound in 2025. Growth is projected to dip to 3.8% in 2024 with a slowdown in industry due to stagnant oil production and then accelerate to 5.3% in 2025 as Tengiz oil field expansion boosts oil production starting in the second quarter of 2025 (Table 2.4.1 and Figure 2.4.7). Growth in services is forecast to slow to 4.7% in 2024 after the record increase in 2023 and then recover to 4.9% in 2025, supported by trade, transport, and hospitality, and benefiting from trade facilitation between Europe and Asia. Growth in industry is forecast to slow to 3.5% in 2024 with smaller gains in mining and accelerate to 5.7% in 2025 as oil production increases. Manufacturing will expand by 3.9% in 2024

Table 2.4.1 Selected Economic Indicators, %

Growth will dip in 2024 and rebound in 2025, with inflation gradually moderating.

	2022	2023	2024	2025
GDP growth	3.2	5.1	3.8	5.3
Inflation	15.0	14.5	8.7	6.3

GDP = gross domestic product.

Sources: Bureau of National Statistics; National Bank of Kazakhstan; Asian Development Bank estimates.

Figure 2.4.7 Growth Domestic Product Growth

Growth is projected to dip in 2024 and rebound in 2025.

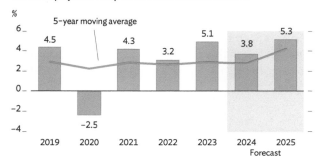

Source: *Asian Development Outlook* database.

and 3.7% in 2025, benefiting from government efforts to accelerate investment inflows. Growth in construction will moderate to 9.4% in 2024 and 8.1% in 2025 as large infrastructure investment projects are completed. Growth in agriculture will rebound to 6.7% in 2024 and reach 7.0% in 2025, following the poor 2023 harvest and government investment to achieve food security.

Despite a slowdown in 2024, consumer spending and investment will support economic growth on the demand side. Growth in consumption is projected to moderate to around 4.0% in 2024 and 2025 as slower growth trims the rise in real disposable incomes. With the completion of large infrastructure projects, investment growth will moderate to 14.5% in 2024 and 9.0% in 2025 despite benefiting from state housing construction support and efforts to attract foreign investment. Net exports are forecast to jump in 2025 as rising oil export volumes from higher production outpace moderate import growth. Downside risks to the outlook include negative spillover from the Russian invasion of Ukraine, slower-than-expected growth in trading partners, and potential disruption to oil exports routes. Further delays of the Tengiz oil field expansion would significantly affect the 2025 growth outlook.

Inflation is projected to slow further in 2024 and 2025 but remain above the central bank target. Amid robust demand and rising fuel and utility prices, inflation is forecast to slow gradually to 8.7% in 2024 and 6.3% in 2025, assuming relatively tight monetary policy and continued exchange rate stability (Figure 2.4.8). Additional state subsidies for farmers are projected to trim food price increases to 9.4% in 2024 and 5.4% in 2025. Government control over energy prices will limit inflation for other goods to 6.7% in 2024 and 6.0% in 2025. Prices for services are projected to become the major source of inflation, rising by 9.8% in 2024 and 8.1% in 2025 because of government-announced increases for utility prices. The central bank will gradually relax monetary policy and lower the policy rate in line with declining inflation and inflationary expectations. Nevertheless, utility price increases and continued strong domestic demand will keep inflation above the central bank's 5% inflation target.

Figure 2.4.8 Inflation

Inflation is projected to diminish in both 2024 and 2025.

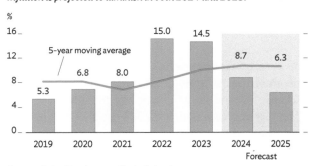

Source: *Asian Development Outlook* database.

The fiscal deficit will widen further in 2024 before narrowing in 2025. Expenditure is forecast to drop to 21.9% of GDP in 2024 and 21.2% in 2025 as the pace of increase in social spending slows. Total revenue is projected to slide to 19.3% of GDP in 2024 and 19.0% in 2025 as transfers from the NFRK decrease. However, tax revenue is projected to rise to 16.2% of GDP in 2025 as it benefits from the rollout of a universal declaration of income and property. With lower NFRK transfers, the budget deficit is projected to widen to 2.6% of GDP in 2024 before narrowing to 2.3% in 2025 with expected higher oil revenues (Figure 2.4.9). The non-oil deficit will widen to 8.3% of GDP in 2024 before narrowing to 7.8% in 2025.

Figure 2.4.9 Fiscal Balance

The fiscal deficit will widen in 2024 before narrowing in 2025.

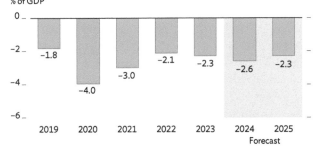

% of GDP

GDP = gross domestic product.
Source: *Asian Development Outlook* database.

Public and external debt are projected to decline further as a percentage of GDP. Government and government-guaranteed debt is projected to stay at 22.3% of GDP by the end of 2024 and decline to 21.9% a year later. Most of the debt is domestic, issued at rates below the key policy rate, which will moderate rising debt servicing costs. External debt is also expected to decline further to about 62% of GDP at the end of 2024 and 56% a year later as foreign-owned subsidiaries repay intercompany debt.

The current account deficit is expected to narrow over the forecast period. Following a marginal export decline in 2024 as lower commodity prices largely offset higher production, the 2025 rise in oil output is projected to raise merchandise exports by 6.4%, while higher domestic demand will boost imports by 2.3% in 2024 and 5.6% in 2025. The service deficit will narrow gradually as revenue rises from transit services. As commodity investors continue to repatriate windfall profits, the primary income deficit will persist. However, outward transfers are expected to decline in 2024 and thereafter, closing the secondary income deficit in 2025. Gross international reserves are projected to reach $37.0 billion in 2024, providing cover for 6.0 months of imports, and $38.2 billion in 2025, or cover for 5.8 months of imports, assuming no intervention in the foreign exchange market. NFRK assets are forecast to rise to $62 billion in 2024 and $65 billion in 2025 as transfers fall below inflows and earnings.

Policy Challenge—Addressing Distortions from Subsidized Lending

State subsidized lending has proliferated since the global financial crisis of 2008–2009. This is because many domestic commercial banks were effectively barred for many years from international financial markets, as they faced mounting nonperforming loans and a volatile exchange rate. Subsidized lending programs have since provided cheap, long-term financing to achieve state priorities in housing, agriculture, small and medium-sized enterprises, and import substitution. Mortgage lending in particular prompted government intervention. In 2018, the state refinanced mortgages originally issued in foreign currency and expanded its subsidized lending programs to reach 82% of the mortgage portfolio by 2022 (Figure 2.4.10).

Figure 2.4.10 Structure of the Mortgage Market by Source of Financing

82% of mortgage loans are subsidized by the government.

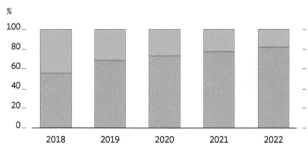

Source: National Bank of Kazakhstan.

Concessional loans undermine monetary policy. After moving in 2015 to a freely floating exchange rate, central bank policy has targeted inflation. However, widespread credit subsidies constrain monetary policy transmission by creating excess liquidity on the market. State-issued subsidies create between the key policy rate and the average lending rate a gap that reached 700 basis points for mortgage loans in December 2022 (Figure 2.4.11). In its long-term Monetary Policy Strategy 2030, the central bank has recognized the need to phase out its subsidized lending programs by 2025.

Figure 2.4.11 Mortgage Interest Rates at Second-Tier Banks

State-issued subsidies create a gap between the key policy rate and the average mortgage rate.

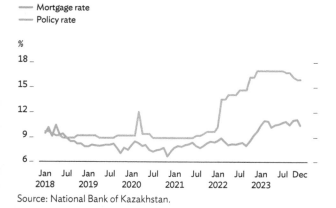

Source: National Bank of Kazakhstan.

Figure 2.4.12 Corporate Lending by Second-Tier Banks

From 2011 to 2022, corporate loans fell from 73% of total credit to 33%.

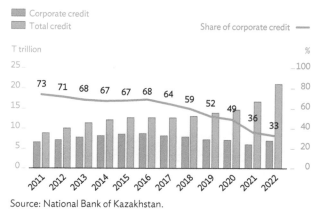

Source: National Bank of Kazakhstan.

Subsidized lending has become a lifeline for the homebuilding industry. In exchange, the industry helps the government achieve its objectives of higher economic growth and better living standards. However, subsidies raise home prices, create dependency, and support otherwise unviable firms. In 2023, the state concessional mortgage program called 7-20-25 reached its earlier set limit of $2.2 billion. Instead of closing the program, though, the government set additional annual limits of $200 million until 2029. Meanwhile, development partners, including the International Monetary Fund, consistently call for streamlining state loan subsidies through structural reforms that strengthen the market orientation of the economy.

Banks have increasingly become intermediaries for subsidized corporate loans. The government-established Damu Fund subsidizes loans for small and medium-sized enterprises though commercial banks to support economic diversification. The local think tank Halyk Finance Research estimated that the state subsidized about 41% of the corporate loan portfolio at the end of 2022. Subsidized lending has led firms to focus on securing subsidies and favors rather than competing on efficiency and quality. However, subsidies seem to have had limited impact, as corporate loans fell from 73% of all bank loans in 2011 to 33% in 2022 (Figure 2.4.12).

Practical measures are available to address the subsidized lending issue. The government needs to disclose both the extent of financial support provided by subsidized lending and its opportunity cost. Alternative financing mechanisms can be deployed by shifting to state guarantees and insurance to cover business risks, rather than subsidizing interest rates. The government needs to adopt a strategy to phase out subsidized lending programs like those of the central bank. Any remaining subsidized lending programs need clearly defined objectives, intended beneficiaries, eligibility criteria, and other appropriate conditions. Binding sunset clauses for subsidized lending programs would encourage periodic review and evaluation and require program closure when objectives are achieved.

KYRGYZ REPUBLIC

Growth remained strong in 2023 with robust gains in almost all sectors but a slowdown in gold production. Inflation subsided with smaller increases in food prices but remained elevated. The current account deteriorated with a surge in imports and large unrecorded reexports. Growth is projected to moderate in 2024 and 2025 with smaller gains in construction and services. Inflation should decline under continued tight monetary policy. Inflation can be tackled with more effective monetary policy.

Economic Performance

Growth slowed but remained robust in 2023.
Growth moderated to 6.2% from 9.0% in 2022, a figure revised up from the previously released 6.3% mainly because the National Statistics Committee recalculated the share of net indirect taxes in GDP. On the supply side, growth in industry slowed from 11.9% in 2022 to 2.7% as metal production, especially gold, fell by 12.8% and expansion in manufacturing plunged from 16.4% in 2022 to 2.0% with lower output of fabricated metals, machinery, and equipment, and despite faster growth in textiles and garments. Growth in services remained robust because of gains in accommodation and food services but slowed somewhat, from 6.8% in 2022 to 6.2%, with slower expansion in transport, storage, information, and communications. Poor rainfall slashed growth in agriculture from 7.3% in 2022 to 0.6% as cereal production fell by 14.6%. Construction growth accelerated from 9.1% in 2022 to 10.3% on higher investment in mining, manufacturing, energy, transport, trade, and housing (Figure 2.5.1).

Slower expansion in consumption trimmed growth on the demand side. According to data available for only the first 9 months of 2023, growth in private consumption fell by half from 16.4% in the same period of 2022 to a still robust 7.9%, sustained by gains in consumer lending, real wages, and net remittances. Expansion in public consumption rose from 0.5% in

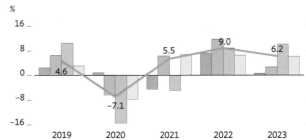

Figure 2.5.1 Supply-Side Growth

Growth moderated but remained robust in 2023 with a pickup in construction and continued gains in services.

Source: National Statistics Committee of the Kyrgyz Republic.

2022 to 1.1% in 2023 because of higher civil service wages. Fixed capital investment rose by 34.6%, mainly from higher domestic spending on energy, water, and education facilities, while foreign investment declined by 26.3%.

Inflation slowed but remained elevated, reflecting strong domestic demand. Average annual inflation slowed from 13.9% in 2022 to 10.8% in 2023. Year-on-year inflation fell by half from 14.3% in

This chapter was written by Nurbek Jenish and Zhamilia Bataeva, Kyrgyz Resident Mission consultants.

December 2022 to 7.3% in December 2023, slightly above the 5.0%–7.0% target range of the National Bank of the Kyrgyz Republic, the central bank (Figure 2.5.2). The decline in inflation came mainly from lower global food prices, seasonal factors that reduced food inflation, and tight monetary policy. The central bank kept its policy rate at 13.0% throughout the year despite slowing inflation. Food inflation similarly fell by half, from 16.2% to 8.4%, but prices rose from 11.1% to 13.3% for other goods and from 9.8% to 10.0% for services, the latter largely reflecting tariff hikes on electricity, other utilities, and transportation.

Gross reserves increased, with a higher share of assets in gold (Figure 2.5.3). The central bank sold $655.7 million in 2023, mainly to smooth excess volatility in the Kyrgyz som as the Russian ruble weakened by about 25% against the dollar. This held som depreciation against the dollar to about 4.0% in 2023. Despite currency interventions, ongoing purchases of domestically mined gold and the conversion of nonmonetary gold on the central bank's balance sheet to foreign exchange enabled gross reserves to rise by about $0.5 billion in 2023 to $3.2 billion at the start of 2024, cover for about 3 months of projected imports.

Strong revenue performance pushed the budget into surplus. The general government fiscal balance moved from a deficit equal to 1.0% of GDP in 2022 to a 1.0% surplus in 2023 as revenue grew faster than expenditure (Figure 2.5.4). Improved tax administration and an expanded tax base boosted revenue from 29.5% of GDP in 2022 to 31.9% in 2023, with gains in both tax and nontax revenue. Gains in tax revenue reflected a 34.2% rise in value-added tax collections on unusually strong imports. Nontax revenue benefited from a more than doubling of revenue from state-owned assets, including dividends from the Kumtor mine and a profit distribution from the central bank. Government spending increased slightly from 30.5% of GDP in 2022 to 30.9% on a higher wage bill and social benefits. With strong nominal GDP growth, public debt declined from 46.9% of GDP at the end of 2022 to 45.5% a year later, with domestic debt rising from 9.2% of GDP to 11.8% and external debt falling from 37.6% of GDP to 33.7% (Figure 2.5.5).

Figure 2.5.2 Monthly Inflation

Headline inflation subsided in 2023 as food price inflation plunged.

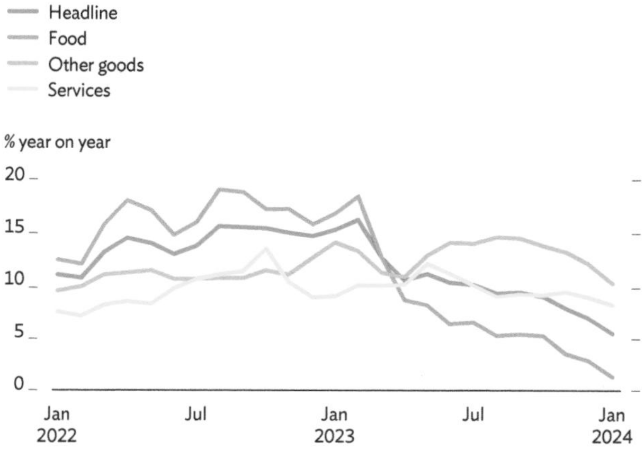

— Headline
— Food
— Other goods
— Services

Source: National Statistics Committee of the Kyrgyz Republic.

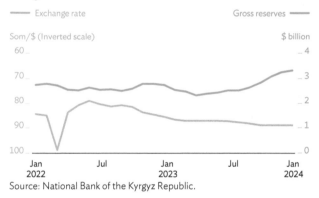

Figure 2.5.3 Exchange Rate and Gross Reserves

The Kyrgyz som depreciated marginally against the dollar in 2023, while gross reserves increased.

— Exchange rate   Gross reserves —

Source: National Bank of the Kyrgyz Republic.

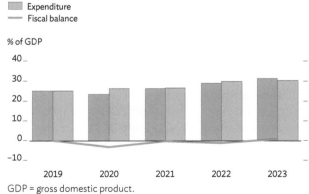

Figure 2.5.4 Fiscal Indicators

The general government fiscal balance improved as revenue rose more than expenditure.

▪ Revenue
▪ Expenditure
— Fiscal balance

GDP = gross domestic product.
Source: National Bank of the Kyrgyz Republic.

Figure 2.5.5 Public Debt

Total debt declined slightly as a percentage of GDP, with more domestic debt and less external.

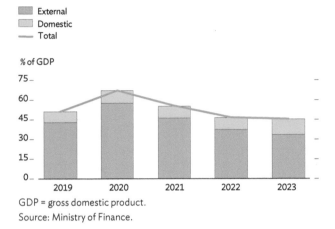

GDP = gross domestic product.
Source: Ministry of Finance.

Figure 2.5.6 Current Account Components

The current account deficit widened in 2022 and the first 9 months of 2023.

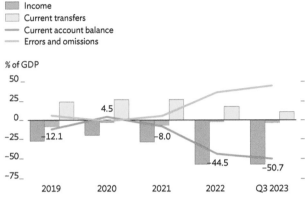

GDP = gross domestic product, Q = quarter.
Note: Preliminary data for 2023 are for the first 9 months and presented as a percentage of annualized GDP.
Source: National Bank of the Kyrgyz Republic.

The banking sector remains sound. Banks remained liquid and well-capitalized, with a capital adequacy ratio of 24.8% and a liquidity ratio of 77.4% at the start of 2024. Nonperforming loans dropped from 12.8% in 2022 to 9.2% at the end of 2023. Credit grew by 26.3% in 2023, with consumer lending up by 68.8% and mortgage lending by 23.2%. Deposits expanded by 27.3%.

The current account deficit widened, while errors and omissions remained large. The recorded deficit, which does not fully count reexports to the Russian Federation because of limited monitoring of trade within the Eurasian Economic Union, surged from 44.5% of GDP in 2022 to 50.7% in the first 3 quarters of 2023, reflecting a larger trade deficit, a smaller surplus in services, and persistently large errors and omissions (Figure 2.5.6). Following an 18.1% drop in exports in 2022, when gold exports dropped hundredfold to $13.1 million, exports surged by 46.8% in 2023 as gold exports rebounded sharply to $1.28 billion. Imports, which rose by 75.7% in 2022, increased a further 26.0% in 2023 because of strong domestic demand and imports of consumer goods and vehicles, mainly from the People's Republic of China, for reexport. After data revision to account for money transferred via mobile phone, the central bank reported a 14.5% increase of net money transfers in 2023, reversing a 14.6% decline in 2022, as outflows declined (Figure 2.5.7).

Figure 2.5.7 Net Money Transfers

Net money transfers increased in 2023 as outflows declined.

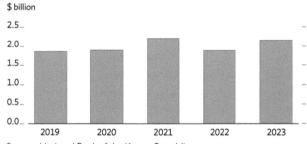

Source: National Bank of the Kyrgyz Republic.

Economic Prospects

Growth is projected to moderate further toward its long-term potential rate. Despite strong growth in January–February 2024 at 8.6%, GDP expansion is expected to decline to 5.0% in 2024 and further to 4.5% in 2025, reflecting slower growth in construction and services (Figure 2.5.8 and Table 2.5.1). Public programs for housing notwithstanding, construction on urban infrastructure, irrigation, and social and industrial facilities will slow to 9.0% in 2024 and stabilize in 2025. Growth in tourism will further support growth in services, though to a lesser extent of 5.0% annually. Gold production is expected to decelerate gradually as the Kumtor mine depletes, though recently announced new technologies for gold extraction may buoy

Figure 2.5.8 Gross Domestic Product Growth

Growth is forecast to moderate in 2024 and 2025 with slower expansion in construction and services.

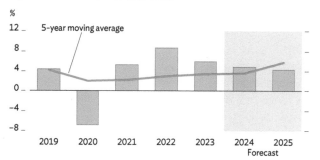

Sources: National Statistics Committee of the Kyrgyz Republic; Asian Development Bank estimates.

Figure 2.5.9 Annual Inflation

Inflation is projected to slow in 2024 and 2025.

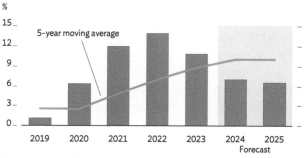

Sources: National Statistics Committee of the Kyrgyz Republic; Asian Development Bank estimates.

Table 2.5.1 Selected Economic Indicators, %

Growth will slow and inflation decelerate in 2024 and 2025.

	2022	2023	2024	2025
GDP growth	9.0	6.2	5.0	4.5
Inflation	13.9	10.8	7.0	6.5

GDP = gross domestic product.
Source: Asian Development Bank estimates.

production. In any case, expansion in manufacturing is projected to accelerate growth in industry to 4.0% in 2024 and 2025. Growth in agriculture is forecast to recover to 2.5% each year, with livestock providing most of the increase, as crop production will continue to face a scarcity of water for irrigation. On the demand side, investment and private consumption will remain the main sources of growth, with higher household incomes supporting private consumption as inflation slows and remittances are projected to remain robust.

Inflation is projected to decelerate further toward the central bank target. It will slow to 7.0% in 2024 and 6.5% in 2025 as an improved global food market and slowing domestic demand reduce inflationary pressures (Figure 2.5.9). The government adopted an action plan to regulate price increases for essential food items during 2024, which is also expected to help curb inflation. In January–February 2024, moderating food prices lowered year-on-year inflation to 5.5%, within the central bank's 5.0%–7.0% target range for the first time since September 2020. The central bank is expected to

maintain a relatively tight monetary policy and continue intervening in the foreign exchange market to smooth exchange rate fluctuations.

Fiscal stimulus will remain limited, while high collections of value-added tax may subside. Improvements to tax and customs administration are expected to continue, but the rate of mandatory social contributions employers pay on wages is likely to fall by half in 2024 in most sectors, from 27.25% to 12.25%. Revenue is projected to moderate to 30.0% of GDP in 2024 and 2025, with a possible slowdown in value-added tax collections on imports if growth in reexports decelerates or reverses. Expenditure is projected as moderating to 29.0% of GDP in both 2024 and 2025, despite higher spending on health, education, the construction and rehabilitation of transport and irrigation infrastructure, and affordable housing. With external debt payments projected at about $400 million annually in 2024–2026, external debt is expected to decline further as a percentage of GDP during this period.

The current account deficit is projected to narrow. This will reflect a further rise in gold exports, slower import growth, and reexports better reflected in external accounts. The trade deficit should shrink as export growth rises with higher gold exports, including sales of gold accumulated by the central bank and expansion in other exports. Imports of vehicles intended for reexport are expected to decline because the reexport of cars from the Kyrgyz Republic to the Russian Federation is likely to become unprofitable from 1 April 2024, when Russian customs clearance for reexported vehicles will increase. Import growth should decline as well because of slower growth in domestic demand.

Downside risks weigh on the outlook. Continuing geopolitical tensions could slow growth in the Russian Federation, reducing trade, investment, and remittances for the Kyrgyz Republic. Slower growth and declines in vehicle imports would also cut revenue, limiting funds to rehabilitate existing infrastructure and finance new infrastructure projects. Power shortages from aging electricity infrastructure and limited water supply, unfavorable weather, and a sustained drop in gold prices would exacerbate these risks.

Policy Challenge—Strengthening Monetary Policy Transmission

Despite a recent decline in inflation, inflation expectations have remained high in the Kyrgyz Republic. Recent external shocks, including a surge in food prices, supply-chain disruptions, and currency depreciation in 2022, have been the main sources of inflationary pressures. Inflation remained high, at 7.3% at the end of 2023. Despite the decline of inflation to 5.5% in February 2024, inflation expectations remain elevated, according to the central bank.

Structural factors hamper the effectiveness of monetary policy. Despite tight monetary policy, with the central bank raising its policy rate six times since 2021 and selling foreign exchange to curb inflation, expectations of high inflation persist. The financial system is shallow and underdeveloped, with a small and uncompetitive banking sector and a nascent stock market. The banking system has continuing excess liquidity, concentrated in a few banks, that is not lent to the private sector or other banks. These features, together with restricted access to international capital markets, limit the central bank's ability to affect lending rates or the exchange rate. Financial literacy also remains low despite central bank efforts to improve it. This hinders the formation of expectations, thwarts communication, and limits the central bank's credibility.

High dollarization weakens monetary policy transmission amid risks of financial stability and currency mismatches. Despite a gradual decline in dollarization over the past 8 years, both the private and the public sector rely heavily on foreign currency borrowing, increasing vulnerabilities in case of exchange rate movements. Historically high reliance on remittances also limits monetary policy. Despite the issuance of long-term government securities in som, local currency debt accounts for only 25.9% of total public debt. Administrative and macroprudential measures in place—such as differentiated minimum reserve requirements with higher reservations for liabilities denominated in foreign currency, higher loss provisions for foreign currency loans, and regulatory limits on commercial banks' net open foreign exchange positions—should be implemented further and complemented with stronger macroprudential policies to reverse dollarization.

Frequent foreign exchange interventions limit how much the exchange rate can be a shock absorber, possibly undercutting monetary policy transmission. According to a study by the International Monetary Fund, currency depreciation in the Kyrgyz Republic by 10 percentage points boosts inflation in the first year by 3 points. The central bank frequently intervenes in the foreign exchange market to smooth exchange rate fluctuations, mainly by selling foreign currency in periods of som depreciation.

Bolstering the credibility and independence of the central bank is crucial. The central bank uses standard channels of announcements and press releases on its website. Better communication achieved by sharing more detailed and transparent information could improve policy predictability and lower inflation expectations. The central bank can benefit from further aligning its communications to best practices, improving public financial literacy, and adopting a forward-looking strategy. Streamlining central bank gold purchases and adhering to rules for profit distribution from the central bank to the budget are essential to strengthen central bank governance and independence.

TAJIKISTAN

Growth accelerated with surges in agriculture and construction as the fiscal deficit widened and the policy interest rate was reduced. Reported inflation hit a decade low amid modest exchange rate volatility. In 2024–2025, growth will decelerate slightly from recent highs as lower remittances subdue demand and expansion in agriculture slows. Inflation should accelerate on increased consumer lending and more expansionary fiscal policy but remain within the central bank's target band. Developing a green economy is important for sustainable development.

Economic Performance

With a wider fiscal deficit and lower policy interest rate, growth accelerated from 8.0% in 2022 to 8.3% in 2023. Expansion in agriculture rose from 8.0% in 2022 to 11.6%, reflecting increases of 15.2% for fruit and 10.7% for grain thanks to favorable weather, and increases in egg and meat production linked to the opening of 54 new micro, small, and medium-sized enterprises in 2023 (Figure 2.6.1). Growth in construction accelerated from 11.4% in 2022 to 12.5% as capacity expansion raised construction for industry and higher bank lending boosted residential construction. Growth in industry fell by half from 15.4% in 2022 to 8.1% because of continued disruption in the supply of inputs for large infrastructure projects. Expansion in services slowed from 16.0% in 2022 to 13.6% with diminished cargo transportation and freight turnover from cross-border trade complications along the country's borders with Afghanistan and the Kyrgyz Republic.

On the demand side, domestic demand was the main growth driver. Growth in investment accelerated from 11.4% in 2022 to 15.8%, primarily in mining and manufacturing, transport, education, and health. Private consumption increased despite a decline in remittances. Public investment spending rose by 24.4%, following 18.0% growth in 2022, to reach 7.9% of GDP.

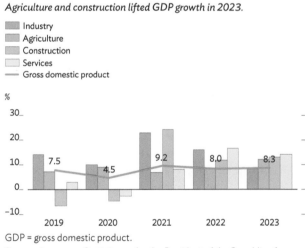

Figure 2.6.1 Supply-Side Growth

Agriculture and construction lifted GDP growth in 2023.

- Industry
- Agriculture
- Construction
- Services
- —— Gross domestic product

GDP = gross domestic product.
Source: Agency on Statistics under the President of the Republic of Tajikistan.

Net exports fell deeper into deficit despite faster growth in exports because their volume is much lower than that of imports.

Average annual inflation fell to its lowest rate in 10 years. The inflation rate slowed from 4.2% in 2022 to 3.8% in 2023, below the central bank's 4%–8% target range (Figure 2.6.2). Food price inflation fell

---

This chapter was written by Shuhrat Mirzoev, Tajikistan Resident Mission consultant.

Figure 2.6.2 Annual Inflation

Inflation decreased further in 2023, with declines in food and services.

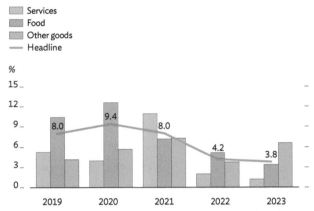

Source: Agency on Statistics under the President of the Republic of Tajikistan.

Figure 2.6.3 Fiscal Indicators

The fiscal deficit widened in 2023 as expenditure outgrew revenue.

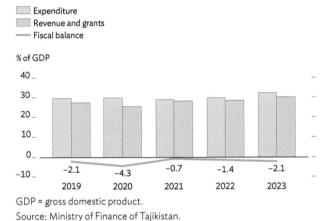

GDP = gross domestic product.
Source: Ministry of Finance of Tajikistan.

Figure 2.6.4 Public Debt

Public debt declined as a share of GDP in 2023 as nominal GDP outgrew nominal debt.

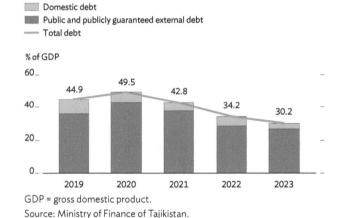

GDP = gross domestic product.
Source: Ministry of Finance of Tajikistan.

from 5.2% in 2022 to 3.4% with significant price cuts for vegetables, vegetable oil, eggs, and flour thanks to a surge in domestic production capacity. Inflation for other goods accelerated from 3.8% in 2022 to 6.6%, with double-digit increases for gasoline and liquefied natural gas, while inflation for services slowed from 2.0% in 2022 to 1.2%. Appreciation of the Tajik somoni against the Russian ruble offset external inflationary pressures on food and fuel, with imports representing nearly 60% of the consumption basket.

The fiscal deficit widened but remained below the government's medium-term target of 2.5% of GDP. The overall fiscal deficit increased from 1.4% of GDP in 2022 to an estimated 2.1% in 2023. Revenue rose significantly from 27.8% of GDP in 2022 to an estimated 29.5% (Figure 2.6.3), reflecting improved tax administration and the delayed effect of tax code changes, despite a further cut in the value-added tax (VAT) rate in 2023 to 14% and the exemption of imported e-vehicles from VAT and excise taxes. Notwithstanding adherence to budget discipline, total expenditure increased from 29.2% of GDP in 2022 to 31.6%, reflecting outlay increases of 36.5% for culture and sport, 27.5% for utility services, and 25.2% for health. Public and publicly guaranteed debt fell from 34.2% of GDP at the end of 2022 to 30.2% a year later as nominal GDP grew faster than nominal debt (Figure 2.6.4). Domestic debt decreased by 6.5% from $424.6 million at the end of 2022 to $396.8 million a year later, or from 5.7% of GDP to 3.3%, reflecting debt service payments and the settlement of nonperforming

loans, with financing secured from the sale of assets of two local banks, Agroinvestbank and Tojiksodirotbank.

Despite several reductions, the policy rate remained well above the inflation rate. With inflationary pressure easing, the National Bank of Tajikistan, the central bank, cut the policy rate from 13.0% in 2022 to 11.0% in February 2023 and further to 10.0% in May, still well above the inflation rate. Broad money contracted by 0.8%, reflecting a 0.3% drop in net foreign assets, and reserve money fell by 5.6%. The drop in reserve money reflected the transition of more than 300 government services to cashless payments, cutting demand for cash from credit institutions, and a surge in deposits by 22.7% compared to 2022. Cuts in the policy rate contributed to a 31.5% jump in credit to the private sector, up from 18.9% in 2022, as reserve requirements remained unchanged (Figure 2.6.5). The somoni depreciated by 7.4% against the US dollar despite central bank interventions, but it appreciated by 15.5% against the Russian ruble.

Figure 2.6.5 Monetary Indicators

Broad money contracted by 0.8% in 2023 as net foreign assets decreased slightly.

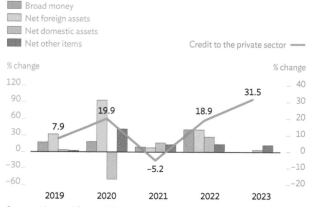

Source: National Bank of Tajikistan.

The banking system remained sound, despite slight deterioration in financial soundness indicators.
The share of nonperforming loans rose slightly from 12.2% of all loans at the end of 2022 to 12.7% in 2023 as credit surged (Figure 2.6.6). Return on bank assets declined from 5.9% to 3.7%, and that on equity from 28.3% to 19.2%, as local financial institutions cut ties

Figure 2.6.6 Banking System Soundness Indicators

In 2023, soundness indicators weakened somewhat, though banks remained quite profitable.

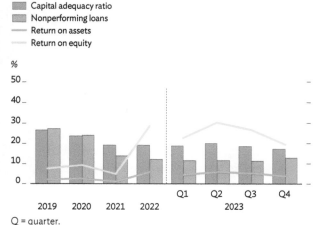

Q = quarter.
Source: National Bank of Tajikistan.

with their sanctioned Russian counterparts. The capital adequacy ratio declined from 19.1% to 17.1% because of higher nonperforming loans and penalties imposed on several banks for compliance issues. The ratio remained well above the minimum prudential norm of 12.0%, though the shares of loans and deposits in foreign currency rose slightly.

The current account reverted after several years of surpluses to a small deficit estimated at 1.0% of GDP as the merchandise trade deficit widened.
Supported by strong domestic output growth and consumption, imports rose by 13.8% or $713 million, while exports rose by 14.3% or $406 million to $2.45 billion. The rise in exports reflected a doubling of growth in exports of gold and other precious metals, along with increases for textiles and clothing at 6.6%, electricity at 3.9%, and other products. These increases offset a 19% drop in machinery exports, which reflected slower growth in manufacturing outside of textiles. Following an unusual spike in 2022 from heavy Russian demand for migrant labor, remittances decreased to their early-2021 level, estimated at 35.0% of GDP in 2023, down from 49.2% in 2022. Gross international reserves decreased from $3.8 billion in 2022 to $2.9 billion in the third quarter of 2023, or cover for 6.6 months of imports (Figure 2.6.7), reflecting the sale of gold reserves and central bank currency interventions.

Figure 2.6.7 Gross International Reserves

Reserves decreased in the first 3 quarters of 2023.

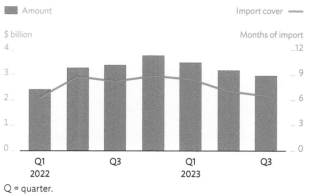

Q = quarter.
Source: National Bank of Tajikistan.

Economic Prospects

Growth is forecast to decelerate to 6.5% in 2024 and 2025 as weak remittances constrain domestic demand (Figure 2.6.8 and Table 2.6.1). The outlook is weighed down by a slowing growth trend in the Russian Federation, limited policy response due to the constrained fiscal space and monetary tools, and weak global demand for the metals and minerals that are Tajikistan's major export commodities. On the supply side, growth will come mainly from services including finance and retail trade, and from industry including energy—notably with the launch of the Rogun hydropower plant's third unit in 2025—and construction. The introduction of new techno-park legislation and incentives for firms will support growth in industry, while the greening of the private sector is expected to attract private investment in 2024–2025. The delayed effect of a more favorable tax regime and continued expansion of production capacity through public investment and public–private partnerships.

will also support growth. Agriculture will continue to expand but at a slower rate following a 150% rise in the price of water for irrigation beginning 1 January 2024 and subdued international prices for key export items in 2024–2025, and as the government continues to prioritize investment in manufacturing in line with its industrialization policy for 2022–2026.

Inflation will accelerate on continued growth in consumer lending, wage increases, and a rise in electricity tariffs. Inflation is expected to reach 5.5% in 2024 and 6.5% in 2025, with increases restrained by currency interventions to counter inflation and exchange rate volatility (Figure 2.6.9). The acceleration reflects expectations of higher lending as deposits increase; an announced 40% increase in pensions, stipends, and public sector salaries beginning on 1 January 2024; and a 16% rise in electricity tariffs effective on the same day. Slower growth in the Russian Federation could again weaken the Russian ruble relative to the Tajik somoni and reduce remittance flows. This would exert downward pressure on the somoni, raising inflation for imported goods.

Figure 2.6.8 Gross Domestic Growth Growth

Gross domestic product growth is projected to moderate to 6.5% in 2024 and 2025.

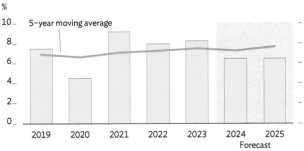

Sources: Agency on Statistics under the President of the Republic of Tajikistan; Asian Development Bank estimates.

Figure 2.6.9 Inflation Forecast

Inflation is projected to increase in both 2024 and 2025.

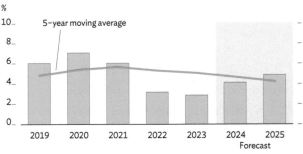

Sources: Agency on Statistics under the President of the Republic of Tajikistan; Asian Development Bank estimates.

Table 2.6.1 Selected Economic Indicators, %

Growth will moderate in 2024 and 2025, with inflation steadily rising.

	2022	2023	2024	2025
GDP growth	8.0	8.3	6.5	6.5
Inflation	4.2	3.8	5.5	6.5

GDP = gross domestic product.
Sources: TAJSTAT; National Bank of Tajikistan; Asian Development Bank estimates.

The government aims to keep the budget deficit below 2.5% of GDP by constraining expenditure in line with revenue. Revenue is projected at 30.0% of GDP in 2024 and 30.5% in 2025, amid a steady rise in the number of taxpayers and an increase in VAT receipts from an expected boost in imports, and despite the negative effects of slower growth and weak remittances. For 2024, the government has introduced a vehicle-scrapping tax, raised the transport tax by 5.88%, implemented a 50% reduction in the VAT rate on the import of natural gas and electricity, and increased revenues from electricity exports, which is likely to raise state enterprise profits. The government plans public investment of $2.1 billion in 2024 and 2025 to boost production capacity in key industries, in line with ongoing industrialization and job creation efforts. Outlays for the Rogun hydropower plant will continue as the availability of concessional financing allows. The deficit is expected to be financed by external sources, with an arrangement under the International Monetary Fund's Policy Coordination Instrument potentially unlocking new funding from investors. Public and publicly guaranteed external debt is estimated to rise to 31.5% of GDP in 2024, primarily reflecting new loans from multilateral institutions, before declining to 27.7% in 2025 because of large scheduled eurobond repayments—unless new concessional financing to complete the Rogun project is received.

The current account is projected to remain in deficit during 2024 and 2025 (Figure 2.6.10). Demand for capital-intensive imports for Rogun and other infrastructure projects will remain strong and widen the trade deficit. Remittances are expected to remain in the range of 30%–35% of GDP, and foreign direct investment is anticipated to show little growth.

Figure 2.6.10 Current Account Balance

The current account deficit is projected to widen further in 2024 and 2025.

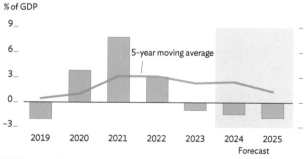

% of GDP

GDP = gross domestic product.
Sources: National Bank of Tajikistan; Asian Development Bank estimates.

Policy Challenge—Developing Tajikistan's Green Economy

Tajikistan faces significant challenges from climate change because of its vulnerability and high dependence on natural resources. The country is among the most vulnerable to climate change, ranking 103rd out of 182 countries on the Notre Dame Gain Index, with little improvement in the past 10 years. At the same time, Tajikistan averages roughly 400 climate-induced incidents each year, severely affecting the national economy and population. With population growing by 2% annually, a shortage of arable land has created high dependency on imported food, weakening food security and increasing the population's vulnerability to natural hazards. The Third National Communication of Tajikistan on Climate Change reported that an estimated 20% of the country's glaciers have been lost in the past 34 years, posing a major threat to the economy because of its dependence on glacier-fed rivers for hydropower generation. These and other critical climate risks could lead to irreversible economic, social, and environmental damage, with a wide range of security implications and a direct impact on welfare and livelihoods.

In response to these challenges, the government has developed and implemented a long-term policy aimed at fostering a green economy. A key milestone was the approval in September 2022 of the Green Economy Development Strategy, 2023–2027 (GEDS), which counts among its 11 priority areas energy efficiency, waste management systems, construction and architecture, the industrial complex, and ecotourism. The government is committed to expanding renewable energy capacity to 10,000 megawatts and achieving by 2037 universal green electricity generation and net-zero emissions. The government submitted in 2021 its updated nationally determined contribution to the Paris Agreement on Climate Change, reiterating its strong commitment to emission reduction, climate adaptation, conservation, and biodiversity.

To further support GEDS implementation, the government should adopt climate-friendly policies. They should include support through incentives and finance to climate-friendly firms and implementing reform to public finance management, which is critical to improving how public resources are planned, budgeted, and executed for the green economy policies set out in the GEDS. Two global agreements—the 2030 Agenda for Sustainable Development and the Paris Agreement—oblige Tajikistan to address inherent challenges to public finance management for green economy development to enable the country to achieve its ambitious economic transformation goals.

Within public finance management, a comprehensive climate fiscal framework and climate-sensitive budgeting should be introduced. This would include technical interventions, such as on-budget climate tagging and a climate-friendly performance orientation for sector and program budgets. Other measures would update public procurement policies and construction standards by integrating green economy principles. Together with other climate-friendly policies, these measures would boost green investment, increase green employment, improve infrastructure governance, strengthen performance orientation, and better align government spending with policy.

TURKMENISTAN

Growth rose slightly in 2023, led by gas exports and public investment. Inflation eased, reflecting tighter credit policy and continued price and foreign exchange controls. A positive outlook for energy and continued public investment indicate accelerating growth in 2024 before it moderates somewhat in 2025. Inflation is projected to rise on structural issues despite continuing price and foreign exchange controls. A young labor force needs expanded education and more high-quality jobs—both essential for inclusive and sustainable growth.

Economic Performance

The government reported growth rising slightly from 6.2% in 2022 to 6.3% in 2023. High gas production and exports were responsible, supported by large public investments.

On the supply side, expansion was reported in all sectors, with industry the main growth driver. Industry expanded by 4.3%, with gas production rising by 3.0% to 80.6 billion cubic meters (Figure 2.7.1). Expansion in industry also benefited from higher output of crude oil, oil products, chemicals, and electricity, along with gains in construction and manufacturing. This included increases in food processing, building materials, and textiles produced mostly under import-substitution programs. Agriculture grew by 4.4% as targets for cotton and wheat production were achieved, and from expansion in horticulture production for domestic and foreign markets. Services expanded by nearly 9.0%, with increases of 8.4% in transportation (including international air and rail services) and communication, 12.8% in trade and catering, and 5.1% in other services.

On the demand side, public investment and net exports were the main drivers of growth. Gross investment in various production facilities and social infrastructure under the President's program for socioeconomic development in 2022–2028 increased by 7.5%, reaching 18.3% of GDP. This was reported to

Figure 2.7.1 Natural Gas Production

Natural gas production rose in 2023.

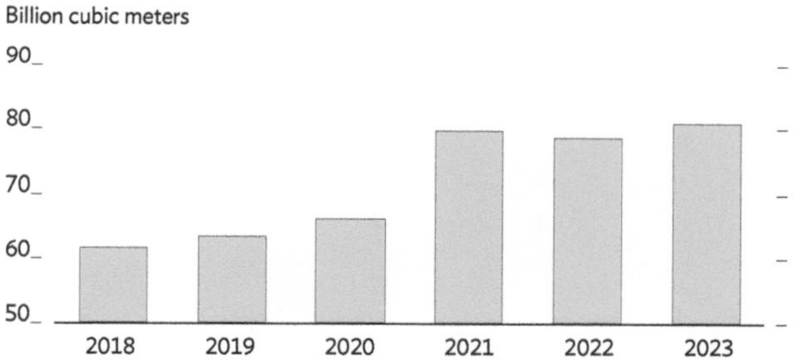

Sources: BP Statistical Review of World Energy 2023; official source.

include new health centers, schools, cultural centers, and residential complexes, as well as continuing phases of the new administrative "smart city" Arkadag, a large construction project. Of total investments, 50.9% was allocated for social infrastructure and the rest for industrial infrastructure.

Inflation eased considerably. Preliminary estimates show average annual inflation falling from 11.2% in 2022 to 5.9% in 2023 as a result of moderating global commodity prices, tighter credit policy, and continued price and foreign exchange controls (Figure 2.7.2). The Central Bank of Turkmenistan maintained its fixed exchange rate regime, which rations foreign currency sales and international money transfers.

This chapter was written by Jennet Hojanazarova of the Turkmenistan Resident Mission, ADB, Ashgabat.

Figure 2.7.2 Average Annual Inflation

Inflation fell sharply in 2023.

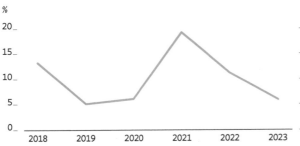

Source: International Monetary Fund. 2023. *Regional Economic Outlook, Middle East and Central Asia*. October.

Most bank lending went to state-owned enterprises in the government's priority sectors, with some credit provided to private firms engaged in import substitution or export promotion.

The state budget surplus is projected to have narrowed from 2.4% of GDP in 2022 to 0.9% in 2023 (Figure 2.7.3). The smaller surplus reflected higher expenditure from increased capital spending. While the state budget does not capture off-budget expenditure, a report by Fitch Ratings in February 2024 estimated public debt to have declined from the equivalent of 5.8% of GDP at the end of 2022 to 4.3% a year later.

Figure 2.7.3 Government Fiscal Indicators

The fiscal surplus is estimated to have narrowed in 2023.

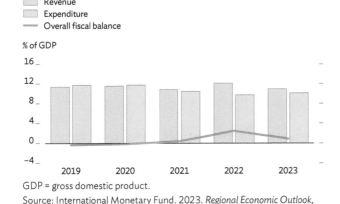

GDP = gross domestic product.
Source: International Monetary Fund. 2023. *Regional Economic Outlook, Middle East and Central Asia*. October.

The current account surplus narrowed from 7.1% of GDP in 2022 to 5.9% in 2023 (Figure 2.7.4). This reflected some relaxation of import controls, along with stable energy prices and exports. Imports rose

Figure 2.7.4 Current Account Balance

The current account surplus narrowed in 2023.

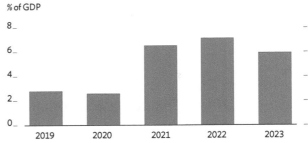

GDP = gross domestic product.
Sources: International Monetary Fund. 2023. *Regional Economic Outlook, Middle East and Central Asia*. October; Fitch Ratings, February 2024.

by 7.6% in 2023, while exports remained essentially unchanged, with earnings mainly from exports of gas to the People's Republic of China (PRC) and additional exports to Azerbaijan and Iran under existing gas swap agreements. With extensive repayment of external loans, external debt in 2023 is estimated to have declined to 5.1% of GDP (Figure 2.7.5).

Figure 2.7.5 External Debt

External debt is estimated to have fallen to 5.1% of GDP in 2023.

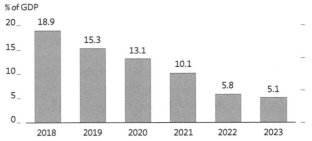

GDP = gross domestic product.
Sources: International Monetary Fund. 2023 *Regional Economic Outlook, Middle East and Central Asia*. October; Fitch Ratings, February 2024.

Economic Prospects

The government projects growth at 6.5% in 2024, with a small deceleration in 2025 from the elevated base in 2024 (Table 2.7.1). This forecast assumes higher capital spending and stable hydrocarbon exports. Gas production is projected to increase gradually through 2025. Faster expansion of gas production and exports, which account for over 60% of total exports, would require new pipeline infrastructure along a regional route yet to be finalized

Table 2.7.1 Selected Economic Indicators, %

Growth is forecast to accelerate modestly in 2024 and then slow in 2025, with higher inflation in both years.

	2022	2023	2024	2025
GDP growth	6.2	6.3	6.5	6.0
Inflation	11.2	5.9	8.0	8.0

GDP = gross domestic product.
Source: Asian Development Bank estimates.

that the PRC is financing, in addition to measures to expand production capacity. Output of gas, oil, and oil products will continue to sustain growth during this period, with expectations of favorable prices and external demand. Activity outside of the large hydrocarbon economy will remain dependent on government support for state-owned enterprises and private firms engaged in import substitution or export promotion.

Strong revenue from hydrocarbons is projected to keep the state budget near balance in 2024 and 2025. While financing for government investment projects will remain sizable, public debt is projected at 4.4% of GDP in 2024, decreasing to 3.9% in 2025 as the government repays external debt on energy projects.

Inflation is projected higher at 8.0% in both years, reflecting higher growth in 2024 and elevated inflation expectations in 2025. The outlook assumes no change in foreign exchange policy or banks' practice of lending mainly to state-owned enterprises. While a large differential between the official and parallel exchange rates has the government examining the costs and benefits of an adjustment, projections assume that the official rate remains unchanged over the forecast period.

The current account surplus is projected to narrow to the equivalent of 3.2% of GDP in 2024 and 2.4% in 2025. Anticipated further relaxation of import constraints will permit higher imports of inputs to export-oriented industries and of consumer goods to the domestic market. At the same time, hydrocarbon exports are projected to keep total export revenue high. External debt is projected to remain below 5% of GDP, reflecting scheduled repayments and the government's aversion to new borrowing.

In February 2024, Fitch affirmed Turkmenistan's long-term foreign-currency issuer default rating *B+* with a positive outlook. This reflects Turkmenistan's extremely strong sovereign balance sheet—with the "B" peer group's highest ratio of sovereign net foreign assets to GDP and lowest public debt—underpinned by the world's fourth-largest natural gas reserves. Factors that could support a further rating upgrade include improvements in governance standards and the business environment, particularly the exchange rate framework, and greater export product and market diversification.

Policy Challenge—Investing in Education and Employment for Youth

Turkmenistan has a large and growing young population, with those aged 15–29 nearing 40% of the population. Through enhanced education, quality work, and social participation, they can contribute to the country's growth and development. Enhancing opportunities for the younger generation and addressing the challenges in their study-to-work transition are essential to make this demographic trend a growth dividend.

The government needs to ensure adequate availability and quality of education and training and create enough high-quality jobs. Large numbers of secondary school graduates, especially women, finish school in Turkmenistan without pursuing further training or finding a job, according to the *United Nations Common Country Analysis 2021 Update*. This indicates underlying structural issues warranting attention and intervention.

The country's 25 tertiary education institutions can enroll annually not more than 15% of school graduates. This does not meet demand for tertiary education. A similar number of graduates enter technical and vocational schools. The bulk of the labor force is thus secondary school graduates with inadequate education and skills to hold highly productive and well-paid jobs. A lot of young people go abroad for study or work, the bulk of them facing various financial constraints and social protection issues that require timely solutions from the government.

More tertiary enrollment is needed to prepare youth for high-skill jobs in more productive sectors. This requires broadening the coverage of existing institutions and opening new ones, including branches of foreign universities. It also requires improving the quality of education through modernized curricula for diverse skills sets in both tertiary education and technical and vocational education, greater spending for research and development, and financing to improve digital and entrepreneurial skills. Achieving these objectives will require greater investment in education to make it more inclusive, competitive, and relevant. Traditionally, education spending has averaged around 3% of GDP, well below outlays in advanced economies.

Job-creation measures are needed to reduce youth unemployment. According to World Bank data based on government statistics, the youth unemployment rate reached 10.6% in 2022, up 0.6 percentage points from 2021 (Figure 2.7.6). Other sources suggest much higher unemployment rates, with youth representing the bulk of the unemployed. The country's undiversified economic structure complicates the creation of quality jobs, with most jobs currently in low-skill agriculture and services. The most productive sectors, such as hydrocarbons, are capital-intensive and require fewer but more highly skilled and technologically advanced workers, with positions usually filled by foreign specialists for lack of local expertise (Figure 2.7.7). The job creation programs would succeed if they are comprehensive and part of a multidimensional approach that combines supply- and demand-side measures.

Figure 2.7.6 Youth Unemployment Rate

Turkmenistan's youth unemployment rate reached 10.6% in 2022.

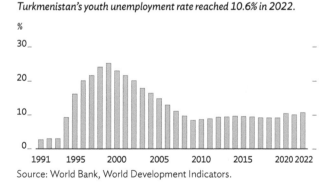

Source: World Bank, World Development Indicators.

Figure 2.7.7 Employment by Sector, 2022

Agriculture remained the largest employer in 2022.

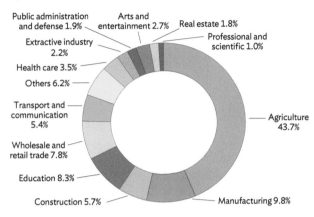

Source: Statistical Yearbook of Turkmenistan, 2023.

Wage subsidies and public employment programs for youth could be useful in the short term. Creating high-quality jobs, however, will require careful policy interventions, which can include efforts to develop high-growth and job-led sectors through rigorous investment programs; improving the business climate for private firms, which currently produce about 35% of GDP; promoting export-oriented industries; improving access to bank finance; and fostering foreign exchange convertibility. A more favorable investment climate would spur foreign direct investment, likely bringing higher technological advancement and demand for skills, enabling higher-paying jobs in competitive industries.

Effective youth empowerment requires public–private collaboration, both national and international. Public–private partnerships can leverage resources, expertise, and networks to support youth initiatives and ensure their sustainability. Investing in joint initiatives such as internship programs, mentorship schemes, and skill development workshops can expose youth to the real world and facilitate their transition to the labor force.

UZBEKISTAN

Growth edged up in 2023 on faster expansion in industry and agriculture. Inflation decelerated with tight monetary policy and continued tax exemption for essential foods. Growth is forecast to slow in 2024 and rise slightly in 2025 as increases in administered prices limit the rise in real disposable household income, cooling demand. Inflation will remain high as structural reforms in energy lead to higher administered prices, despite continued monetary tightening. Green development policy is critical for accelerating the transition to a green economy.

Economic Performance

Faster expansion in industry and agriculture helped accelerate economic growth. The State Statistics Agency reported growth rising from 5.7% in 2022 to 6.0% in 2023 (Figure 2.8.1). On the supply side, expansion in industry increased from 5.3% in 2022 to 6.0% as healthy external and domestic demand led to gains in metal and food processing and textile manufacturing. Mining and quarrying grew by a modest 1.0% as reserve depletion caused the extraction of oil and gas to plummet. Coal output, in contrast, expanded with increased demand for household heating during the cold season. Growth in agriculture accelerated from 3.6% in 2022 to 4.0% with healthy demand for cotton from textile-exporting enterprises, gains in wheat and livestock production for domestic consumption, and increased horticulture output from greater crop diversification. Expansion in construction slowed marginally, from 6.6% in 2022 to 6.4%, with similar growth in new buildings and structures. Growth in services slowed from 8.5% in 2022 to 6.8% as expansion in accommodation and food services, transportation, and storage declined with slower expansion in private consumption and cooling business activities, despite a 27% rise in tourist arrivals.

Higher investment boosted growth on the demand side. Growth in private consumption fell from 11.0% in 2022 to an estimated 6.3% in 2023 as high inflation

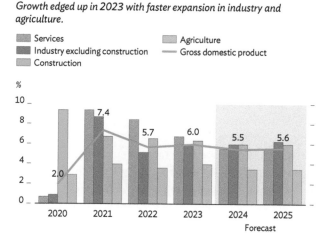

Figure 2.8.1 Supply-Side Growth

Growth edged up in 2023 with faster expansion in industry and agriculture.

Source: Statistics Agency of Uzbekistan.

and a 32.9% drop in cross-border transfers trimmed real household income growth, despite increases in nominal public wages, pensions, and social assistance. Public consumption growth slowed from 3.5% in 2022 to an estimated 2.9%, reflecting a cut in public spending in the second half of 2023. Expansion in investment surged from 3.1% to 22.1%. This reflected greater private investment, including a jump in foreign direct investment, to upgrade manufacturing, as well as heavy public investment in electricity and natural gas supply

---

This chapter was written by Begzod Djalilov of the Uzbekistan Resident Mission, ADB, Tashkent.

networks and urban infrastructure. The deficit in net exports of goods and services widened by 24.3% as growth in imports of petrochemicals, machinery, and equipment, mainly for industry, outpaced growth in exports, notably services and gold.

Inflation slowed in 2023 as monetary policy remained tight and the government retained a tax exemption for essential foods. Inflation decreased from 11.4% in 2022 to 10.0% in 2023 as the Central Bank of Uzbekistan kept monetary policy tight, lowering its policy rate by only 100 basis points, from 15.0% to 14.0%, in March 2023. In addition, the government extended the exemption of essential food products from value-added tax and custom duties. Inflation declined from 15.3% in 2022 to 12.1% for food and from 10.0% to 8.5% for other goods. However, inflation in services surged from 7.0% to 8.2% because of demand-side pressures, including an October rise in administered energy prices. In December 2023, year-on-year inflation decreased to 8.4%, close to the central bank target, though a rise in energy prices may make the slowdown temporary.

The fiscal deficit expanded from 3.9% of GDP in 2022 to an estimated 5.5% as spending outgrew revenue. With improved tax collection and a broadening of the tax base, revenue rose from 29.7% of GDP to an estimated 33.0% in 2023. Stable prices for gold, copper, petrochemicals, and other key commodities produced by state enterprises, the largest taxpayers, sustained a steady revenue stream to the budget. Outlays rose from 33.9% of GDP to an estimated 38.5%, reflecting increased social spending, higher subsidies for state-owned enterprises, and increased public wages and pensions. Most of the fiscal deficit was financed by external borrowing, raising public debt from 36.4% of GDP to 37.7%. In October 2023, Uzbekistan issued $349.1 million in green sovereign international bonds denominated in Uzbek sum on the London Stock Exchange, along with conventional international bonds valued at $660 million.

Bank lending to the economy expanded further in 2023. Credit to the economy rose by 23.3%, up from 21.4% a year earlier, on rising demand from industry, services, and higher mortgage lending. The share of nonperforming loans moderated from 3.6% of all loans in 2022 to 3.5% in 2023. Growth in broad money

plunged from 30.2% in 2022 to 12.2% as expansion of the local currency money supply slowed by more than half from 39.0% in 2022 to 18.4% and growth in foreign currency deposits slowed equally steeply from 10.8% to 5.1% (Figure 2.8.2).

Despite a surge in gold exports, the current account deficit widened as imports rose faster than exports (Figure 2.8.3). High gold prices helped total exports rise by 23.8%, up from 15.9% in 2022, as non-gold exports increased by 4.2%. With robust domestic demand, import growth accelerated to 24.0% from 20.6% in 2022, driven by imports of cars, equipment, and petroleum products, alongside 9.8%

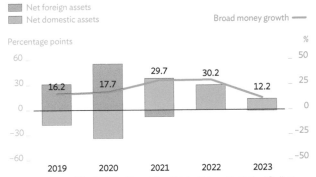

Figure 2.8.2 Contributions to Money Supply Growth

Broad money growth slowed in 2023, reflecting smaller expansion in net domestic assets and a decline in net foreign assets.

Sources: Central Bank of the Republic of Uzbekistan. Statistical Bulletin: January–December 2023; Asian Development Bank estimates.

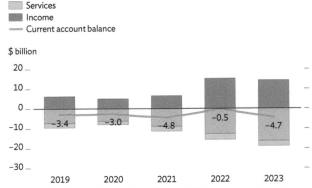

Figure 2.8.3 Current Account Components

The current account deficit widened significantly in 2023 as the merchandise trade deficit deepened.

Sources: The Central Bank of Uzbekistan. 2023. Preliminary Data of Current Account Balance for 2022; Asian Development Bank estimates.

depreciation of the currency against the US dollar. Growth in remittances returned to its medium-term trend, dropping to 12.6% of GDP after 19.2% growth in 2022, as the number of migrant workers decreased and the Russian ruble depreciated. Gross foreign reserves edged down from $35.8 billion at the end of 2022 to $35.6 billion a year later, providing cover for 9 months of imports, with a 6.8% rise in gold reserves largely offsetting a 19.5% decline in foreign currency reserves (Figure 2.8.4).

Figure 2.8.4 Gross International Reserves

Gross foreign reserves edged down in 2023 as foreign currency reserves declined.

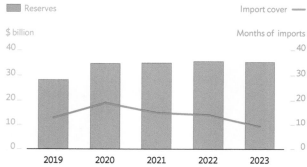

Sources: Statistics Agency of Uzbekistan; Asian Development Bank estimates.

Figure 2.8.5 Gross Domestic Product Growth Forecast

Growth is forecast to decrease in 2024 and rise slightly in 2025 with slower expansion in private consumption and services.

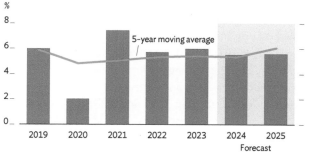

Sources: Statistics Agency of Uzbekistan; Asian Development Bank estimates.

Table 2.8.1 Selected Economic Indicators, %

Growth will rise slightly in 2024 and further in 2025 as transportation expands, with moderating inflation.

	2022	2023	2024	2025
GDP growth	5.7	6.0	5.5	5.6
Inflation	11.4	10.0	10.0	9.5

GDP = gross domestic product.
Sources: State Statistics Agency; Central Bank of Uzbekistan; Asian Development Bank estimates.

Economic Prospects

Growth is forecast to weaken, especially in services and agriculture, as administered price increases limit a rise in real domestic demand. It will slow to 5.5% in 2024 before rising slightly to 5.6% in 2025 from a pickup in industry (Figure 2.8.5 and Table 2.8.1). On the supply side, growth in services is anticipated to decelerate to 5.5% in both years with cooling demand for food and accommodation, storage, and transportation services. Expansion in agriculture is projected slowing to 3.5% in both years because of expected shortages of water for irrigating cotton and wheat. Growth in construction is forecast to decelerate to 6.0% in both years, reflecting slower expansion in housing, local infrastructure, and upgrades to manufacturing plants. Rising external demand for food and textiles and domestic demand for mining and quarrying are projected to sustain industry growth at 6.0% in 2024 and raise it to 6.3% in 2025.

On the demand side, private consumption and investment growth will slow. Ongoing structural reforms involving domestic price increases for energy in 2024 and 2025 are forecast to trim real disposable household income growth. This will cool demand and moderate growth in private consumption to 5.0% in 2024 and 5.3% in 2025 despite planned periodic adjustments of public wages and pensions to keep pace with inflation. In addition, commercial banks are expected to limit consumer lending and mortgages to slow rapid growth in credit to the economy. Public consumption is forecast to grow by a modest 1.0% yearly on slightly higher spending to operate and maintain social sector institutions amid anticipated fiscal consolidation during 2024–2025. With planned higher public and private investment in health care, education, urban infrastructure, and industrial facility expansion, investment is projected to grow by 8.0% in both years, down slightly from 2023. Higher imports of capital and intermediate goods for industry and transport services are expected to widen the deficit in net exports, offsetting gains in exports of textiles, food, and tourism services.

Inflation is projected little changed, despite continuing tight monetary policy, as structural reforms in energy raise administered prices. Year-on-year inflation slowed to 9.1% in January 2024 from 12.1% a year earlier as the central bank maintained its policy rate at 14.0%. However, inflation is anticipated to remain at 10.0% in 2024 and moderate only to 9.5% in 2025, reflecting the lagged impact of energy price hikes in October 2023 and expected further domestic energy price increases in 2024 and 2025 (Figure 2.8.6). To curb inflationary pressure by slowing credit growth, commercial banks are expected to continue limiting microcredit and consumer lending, including auto loans. Moreover, the government is expected to reduce energy subsidies and policy lending, and improve the targeting of social protection payments, to narrow the fiscal deficit to 4.0% of GDP in both years.

Structural reforms and expanding social spending will limit fiscal consolidation and deficit reduction. The fiscal deficit is projected at 4.0% of GDP in 2024, narrowing to 3.5% in 2025 (Figure 2.8.7). Revenue is expected to remain at 33.0% of GDP in 2024 and 2025 with steady tax revenue from state-owned enterprises in mining and quarrying that benefit from high prices for gold, copper, and petrochemicals. The government aims to maintain high spending for capital projects, education, health care, and social protection, while strengthening fiscal discipline by curbing outlays for unanticipated public activities and subsidies to state-owned enterprises. Expenditure is forecast as moderating to the equivalent of 37.0% of GDP in 2024 and 36.5% in 2025.

Cooling income inflows and increasing imports will expand the current account deficit. The current account deficit is forecast to widen to around 5.0% of GDP in 2024 and 2025 on rising imports and declining remittance inflows from the Russian Federation (Figure 2.8.8). Higher demand for imported consumer products, capital and intermediate goods, and transport services is anticipated to keep import growth higher than the expansion of exports of goods and services.

Rising gold reserves are expected to raise gross foreign reserves to $36 billion in 2024 and 2025. These reserves will provide cover for 11 months of imports in 2024 and 10 months in 2025. The authorities set a $5 billion ceiling on external borrowing in 2024 to keep total public debt below 60.0% of GDP in 2024

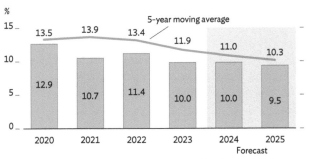

Figure 2.8.6 Inflation Forecast

Inflation will remain high in 2024 with energy price increases and decrease slightly in 2025 from anticipated monetary tightening.

Sources: Statistics Agency of Uzbekistan; Asian Development Bank estimates.

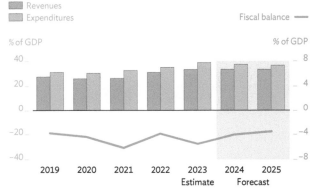

Figure 2.8.7 Fiscal Indicators Forecast

The fiscal deficit is forecast narrowing to 4.0% of GDP in 2024 and 3.5% in 2025 with fiscal consolidation.

GDP = gross domestic product.
Sources: International Monetary Fund; Asian Development Bank estimates.

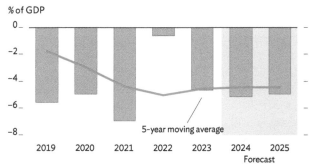

Figure 2.8.8 Current Account Forecast

The current account deficit will widen in 2024 on rising imports.

GDP = gross domestic product.
Sources: International Monetary Fund; Asian Development Bank estimates.

Figure 2.8.9 Public External Debt Forecast

The ratio of public debt to GDP will change little in 2024–2025.

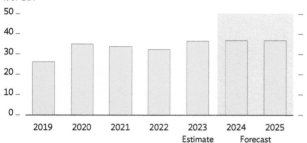

GDP = gross domestic product.
Sources: Statistics Agency of Uzbekistan; Asian Development Bank estimates.

and 2025. External public debt is currently below 38.0% of GDP and is expected to stay at about 37.0% in 2024 and 2025 (Figure 2.8.9). With capital investment in petrochemicals, mining, and quarrying, foreign direct investment is projected to grow by 10.0% each year.

Risks to growth stem primarily from possible slowdown in Uzbekistan's major trading partner.
Slowing growth in the Russian Federation, the main destination of migrant workers and exports of food and textiles, would weaken external demand for Uzbekistan's processed food and garments and its migrant workers. The drop in remittance inflow would trim households' income, slowing private consumption growth. Tightened external financial conditions would further raise the cost of external borrowing for capital investment projects and business activities. Growing contingent liabilities from state-owned enterprises, expanding public–private partnerships, and climate change would also pose risks to growth and fiscal sustainability.

Policy Challenge—Green Development Policy

A green development policy is critical for accelerating a transition to a green economy. In its nationally determined contributions to 2030, Uzbekistan aims to generate at least 30.0% of its electricity from renewable sources and cut greenhouse gas emissions by 35.0% per unit of GDP from 2010 levels. According to Our World in Data, as of 2020, Uzbekistan's total emissions were 184.15 million tons of carbon dioxide

equivalent, or 0.39% of global emissions, ranking the country 42nd out of 198 countries. Emissions per million dollars of GDP were 3,074 million tons, 23rd highest of 198 countries.

The government has adopted a Strategic Framework for Transitioning to a Green Economy. The framework reflects its national commitments to the Paris Agreement and its national development strategy 2030. The government has set up the Ministry of Ecology, Environmental Protection, and Climate Change to govern climate issues. Green transitioning and fulfilling national climate commitments warrant a consolidated green development policy with cross-sectoral coordination and public participation. Uzbekistan is progressing toward diversifying its electricity generation with renewable sources and greening its public finance management.

Green development policy is fragmented among various ministries and agencies, risking inefficiency in pursuing a green economy. The Ministry of Energy and the Ministry of Investment, Industry, and Trade both lead policy on expanding electricity generation with renewable sources, for example, while the Ministry of Economy and Finance sets strategic directions for transitioning to a green economy and oversees the adoption of green practices in public finance management. Green development policy, however, requires an institution with a mandate to coordinate and monitor the work of different ministries.

Institutionalizing a climate policy council could provide a solution. Ideally, the Cabinet of Ministers or a similarly high-ranking government institution should lead such a council, with representatives from line ministries, the private sector, civil society organizations, and think tanks. The council's coordinating activities could include the following: (i) adapting the service sector to climate change, (ii) training specialists with green skills to ensure labor productivity and competitiveness in a future green economy, (iii) revising and harmonizing technical regulations and standards for industrial goods with international and regional green standards and practices, (iv) adapting public transport infrastructure to electric-powered mobility and other decarbonized modes of logistics, (vi) providing transboundary management of regional public goods such as water resources due to climate change, and (vii) adapting the healthcare system to increasingly frequent heatwaves.

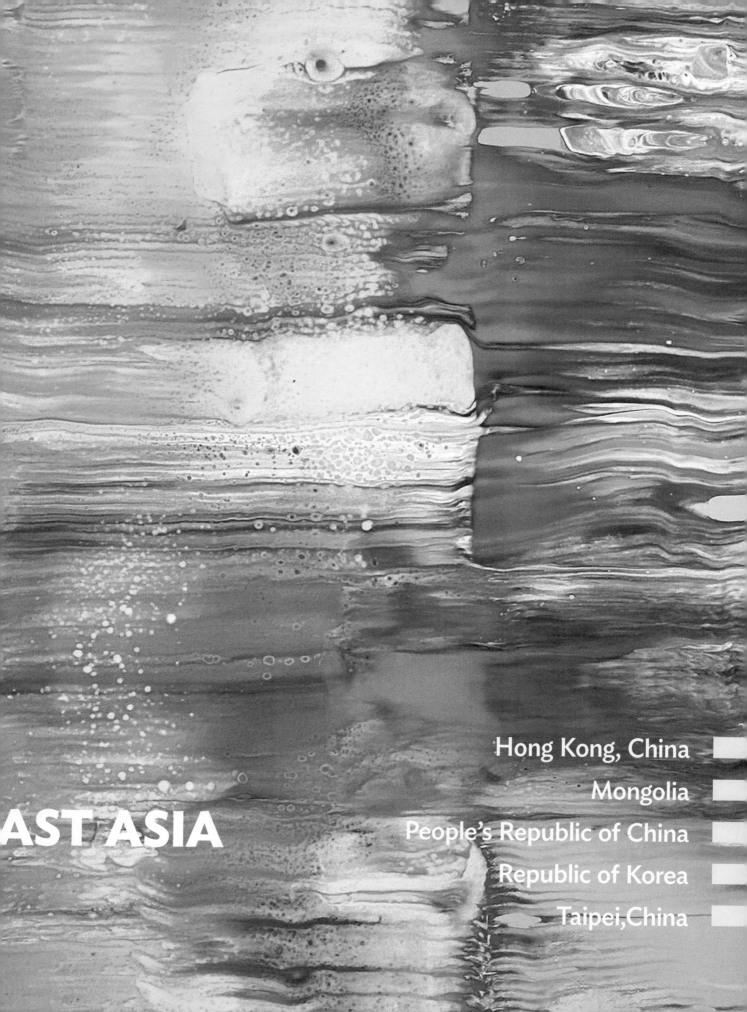

EAST ASIA

Hong Kong, China
Mongolia
People's Republic of China
Republic of Korea
Taipei,China

HONG KONG, CHINA

Private consumption, investment, and tourism buttressed a growth rebound in 2023 following an average contraction of 1.4% in 2019–2022. Growth is expected to moderate this year and next as impetus from the post-pandemic reopening fades and activity in the People's Republic of China (PRC) weakens. Inflation will likely remain moderate over the forecast horizon. In the medium term, diversification within and outside the financial sector is crucial to sustain growth.

Economic Performance

Growth resumed in 2023 with GDP rising by 3.2%, following a 3.7% contraction in 2022. Despite last year's growth, real GDP remained 2.7% lower than in 2018, diverging from the other advanced Asian economies that rely more on high-technology exports (Figure 2.9.1). The lifting of COVID-19 restrictions at the start of the year boosted private consumption and tourism spending. These tailwinds, however, were curtailed by tight financial conditions and weakening demand from the PRC (Figure 2.9.2). Private consumption picked up by 7.3%, as retail sales grew by 16.2% and restaurant sales by 26.1% (Figure 2.9.3). The government supported the consumption rebound by extending through 2023 the "Consumption Voucher Scheme" initiated during the pandemic. Labor market conditions also supported private consumption as unemployment fell to just 2.9% in the fourth quarter of 2023 from a year earlier, while wages continued to rise (Figure 2.9.4). The impact, however, was weakened by the shrinking of the overall labor force, by 4.8% in the fourth quarter of last year from its peak in June–August, due to aging and emigration. Gross fixed capital formation expanded by 10.8%, reversing a 7.4% contraction in 2022. This was driven by private investment rising 16.1% as purchases of machinery and equipment resumed along with construction. Driven by a 13.8% fall in exports to the PRC, merchandise exports plummeted by 10.3% while imports contracted by 8.6%. Although net services exports expanded as tourism

Figure 2.9.1 Quarterly Gross Domestic Product, Selected Asian Economies

Real GDP growth diverged from other advanced Asian economies that focus more on high-tech exports.

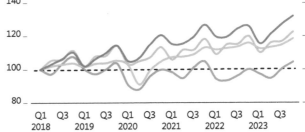

— Hong Kong, China
— Republic of Korea
— Singapore
— Taipei,China

GDP = gross domestic product, Q = quarter.
Source: CEIC Data Company.

rebounded, net exports subtracted 2.5 percentage points from growth. The fall in exports narrowed the current account surplus to 9.3% of GDP in 2023, from 10.2% in 2022.

Outbound tourism strongly recovered last year surpassing the rebound in inbound tourism, but net services receipts increased. The rapid rise in outbound tourism was driven by pent-up demand and

---

This chapter was written by Jules Hugot of the Economic Research and Development Impact Department (ERDI), ADB, Manila, and Michael Timbang, ERDI consultant.

Figure 2.9.2 Quarterly Gross Domestic Product Growth
Rate, 2023

Growth accelerated in the second half of 2023.

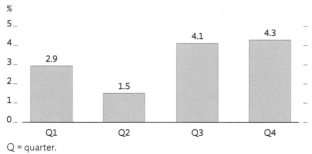

Q = quarter.
Source: Census and Statistics Department.

Figure 2.9.3 Restaurant and Retail Sales

Restaurant and retail sales rebounded in 2023, but remain below pre-pandemic levels.

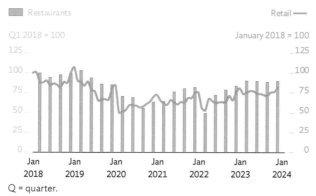

Q = quarter.
Source: Census and Statistics Department.

Figure 2.9.4 Labor Market Indicators, 3-Month
Moving Average

*The labor market tightened in 2023, with about 5% fewer workers than
in 2018.*

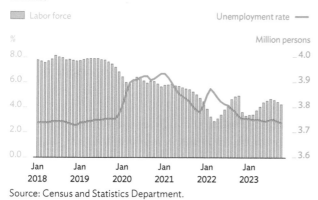

Source: Census and Statistics Department.

easier access to the Greater Bay Area (GBA) since the
2018 commissioning of the Guangzhou–HKG high-
speed railway and bridge to Macau, China. Shopping
in the PRC also became more attractive due to the
11% appreciation of the Hong Kong dollar against
the yuan during March 2022–December 2023. And
services consumption in the PRC also became more
attractive with the development of a higher-quality
services offering, including car maintenance, dental
services, or spas. Tourist arrivals in 2023 recovered
to 52% of their 2018 levels as visitors from the PRC
returned, accounting for 79% or the total (Figure 2.9.5).
Tourism receipts rose to 54% of 2018 levels, but average
per capita spending of same-day visitors fell by 40%
compared to 2018 (Figure 2.9.6). Meanwhile, per capita
spending of overnight visitors increased by only 5% over
the same period. This could imply that Hong Kong,
China is becoming a less attractive shopping destination
partly due to the Hong Kong dollar appreciation, but
also because of the gradually expanding alternatives in
the GBA. Overall, services exports grew by 21.2% last
year, driven by a rebound in exports of travel services to
48% of 2018 levels (Figure 2.9.7). Exports of business
and other services, however, grew by just 2.2%, while
exports of financial services declined by 4.1% on
subdued cross-border trade, financial, and commercial
activities involving the PRC.

**Monetary tightening dampened the stock market
and the real estate market.** The Hong Kong
Monetary Authority raised its base rate four times

Figure 2.9.5 Tourist Arrivals, by Origin

*Tourist arrivals recovered in 2023, but PRC arrivals remain about a
third below pre-pandemic levels.*

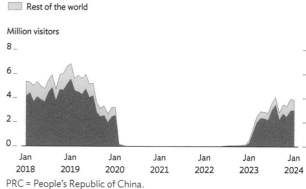

PRC = People's Republic of China.
Source: CEIC Data Company.

Figure 2.9.6 Tourism Receipts

Tourism receipts remained below pre-pandemic levels.

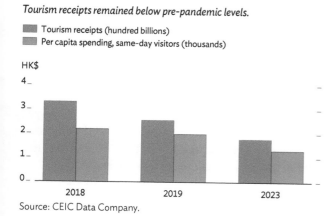

Source: CEIC Data Company.

Figure 2.9.7 Services Exports

Receipts from travel services rebounded sharply in the first quarter of 2023.

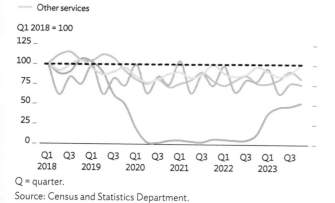

Q = quarter.

Source: Census and Statistics Department.

last year to sustain the Hong Kong dollar peg to the US dollar. This, together with concerns over the PRC outlook, dampened the stock market. As a result, the Hang Seng Index fell by 24.4% at the end of February 2024 from end-January 2023, reaching its lowest level since 2009. This also constrained demand for residential property, pushing prices down 6.9% in December year on year, and 21.8% since their peak in September 2021.

The government budget remained in sharp deficit with revenue and expenditure both contracting.
Government revenue fell by an estimated 10.9% in fiscal year 2023 (FY2023; ended 31 March 2024) as revenue from land premiums paid to change land use rights and stamp duties on property transaction

values contracted sharply (Figure 2.9.8). Declining revenues were roughly matched by a 10.2% decrease in expenditure, driven by reduced pandemic-related spending. As a result, the budget recorded a deficit equivalent to 5.8% of GDP—a slight improvement from 6.7% in FY2022, but still in marked deficit.

Figure 2.9.8 Fiscal Indicators

The fiscal balance remained in sharp deficit in FY2023.

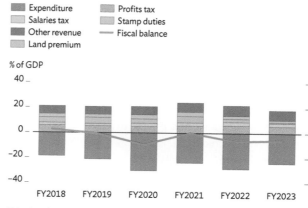

FY = fiscal year, GDP = gross domestic product.
Note: Fiscal balance is computed as total government revenue minus expenditure.
Source: Financial Services and the Treasury Bureau.

Inflation edged up but remained moderate at 2.1% last year, despite the economic rebound.
Restaurant and takeaway prices contributed most to inflation as reopening boosted demand while a number of establishments did not reopen after the pandemic (Figure 2.9.9). This was also supported by

Figure 2.9.9 Headline Inflation

Inflation edged up in 2023 as rental prices picked up.

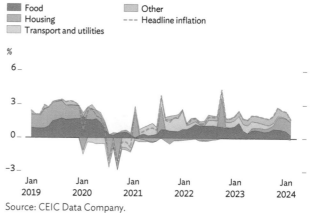

Source: CEIC Data Company.

the tighter labor market. Energy prices contributed marginally to inflation in the first half of the year, while housing prices picked up in the second half as the waiver granted on public housing rent increases during the pandemic expired. Netting out the unwinding of one-off pandemic relief measures, underlying inflation remained at 1.7% last year, the same as in 2022.

Economic Prospects

GDP growth is forecast to moderate to 2.8% in 2024, edging up to 3.0 in 2025 (Table 2.9.1 and Figure 2.9.10). Growth will start to normalize as private consumption and the tourism boost from reopening fades and the fiscal deficit narrows. Meanwhile, exports and imports will improve this year and next, while public and private investment will pick up further amid expected interest rate cuts and resuming government investment.

Private consumption growth will slow down but will continue to benefit from rising incomes. This will be driven by the continuing tight labor market.

Table 2.9.1 Selected Economic Indicators, %

Growth will moderate this year, while inflation will edge up slightly.

	2022	2023	2024	2025
GDP growth	–3.7	3.2	2.8	3.0
Inflation	1.9	2.1	2.3	2.3

GDP = gross domestic product.
Sources: Census and Statistics Department; Asian Development Bank estimates.

Figure 2.9.10 Gross Domestic Product Growth

Growth will moderate in 2024 and edge up in 2025.

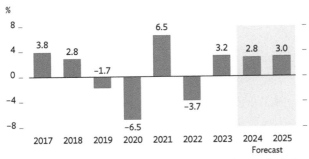

Sources: Census and Statistics Department; *Asian Development Outlook* Database.

However, wage increases will slow as easier entry for migrants through the Top Talent Pass Scheme and Enhanced Supplementary Labor Scheme will alleviate the labor shortage.

The tourism recovery will lose steam despite efforts to attract new visitors. As tourist spending on shopping declines, the government will increasingly invest in cultural and sporting events. The shift aims to attract tourists, including from the PRC, but also to offer residents a reason to spend weekends at home rather than elsewhere. Entry restrictions were also relaxed for the residents of two provinces in the PRC, but these marginal adjustments are not likely to boost tourism much. Despite these efforts, visitor arrivals are not expected to recover to their 2018 peak over the forecast horizon.

Government expenditure will likely decline further after a period of pandemic-related spending. The fiscal deficit is projected to narrow to 1.5% of GDP in FY 2024, before returning to surplus in FY 2025. The government expects revenue to increase by 14.1% this year with sharp rebounds in land premiums and stamp duty receipts as the property market revives. In contrast, government expenditure should rise by just 6.7%. This year's deficit will marginally lower fiscal reserves to 21.7% of GDP, still covering a comfortable 11 months of government expenditure.

Investment growth will pick up on the anticipated property market rebound and government infrastructure initiatives. All residential property demand management measures—including restrictions on non-resident property purchases and their resale within 2 years—were removed in February. This will stimulate transaction volumes and consequently boost government revenue. Property prices, however, are expected to further decline this year—due to persistently high borrowing costs and a backlog of unsold properties—before stabilizing in 2025 on monetary policy easing. This stabilization, coupled with a reduction in labor shortages in construction, is expected to bolster private investment in the sector. Public investment will also rise, notably around the Northern Metropolis. A 900,000-home development centered around a technology and innovation hub near Shenzhen and slated to begin this year.

Inflation is forecast to edge up slightly to 2.3% in 2024 and remain unchanged in 2025. Domestic prices, such as commercial rentals and labor costs, will face some upward pressure this year as the economy recovers further. But the impact will be limited as the economy continues to operate below capacity. In addition, external price pressures will ease further as the global monetary policy stance remains tight, particularly in the first half of the year. On balance, this will result in a mild, broad-based increase in prices.

Risks are mostly related to developments in the PRC. A sharper-than-expected slowdown in the PRC would dampen tourism. It would also curtail merchandise and financial services exports, and investment from non-residents, notably in residential property. Greater tensions between the PRC and US in the context of the US presidential election in November are also a threat for Hong Kong, China, given its strong economic links with both. Given the peg to the US dollar, prolonged monetary tightening in the US would also worsen prospects, particularly in the housing sector.

Policy Challenge—Diversifying Within and Outside the Financial Sector

With the financial sector facing external headwinds, diversification should be prioritized. Financial services have supported Hong Kong, China's economic growth, with its share of GDP increasing from 12.3% in 2002 to 22.4% in 2022 (Figure 2.9.11). This is primarily due to Hong Kong, China's unique legal status, which made it a bridge between global investors and a rapidly industrializing PRC. However, long-term prospects of an economic slowdown in the PRC, growing onshore financial markets, and geopolitical tensions with the US require a strategic reassessment of the economy's heavy reliance on the finance sector. To ensure sustained prosperity, preserving the city's competitive edge in finance must be balanced with fostering diversification into other high-value activities.

Opportunities remain in the corporate green bond market. Transactions on the Hong Kong Exchanges and Clearing was overtaken by the Shenzhen Stock Exchange in 2021 and India's stock market in January

Figure 2.9.11 Top Four Sector Shares of Gross Domestic Product

The financial services share of GDP has almost doubled over the past 2 decades.

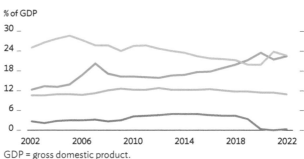

GDP = gross domestic product.
Source: Census and Statistics Department.

this year. Preserving an edge in financial services requires gaining market share in areas that outpace the market, such as green and sustainable finance. While Hong Kong, China ranks third in Asia for green bond issuance, the majority are government-issued and primarily for low-carbon buildings (Figure 2.9.12). For corporate green bonds issuance, Hong Kong, China follows the PRC, Japan, the Republic of Korea, and Singapore. Still, Hong Kong, China has pioneered green bond initiatives, including the world's largest retail green bond and the first government tokenized green bond issue, with interests recorded on a blockchain. To enhance its appeal on this market, it needs to keep pace with legal, regulatory, and business

Figure 2.9.12 Green Bond Issuance in the Top Six Asian Markets, 2023

Hong Kong, China is Asia's largest issuer of sovereign green bonds, but it lags behind in corporate green bond issuance.

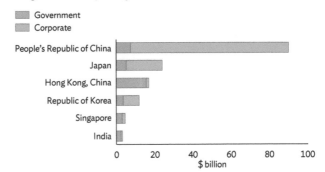

Sources: *AsianBondsOnline*; Bloomberg.

environment policies in competing markets. There is also potential for developing carbon markets especially in the GBA.

Success in fintech has been limited, but current initiatives may help the sector take off. Despite Hong Kong, China's strong background in finance, fintech success has been limited largely due to concerns over data sovereignty. And digital literacy has caught up in other regional markets: only 25% of customers in Hong Kong, China used e-banking services frequency in the latter half of 2022, compared to 35% in Singapore. Still, the financial sector is well-positioned to develop fintech ventures, capitalizing on its expertise, client base, and unique access to the PRC market. Current initiatives aim to establish Hong Kong, China as a cryptocurrency hub. To this end, the Securities and Futures Commission is accepting applications for crypto trading platform licenses and the Hong Kong Monetary Authority is collaborating with the Central Bank of the United Arab Emirates to set common standards.

Hong Kong, China is underutilizing its potential for innovation and new technologies. The economy boasts a renowned legal system, excellent global connectivity, appeal to regional and international talent, and a dynamic financial sector. It also enjoys connectivity within the GBA, with a market of nearly 90 million people and extensive manufacturing capacity. Yet, despite this favorable environment, just 1% of the economy's GDP was devoted to research and development in 2021—less than half the rate in Japan, the Republic of Korea, Singapore, and the PRC. This suggests much room to grow for high-tech industries.

Biotech is promising, given Hong Kong, China's comparative advantage. With intense global competition and a relatively small market, efforts should focus on nurturing sectors already enjoying comparative advantage, notably biotech. Hong Kong, China can boast about its leading global universities, over 250 biopharma companies, and a promising domestic healthcare market due to high income and population aging. As a result, it has emerged as Asia's largest center for initial public offerings of biotech firms. In October last year, its Chief Executive announced the establishment of the Greater Bay Area International Clinical Trial Institute—a platform aiming to capitalize on top-tier clinical research standards and access to clinical testing networks in the GBA. This holds the potential to bolster the economy's biotech ambitions.

MONGOLIA

The economy had robust growth in 2023 as mineral output and exports increased, leading to current account and fiscal surpluses, as well as larger international reserves. Inflation receded but remained elevated. Mining should continue driving growth in 2024 and 2025, while agriculture, confronting unusually harsh weather, will likely contract in 2024 before recovering modestly in 2025. Inflation should continue to ease and the current account will return to deficit. Mongolia needs to accelerate investment in climate change mitigation and adaptation to meet its targets and build economic resilience, for which improved institutional capacity and investment climate are both required.

Economic Performance

The economy grew by 7.0% in 2023, supported by mining and the full border reopening with the People's Republic of China (PRC). Mining, accounting for about 28% of GDP, expanded by 23.4% as coal production and exports surged to multi-year highs. It contributed 2.6 percentage points to economic growth. Improved border processing and transport infrastructure, including additional truck lanes and simplified customs clearance procedures, along with sustained demand from the PRC, pushed coal exports to 69.6 million tons in 2023 from 31.7 million tons in 2022. Copper production and exports also rose as the underground section of the Oyu Tolgoi mine, responsible for around half of Mongolia's copper production, began operations in March 2023. Agricultural production contracted by 8.9% primarily due to harsh winter conditions that resulted in significant loss of livestock, cutting 1.3 points from growth. Services, which account for 40.1% of GDP, grew by 9.2%, contributing 4.3 points to growth. Within services, transportation and storage grew by 39.3% due to increased mining activity, contributing 1.8 points (Figure 2.10.1). On the demand side, export growth lifted net exports' contribution to GDP growth to 5.2 percentage points. Private consumption also rose with the improved economic situation, raising growth by 4.8 points, while government consumption added another 1.3 points.

Figure 2.10.1 Supply-Side Contributions to Growth

GDP surged in 2023 as expanded mining activity drove services up.

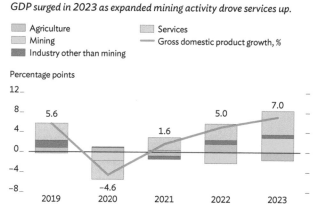

GDP = gross domestic product.
Sources: National Statistics Office of Mongolia. Statistical Information Services; Asian Development Bank estimates.

However, investment declined by 4.3 percentage points partly due to reduced outlays at the Oyu Tolgoi mine (Figure 2.10.2).

Inflation moderated in 2023, but remained elevated. Average consumer price inflation fell to 10.4% in 2023, compared to 15.2% in 2022, with the year-end inflation rate dropping to 7.9% compared to 13.2% in 2022 (Figure 2.10.3). The moderation came as supply shocks associated with trade disruptions

---

This chapter was written by Edward Faber of the Mongolia Resident Mission, ADB, Ulaanbaatar.

Figure 2.10.2 Demand-Side Contributions to Growth

Net exports and private consumption drove growth.

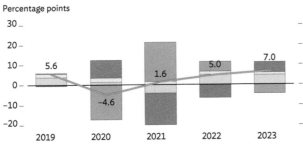

Sources: National Statistics Office of Mongolia. Statistical Information Services; Asian Development Bank estimates.

Figure 2.10.3 Inflation

Consumer price inflation moderated but remained elevated.

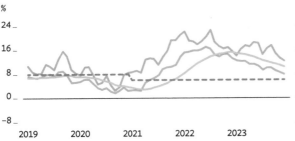

Sources: National Statistics Office of Mongolia. Statistical Information Services; Parliament Resolutions on Monetary Policy Guidelines, 2015–2022; Asian Development Bank estimates.

Figure 2.10.4 Exchange Rates

The Togrog stabilized against the US dollar.

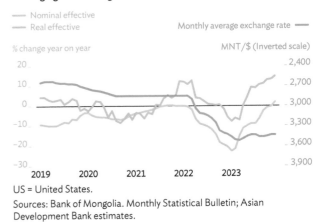

US = United States.
Sources: Bank of Mongolia. Monthly Statistical Bulletin; Asian Development Bank estimates.

Figure 2.10.5 Current Account Balance

The current account recorded a surplus for the first time since 2007.

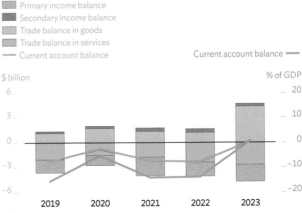

GDP = gross domestic product.
Sources: Bank of Mongolia. Balance of payments statistics; Asian Development Bank estimates.

from the pandemic and the Russian invasion of Ukraine dissipated, the PRC border fully reopened, tight monetary policy continued (with the central bank policy rate held at 13%), and the togrog appreciated by 1.0% against the US dollar (Figure 2.10.4). However, upward inflationary pressures came from faster economic growth and increased government expenditure, as well as the agricultural challenges affecting food prices, which rose by 12.2%, driven by a 16.2% increase in meat prices.

The current account balance shifted into surplus for the first time since 2007, equivalent to 0.7% of GDP. The balance turned positive due to the

large trade surplus (Figure 2.10.5). Merchandise exports rose by 41%, while merchandise imports grew by only 10%, partly due to weaker global food and energy prices, increasing the trade surplus to 21.5% of GDP. However, trade in services recorded a deficit of 12.8% of GDP, with tourism and transport services accounting for a large share, while the income account deficit rose to 8.0% of GDP, with interest payments on foreign debt a significant component. Net capital inflows declined to 7.9% of GDP, as foreign direct investment (equivalent to 8.3% of GDP) fell to $1.7 billion from $2.4 billion a year earlier. Overall, the balance of payments posted a surplus of 7.2% of GDP and international reserves increased from

$3.4 billion at the end of 2022 to $4.9 billion at the end of 2023, equivalent to 4.3 months of imports (Figure 2.10.6).

The fiscal balance recorded a surplus of 2.7% of GDP in 2023 (Figure 2.10.7). Government revenues grew by 30.7% to 35.3% of GDP as tax revenue rose to 31.0% of GDP on improved economic activity, especially in the mineral sector. Expenditure increased by 23.5% to 32.6% of GDP as both capital and recurrent expenditure grew, the latter due to large increases in public sector wages. Public debt—excluding a

Figure 2.10.6 Gross International Reserves

Foreign exchange reserves rebounded in 2023 as exports surged.

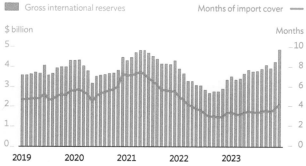

Sources: Bank of Mongolia. External sector statistics; Asian Development Bank estimates.

Figure 2.10.7 Government Budget

All fiscal balances were in surplus in 2023.

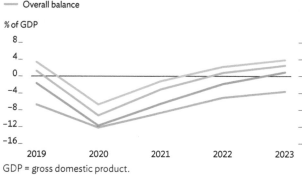

GDP = gross domestic product.

Notes: The primary balance is the gap between revenue and expenditure, adjusted by interest expenditure. The structural balance is the gap between expenditure and the revenue trend over the longer term, the ceiling for which is set by the Fiscal Stability Law subject to parliamentary amendment.

Sources: National Statistics Office of Mongolia. Statistical Information Services; Parliament resolutions on government budget, 2015–2022; Asian Development Bank estimates.

$1.7 billion swap between the central bank and the PRC—fell to 44.7% of GDP, down from 59.3% of GDP in 2022, primarily because of robust GDP growth, but also due to a 3.7% decline in debt stock. Mongolia issued two dollar-denominated sovereign bonds, one in January 2023 for $650 million, with the second in December for $350 million, to roll over expiring maturities, with both bonds well over-subscribed.

Broad Money supply (M2) increased by 26.8% during 2023 and credit grew by 23.1% (Figure 2.10.8). The central bank policy rate remained high, as did bank lending rates, which averaged close to 16% at the end of 2023 compared to 15% at end-2022. The banking sector nonperforming loan ratio fell to 7.5% of total loans at year-end, compared to 9.1% a year earlier. During 2023, all systemically important banks complied with the 2021 amendment to the banking law requiring banks to be publicly listed by June 2023.

Figure 2.10.8 Money and Credit

Credit and broad money grew in 2023.

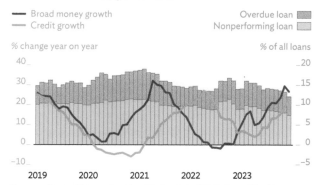

Sources: Bank of Mongolia. Monthly Statistical Bulletin and Banking Sector Consolidated Balance Sheet; Asian Development Bank estimates.

Economic Prospects

GDP growth is forecast to moderate to 4.1% in 2024 before rising again to 6.0% in 2025 (Table 2.10.1). Mining will drive growth in both years, particularly the Oyu Tolgoi mine, which is projected to double its concentrate production by 2025, with most of the increase expected in 2025. Mining is projected to contribute 1.5 percentage points to growth in 2024 and 2.6 points in 2025. However, agriculture will contract again in 2024, pushing down GDP growth, as Mongolia suffers from one of its worst winters in recent memory—over 5 million head of livestock perished

Table 2.10.1 Selected Economic Indicators, %

Growth will remain robust in 2024 and 2025 supported by mining, while inflation should moderate but remain elevated.

	2022	2023	2024	2025
GDP growth	5.0	7.0	4.1	6.0
Inflation	15.2	10.4	7.0	6.8

GDP = gross domestic product.
Sources: National Statistics Office of Mongolia. Statistical Information Services; Asian Development Bank estimates.

as of March, with the number expected to grow. A recovery in agriculture, mining expansion and services growth supported by a mining spillover to other sectors will push up GDP growth in 2025.

On the demand side, government operations will support growth in 2024. According to the 2024 budget, government expenditure will increase by 21.8% as recurrent expenditure grows on higher wages and pensions for public servants along with capital expenditure on accelerated investments under the government's New Recovery Policy. The challenges in agriculture will likely drag on private consumption in 2024, particularly for the 30% of the population that relies on agriculture for income. Investment is forecast to decline in 2024 with falling capital investment associated with the Oyu Tolgoi mine, but it should increase in 2025 supported by a recovery in agriculture. Net exports should contribute positively in both years, particularly in 2025 as mineral exports rise.

Inflation is expected to stabilize in 2024, although it will remain elevated, and is projected to recede in 2025. While the overall recent trend in inflation has been downward, the challenging winter conditions will put upward pressure on meat prices, and higher government expenditure will have an inflationary effect. The central bank policy rate was reduced from 13% to 12% in March 2024, but it remains well above the current rate of inflation and will likely have a downward effect on prices. Therefore, average inflation is forecast at 7.0% in 2024 and 6.8% in 2025.

The current account is likely to return to deficit in both 2024 and 2025. Imports are expected to increase due to higher government expenditure and more buoyant economic activity following recent strong growth, while export value should stabilize on increased

export quantity but softer commodity prices. However, the current account deficit should narrow in 2025 as copper concentrate exports increase with greater production from the Oyu Tolgoi mine.

Risks to the outlook are balanced. Downside risks include the ongoing climate-related disaster in agriculture, which will affect tax revenue, along with any reduction in coal purchases by the PRC or lower commodity prices for key exports. In addition, Mongolia's susceptibility to shocks and its narrow and small economy means that the fiscal balance can diverge significantly from budgeted amounts, affecting growth and inflation. Upside risks include upward movements in commodity prices, the potential for expanded coal sales, or a faster-than-expected ramp up of production from the Oyu Tolgou mine, all of which can push growth higher over the forecast horizon.

Policy Challenge—Increasing Climate Investment

Mongolia is committed to reducing its greenhouse gas emissions and increasing resilience to climate change by investing in climate change mitigation and adaptation. Climate change mitigation poses a significant challenge, with Mongolia the 17th highest per capita contributor of greenhouse gas emissions, of which 44.8% is related to generating energy from coal and 52% from agriculture. The nation is also particularly vulnerable to the impacts of climate change, with rising temperatures and increasing aridity threatening the traditional nomadic herding lifestyle that many Mongolians depend on. The average air temperature increased by 2.5°C over the past 80 years in Mongolia, and climate model projections suggest it will warm up to 4.5°C by 2050. Under its nationally determined contribution (NDC) under the Paris Agreement, Mongolia is targeting a 22.7% reduction in emissions by 2030, compared to the business-as-usual scenario and significant investments in climate resilience.

Achieving the NDC goal requires substantial investment financing which is far from assured. It is estimated that Mongolia needs $11.5 billion in climate investments, of which $5.2 billion is for adaptation and $6.3 billion for mitigation. However, accelerating climate investments is not without its challenges. The country faces several barriers to attract the necessary funding, including a lack of institutional capacity, limited experience with climate finance, and a regulatory environment not always conducive to investment. In addition, the country's heavy reliance on fossil fuels, particularly coal, makes the transition to a low-carbon economy particularly complex, and the economy's dependence on revenues from coal exports introduces new economic vulnerabilities resulting from the global shift to net-zero.

Despite these challenges, there are significant opportunities for increasing and speeding up climate-related investments. The country has abundant renewable energy resources—including solar, wind, and hydropower—which could provide a sustainable low-carbon alternative to fossil fuels. Mongolia's vast grasslands also offer opportunities for carbon sequestration through improved livestock management and restoration of degraded lands.

To capitalize on these opportunities, Mongolia must strengthen its institutional capacity and improve its investment climate. This could include reforms to streamline regulatory processes, enhance transparency, and provide greater certainty for investors. The country is considering introducing a climate law, which can serve as a powerful tool to drive climate action and facilitate investment in low-carbon development. By establishing clear emission reduction targets, creating a comprehensive policy framework that incentivizes climate-friendly practices, and strengthening institutional arrangements, the law can foster an environment that promotes sustainable growth. In addition, the law can ensure transparency and accountability through reporting requirements and independent reviews, while also demonstrating the government's commitment to addressing climate change. Mongolia can also integrate NDC priorities into its public investment program and support sector agencies to identity, prioritize, and design annual and medium-term climate investments. Mongolia has already developed a green taxonomy—a classification system that defines and categorizes economic activities, investments, or projects based on their environmental impact and sustainability—which could be expanded to include economic activities aligned with sustainable development goals. Finally, Mongolia can explore innovative financing mechanisms, such as green bonds or public-private partnerships, to attract the necessary capital.

International support will be crucial in helping Mongolia accelerate climate investment. Multilateral development banks can provide financing and technical assistance to help the country build capacity and develop low-carbon infrastructure. In addition, Mongolia can learn from the experience of other countries that have successfully attracted climate finance and implemented low-carbon development strategies.

PEOPLE'S REPUBLIC OF CHINA

Following an uptick in 2023, economic growth will likely moderate in 2024 and 2025 with persistent deflationary pressures a continuing concern until there is a substantial revival in domestic and global demand. Growth this year and next will be driven by continued fiscal support, but could accelerate if the property sector correction is largely addressed. There is a pressing need to address the property sector and local government finance issues.

Economic Performance

Economic growth rebounded to 5.2% in 2023 from 3.0% in 2022 on a robust expansion in services and consumption after COVID-19 restrictions were lifted in late 2022 (Figure 2.11.1). However, the rebound was bumpy. GDP growth fell from 6.3% in the second quarter (Q2) to 4.9% in Q3 with the property market weakening more than expected. GDP growth recovered to 5.2% in Q4 after a series of stimulus packages were introduced in the second half (H2) of the year, financed by additional sovereign bond issuance, the further easing of monetary policy, and policies supporting the property market.

On the demand side, consumption, especially services expenditure, drove the post-pandemic recovery. Household consumption recovered as disposable household income per capita grew by 6.1% in real terms (Figure 2.11.2). Consumption's contribution to growth increased sharply from 1.2 percentage points in 2022 to 4.3 points in 2023. Spending on services such as dining rebounded after COVID-19 mobility-related restrictions were lifted in late 2022. However, spending on consumer goods did not grow as much as services, suggesting that household confidence has yet to recover fully.

Investment grew by 3.0% in 2023 as solid growth in manufacturing and infrastructure investment offset the decline in property investment. Investment contributed 1.5 percentage points to growth in

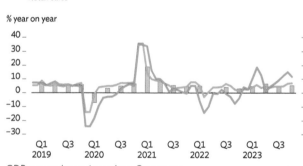

Figure 2.11.1 Real Economic Growth

GDP growth picked up in 2023, boosted by a recovery in consumption.

- Gross domestic product
- Industrial sector value added
- Retail sales

% year on year

GDP = gross domestic product, Q = quarter.
Sources: CEIC Data Company; Asian Development Bank estimates.

2023 (similar to the 1.4 points in 2022) as policy measures boosting high technology manufacturing, public infrastructure projects, and disaster rebuilding offset the property market downturn. Manufacturing investment, especially in high-tech industries, grew by 6.5% in 2023, supported by rising bank credit. Infrastructure investment also grew by a robust 5.9%, but real estate investment contracted by 9.6% (Figure 2.11.3). New construction remained subdued in most cities as homebuyer confidence has yet to recover and property developers continue to struggle with debt servicing and a large backlog of unfinished projects.

This chapter was written by Yothin Jinjarak, Wen Qi, Akiko Terada-Hagiwara, and Yajing Wang of the People's Republic of China Resident Mission, ADB, Beijing.

Figure 2.11.2 Real Growth in Income and Consumption per Capita

Growth in consumption rebounded in 2023 while income grew steadily.

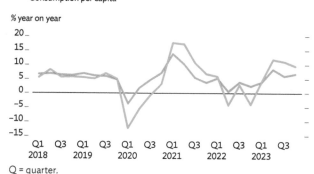

— Income per capita
— Consumption per capita

% year on year

Q = quarter.

Sources: CEIC Data Company; Asian Development Bank estimates.

Figure 2.11.3 Growth in Fixed Asset Investment

Solid growth in manufacturing and infrastructure investment offset the decline in property investment.

— All fixed assets   — Infrastructure
— Manufacturing   — Real estate

% year on year, year to date

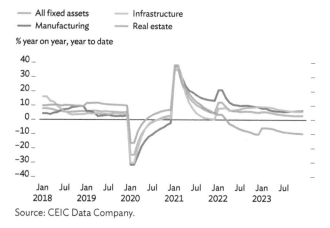

Source: CEIC Data Company.

Figure 2.11.4 Demand-Side Contributions to Growth

Consumption and investment drove the economic recovery in 2023.

▓ Consumption
▓ Investment
▓ Net exports
— Gross domestic product growth, %

Percentage points

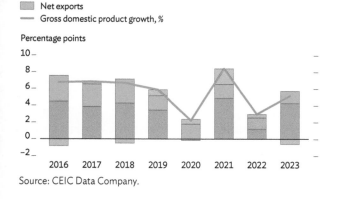

Source: CEIC Data Company.

Net exports weighed down growth amid slowing global demand (Figure 2.11.4). Net exports finished the year subtracting 0.6 percentage points from growth, compared to a positive 0.4 points contribution in 2022 after a good start early in the year and some tailwinds from electric vehicle and technology product exports.

On the supply side, the tertiary sector rebounded in 2023. It grew by 5.8% and contributed 3.1 percentage points to GDP growth, up from 1.7 points in 2022 (Figure 2.11.5). Accommodation and catering, information and technology services, and transportation led the recovery, but real estate services contracted. Secondary industry grew by 4.7% in 2023 and contributed 1.8 points to growth. High-tech manufacturing expanded rapidly, with the production of solar cells, new energy devices, and power-generating units growing in the double digits. The contribution of primary industry to growth remained unchanged at 0.3 points.

The labor market improved in 2023. The surveyed urban unemployment rate decreased from 5.5% in January to 5.1% in December 2023 and new urban jobs increased from 12.1 million in 2022 to 12.4 million in 2023. However, imbalances remained as young workers still faced multiple challenges such as limited job creation in private business and skill mismatching. The youth unemployment rate (ages 16–24) peaked at 21.3% in June 2023. Excluding university students, the rate was 14.9% in December. Migrant workers benefitted from the economic recovery, especially in the low-paid services. The unemployment rate for migrant workers from rural areas working in urban areas dropped to a historical low of 4.3% in December 2023.

Inflation remained subdued in 2023, dragged down by food deflation and softer energy prices. Consumer price inflation averaged 0.2% in 2023, down from 2.0% in 2022, driven by food deflation and lower energy prices (Figure 2.11.6). Food prices declined by 0.3% with pork prices falling 11.3%. Non-food inflation dropped to 0.4%, reflecting weak demand and softer global energy prices. Core inflation (excluding energy and food prices) was 0.7%. The producer price index declined by 3.0% in 2023 after increasing by 4.2% in 2022, as commodity and raw material prices decreased and domestic and external demand remained weak. Prices for newly constructed homes in the top 70 cities

Figure 2.11.5 Supply-Side Contributions to Growth

With business back to normal, services rebounded strongly.

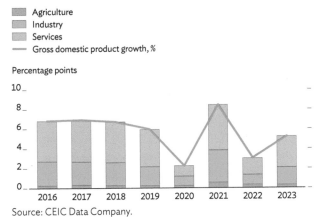

Source: CEIC Data Company.

Figure 2.11.6 Monthly Inflation

Consumer price inflation remained subdued in 2023 dragged down by food deflation and lower energy prices.

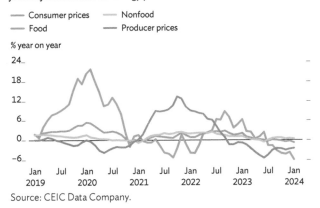

Source: CEIC Data Company.

Figure 2.11.7 Prices for Newly Constructed Homes

Housing prices were on a declining trend in 2023.

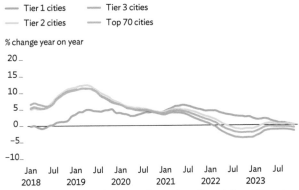

Note: Tier-1 cities include Beijing, Guangzhou, Shanghai, and Shenzhen; tier 2 includes 31 provincial capitals and larger municipalities; and tier 3 includes 35 other cities.
Sources: CEIC Data Company; Asian Development Bank estimates.

Figure 2.11.8 Banking Lending and Policy Rates

Monetary policy was accommodative as key rates were trimmed despite multiple constraints.

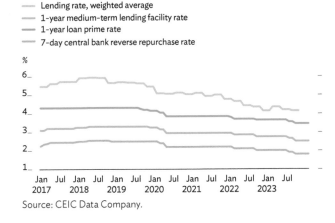

Source: CEIC Data Company.

declined by an average 0.9%, with prices in tier 3 cities declining the most and those in top tier 1 cities rising (Figure 2.11.7).

Monetary policy was accommodative amid multiple constraints. The People's Bank of China (PBOC), the central bank, trimmed the 1-year medium-term lending facility rate twice for a total of 25 basis points to 2.50% in 2023, even though concerns over bank profits, pressures from currency depreciation, and capital outflows had increased (Figure 2.11.8). As a result, the 1-year loan prime rate moderated from 3.65% at the end of 2022 to 3.45% at the end of 2023. The PBOC also reduced the required reserve ratio for commercial banks twice to free up additional funds for lending and lowered the 5-year loan prime rate used for mortgage pricing by 10 basis points to 4.20% to support the stressed real estate sector.

Credit supply ticked up in 2023 on strong government bond issuance. Total social financing—an aggregate that includes bank loans, shadow bank financing, government and corporate bonds, and equity financing—grew by 9.8% in 2023, up from 9.6% a year earlier (Figure 2.11.9). Government bonds outstanding increased by 15.9% at the end of 2023 as local government special bond issuance accelerated in H2 and loans outstanding increased by 10.7% by year-end. Banks reallocated credit from the property sector to manufacturing. Medium- and long-term loans to manufacturing grew by 31.9%, but those to the property sector declined by 1.0% at the end of 2023.

Figure 2.11.9 Growth in Broad Money, Credit Outstanding, and Government Bonds Outstanding

Thanks to strong government bond issuance, credit expansion ticked up in 2023.

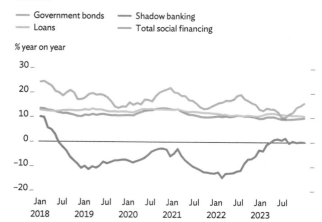

Note: Shadow banking includes entrust loans, trust loans, and bank acceptance bills.
Sources: CEIC Data Company; Asian Development Bank calculations.

Fiscal policy was supportive in 2023 although the budget deficit narrowed slightly. The deficit fell from 4.7% of GDP in 2022 to 4.6% of GDP in 2023 on improving fiscal revenue and slowing expenditure growth. Fiscal revenue recovered from last year's COVID-19 shock and value-added tax credit refunds increased by 6.4%, driven by an 8.7% increase in tax revenues (Figure 2.11.10). Meanwhile, the continuing property sector correction dampened local government revenue from land sales which constrained their spending. The growth in fiscal expenditure of general government (including central and local governments) declined to 5.4% in 2023 from 6.1% in 2022. In H2 of 2023, fiscal support increased, as the authorities issued a CNY1 trillion sovereign bond (equivalent to around 0.8% of GDP) to finance local government disaster prevention and recovery spending. New local government special bond issuance—typically not included in the general budget—also accelerated significantly in H2 and reached nearly CNY4.0 trillion (around 3.2% of GDP) by the end of the year in a concerted effort to boost public infrastructure investment.

The current account surplus narrowed driven by a lower merchandise trade surplus and a wider services trade deficit. The surplus decreased from 2.2% of GDP in 2022 to 1.5% of GDP in 2023

Figure 2.11.10 General Government Fiscal Revenue and Expenditure

Fiscal policy stepped up in the second half to support the 2023 economic recovery.

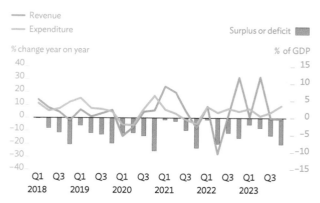

GDP = gross domestic product, Q = quarter, yoy = year on year.
Note: Public finance budget only.
Sources: CEIC Data Company; Asian Development Bank calculations.

(Figure 2.11.11). The merchandise trade surplus decreased from 3.7% of GDP in 2022 to 3.4% of GDP in 2023 on weak exports. Despite the lift from a 73.4% growth in electric vehicle exports, overall merchandise exports declined by 5.0% amid weak global demand and geopolitical uncertainties. Geographically, exports fell across major trade partners, including Southeast Asia by 6.0%, the United States (US) by 13.0%, Japan by 8.7%, and the European Union (EU) by 10.2%.

Figure 2.11.11 Current Account Balance and Merchandise Trade

The current account narrowed as the merchandise trade surplus decreased and services trade deficit normalized.

GDP = gross domestic product, Q = quarter.
Note: January and February data are combined to exclude the Lunar New Year effect.
Sources: CEIC Data Company; Asian Development Bank calculations.

Imports also dropped by 4.0% on weak domestic demand and lower commodity prices. Thanks to the resumption of cross-border travel, the services trade deficit widened from 0.5% of GDP in 2022 to 1.3% of GDP in 2023, recovering to 87.8% of the 2019 pre-pandemic level.

Foreign direct investment (FDI) inflows decreased in 2023 amid weaker confidence and geopolitical tensions. Increased geopolitical tensions and economic slowdown concerns dampened foreign company confidence, while a wider positive interest rate spread between the US and the PRC made investment in the PRC less attractive. As a result, FDI inflows decreased by 81.7%, resulting in a net outflow equal to 0.9% of GDP, compared to a net inflow of 0.2% of GDP in 2022. Meanwhile, net portfolio investment outflows reached 0.8% of GDP in the first 3 quarters of 2023, lower than 2.0% of GDP during the same period in 2022 (Figure 2.11.12). Reserve assets increased by $143 billion and stood at $3.45 trillion at end-2023. The renminbi depreciated by 1.7% against the US dollar over the year (Figure 2.11.13). It depreciated by 1.3% in nominal effective terms (against a trade-weighted basket of currencies) and by 5.5% in real effective terms (taking inflation differentials into account).

Figure 2.11.12 Balance of Payments

FDI inflows decreased significantly in 2023 amid weaker confidence and increased geopolitical tensions.

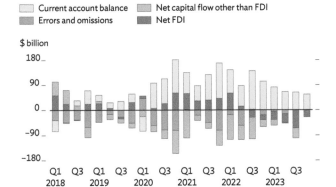

FDI = foreign direct investment, Q = quarter.
Note: Only current account balance and net FDI data available are for Q4 2023.
Sources: CEIC Data Company, Asian Development Bank calculations.

Figure 2.11.13 Renminbi Exchange Rates

The renminbi depreciated against the US dollar for most of 2023 before recovering toward the end.

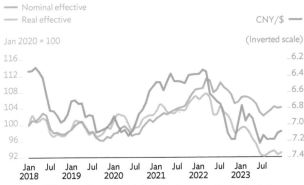

Sources: CEIC Data Company; Asian Development Bank calculations.

Economic Prospects

Economic growth is expected to moderate in 2024 and 2025. GDP is forecast to grow by 4.8% in 2024 reflecting the ongoing property market adjustment and weak external demand. Growth will further moderate to 4.5% in 2025 (Table 2.11.1). Last year's support for the housing market—including lower down payment rates and lower buying restrictions—along with accommodative monetary policy through lower reserve requirement ratios and policy rates, and fiscal stimulus to rebuild disaster-affected areas could have some near-term effects. Household consumption should help drive economic recovery in 2024 as the labor market and household income improve. Investment will be supported by strong public infrastructure growth boosted by fiscal expansion, while high-tech and other manufacturing investments should continue to grow solidly due to policy support. However, low consumer and investor sentiments in the property sector are expected to persist, tamping down consumer spending

Table 2.11.1 Selected Economic Indicators, %

Growth will moderate in 2024 and 2025, while inflation rises.

	2022	2023	2024	2025
GDP growth	3.0	5.2	4.8	4.5
Inflation	2.0	0.2	1.1	1.5

GDP = gross domestic product.
Sources: CEIC Data Company; Asian Development Bank estimates.

and private investment. Real estate investment will also remain a drag due to sluggish housing demand, especially as the backlog of unfinished projects and concerns over debt repayment weaken developers' investment appetite. Weak external demand, together with increased trade tensions will dampen demand for PRC exports with net exports continuing to drag down growth.

Supportive policies are essential to bring the economy back on solid footing. To revive growth momentum, effective measures to resolve property sector problems and strengthen private investment and household consumption should be enhanced in the policy pipeline this year. More targeted fiscal and monetary policies supplementing those announced and implemented in 2023, as well as the effective use of ultra-long special treasury bonds announced in March 2024, are necessary to address the challenges of persistently tepid external demand, high local government debt, deflationary pressure, geopolitics risks, and new sources of productivity gains amid demographic changes and an aging population.

Policy support to selected industries will drive the supply side despite excess capacity in certain sectors. Growth in services will moderate in 2024 as the post-COVID recovery boost fades. However, credit support, tax breaks, and grants for technology sectors, including semiconductors, high-tech equipment, and artificial intelligence, along with demand for low-carbon technologies, including electric vehicles, batteries, and renewables, will likely continue in 2024. Construction will be supported by infrastructure investment and public projects. Excess capacity concerns increased as the industrial capacity utilization rate dropped from 75.6% in 2022 to 75.1% in 2023. Inventory drawdowns as consumption rises and a pickup in new orders should lessen excess capacity in some manufacturing industries, such as automobile, pharmaceutical, electric machinery, and equipment, where capacity utilization rates dropped in recent years.

The labor market should improve but youth unemployment challenges will likely remain. The labor market should improve in line with a pickup in household consumption and a step up in policy, especially fiscal support. Jobs created in construction and services will continue to benefit low and medium-skilled labor, especially migrant workers.

However, youth unemployment will likely remain as the government expects a record high of 11.8 million new college and university graduates in 2024.

Inflation is forecast to rise to 1.1% in 2024 and 1.5% in 2025 as the economy continues to recover. The lingering effects of overcapacity in some manufacturing companies should tamp down price increases this year, and continued weakness in domestic and external demand will likely put downward pressure on producer prices and core inflation. However, with pork prices bottoming out and energy prices increasing, overall price movements should steer away from outright deflation. Inflation should increase further in 2025 assuming domestic demand, especially in the property sector, continues to recover.

Monetary policy will remain accommodative. In early January 2024, the PBOC announced a further reduction in the bank reserve requirement ratio (RRR) by 50 basis points that took effect on 5 February, doubling the size of typical RRR cuts, and signaled increased efforts to shore up credit supply. The central bank also injected CNY350 billion into policy banks via the Pledged Supplementary Lending facility likely to provide low-cost funding to social housing and infrastructure. To support the property market, the PBOC lowered the 5-year loan prime rate—mortgage reference rate—by 25 basis points to 3.95% in February 2024.

Fiscal policy will support growth. The higher new local government special bond issues quota (CNY 3.9 trillion in 2024) and CNY1 trillion ultra-long special government bond issuance announced in March 2024 should support economic growth. Fiscal policy measures are expected to be targeted and focused on strategic industries, affordable rental housing projects, urban renovation, and rebuilding disaster-affected areas. In addition, the central government is expected to take a bigger role in fiscal spending to help ease the financing burden of local governments. While the economy is expected to continue expanding in 2025, the fiscal spending will likely moderate after years of high fiscal deficit and rising local government debt, which have increased from 21.6% of GDP in pre-pandemic 2019 to 32.3% in 2023. COVID-related expenditure and reduced land sales have increased the financial strain faced by local governments and made it difficult for them to service their debt.

The current account surplus is projected to decrease slightly due to tepid external demand and resumption of outbound travel. The expected easing of growth in advanced economies and ongoing global trade slowdown will dampen demand for PRC exports. While exports from new industries such as electric vehicles, batteries, and renewables are bright spots, they will face headwinds from growing trade tensions with their Europe and US counterparts. Meanwhile, the services trade deficit will likely increase as outbound travel, which has yet to return to pre-pandemic levels, can be expected to pick up. FDI will likely continue its downward trend, but should remain strong in high-tech sectors. Outward direct investment could pick up in new sectors as offshoring to improve efficiency and gain higher market share gradually occurs. Capital outflow pressure is expected to ease as US interest rates trend downward.

Risks to the outlook are balanced. Downside risks include further deterioration in the property market, undermining financial stability, and threatening the growth outlook. Longer-than-expected financial market turbulence can dampen consumer sentiment as happened following the recent stock market slump. External risks include increased trade tensions with the US and EU further weakening PRC's exports, escalated geopolitical tensions that could disrupt supply chains, renewed energy challenges triggered by geopolitical conflict, and fragmentation of the global economy. Full and effective implementation of government fiscal and monetary measures as announced along with additional policy support could raise private sector confidence faster-than-expected, resulting in higher growth and inflation than forecast.

Policy Challenge—How Stimulating is Government Spending?

How effective has large fiscal spending been in stimulating growth remains a largely open question. During the 2008–2009 global financial crisis, the government rolled out a fiscal stimulus package equivalent to nearly a fifth of GDP. To boost the property sector in 2015, it subsidized interest rates on loans by policy banks. As the pandemic struck in 2020, it guided the policy bank financing for infrastructure projects

and issued special sovereign bonds. These packages substantially raised fiscal deficits. Understanding the extent to which these large stimulus packages have been effective in achieving their objectives has become increasingly relevant as the economy continues to face many headwinds, including the property sector downturn, local government debt, deflationary pressures, uncertainty in global markets, lukewarm confidence among the private sector and households, overcapacity in some sectors, and aging population and productivity issues. It is thus important to assess the lessons learned from past government stimulus spending to inform the design and implementation of future policies.

Concerns over public debt levels imply that the scope for additional borrowing is narrowing and new loans should be more productive. According to official statistics (IMF 2024), at the end of 2023 central government debt was estimated to equal 23.8% of GDP, with local government debt the equivalent of 32.3%. It is estimated that off-balance sheet liabilities from local government financing vehicles (LGFVs)—set up to finance public infrastructure projects—could be as large as 48.1% of GDP. Together, the augmented debt of central and local governments grew from 80.8% of GDP in 2018 to 116.2% in 2023. Since the property market downturn started in 2021, local governments have also faced hard budget constraints as their own-source revenues declined with the sale of land-use rights to property developers. At the same time, local governments shared the significant burden of pandemic-related health and medical expenditure. With local government debt still large and their ability to raise revenue limited, the central government will likely assume some local government responsibilities, which in turn will require additional fiscal packages that will affect debt sustainability. Therefore, it is essential to ensure that these fiscal injections are designed and implemented so they are effective in meeting their objectives.

Measured by the usual fiscal multiplier yardstick, several studies on the impact of local authority expenditures indicate that these fiscal impulses have been reasonably effective. The studies used provincial data to show that the fiscal multiplier was positive, as an increase in government spending did indeed lead to positive output growth. The analyses yielded a range of local fiscal multipliers from 0.6 (Guo et al. 2016) to 1.0 (Chen et al. 2021), indicating that a 1% increase in government spending leads to an increase in output between 0.6%–1.0%. The results varied across localities, however, with spending by localities receiving larger transfers from the central government not necessarily yielding larger multipliers. A more recent study of local fiscal multipliers in the PRC yielded a multiplier of 0.7 (Dong et al. forthcoming). However, this study also showed that if fiscal spending does not lead to a deterioration of the fiscal balance, the multiplier is 2.9, and 0.2 if the financing is by increasing fiscal deficits. Thus, to raise the effectiveness of government spending, local governments should reduce the deficit by raising revenues. These findings point to the dependence of local government on land and other property sales, which is their main source of revenue, and the detrimental effect of local government borrowing on the efficacy of fiscal policy as measured by local fiscal multipliers.

The results of the fiscal multiplier studies also varied by targeted economic sector. Government spending on investment had a multiplier of 0.6, but investment in technology yielded a fiscal multiplier of 8.6, much higher than the infrastructure spending multipliers of 0.4 and 0.1 for construction and real estate-related industries. These results and the correction in the housing market that has led to fragility of LGFVs and debt-ridden local governments indicate that growth fuelled by fiscal resources directed toward infrastructure investment and the property sector is unsustainable.

The more effective the fiscal policy supporting consumption, the higher and more sustainable the quality of long-term development. Economic growth must also rely on domestic demand to maintain its momentum amid uncertainty in the global environment. As income levels increase in the PRC, consumption of goods and services will likely play an increasing role in driving GDP growth and the long-term sustainability of economic development. However, the fiscal multiplier on private consumption is shown to be small, but at the same time, raising the effectiveness of government support for consumption is becoming more urgent given ongoing demographic changes, including declining fertility, an aging population, and urban-rural migration. Thus, several policy measures and reforms are needed. In the near term, the property sector problems should be addressed as private consumption depends on household wealth, which is stored in the housing market. In addition, policies targeted at strengthening social safety nets, particularly pension insurance, unemployment insurance, and medical insurance—along with improving the effectiveness of government spending in these areas—will increase household consumption, thereby raising the fiscal multiplier of government consumption incentives.

REPUBLIC OF KOREA

Economic growth will accelerate from 1.4% in 2023 to 2.2% in 2024, driven by higher exports, and then moderate to 2.3% in 2025 amid a tepid global recovery. Domestic demand will remain subdued in 2024 due to tight monetary and fiscal policies, then improve in 2025 as inflation continues to moderate and global oil prices stabilize. Containing the high level of household debt and debt service costs is a policy challenge, especially in a high interest rate environment.

Economic Performance

GDP growth decelerated to 1.4% in 2023 from 2.6% in 2022 (Figure 2.12.1). GDP growth in the Republic of Korea (ROK) averaged 0.9% year on year in the first half of 2023. It picked up in the second half driven by a rebound in exports, with third quarter growth at 1.4%, followed by a 2.2% expansion in the final quarter. Strong external demand for semiconductors, ships or vessels, and automobiles supported the export recovery after a year of decline (Figure 2.12.2). Total imports moderated in 2023 due to a decline in merchandise imports, resulting in a negligible contribution of net exports to growth. By contrast, domestic consumption remained tepid. Despite fuel tax cuts and discount coupons on some food items to cushion the impact of inflation on household spending, consumer sentiment weakened due to persistently high prices and high borrowing costs. Private consumption growth slowed to 1.8% in 2023 from 4.1% in 2022, reducing its contribution to GDP growth to 0.9 percentage points (Figure 2.12.3). Public consumption's contribution to growth also fell to 0.2 points as the government adopted a tight fiscal policy. Gross fixed capital formation rose by 1.1% in 2023 after contracting in 2022, contributing 0.4 points to

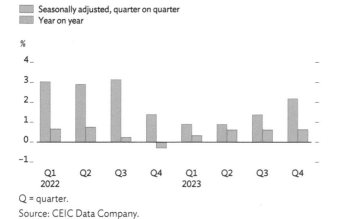

Figure 2.12.1 Quarterly Gross Domestic Product

Economic growth slowed in 2023 with an upward quarterly trend.

Q = quarter.
Source: CEIC Data Company.

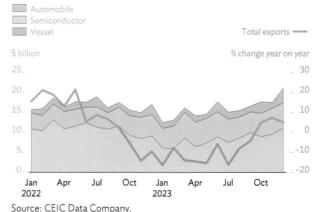

Figure 2.12.2 Value of Major Commodity Exports

Exports of major commodities improved in the latter part of 2023.

Source: CEIC Data Company.

This chapter was written by Madhavi Pundit and Melanie Quintos of the Economic Research and Development Impact Department, ADB, Manila.

Figure 2.12.3 Demand-Side Contribution to Growth

Weak domestic demand dampened growth.

- Private consumption
- Government consumption
- Fixed capital
- Change in stocks
- Net exports
— Gross domestic product growth, %

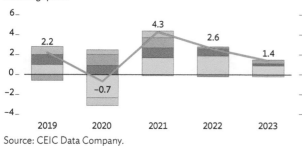

Source: CEIC Data Company.

Figure 2.12.4 Inflation

Inflation eased due to declining fuel prices.

— Core
— Headline
-- Target

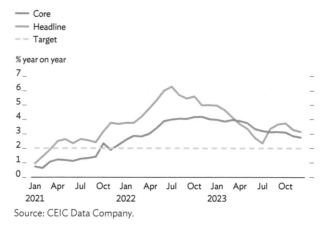

Source: CEIC Data Company.

growth. This was mainly driven by higher investments in construction and equipment as both private and public investments picked up slightly.

On the supply side, muted performance across sectors hindered growth in 2023. Services, which holds the largest share of GDP, grew by 2.1% in 2023 from 4.2% in 2022, contributing 1.2 percentage points to growth. Faster growth in transportation, storage, and real estate were offset by a decline in wholesale and retail trade due to weak domestic demand. Meanwhile, manufacturing growth remained muted at 1.0%, contributing only 0.3 points to growth. Agriculture declined by 2.4% due to unfavorable weather conditions.

The labor market had its strongest recovery since the pandemic. The unemployment rate dropped to a low of 2.7% in 2023. The labor force participation rate improved to 64.3%, driven by a rise in the female participation rate to a high of 55.6%. Notably, based on data from Statistics Korea, jobs created were mostly in services, particularly in business, personal, and public service; health and social work; and accommodation and food service.

Headline inflation eased to 3.6% in 2023 but remained above the central bank's target of 2% (Figure 2.12.4). As global oil prices declined, inflation moderated from its year-on-year peak of 6.3% in July 2022. Transport costs fell, while food and restaurants and hotels recorded slower price increases. Core

inflation, which excludes highly volatile food and energy, averaged 3.4% in 2023, lower than the 3.6% average in 2022.

Monetary policy remained tight amid sticky inflation. After raising its key policy rate by 25 basis points in January 2023 to 3.5%, the central bank kept the rate unchanged for the rest of the year. As a result, the average bank lending rate increased from 4.3% in 2022 to 5.2% in 2023, its highest in 11 years. At the same time, total outstanding loans rose by 5.1% by end-December 2023, higher than the 4.8% increase in 2022. The increase was driven in part by a rise in household mortgages following the introduction of 50-year mortgage loans by banks and the government's provision of housing assistance to targeted groups.

The government pursued fiscal consolidation by reducing expenditure. For 2023, the budget signaled a shift in government priority to reduce the fiscal deficit to 2.6% of GDP from 5.4% in 2022. The policy aimed to reduce the debt to GDP ratio, which rose to 49.4% in 2022 from 37.6% in 2019, due to pandemic-induced fiscal expansion. As of September, the latest data available for 2023, the fiscal deficit stood at 4.3% of GDP while the debt to GDP ratio reached 49.9%.

The current account surplus widened to 2.1% of GDP due to the rebound in exports. Merchandise exports improved in the latter part of the year led by semiconductors, while subdued domestic demand pulled down imports. This resulted in a merchandise trade surplus of $34.1 billion or 2.0% of GDP. By destination, shipments to the United States (US) grew by double-digits in the fourth quarter. Merchandise exports to Japan and ASEAN increased, while those to the People's Republic of China (PRC) declined (Figure 2.12.5). However, the services deficit widened to 1.5% of GDP in 2023 as outbound tourism increased. The nominal exchange rate depreciated by 1.1% against the US dollar in 2023, while the real effective exchange rate (accounting for inflation differentials with trade partners) appreciated by 1.8%. Official foreign exchange reserves rose to $420 billion in December 2023, equivalent to 7.4 months of import cover.

Table 2.12.1 Selected Economic Indicators, %

Growth is expected to pick up while inflation will trend down this year and next.

	2022	2023	2024	2025
GDP growth	2.6	1.4	2.2	2.3
Inflation	5.1	3.6	2.5	2.0

GDP = gross domestic product.
Source: Asian Development Bank estimates.

Figure 2.12.5 Merchandise Exports by Destination

Exports to major destinations are trending upward.

— PRC
— US
— EU 27
— Japan
— ASEAN

% change year on year

PRC = People's Republic of China, US = United States, EU = European Union, ASEAN = Association of Southeast Asian Nations.
Source: CEIC Data Company.

Economic Prospects

Growth is forecast to pick up to 2.2% in 2024 and edge higher to 2.3% in 2025 on rising exports (Table 2.12.1). In the near term, growth will remain below the pre-pandemic trend and with an uneven recovery as domestic demand remains weak. Sustained demand for semiconductors globally, supported by expanding artificial intelligence (AI) services and cloud server business, will drive growth in 2024 (*Special Topic on Asia's Rebounding Semiconductor Sector and the Role of Artificial Intelligence*).

Consumption will remain subdued amid tight monetary and fiscal policies. Household demand for goods and services will remain sluggish in the first

half of 2024 amid a high inflation and interest rate environment that will continue to affect debt servicing capacity. In the second half of 2024, consumption is expected to pick up slightly as inflationary pressures dissipate, leaving room for monetary and financial conditions to loosen. In addition, an increase in labor supply, particularly from women and the elderly, can augment household income. Government consumption will be contained under the 2024 budget with expenditure rising 2.8%, the slowest increase since 2005. However, given lower expected revenues, the deficit is forecast to be 3.9% of GDP. The government plans to implement 65% of the budget in the first half of 2024, focusing on support for low-income and disadvantaged groups, job creation, and public infrastructure projects.

Investment growth will remain moderate, dragged down by a weak property sector. Moderate improvement in manufacturing activity and facilities investment will be driven by the export recovery. The seasonally adjusted manufacturing purchasing managers' index of 50.7 in February 2024 on top of the

Figure 2.12.6 Manufacturing Indicators

Recent surveys point to an upbeat outlook for manufacturing.

Source: CEIC Data Company.

18-month high of 51.2 in January indicated sustained expansion (Figure 2.12.6). The Business Survey Index for manufacturing also improved to a 7-month high in February as sentiment among export-oriented firms indicated a more upbeat outlook. On the downside, housing and construction investments are set to decrease amid high borrowing costs, tight credit conditions, and risks of project financing-related losses. Unsold residential properties remain high and forward-looking indicators, including approved building permits and housing starts, have been on a downtrend (Figure 2.12.7). Housing prices and rents that spiked during 2020–2021 declined during the pandemic and remain low, partly due to a mismatch in demand and supply of units.

Figure 2.12.7 Property Indicators

The property sector continues to face headwinds.

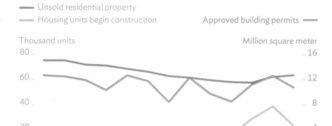

Source: CEIC Data Company.

Inflation is expected to continue trending downward as global oil prices stabilize, monetary policy remains tight, and some consumption taxes are cut. Headline inflation is projected to average 2.5% in 2024 and 2.0% in 2025 as global oil prices ease along with domestic demand. In February 2024, inflation rose to 3.1% year on year from 2.8% in January due to higher food costs, but core inflation remained unchanged at 2.5%, indicating that underlying pressures are easing. The central bank held its policy rate steady in February at 3.5% and signaled it will maintain a restrictive policy stance until inflation meets its target level of 2%. The government also plans to implement price controls, exempt and reduce tariffs for several fruit items, keep public utility fees unchanged for the first half of the year, and extend a fuel tax cut.

The current account surplus is expected to widen in 2024 but may narrow in 2025 as domestic demand picks up. The widening trend is already apparent. In January 2024, the current account remained in surplus for the ninth consecutive month supported by goods exports. Merchandise exports expanded by 4.8% over the previous year in February 2024, following an increase of 18.0% in January 2024 and a recovery from the 7.7% decline in the same period last year. This was mainly driven by a growth in exports of semiconductors (66.7%) and vessels (27.7%). Exports to major markets started improving since the turn of the year—shipments to the US rose by an average 18.1% in the first 2 months of 2024, and exports to the PRC increased by 6.8%. The forecast trend in demand for semiconductors and overall exports, and consequently growth prospects, assume a continuing global recovery.

Risks to the outlook are tilted to the downside. The growth outlook hinges largely on the strength of a rebound in global demand for exports from the ROK, particularly semiconductors. Fragile external demand and geopolitical tensions can weaken growth prospects. High household and corporate debt amid a prolonged tight monetary policy stance can constrain consumption and investment. The recent downturn in the real estate sector, if continued, could also drag down growth in the near term. In addition, political uncertainty from international and local elections could affect growth, as investors may take a wait-and-see attitude in succeeding months. On the upside, growth could be higher than projected if inflation declines faster and a stronger export rebound materializes.

Policy Challenge—Rising Household Debt

Household debt has grown rapidly in the last decade and poses a risk for the economy. As a percentage of GDP, household debt in the ROK increased from 76.0% in 2010 to 107.7% in 2022, with sharp increases during the COVID-19 pandemic, making it one of the highest among Organisation for Economic Co-operation and Development countries. It gradually edged down to 104.5% in September 2023 as the central bank tightened monetary policy beginning in August 2021 to curb inflation. At the end of December 2023, credit to households was mostly in mortgage loans (56.4%), followed by other personal loans (37.3%), and merchandise credit which included credit card transactions (6.3%) (Figure 2.12.8). A high share of mortgage loans is linked to home purchases and jeonse, or home rental deposits. Among outstanding loans, almost 70% carry floating interest rates, mostly linked to either deposit rates or market interest rates.

Figure 2.12.8 Household Credit in 2023

Mortgage loans comprise the largest type of credit to households.

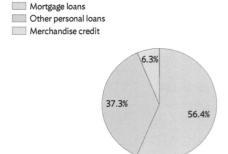

Source: CEIC Data Company.

The household debt service burden has been increasing sharply with rising interest rates, especially for low-income groups. Based on the 2022 Survey of Households Finances and Living Conditions, debt payments on average claim 23% of indebted households' regular income—44% for the poorest quantile. In addition, the proportion of vulnerable borrowers—defined as low-income borrowers or those with low credit scores and holding multiple loans—has increased slightly as of September 2023 (Figure 2.12.9). Although household loans overdue by at least 1 month, an indicator of delinquency, accounted for only 0.4% of total loans as of December 2023, they are on a rising trend. Moreover, as most outstanding loans carry floating rates, the debt service burden will grow as interest rates increase. While there is no imminent systemic risk to the financial system, given the low level of delinquencies and high bank capital adequacy ratios, the rising debt burden will further dampen private demand in the near term and weaken economic recovery.

Figure 2.12.9 Proportion of Vulnerable Borrowers

The proportion of vulnerable borrowers is rising moderately.

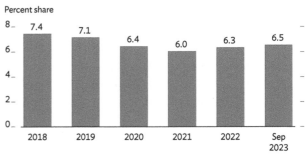

Note: Vulnerable borrowers are defined as low-income borrowers or those with low credit scores and holding multiple loans.
Source: Bank of Korea Financial Stability Report.

To manage household debt, the government introduced tighter loan regulations. In September 2023, the Financial Services Commission (FSC) announced stricter regulations to ensure that a borrower's repayment capacity is taken into account by banks in their lending operations. For floating loans, the FSC will gradually introduce a stressed debt-to-service ratio (DSR) limit for lenders that accounts for the lender's exposure risk to borrowers in case of interest rate fluctuations. The eligibility criteria for special household mortgage loans were also tightened and targeted toward lower income households to prevent speculative homebuyers. For long-term mortgage loans, the government will closely monitor banks to ensure strict adherence to lending procedures, strengthen DSR rules, and improve regulations as necessary to better manage household debt.

The planned measures are needed to manage the debt situation along with rigorous risk monitoring to prevent banking system fragility. Monitoring should cover household, corporate, and project financing. Also, because household loans are closely related to the real estate sector, sudden changes in loan volume can affect an already fragile property market. Identifying and prioritizing policies that align household debt growth to nominal GDP growth and raise the share of fixed-rate loans for mortgage loans, as outlined in the 2024 Economic Policy Directions, are important next steps. In the near-term, policymakers should continue to implement targeted financial support while balancing growth considerations and orderly deleveraging to safeguard long-term growth.

TAIPEI,CHINA

With demand for exports weakening, growth slowed in 2023 and inflation edged down. Growth is expected to rise in 2024 as exports and investment pick up and then fall slightly in 2025 as consumption moderates. Inflation will moderate as supply shocks from the October typhoon dissipate and global commodity prices moderate. Policies are needed to prevent housing from becoming increasingly unaffordable.

Economic Performance

After contracting in the first half of 2023, the economy picked up on strong consumer spending. GDP contracted by 1% in the first half of the year following a mild contraction in the fourth quarter of 2022. Strong consumption growth and a modest recovery in exports in the second half of 2023 (following a 10% drop in the first half) pushed GDP growth to 1.3%, its slowest pace since 2015 (Figure 2.13.1). With mobility restrictions gone, "revenge spending" on services drove consumption in 2023. Consumption also benefited from one-off cash payments to individuals and other stimulus from the post-pandemic special budget for 2023–2025 which, overall, amounted to roughly 1.6% of 2023 GDP. Private spending on services, after growing by almost 5% in 2022, rose by 13% last year. By contrast, private spending on goods grew by just 2% in both 2022 and 2023. Overall, private consumption growth accelerated to 8.3%, up from 3.7% in 2022, and contributed 3.8 percentage points to GDP growth. Public consumption spending was tepid, growing by less than 1%.

Weak external demand pushed down exports and investment. Exports fell by 4.3% in 2023 as demand faltered for electronics and high-tech products, which account for about 25% of GDP. Demand was weak in the economy's two largest markets. In the People's Republic of China (PRC), spending was modest due to slower growth and uncertainty surrounding its property

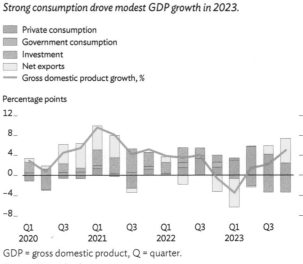

Figure 2.13.1 Demand-Side Contributions to Growth

Strong consumption drove modest GDP growth in 2023.

- Private consumption
- Government consumption
- Investment
- Net exports
- Gross domestic product growth, %

GDP = gross domestic product, Q = quarter.
Source: Haver Analytics.

market. In the United States (US), the demand for electronics slowed as consumers continued shifting back to services. However, imports contracted more, by 5.7%, leaving net exports with a small positive impact on growth. Weak external demand also held down investment as firms postponed capacity expansion. The resulting weak business confidence and bloated inventories led in turn to an 8.7% fall in fixed investment and a drawdown of inventories, leaving a negative 0.5 percentage points impact on growth.

This chapter was written by David Keith De Padua and Henry Ma of the Economic Research and Development Impact Department, ADB, Manila.

The improvement in the trade balance in the second half of 2023 widened the current account surplus. Supported by a depreciation in the NT dollar from an average of NT$29.8 per US dollar in 2022 to NT$31.1 in 2023, a gradual increase in exports later in the year combined with the sustained import contraction raised the trade surplus to 12.7% of GDP from 9.0% of GDP in 2022. This offset a decline in net services receipts, which fell from 1.7% of GDP to 1.3% in 2023 due to flourishing outbound tourism. On balance, the current account surplus increased from 13.3% of GDP in 2022 to 13.9% of GDP in 2023. There remained ample foreign currency reserves by end-2023, covering roughly 20 months of imports.

Consumer demand and supply shocks drove inflation. Headline inflation was on a downward trajectory in the first half of 2023 and came in below 2% in June and July (Figure 2.13.2). In October, however, Typhoon Koinu damaged crops, driving up food prices and inflation to 3.0%, leaving the average full-year inflation at 2.5%. Inflation slowed in January this year, but renewed seasonal pressures from the lunar holiday drove food prices and miscellaneous services higher.

Monetary policy was tightened in response to higher inflation, and the financial system remained solid. The central bank hiked its policy rate in March 2023, bringing it to 1.87%. Since then, despite a spike

in inflation in December, the central bank has kept the policy rate constant, judging that price pressures were temporary. Broad money growth slowed from 7.0% in 2022 to 5.3% in 2023, while credit growth crept up from 6.4% to 6.5%. Nonperforming loans were 0.1% of total loans and the average capital adequacy ratio was 14.7% in 2022, relatively unchanged since 2020. Banks' pretax earnings were at a record high.

Fiscal policy was modestly expansionary. Higher public spending on infrastructure and on research and development along with slightly lower revenues turned the fiscal balance from a surplus of 0.3% of GDP in 2022 to a deficit of 1.0% of GDP in 2023. Public debt decreased and remained manageable at 26.6% of GDP at the end of 2023.

Despite slower growth, labor market indicators improved, but inflation eroded real wages. Unemployment slid to 3.3% in 2023 from its recent peak of 3.9% in 2020–2021 during the worst of the COVID-19 pandemic. The labor force participation rate, after marginally falling in 2021, regained its upward trend and reached a historic peak of 59.2% in 2023. The steady increase since 2010 has been attributed to increased female participation. Higher inflation, however, led to the average real monthly wage falling by about 1%, the first decline since 2016.

Economic Prospects

The economy faces significant long-term challenges. Its current advantages include a highly skilled labor force, strategic location for trade, and strong base of high-tech industries. Its prudent macroeconomic policies will also help, although there may be some concerns arising from the long-term performance of state-owned enterprises, pension funds, and the health insurance system. Nevertheless, estimates point to potential growth slowing from 3.5% to 3.0% due to population aging and increasing constraints to investment and trade as geopolitical tensions continue. Climate change risks will also increase. For example, changing rainfall patterns could negatively affect water-intensive chip production. The authorities are taking steps to mitigate other risks, including managing the inflow of migrant labor, helping youth acquire skills through enterprise apprenticeships, and promoting female labor force participation.

Figure 2.13.2 Monthly Inflation

Food prices have pushed inflation higher in recent months.

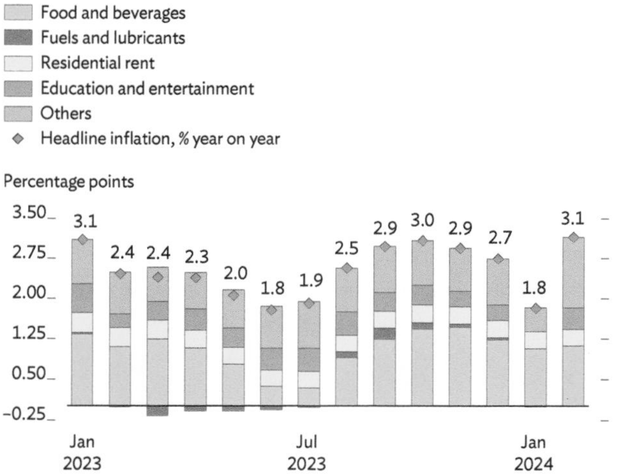

- Food and beverages
- Fuels and lubricants
- Residential rent
- Education and entertainment
- Others
- ◆ Headline inflation, % year on year

Percentage points

Source: Haver Analytics.

In the near term, economic growth will pick up.
The economy is projected to grow by 3.0% in 2024 as exports and investment expand (Table 2.13.1). The 1.1% growth of merchandise exports in the fourth quarter of 2023—after contracting the previous 4 quarters—suggests the sector has bottomed out. The boom in artificial intelligence is expected to boost demand for semiconductors. Exports to the US grew by 57% in January and to the PRC by 22%. Export orders point to a continued recovery (Figure 2.13.3), which will in turn help investment bounce back. The pickup in the leading indicators index and purchasing managers' index supports this outlook. Consumption growth will already start to moderate this year and continue to slow through 2025, slowing growth to 2.7% in 2025. An early indication is that retail sales fell by 1.5% in December after averaging 5.5% growth in January-November. Consumer spending will also be held back by weak growth in real earnings.

Table 2.13.1 Selected Economic Indicators, %

Growth will rebound then moderate, and inflation will slow.

	2022	2023	2024	2025
GDP growth	2.6	1.3	3.0	2.7
Inflation	2.9	2.5	2.3	2.0

GDP = gross domestic product.
Source: Asian Development Bank estimates.

Figure 2.13.3 Export Orders

Export orders, a leading indicator for exports, have been trending upwards.

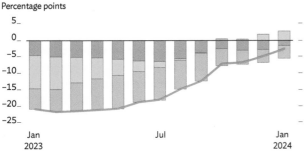

HKG = Hong Kong, China, PRC = People's Republic of China, US = United States.
Source: CEIC Data Company.

The near-term inflation outlook is sanguine.
As consumption slows and supply shocks from the typhoon and higher global commodity prices wane, inflation should moderate. The central bank is also likely to maintain its monetary policy stance. Food and beverage prices accounted for over a third of headline inflation, and continue to be its main driver. The contribution of fuel and lubricants has been negligible with oil prices relatively stable and government price controls minimizing fuel price volatility. Inflation is thus projected to fall to 2.3% in 2024 and 2.0% in 2025 (Figure 2.13.4).

Figure 2.13.4 Headline and Core Inflation

Inflation moderated in 2023 and will continue to decline.

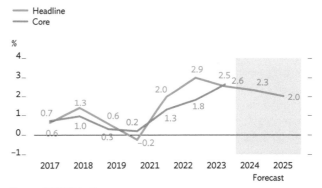

Source: CEIC Data Company.

Policy Challenge—Affordable Housing

House prices have climbed faster than incomes over the past decade, raising concerns among policymakers over housing affordability for a large part of the population. The average price of a residence grew by an average 4.3% annually during 2013–2023. House prices are now among the highest in the region and comparable to prices in high-income economies. During the same period, the average nominal wage grew by only about 1.9% annually. The ratio of house prices to incomes has climbed from 4.5 in 2002 to nearly 10 in 2023 (Figure 2.13.5). In response, people are delaying home purchases. In 2013, the average homebuyer was from 30 to 35 years old; in 2023 it was 35 to 40 years old.

Figure 2.13.5 House Price to Income Ratio

The house price to income ratio has more than doubled since 2002.

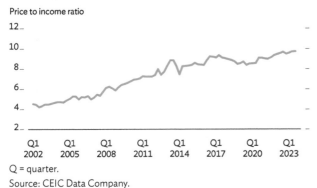

Q = quarter.
Source: CEIC Data Company.

Figure 2.13.6 Housing Loan Payments to Income Ratios

Housing loan payments have increased and are above the affordability benchmark across most cities.

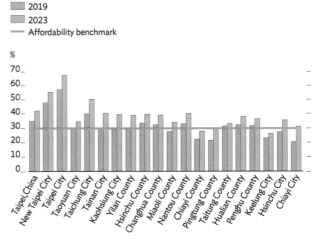

Source: CEIC Data Company.

Despite high prices, home ownership remains prevalent. In 2019, the home ownership rate was about 85%. There is a strong preference for buying a home instead of renting, and property is generally seen as a good investment asset. Government policies also play a part, through mortgage subsidies and low property taxes that incentivize home ownership. Although the population is aging, the number of households continues to grow. In January 2023, they grew by 1.6%, or about 150,000 more households, compared to the same month in 2022. Roughly 36% of the population remains below the age of 35, so housing demand will likely remain robust in the near future.

Mortgage debt service is also rising. Mortgage debt reached 48.3% of GDP in 2023, an all-time high and higher than the Republic of Korea (35%) and Singapore (40%). Consequently, the cost of servicing housing loans rose from an already substantial 35% of income in 2019 to 42% in 2023, well above the widely used international affordability benchmark of 30% (Figure 2.13.6). As a result, the number of households seeking relief increased to 18,633 in 2021, more than double the annual average of 7,300 applicants during 2010–2020.

The high cost of housing has negative economic and social implications. The increasing share of income that goes to debt service reduces consumer spending on other items. It can also discourage fertility, especially among younger couples, contributing to population aging. More broadly, household debt remained high at 88.7% of GDP in 2022, with the higher interest rate environment and variable mortgage rates making some households vulnerable to shocks.

The authorities are taking measures to address the problem but there is scope for enhancement. To increase supply, the Housing Act was revised in 2017 with a target of building 200,000 social housing units. As of February 2024, 168,000 have been built and the target is expected to be met by end-2024. But the target may now be outdated and insufficient. The government should assess whether more socialized housing is needed, potentially expand the program, and expedite construction to ensure there is adequate supply of affordable housing. To help moderate demand and speculation, the Ministry of Finance will raise the tax on non-owner occupied homes to 2.0%–4.8% from 1.5%–3.6%, and reduce the tax on owner-occupied homes to 1.0%. The tax on homes for lease will be reduced, which should help increase the supply of rental units. Mortgage subsidies should be reexamined and rationalized as well. The rental market also remains small in scale and underregulated. Policies that encourage renting properties, such as tax incentives, would expand the rental market and encourage the creation of more professional rental companies. As the rental market expands, it should be complemented with enhanced regulations that safeguard landlord and tenant rights.

SOUTH ASIA

Afghanistan

Bangladesh

Bhutan

India

Maldives

Nepal

Pakistan

Sri Lanka

AFGHANISTAN

Drought, cold, disasters, and a weak investment climate brought a third consecutive year of economic contraction. In the medium term, modest economic growth could resume with better security, domestic revenue mobilization, expanding trade, and improved agriculture as El Niño boosts precipitation. Deflation that occurred due to a strong local currency and falling global commodity prices will give way to inflation as pressure for currency appreciation recedes. Inclusive growth requires improved access to finance.

Economic Performance

Drought, cold weather, disasters, and a weak investment climate led to a third consecutive year of contraction. However, with continued international humanitarian assistance and support for basic needs, the decline in real GDP diminished from 20.7% in 2022 (years designating, unless otherwise specified, the fiscal year ending on 20 March of that year) to 6.2% in 2023. Data from the de facto National Statistics and Information Authority showed activity declining in agriculture, industry, and services, with each contracting by 5%–7% (Figure 2.14.1). Accompanying the declines was a substantial change in the sector composition of GDP. From 2021 to 2023, the share of services declined by 14.3% to 45.0% of GDP, while the share of agriculture grew by 12.4% to 33.7% of GDP and that of industry by 23.9% to 16.1%, despite declining output in each sector.

Services, the largest sector of the economy, accounted for nearly half of the GDP decline. They contracted a further 6.5% in 2023, following a 30.1% decline in 2022, reflecting significant decreases in all leading service industries. Wholesale and retail trade each contracted by 8.6%, finance and insurance by 6.6%, health and social services by 5.9%, real estate by 5.2%, restaurants and hotels by 4.9%, and post and telecommunication by 4.7%. Only education expanded, by a modest 0.7%.

Figure 2.14.1 Supply-Side Growth

The economy shrank for 3 consecutive years with declines in all three major sectors.

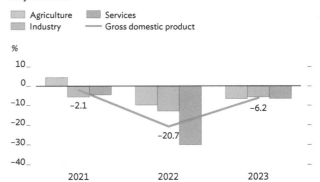

Note: Years are fiscal years ending 20 March of that year.
Source: National Statistics and Information Authority.

Another 35% of the decline in GDP came from agriculture, which contracted by 6.6%. Significant crop losses were caused by the current multiyear drought, the most severe in the past 3 decades; an extreme cold wave during December 2022 and January 2023; and earthquakes and flooding. In addition, scarcity of seeds and other agricultural inputs, restricted market access, and supply chain disruption reduced the area under cultivation. Livestock

---

ADB placed on hold its regular assistance in Afghanistan effective 15 August 2021.

production suffered from high feed prices, disease, adverse weather, poor-quality forage, and limited access to veterinary services and water.

A sharp worsening of the investment climate and collapsing business confidence contributed to the decline in industry. Industry contracted by 5.6% as the sector shifted toward resource-intensive primary activities such as mining and quarrying, which expanded by 4.1%. The move away from more diversified and skill-intensive activities reflected brain drain and commercial pessimism from weak governance and policy uncertainty, macroeconomic instability, chronic illiquidity, and elevated risk premiums required for formal finance.

Rising global prices for food and petroleum, drought, and supply chain difficulties brought double-digit inflation. Inflation averaged 10.8% in 2023, with food prices rising by 14.6% and prices of other goods rising by 7.0% (Figure 2.14.2). Year-on-year inflation peaked in July 2022 at 18.3%, reflecting increases of 25.0% for food and 11.6% for other items. Inflation slowed to 3.1% in the fourth quarter of 2023 with an easing of international supply chain bottlenecks and stabilization of the afghani, the local currency.

The formal finance sector performed well below its potential to support economic recovery, constrained by real and perceived illiquidity risks. International humanitarian assistance, especially the attendant inflow of US dollar banknotes for humanitarian purposes, and robust revenue collection have moderately improved liquidity. Bank deposits rose by 2.4% in 2023 (Figure 2.14.3). However, total loan volume fell by 18.3%, with a perceived substantial increase in nonperforming loans. This reflects the adverse effect of 3 years of economic contraction on the capacity of borrowers to service debt, which has weakened bank balance sheets.

The trade deficit widened sharply as rising global prices for oil and food caused imports to grow much more than exports. The trade deficit ballooned from $4.4 billion in 2022 to $6.2 billion in 2023 as merchandise imports rose by 44.6% to $7.1 billion (Figure 2.14.4). Food accounted for 22.2% of imports, petroleum and oil 19.0%, and machinery and spare parts 8.3%. Merchandise exports rose by 116.1% from

Figure 2.14.2 Monthly Inflation

Inflation peaked in July 2022 and has declined since then.

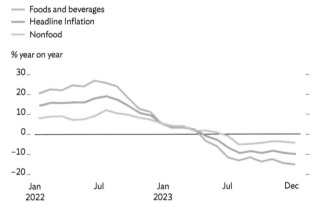

Source: Data collected from official sources.

Figure 2.14.3 Bank Deposits and Credit

Credit from banks declined under economic contraction.

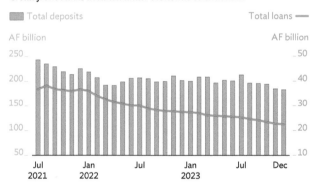

Source: Data collected from official sources.

Figure 2.14.4 Merchandise Exports and Imports

Imports have remained far larger than exports.

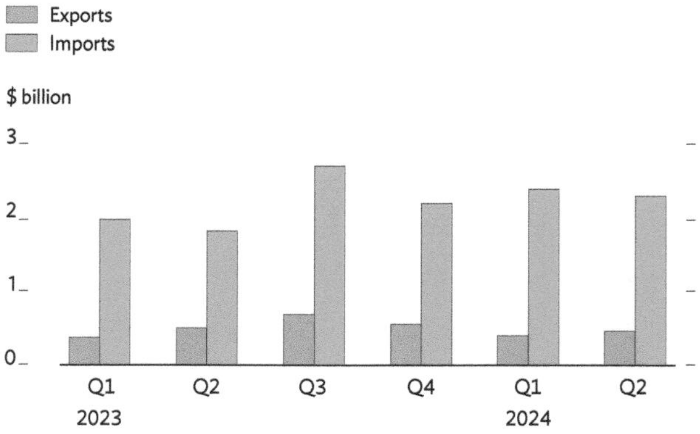

Q = quarter.
Note: Years are fiscal years ending 20 March of that year.
Source: Data collected from official sources.

Figure 2.14.5 Afghani Exchange Rates

The afghani showed little change against major world currencies but appreciated against the Pakistan rupee and the Iranian riyal.

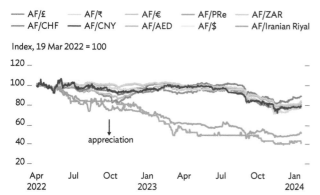

Notes: Afghanis per unit of foreign currency, so a downward slope indicates afghani appreciation. Readings were on the 19th day of each month.

Source: Data collected from official sources.

$0.85 billion to $1.83 billion in 2023, with a 500% rise in coal and an 80% jump in food registering the main increases.

Afghani exchange rates with the currencies of major advanced economies remained relatively stable. However, the afghani appreciated against the Pakistani rupee and the Iranian riyal, the currencies of the country's main import suppliers (Figure 2.14.5).

Economic Prospects

Modest economic growth is possible in 2024 and 2025. This assumes sustained international humanitarian assistance and support for basic needs. Growth would depend on improved security, higher domestic revenue mobilization, expanded trade, and better performance in agriculture. Inflows of US dollars for humanitarian purposes help stabilize the economy, providing needed liquidity to banks, supporting purchasing power, and reaching needy households.

Output in agriculture is likely to increase somewhat, with above-average precipitation from the current El Niño weather cycle. According to the Famine Early Warning Systems Network, moderate to heavy precipitation in the winter of 2024 may ease groundwater shortfalls in Afghanistan's central region. Supported by irrigation in the country's center and south, production is likely to increase, though

past water deficits may continue to inhibit rainfed crops. Meanwhile, a drug ban imposed in April 2022 is projected to slash opium cultivation by 95% and eliminate more than $1 billion in rural income annually.

Likely deflation in 2024 reflects a strong afghani and falling global commodity prices, but inflation could return in 2025. Deflation began in April 2023 and continued for the first 3 quarters of the fiscal year, with year-on-year decreases in prices for both food and other items. In calendar 2023, a year-on-year decline in food prices averaged 7.4%, while deflation for other items was 1.2%. Given high pass-through of exchange rate changes into inflation, appreciation of the afghani against the Pakistani rupee and Iranian riyal likely maintained deflation for the whole of fiscal 2024. Inflation could rise to middle single digits in 2025 with no further appreciation of the afghani.

Fiscal space to support development projects will likely remain tight. With Afghanistan receiving only humanitarian aid and no assistance for development projects, the budget for development spending is reduced. Future ability to support investment, directly or through public–private partnerships, remains uncertain, particularly given weak capitalization in domestic banks.

Higher imports are likely to spell a wider trade deficit in 2024. In the first half of the fiscal year, merchandise imports surged by 23.8% over the same period in 2023, reaching $3.8 billion. Merchandise exports in the same period were 7.4% below those in the first half of 2023 to $720 million. The rise in imports reflected higher demand for essential goods financed by humanitarian support and real appreciation of the afghani against the currencies of Afghanistan's major trade partners. An informal system of money transfer called hawala has proved resilient in financing imports but exposes the country to greater economic vulnerability.

This outlook faces significant downside risks. Besides institutional uncertainties and economic vulnerabilities, risks include a potential reduction in international humanitarian assistance and support for basic needs; possible further restrictions on education and employment for women; and continued drought, flooding, and landslides. If these risks materialize, the economy will contract further, and unemployment, poverty, and food insecurity will worsen.

Policy Challenge—Improving Access to Financial Services

Access to finance services is essential to support inclusive and sustainable growth. A well-functioning formal financial system provides intermediation that boosts access to financing and investment. It also helps firms and households manage risk, financial volatility, and economic vulnerability. Financial inclusion enables households to invest in education and health and obtain access to savings, credit, and insurance, and firms to access capital for investment and growth. Despite 2 decades of significant advances in the country's formal financial system from calendar years 2002 to 2021, around 90% of adult Afghans lack access to financial services (Figure 2.14.6), with a large and expanding gender gap in account ownership (Figure 2.14.7). From 2017 to 2021, women's already small share of financial account ownership fell by a third, from 7% to 5%, far below peer and regional economies. Furthermore, the share of financing for micro-, small, and medium-sized enterprises (MSMEs) and agriculture lags that in other conflict-affected low-income countries. Loans for MSMEs equaled only 0.17% of GDP in 2018, while lending for agriculture including livestock was only 4.2% of GDP, despite agriculture then providing 22% of GDP.

Figure 2.14.6 Bank Account Ownership

Account ownership in Afghanistan lags the rest of the world, including the average for transitional countries in Europe and Central Asia.

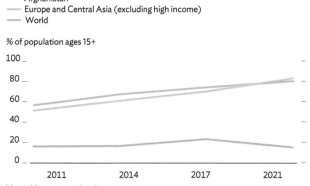

Note: Years are calendar years.
Source: World Bank, World Development Indicators.

Figure 2.14.7 Gender Gap in Account Ownership

A far smaller percentage of women in Afghanistan have bank accounts than the average for transitional countries in Europe and Central Asia.

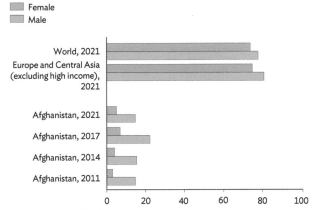

Note: Years are calendar years.
Source: World Bank. World Development Indicators database.

Both demand- and supply-side barriers limit the access of individuals and firms to financial services. Demand-side obstacles include low financial literacy, limited and asymmetric information, high interest rates, heavy documentation requirements, and lack of trust. In addition, most households lack the funds needed to open a bank account. On the supply side, commercial and state-owned banks do not understand the needs and business models of MSMEs. Weak property rights severely limit collateralization and opportunities for contracting, while high trade and transport margins shorten the horizon of profitable market access and increase risk. Other issues include the lack of a transparent and credible legal and regulatory framework, poor infrastructure, substandard accounting and auditing standards, weak formal credit services, and high costs attributable to locally monopolistic money lending, high security expenses, and corruption. These barriers disproportionally affect the poor, youth, women, and the internally displaced.

Innovative business models and financial services could alleviate these constraints. This would require tailoring them to the needs of MSMEs, particularly those owned by women. Accompanying these changes should be legal and regulatory reforms ensuring contract transparency and enforcement, secured transactions, data privacy, and compliance with credit reporting regulations. Improving financial literacy could mitigate information failures and asymmetries, reduce monitoring costs, and greatly improve risk perceptions for small entrepreneurs, individuals, and households. International experience suggests that financial literacy is strongly linked with the business performance of young entrepreneurs, since it enables individuals and firms, particularly MSMEs, to use debt, credit, and strategic investment more creatively and allow more proactive and complex financial decisions.

Digitizing payment systems, particularly through mobile phones, could prompt millions of unbanked Afghans to use formal financial services. According to the New York Times, in 2023 around 70% of the Afghan population had access to mobile phones, and an even higher percentage of adults. Mobile payment systems can achieve much greater geographical coverage for financial services, are far more competitive than local informal lending, and can deliver benefits to those whose limited mobility and cash assets currently prevent them from opening bank accounts. Developing and expanding interoperable payment infrastructure to facilitate transactions and financial transfers among mobile money providers, banks and other lenders, and public agencies can promote broader, lower-cost access to a wider range of financial services.

BANGLADESH

Growth moderated in fiscal 2023 as monetary tightening in the advanced economies lowered external demand. Inflation rose significantly, and the current account deficit narrowed. Despite macroeconomic headwinds, GDP expansion is expected to accelerate gradually this year and next with resilient exports and the government committed to structural reform. Inflation will gradually moderate, while the current account turns into small surpluses. Reforms to enhance Bangladesh's competitiveness will be critical for the country's smooth graduation from least-developed country status.

Economic Performance

GDP expansion moderated to 5.8% in fiscal year 2023 (FY2023, ended 30 June 2023) from 7.1% in the previous year. The slowdown hit both industry and services (Figure 2.15.1). Growth in industry slowed to 8.4% from 9.9% in FY2022, reflecting reduced export demand and domestic shortages of electricity and fuel, with large-scale manufacturing production growth falling to 8.4% from 15.7% in FY2022. Services growth also slowed, to 5.4% from 6.3%, reflecting lower growth of domestic demand due to high inflation. However, growth in agriculture increased to 3.4% from 3.1% in the previous year despite inclement weather patterns.

On the demand side, slower rises in private consumption and investment dragged down GDP growth. High inflation hit private consumption, while public consumption expanded with higher expenditure on subsidies and current transfers. The high cost of production and difficulties in opening import letters of credit constrained the growth of private investment. Growth in public investment slowed as only 84.2% of the annual development program was implemented in FY2023, compared with 92.7% in FY2022. With a sharp decline in imports, net exports added to growth.

Inflation surged to an average of 9.0% in FY2023 from 6.2% in FY2022. It was driven by high and volatile food, fuel, and fertilizer prices, and the depreciation

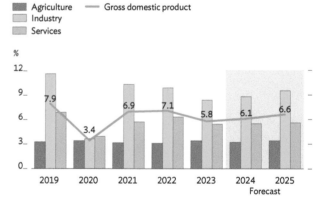

Figure 2.15.1 Supply-Side Growth

Growth slowed with lower industry and services expansion in FY2023 but will turn higher with sectoral rebounds in FY2024.

FY = fiscal year.
Note: Years are fiscal years ending on 30 June of that year.
Sources: Bangladesh Bureau of Statistics; Asian Development Bank estimates.

of Bangladesh taka against the dollar. Year-on-year headline inflation reached 9.7% in June 2023 from 7.6% in June 2022. Food inflation accelerated to 9.7% year on year in June 2023 from 8.4% in June 2022, and nonfood inflation to 9.6% from 6.3%, due to upward adjustments in domestic fuel and energy prices and marked depreciation of the taka against the dollar (Figure 2.15.2).

This chapter was written by Barun K. Dey and Mahbub Rabbani of the Bangladesh Resident Mission, ADB, Dhaka.

Figure 2.15.2 Monthly Inflation

Price pressures rose in FY2023.

— Food
— Nonfood
— Overall

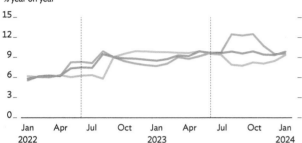

FY = fiscal year.
Source: Bangladesh Bank. 2024. Monthly Economic Trends. February.

Monetary policy was tightened in FY2023 to restrict credit growth and contain inflation.
Bangladesh Bank, the central bank, raised its policy repo rate by 0.5 percentage points to 6.0% in FY2023 and 8.0% in January 2024. It replaced the capped lending rate with a market-driven lending rate for bank loans based on the 6-month moving average rate of Treasury bills and, further, imposed fees on loans to micro and small enterprises. Private sector credit grew more slowly as interest rates rose and as political uncertainty surrounding a general election in January 2024 reduced private sector appetite for loans. Meanwhile, credit to the public sector rose substantially, by 35.0%, while the issuance of national savings certificates was curtailed. As a result, broad money grew by 10.5%, compared to 9.4% in FY2022, and rose by 8.6% year on year in December 2023 (Figure 2.15.3).

Fiscal policy supported growth in FY2023. Revenue grew by 9.5% and was equivalent to 8.2% of GDP, lower than 8.4% in FY2022. Income and value-added tax, accounting for 64.0% of total revenues, grew by 9.5%. Significantly slower growth in capital expenditure, down from 15.7% in FY2022 to 4.6% in FY2023, tamped down government expenditure to 12.6% of GDP from 13.0% in FY2022. On balance, the fiscal deficit declined to 4.4% of GDP from 4.6% in the previous year.

Bangladesh remains at a low risk of external and overall debt distress. The ratio of public debt to GDP increased from 37.9% in FY2022 to 39.8% in FY2023, with external debt rising from 15.4% of GDP

Figure 2.15.3 Monetary Indicators

Overall credit growth moderated in FY2023 as contractionary monetary policy took effect.

— Broad money
— Credit to the private sector
— Credit to the public sector

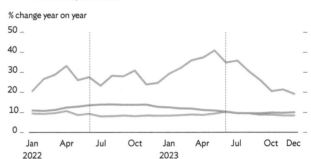

FY = fiscal year.
Source: Bangladesh Bank. 2024. Major Economic Indicators: Monthly Update. January.

to 17.7% (Figure 2.15.4). The government continued to seek mainly concessional external borrowing, especially to finance infrastructure projects. With the government's reduced reliance on national savings certificates without increased recourse to bank credit, domestic public debt decreased from 22.5% of GDP to 22.1%. Several reforms being implemented—notably automation in revenue administration, such as electronic tax filing and payment of return, tax deduction at sources, and implementing a new income tax law—should ensure fiscal and debt sustainability. Increasing the ratio of revenue to GDP will be critical to support much-needed social, development, and climate spending.

Figure 2.15.4 Government Debt

Government debt continued to rise.

■ Domestic
■ External

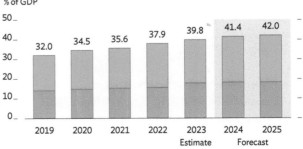

GDP = gross domestic product.
Note: Years are fiscal years ending 30 June of that year.
Source: International Monetary Fund.

Export growth decelerated sharply. It slowed from 33.4% in FY2022 to 6.3% in FY2023 and 2.5% in the first 7 months of FY2024, from 9.8% during the same 7 months in FY2023 (Figure 2.15.5). Export growth in FY2023 was entirely due to expansion in garment exports, which grew by 10.3% as other exports declined by 9.5%. The marked economic slowdown in the European Union and the United States were mainly responsible for the sharp deceleration of export growth, but domestic fuel and electricity shortages in factories also played a role.

Figure 2.15.5 Export Growth

Merchandise exports have grown more slowly since the beginning of FY2024 on lower demand in advanced economies.

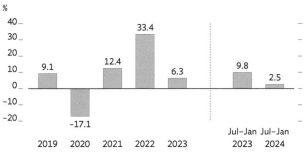

FY = fiscal year.
Note: Years are fiscal years ending on 30 June of that year.
Sources: Bangladesh Bank; Export Promotion Bureau, Bangladesh.

Imports declined across the board in FY2023. This occurred in tandem with slower GDP growth and as central bank restrictions on opening letters of credit aimed to stem a marked decline in foreign exchange reserves. Imports of intermediate goods decreased sharply in line with curtailed manufacturing. Imports of capital goods and petroleum goods also declined. However, fertilizer and rice imports increased under government efforts to ensure food security. Total imports contracted by 15.8% from a marked 35.9% expansion in FY2022 and by 18.3% in the first 7 months of FY2024 from 5.7% contraction in the same period of FY2023.

The current account deficit narrowed sharply to 0.7% of GDP in FY2023 from 4.1% in FY2022 (Figure 2.15.6). The improvement resulted from a lower trade deficit, as imports declined sharply while exports expanded moderately, and from rising remittances. A

Figure 2.15.6 Current Account Components

Lower imports and high remittance inflows narrowed the current account deficit significantly.

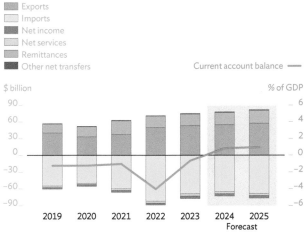

GDP = gross domestic product.
Note: Years are fiscal years ending on 30 June of that year.
Source: Bangladesh Bank.

sharply depreciated taka, government cash incentives, and increased ease of transfer through mobile financial services led to an increase of 3.7% in remittances in the first 7 months of FY2024, slightly below 4.3% growth in the same period a year earlier (Figure 2.15.7).

Foreign exchange reserves fell significantly in FY2023, leading to a squeeze on imports and pressure on the exchange rate. Even with a significantly reduced current account deficit, sharply reduced financial inflows including a decline in medium- and long-term loans led to gross foreign

Figure 2.15.7 Growth in Remittances

Remittances grew more slowly in the first half of FY2024.

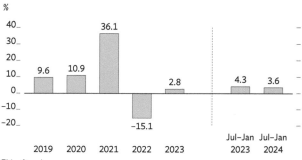

FY = fiscal year.
Note: Years are fiscal years ending on 30 June of that year.
Source: Bangladesh Bank.

exchange reserves falling by 25% to $31.2 billion at the end of FY2023 and to $25.1 billion at the end of January 2024, covering about 4.1 months of imports (Figure 2.15.8).

The taka depreciated by 11.8% against the dollar in FY2023. It depreciated by a further 9.1% to the end of January 2024 from January 2023 as adjustment toward a market-determined rate continued (Figure 2.15.9). It depreciated in real effective terms by 8.3% in FY2023 and by 0.5% in calendar year 2023. Central bank net sales of foreign exchange worth $13.4 billion to commercial banks were intended to curb excessive exchange rate fluctuations in FY2023. Bangladesh aims to move toward a more market-oriented exchange rate system by initially adopting a crawling peg arrangement.

Economic Prospects

Growth is projected to edge up to 6.1% in FY2024 and 6.6% in FY2025 on resilient export growth (Figure 2.15.10 and Table 2.15.1). Despite weaker global demand, exports of Bangladesh's traditional low-end garments will continue to grow, as exporters use domestic yarn and fabric due to the dollar crisis. Private consumption is expected to rise with easing inflation, while public consumption is expected to witness moderate growth on lower subsidy spending and continued austerity measures already announced by the government. Public investment will increase with ongoing priority mega infrastructure projects in energy and railways. Growth in private investment is expected to edge up as uncertainty diminishes

Figure 2.15.8 Gross Foreign Exchange Reserves

Foreign exchange reserves trended lower.

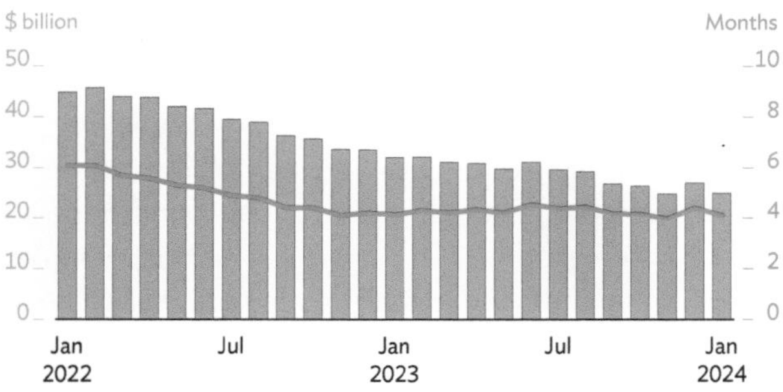

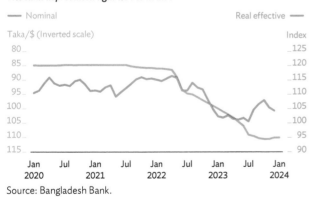

Source: Bangladesh Bank.

Figure 2.15.9 Exchange Rates

The taka depreciated against the dollar.

Source: Bangladesh Bank.

Figure 2.15.10 Demand-Side Contributions to Growth

Subdued consumption pulled down growth in FY2023.

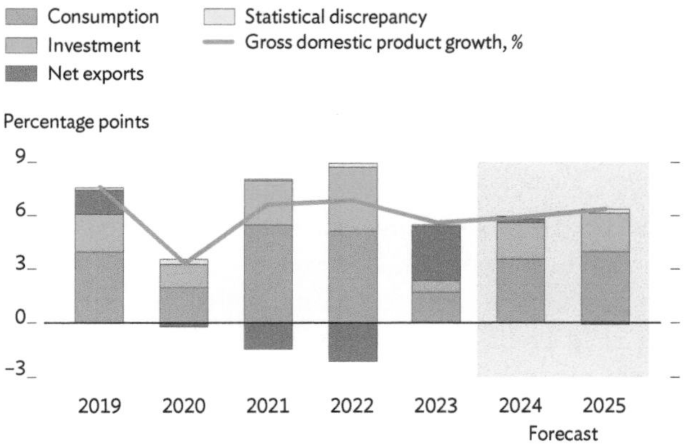

FY = fiscal year.
Note: Years are fiscal years ending on 30 June of that year.
Sources: Bangladesh Bureau of Statistics; Asian Development Bank estimates.

Table 2.15.1 Selected Economic Indicators, %

Economic growth is forecast to edge up.

	2022	2023	2024	2025
GDP growth	7.1	5.8	6.1	6.6
Inflation	6.2	9.0	8.4	7.0

GDP = gross domestic product.
Note: Years are fiscal years ending on 30 June of that year.
Sources: Bangladesh Bureau of Statistics; Asian Development Bank estimates.

following the general election in January 2024. Growth will rise further in FY2025 on a continuing rebound in exports due to economic recovery in major importing countries, an easing in energy costs, and reduced import restrictions, aided by gradual improvement in foreign exchange reserves. Private consumption will be buoyed by an increase in remittances. Private investment is expected to rise along with consumer and investor confidence as inflation further eases, and public investment will rise as fast-tracked projects are implemented.

On the supply side, a rebound in industry and services will contribute to higher GDP growth. Agriculture is expected to maintain its trend growth of 3.2%, reflecting a good crop outlook and better market prices encouraging farmers to produce more. While inadequate rainfall during the monsoon severely affected the summer crop, the wet monsoon crop was cultivated on a planted area larger than earlier projected and is anticipated to have high yields. Barring natural calamities, winter crop production is also expected to rise with government support for farmers' use of subsidized harvesters and modern seeds. Industry is projected to grow faster at 8.8% with a rebound in manufacturing aided by resilient exports. The index of large-scale manufacturing production grew by 15.0% in the first quarter of FY2024 compared to the same period of the previous year, indicating a rebound. Service sector growth is expected to increase to 5.5% in FY2024, following the trend in industry. Similar factors will raise sector growth in FY2025.

Inflation is projected to moderate, averaging 8.4% in FY2024 and 7.0% in FY2025. Year-on-year monthly headline inflation exceeded 9.0% in the first 7 months of FY2024. Though nonfood inflation moderated as monetary policy was tightened, food inflation reversed unexpectedly, keeping headline inflation elevated. However, inflation is expected to moderate in the remaining months of the fiscal year and edge down to the projected rate for the whole year on continued monetary tightening, expected decline in global oil and commodity prices, and a better crop outlook. The government's plans to reduce exchange rate volatility and eliminate structural subsidies for petroleum products while keeping the budget deficit unchanged will, if successfully implemented, ease inflation. Assuming favorable

weather, inflation is projected to moderate further in FY2025 under continued monetary policy tightening and fiscal consolidation.

The current account should move into surplus in FY2024 and FY2025 on a narrowing trade deficit and rising remittances (Figure 2.15.6). The surplus is expected to grow from 0.8% of GDP in FY2024 to 0.9% in FY2025 on modest growth in remittances and exports. With a growth slowdown in key export destinations, restrictions on opening letters of credits affecting imports of key inputs, and shortages of electricity and fuel, export growth is projected to be slower in FY2024. It will rise further in FY2025 on improving energy supply, strong growth in new markets for garments, and measures aimed at easing access to trade financing. Imports are forecast to contract in FY2024 but rise in FY2025—assuming a relatively stable exchange rate, stronger foreign exchange reserves, and reduced geopolitical tensions—as central bank restrictions are lowered. Remittances are forecast to increase in FY2024 and further in FY2025 driven by cash incentives, the availability to residents of foreign exchange savings accounts, and the increased use of mobile financial services for remittance transfers. However, the wide difference between official and market exchange rates will still encourage remittance transfers through unofficial channels. The gradual move toward a market-driven exchange rate should alleviate this problem.

The fiscal deficit is forecast unchanged at 4.5% of GDP in FY2024 and FY2025, compared to 4.4% in FY2023. Revenue collection is projected at 8.8% of GDP in FY2024, as tax collections by the National Board of Revenue grew by only 14.8% in July 2023–January 2024, representing only 40% of the overall revenue target for the year, owing to uncertainty in the run-up to the January 2024 general election. Total fiscal spending is projected to rise to 13.3% of GDP, as government expedites implementation of priority mega projects.

The ratio of public debt to GDP is expected to remain relatively stable in the near-to-medium term. The government remains cautious about contracting external debt, especially commercial debt. The ratio of public debt to GDP is forecast to increase to 41.4% in FY2024 from 39.8% in FY2023, with external debt rising to 18.1% of GDP from 17.7% and domestic debt growing to 23.3% from 22.1% in FY2023.

Policy Challenge—Overcoming the Challenges of Graduation from Least-Developed Country Status

Bangladesh is on track to graduate from the group of least-developed countries (LDCs) in 2026, but the transition poses challenges. This milestone in the country's economic development necessitates careful preparation, as the post-LDC period involves the conclusion or significant reduction of many international support measures received as an LDC. Graduation involves three key economic implications that affect the nation's capacity to export and attract investments. First, policy flexibility granted under special treatment in World Trade Organization (WTO) agreements may be lost. LDC graduation would limit policy space and flexibility in compliance with WTO rules. Subsidies for exporters may cease due to WTO subsidy rules, and full enforcement of trade-related aspects of intellectual property rights could hinder Bangladesh's pharmaceutical self-sufficiency, jeopardizing 98% of local demand previously met through patent waivers. Second, some development financing may shift from grants to loans on concessional terms, though grant assistance could still be available depending on the areas of cooperation. After graduation, Bangladesh may encounter challenges in accessing certain LDC-specific funds unless terms of engagement are adjusted in response to a reduction in the overall number of LDCs. Third, and perhaps more importantly, preferential access to export destinations, including through duty-free and quota-free schemes and LDC-specific preferential rules of origin, may be lost.

As more than 70% of merchandise exports currently enjoy trade preferences, imminent graduation poses significant concerns for exports. This especially applies to the country's ready-made garments, which constitute more than 83% of total exports. This industry has successfully expanded its market share in major importing countries, capitalizing on trade preferences (Figure 2.15.11). Following graduation, Bangladesh may lose these preferences and face less-favorable trade conditions, or most favored nation tariff rates, contingent on the trade policies of receiving countries (Table 2.15.2). According to a WTO estimate, post-graduation tariff hikes could lead to a 14% decline in exports.

Figure 2.15.11 Apparel Market Share in Major Countries

Bangladesh's share of ready-made garment imports has expanded in major markets on trade preferences for least-developed countries.

Note: The European Union market share includes trade within the union. The US does not provide any trade preference for Bangladesh, but preferences offered by other countries strengthen Bangladesh's exports.
Source: Razzaque M. A., H. Akib, and J. Rahman. 2020. Bangladesh's Graduation from the Group of LDCs: Potential Implications and Issues for the Private Sector. In Razzaque, M. A., ed. *Navigating New Waters: Unleashing Bangladesh's Export Potential for Smooth LDC Graduation.* Bangladesh Enterprise Institute.

Table 2.15.2 Change in Post-Graduation Tariff Rates in Major Export Markets

After graduation, Bangladesh to face high tariff rates.

Countries	Share of Exports from Bangladesh in Fiscal 2023, %	Current Tariffs on Bangladesh as an LDC	Average Post-Graduation Tariff Rates
European Union	45.4	0	12.00[a]
United States	17.5	15[b]	15.00
United Kingdom	9.6	0	0.00[c]
India	3.8	0	8.61
Japan	3.4	0[d]	8.71
Canada	3.1	0	17.00
PRC	1.2	0[d]	16.20

LDC = least developed country, PRC = People's Republic of China.
[a] Not yet settled.
[b] Bangladesh does not enjoy any tariff preference in the United States.
[c] But with more stringent rules of origin.
[d] On 98% of products.
Sources: Export Promotion Bureau of Bangladesh, 2023; World Integrated Trade Solution.

Smooth and sustainable graduation would require enhanced trade and investment competitiveness. This task becomes exceedingly challenging without substantial foreign direct investment (FDI), considering that current FDI equals less than 1% of

GDP (Figure 2.15.12). Inadequate infrastructure, underdeveloped logistics, cumbersome border processes, an opaque regulatory environment, and a lack of integration between trade and industrial policies are major deterrents to FDI. A high tariff regime poses a significant constraint to the goal of fostering a diversified, export-oriented industry base through FDI and collaboration between foreign and domestic investors.

Figure 2.15.12 Net Foreign Direct Investment Inflows

Foreign direct investment has been below 1% of GDP in most years.

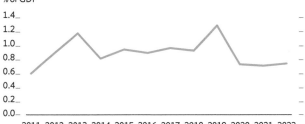

% of GDP

GDP = gross domestic product.

Note: Years are fiscal years ending on 30 June of that year.

Sources: Bangladesh Bank; World Bank. World Development Indicators database.

Recognizing the need for competitiveness, the authorities are taking necessary steps. Seven subcommittees under the Prime Minister's office are addressing market access and trade agreements, intellectual property rights, WTO issues, investment, domestic market development, export diversification, internal resource mobilization, tariff rationalization, and branding. The government has adopted for the first time a National Tariff Policy, 2023 (NTP 2023) to address various policy-induced disincentives and undertake pertinent reform measures to comply with WTO obligations. The Bangladesh Investment Development Authority has initiated its Business

Investment Climate Improvement Program. The Bangladesh Economic Zones Authority is developing 100 special economic zones. The government is developing a model bilateral investment treaty to facilitate negotiations. To graduate with momentum, Bangladesh is preparing a smooth transition strategy that will guide the various policy actions.

Additional measures are required to tackle graduation challenges. The implementation of NTP 2023 needs to be closely monitored by the LDC graduation subcommittee on internal resource mobilization and tariff rationalization, as trade liberalization and tariff rationalization are two primary objectives of the policy. Through tariff rationalization, the NTP 2023 can help tackle various policy-induced disincentives to exports, reduce tariff complexity, and ensure a WTO-compliant tariff regime. Proper implementation of the NTP 2023 will contribute to establishing a predictable tariff regime, as envisioned in the policy, which will further attract investment. Proactive and bilateral engagement with key export markets should be ensured to retain favorable market access terms even after LDC graduation. To provide WTO-compliant export support measures, it would be helpful to learn from experience of other developing countries, such as the People's Republic of China and Viet Nam. Further, the implementation of the Business Investment Climate Improvement Program should be accelerated to facilitate investment and boost investor confidence. Existing investment treaties should be modernized and considered for renegotiation in line with the evolving market dynamics. Focus should be given to fully operationalizing a few economic zones to set examples for future ones. To prepare for LDC graduation and beyond, Bangladesh should undertake a comprehensive capacity-building program in such areas as trade policy and negotiation, investment, logistics, standards and testing, and intellectual property rights.

BHUTAN

Growth decelerated in 2023 as industrial output contracted. Inflation eased and the fiscal deficit moderated, but the current account deficit remained elevated. Growth will revive in 2024 and accelerate in 2025 as a major hydropower plant comes onstream. Inflation will edge up this year before moderating in 2025, as will the current account deficit. To achieve the goal of becoming a more prosperous economy by 2034, Bhutan needs to adopt an innovative and inclusive financing strategy that engages the private sector.

Economic Performance

Economic growth slowed from 5.2% in 2022 to 4.0% in 2023, primarily because of contraction in industry. Industrial output contracted by 4.4% owing to a credit moratorium on commercial housing and hotel construction that was imposed in mid-2023 to conserve foreign exchange reserves, and due to contraction in hydropower output because of suboptimal hydrological flow (Figure 2.16.1). Services expanded by an estimated 9.4%, underpinned by strong expansion in accommodation and food services, transport, and public administration. Agriculture grew by a modest 1.3% due to an erratic monsoon and a shortage of fertilizer. The sector employs over 40% of the labor force but continues to be hampered by low labor productivity due to reliance on traditional farming methods, challenging topography, and erratic weather exacerbated by climate change.

On the demand side, growth was supported by continued expansion in consumption expenditure. This was underpinned by a marked increase in civil servants' salaries and wages and an election year boost in government expenditure in the second half of 2023 (Figure 2.16.2). Private consumption expenditure expanded by 3.5%, and public consumption by 2.4%. The transition from the 12th to the 13th Five-Year Plan delayed investment outlays in the second half of 2023 and the credit moratorium on commercial housing and hotel construction hampered private sector investment. As a result, gross fixed investment contracted by an estimated 4.9% in 2023.

Figure 2.16.1 Supply-Side Contributions to Growth

Gross national product growth moderated in 2023 as industry output slumped.

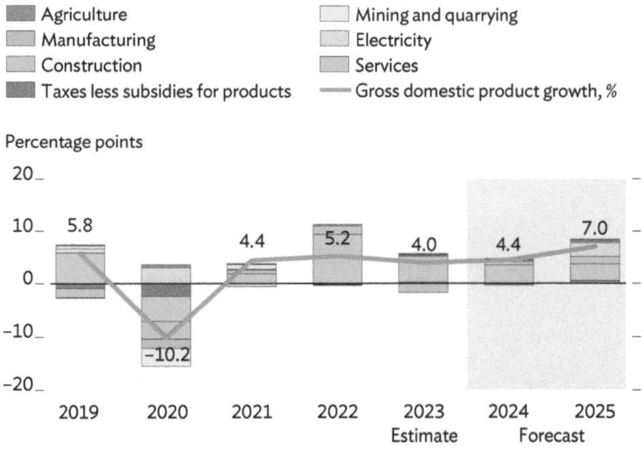

Legend:
- Agriculture
- Manufacturing
- Construction
- Taxes less subsidies for products
- Mining and quarrying
- Electricity
- Services
- Gross domestic product growth, %

Percentage points

Values shown: 5.8 (2019), −10.2 (2020), 4.4 (2021), 5.2 (2022), 4.0 (2023 Estimate), 4.4 (2024 Forecast), 7.0 (2025 Forecast)

Sources: National Statistics Bureau; Haver Analytics; Asian Development Bank estimates.

A slowdown in nonfood price inflation moderated average inflation to 4.2% in 2023 from 5.6% in 2022. A midyear fall in fuel prices offset some of the price increases in health care, housing, utilities, and recreation and culture. The salary and wage increase for public servants and higher food prices in the second half of 2023 led to an uptick in inflation in the fourth quarter of 2023 (Figure 2.16.3).

The budget deficit narrowed on higher revenue and grants. It fell from 7.0% of GDP in fiscal year 2022 (FY2022, ended 30 June 2022) to 6.7% in FY2023

This chapter was written by Sonam Lhendup of the Bhutan Resident Mission, ADB, Thimphu.

Figure 2.16.2 Demand-Side Contributions to Growth

Gross domestic product growth moderated in 2023 as investment slumped.

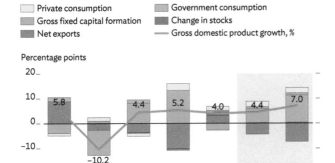

Sources: National Statistics Bureau; Haver Analytics; Asian Development Bank estimates.

Figure 2.16.3 Inflation

Inflation moderated in 2023 as global fuel prices decreased.

Sources: National Statistics Bureau; Haver Analytics.

as revenue and grants expanded from 25.1% of GDP in FY2022 to 25.7% in FY2023, owing to marginally improved inflow of budgetary grants and transfers (Figure 2.16.4). Government spending increased from 32.1% of GDP in FY2022 to 32.4% in FY2023 as both current and capital expenditure grew. While increased tax revenue effectively covers current expenditures, Bhutan still grapples with adequately financing development activities due to a narrow tax base. Domestic public debt decreased to 11.4% of GDP in 2023 on improved revenue from direct taxes and the settlement of outstanding facilities. Debt service equals 32.4% of domestic revenue, indicating moderate risk of debt distress.

Figure 2.16.4 Fiscal Indicators

The fiscal balance improved slightly in 2023 as revenues increased.

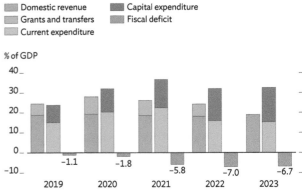

GDP = gross domestic product.
Sources: National Statistics Bureau; Haver Analytics; Asian Development Bank estimates.

Monetary policy remained accommodative in 2023.
While the net foreign assets of the banking system declined by 21%, money supply expanded by 6.7%, primarily on expansion of domestic credit despite the moratorium on construction credit (Figure 2.16.5). Credit to the private sector increased by 15.5%, indicating heightened demand for private investment.

The current account deficit narrowed to an estimated 25.2% of GDP in 2023, down from 31.2% in 2022. This reflected narrower deficits in both goods and services trade (Figure 2.16.6). A sharp fall in electricity exports by 23% offset growth in other exports of 5.4%, while imports of bitcoin processing units and machinery and mechanical

Figure 2.16.5 Monetary Indicators

Monetary policy was accommodative in 2023.

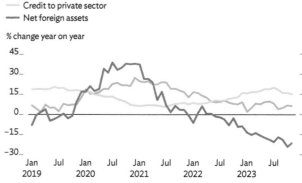

Sources: National Statistics Bureau; Haver Analytics; Asian Development Bank estimates.

appliances sharply fell, lowering total imports. The large current account deficit led to a drop of 20% in foreign exchange reserves. Since the bulk of Bhutan's imports are denominated in Indian rupees, a decline in rupee earnings from hydropower exports is a matter of concern. In 2023, public external debt dropped by 2.9 percentage points to equal 101.9% of GDP, of which hydropower debt accounted for 66.3%. About 64.3% of the public external debt was owed to India, of which 93.8% was hydro debt, considered self-liquidating under a long-term power purchasing agreement with India (Figure 2.16.7).

Figure 2.16.6 Components of the Current Account

The current account improved as deficits in both goods and services moderated.

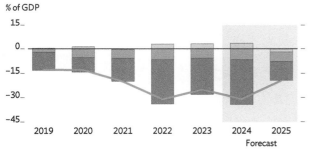

GDP = gross domestic product.
Sources: National Statistics Bureau; Haver Analytics; Asian Development Bank estimates.

Figure 2.16.7 Government Debt

Public debt remained high in 2023.

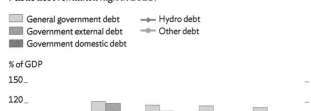

GDP = gross domestic product.
Sources: Ministry of Finance; Haver Analytics; Asian Development Bank estimates.

Economic Prospects

Modest growth of 4.4% is forecast in 2024 before marked acceleration to 7.0% in 2025 (Table 2.16.1). Services growth will underpin 2024 GDP growth, and greater hydropower generation in 2025 will boost growth in 2025. Services are forecast to expand by 6.5% in 2024 as tourist arrivals reach 60% of the 2019 level before the pandemic. Industry output will rebound to 2.5% on an upswing in all its constituents aside from construction. A contribution from the newly commissioned Nikachhu hydropower plant in early 2024 will add to growth. However, the continuation of the credit moratorium on the construction of commercial buildings and real estate until mid-2024 and a slow start to 13th Five-Year Plan activities will drag down construction by 2.2% in 2024, before a rebound in 2025. Agriculture growth will remain steady but sluggish at 1.4% in the forecast years. The contribution from services will remain strong in 2025, with services forecast to grow at 5.7% on steady growth in tourist arrivals. Industry output is forecast at 15.6% in 2025, driven by double-digit growth in electricity and construction, supported by resumed construction on the 600-megawatt Kholongchhu hydropower plant in 2025. The expected full commissioning of the Punatsangchhu II hydropower plant will raise industrial output markedly and add close to 5 percentage points to GDP growth in 2025. India's robust growth in the forecast years will drive Bhutan's growth through increased exports of goods and services, as the two economies share strong economic ties.

Steady growth in domestic demand will remain the main growth driver in 2024 and 2025. Private consumption will grow by 4.6% in 2024 on higher tourism earnings and the increase in civil service salaries. Consumption growth is estimated to hold

Table 2.16.1 Selected Economic Indicators, %

Inflation will rise this year before moderating in 2025, as growth accelerates in both years.

	2022	2023	2024	2025
GDP growth	5.2	4.0	4.4	7.0
Inflation	5.6	4.2	4.5	4.2

GDP = gross domestic product.
Sources: Ministry of Finance; National Statistics Bureau; Asian Development Bank estimates.

steady in 2025 on continued credit expansion to the private sector and steady remittances. Public consumption growth is forecast to stabilize around 4.0% in the forecast years on expansion in recurrent expenditure. Fixed investment will rebound markedly in the forecast years from contraction by 4.9% in 2023 as private investment rises on steady credit growth and public investment grows as the government implements the 13th Five-Year Plan. The budget deficit is projected to widen to 8.3% of GDP in FY2024 due to a drop in grants and transfers to less than half of the previous fiscal year. It will narrow to 2.4% in FY2025 on a near tripling of grants already committed for the implementation of the 13th plan and on transfers from full operation of the Punatsangchhu II plant.

The current account deficit will widen in 2024 before narrowing in 2025. The deficit is projected at 28.8% of GDP in 2024, 3.7 percentage points wider than in 2023, largely on a growing trade deficit, particularly with India, and lower budgetary grants and transfers. The deficit will narrow to 15.7% of GDP in 2025 largely due to a surge in hydropower exports coming from the newly commissioned hydropower plants.

Headline inflation is projected to rise slightly to 4.5% in 2024 and moderate to 4.2% in 2025. Inflation will closely track global prices for petroleum, food, and other commodities that are prominent in Bhutan's import basket. A rise in inflation from 4.2% in 2023 to 4.5% in 2024 is also reflective of increased spending propensity driven mainly by the civil servant's salary increase in mid-2023. However, as Indian imports constitute about half of Bhutan's consumer price index, continuing moderation of inflation in India will help contain inflation in Bhutan. With improvements in the global supply chain and moderate inflation in India, average inflation in Bhutan will moderate in 2025.

Risks to the outlook are largely skewed to the downside. Growth in foreign currency reserves is expected to be subdued in 2024 because of lower inflow of grants and transfers, but persistent decline in foreign currency reserves could pose a risk (Figure 2.16.8). Lower-than-expected tourist arrivals would derail growth projections and adversely affect foreign currency reserves. Erratic monsoons or floods

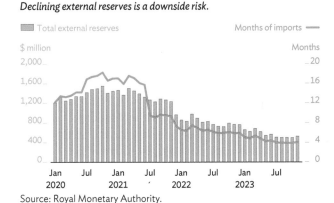

Figure 2.16.8 External Reserves

Declining external reserves is a downside risk.

Source: Royal Monetary Authority.

could depress farm output and hydropower energy generation, as well as damage infrastructure. Domestic risks include delays in the commissioning of the hydropower plants, tighter-than-expected fiscal space, continuing attrition of employees from both the public and the private sector, and the mass outmigration of youthful talent to developed economies.

Policy Challenge—Innovative Financing for Growth

The 13th Five-Year Plan acknowledges the importance of public–private partnership (PPP) to finance infrastructure development and service delivery. To overcome the plan's resource gap, estimated at 9% of GDP, and to achieve the goal of transforming Bhutan into a high-income economy by 2034, Bhutan needs to adopt an innovative financing strategy involving all stakeholders, including the private sector. Globally, PPPs have proven vital for leveraging private finance and addressing financing gaps. The World Bank's Private Participation in Infrastructure Report 2023 highlights that PPPs mobilized $36.4 billion across 44 economies in the first half of 2023, covering energy, health care, transport, waste, sewerage, and greenfield projects. In South Asia, PPPs attracted $1.8 billion, with India leading in implementing PPP projects. By leveraging the potential of PPPs and attracting private sector participation, Bhutan can bridge the fiscal gap for sustainable development, generate employment, and foster partnerships.

Despite political commitment and a favorable legal framework in Bhutan, progress in PPP implementation has been limited. Challenges to implementing PPP projects in Bhutan include complex institutional settings, the absence of provision for unsolicited proposals, centralized approval procedures, a small market with a nascent private sector, dominant state-owned enterprises, limited awareness of PPPs, and a scarcity of successful examples. Owing to these shortcomings, Bhutan's only PPP, the Multi-Level Car Park in Thimphu, has not spurred further PPP development. A revised PPP policy, awaiting cabinet approval, aims to address these challenges and create a conducive environment for the smooth implementation of PPP projects. The updated policy seeks to streamline the approval process and framework, categorize projects by size for quicker approval, integrate PPP into sectoral plans, and allow unsolicited project proposals, among other enhancements.

Achieving PPP success in Bhutan requires enhanced capacity to structure and negotiate contracts. To this end, the country needs a risk-sharing formula and a robust mechanism for assessing and mitigating various risks. Given Bhutan's small market and private sector, the government must actively promote a PPP agenda to attract private sector participation. It should develop capacity to assess and ensure the financial viability of PPP deals. Implementing PPP projects necessitates a robust regulatory and institutional framework, a conducive business environment, prudent fiscal management, and government commitment to reducing its sizeable contingent liabilities. Increasing access to long-term finance through domestic markets is crucial. Capacity, consensus building, and sector-wide support at all implementation levels are essential for overseeing, selecting, monitoring, and implementing PPPs. Implementing PPPs can entail complex contract structuring, negotiation, and follow-up with sometimes substantial budgetary costs. To contain these costs, the PPP program should be included in a medium-term fiscal framework. Reform of state-owned enterprises and their selective privatization are also necessary. According to the World Bank report mentioned above, such reforms have played a pivotal role in fostering the PPP process in Brazil, Colombia, and the Philippines. Experience with waste management and waste-to-energy PPP projects in Bangladesh, India, the People's Republic of China, and the Philippines emphasize the need for robust and transparent tendering and contracting processes to realize PPP benefits. Achieving these reforms and establishing the necessary frameworks for PPPs will take time. Given the importance of this type of development financing, implementing the necessary reforms should start now.

INDIA

The economy grew robustly in fiscal 2023 with strong momentum in manufacturing and services. It will continue to grow rapidly over the forecast horizon. Growth will be driven primarily by robust investment demand and improving consumption demand. Inflation will continue its downward trend in tandem with global trends. To boost exports in the medium term, India needs greater integration into global value chains.

Economic Performance

Growth increased to 7.6% in fiscal year 2023 (FY2023, ended 31 March 2024), driven by manufacturing, construction, and services (Figure 2.17.1). Agriculture growth dropped sharply due to the impact of erratic rainfall. This was compensated by an increase in manufacturing growth to 8.5%. Construction also grew rapidly by 10.7% due to strong housing demand. Services, which account for 50% of GDP, grew by 7.5%, led by financial, real estate,

and professional services. Net indirect taxes also got a boost in FY2023 due to declining central government subsidy expenditure following high fertilizer subsidies in FY2022.

Strong investment drove GDP growth in FY2023 as consumption was muted (Figure 2.17.2). Gross capital formation increased by 10.2% in FY2023 to contribute 3.4 percentage points to GDP growth as

Figure 2.17.1 Supply-Side Contributions to Growth

Strong expansion in services and industry supported growth in 2023.

- Agriculture
- Services
- Industry
- Net taxes on products
- — Gross domestic product growth, %

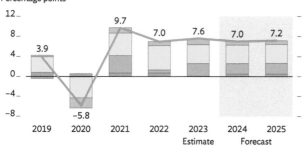

Percentage points

Notes: Years are fiscal years ending on 31 March of the next year. Growth rates are year on year. Net taxes on products are tax receipts minus subsidies.
Sources: Ministry of Statistics and Programme Implementation; CEIC Data Company.

Figure 2.17.2 Demand-Side Contributions to Growth

Investment drove economic growth in FY2023.

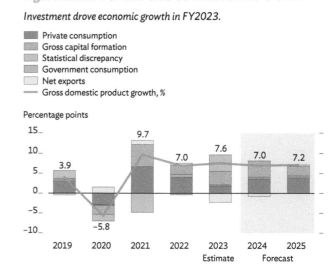

- Private consumption
- Gross capital formation
- Statistical discrepancy
- Government consumption
- Net exports
- — Gross domestic product growth, %

Percentage points

Note: Years are fiscal years ending on 31 March of the next year.
Sources: Ministry of Statistics and Programme Implementation; CEIC Data Company.

This chapter was written by Chinmaya Goyal of the India Resident Mission (INRM), ADB, New Delhi, and Simran Uppal, INRM consultant.

public and private sector capital expenditure grew strongly. Consumption remained subdued, however, with growth falling to 3.0% because of weak rural demand and tepid growth in public consumption under fiscal consolidation, adding 2.1 points to growth. Exports also grew modestly at 1.5% in real terms, while imports grew by 10.9%, driven by greater domestic demand for inputs and capital goods. As a result, net exports declined, deducting 2.3 percentage points from growth.

Consumer inflation moderated in FY2023 despite higher food inflation. It averaged 5.4% during April 2023–January 2024, compared to 6.8% in the corresponding period in FY2022 (Figure 2.17.3). After a spike in July 2023 led by food prices, consumer inflation moderated in the remainder of the year, driven by declining commodity prices and relatively lower food inflation. Core inflation, which was sticky until February 2023, also trended down to record a 4-year low of 3.6% in January 2024 owing to wholesale price deflation from April to October 2023. However, food inflation has remained elevated, mainly from higher prices for pulses, vegetables, sugar, and cereals (Figure 2.17.4). To ease price pressure on cereals and pulses, the government extended duty-free imports until March 2025 for certain pulses and introduced new restrictions on rice exports.

The policy interest rate has remained unchanged at 6.5% since February 2023. To combat inflation, the Reserve Bank of India, the central bank, had earlier raised its policy repo rate by 250 basis points from April 2022 to February 2023 (Figure 2.17.5). Even though core inflation has moderated, the policy rate has remained unchanged to let inflation fall further. As a result, banks' lending rates increased by an average of 194 basis points from April 2022 to January 2024.

Bank credit growth remained robust in FY2023, driven by demand for services and personal loans. Bank credit growth was the highest in a decade, supported by structural factors: lower nonperforming loans, corporate deleveraging, and improved capability to service debt. Outstanding bank credit, excluding public loans to buy crops from farmers, was higher by 16% at the end of January 2024 compared to a year earlier (Figure 2.17.6). Growth in credit to industry was relatively muted. Instead, growth came from loans to the service sector and personal loans such

Figure 2.17.3 Consumer Inflation

Key inflation indicators softened except for food.

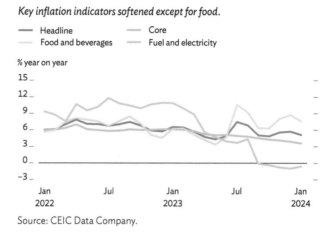

Source: CEIC Data Company.

Figure 2.17.4 Sources of Food Inflation

Inflation has remained high for cereals, milk, and many other food items.

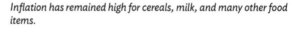

Source: CEIC Data Company.

Figure 2.17.5 Interest Rates

Commercial bank interest rates rose in 2023.

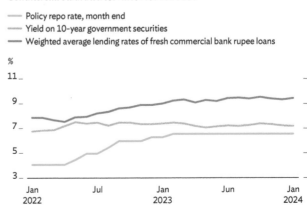

Source: CEIC Data Company.

Figure 2.17.6 Growth in Bank Credit

Demand from services and for personal loans drove growth in credit.

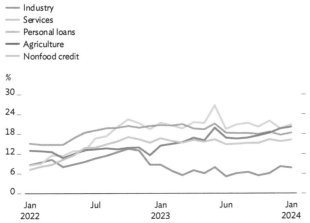

— Industry
— Services
— Personal loans
— Agriculture
— Nonfood credit

%
30
24
18
12
6
0

Jan 2022   Jul   Jan 2023   Jun   Jan 2024

Note: Excludes public loans to buy crops from farmers and the impact of a merger combining HDFC, a large bank, with a nonbank financial corporation, which drove up outstanding bank credit.
Sources: CEIC Data Company; Reserve Bank of India.

Figure 2.17.7 Central Government Fiscal Deficit

Fiscal deficit moved closer to pre-pandemic levels.

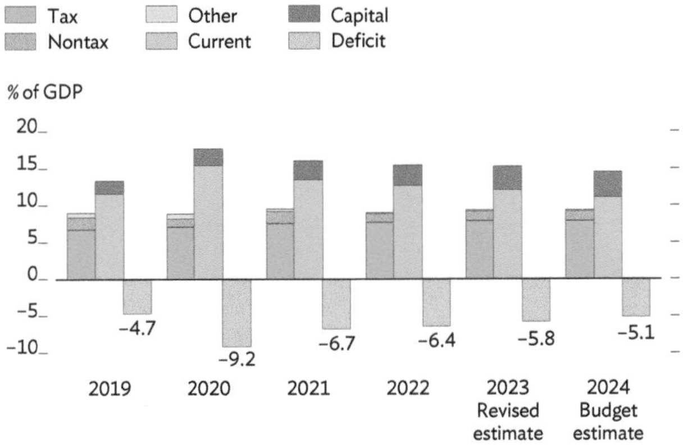

■ Tax   □ Other   ■ Capital
■ Nontax   ■ Current   □ Deficit

% of GDP
20
15
10
5
0
-5
-10

-4.7   -9.2   -6.7   -6.4   -5.8   -5.1

2019   2020   2021   2022   2023 Revised estimate   2024 Budget estimate

GDP = gross domestic product.
Note: Years are fiscal years ending on 31 March of the next year.
Source: Ministry of Finance Union Budget.

as home and auto loans and unsecured credit card debt. The acceleration of unsecured consumer credit prompted the central bank to impose various prudential measures including higher risk weights on certain types of consumer credit and credit card receivables, and to require regulated entities to establish sector limits on their exposure to consumer credit.

The overall health of the banking sector remains robust. The Indian banking sector continued to show improved asset quality with gross nonperforming assets declining to a 10-year low of 3.2% at the end of September 2023 from 3.9% at the end of March 2023. This decline occurred across productive sectors and industries, with the gross nonperforming asset ratio lowest for personal loans.

The central government fiscal deficit shrank from 6.4% of GDP in FY2022 to an estimated 5.8% in FY2023. Better-than-expected revenue performance pushed the deficit lower than the budget target of 5.9% of GDP in FY2023 (Figure 2.17.7). Personal income tax collections are estimated to have grown by 23.0% in FY2023, which highlighted surging incomes for salaried professional and government efforts to widen the tax base by keeping tax exemption limits stable and using digital tools to prevent tax leakage. On the expenditure side, government capital expenditure rose by 28.0%

while current expenditure grew by only 2.5%. As a result, overall expenditure shrank as a share of GDP, even as receipts grew.

Merchandise exports contracted in FY2023 as global trade remained weak, but the current account deficit narrowed. A decline in goods exports by 3.5% in the first 11 months of FY2023 was driven by lower exports of petroleum crude and products, metals, and gems and jewelry, while growth was noted in electronic and pharmaceutical exports. Goods imports also contracted in the period, by 5.3% year on year, with lower prices for energy and food commodities, even as imports of capital goods, iron and steel, pulses, and electronics surged. Falling imports narrowed the merchandise trade deficit by 8.4%. Service export growth moderated to 6.8% compared to the same period of the previous year, while service imports fell by 2%. These developments and continued strong inflow of remittances narrowed the current account deficit from 2.0% of GDP in FY2022 to an estimated 1.2% in FY2023 (Figure 2.17.8).

Foreign exchange reserves increased in the first 11 months of FY2023 as the exchange rate remained relatively stable. Net foreign portfolio investment turned positive, registering net inflow of $32.3 billion in the first 9 months of FY2023, after recording net outflow of $3.5 billion in the same period of FY2022, and foreign direct investment (FDI) net

Figure 2.17.8 External Current Account

The current account deficit narrowed in FY2023 due to lower imports.

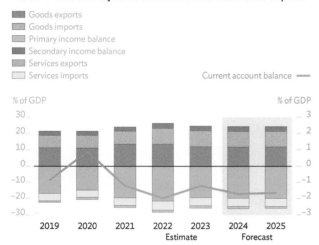

- Goods exports
- Goods imports
- Primary income balance
- Secondary income balance
- Services exports
- Services imports
- Current account balance ——

GDP = gross domestic product.
Note: Years are fiscal years ending on 31 March of the next year.
Sources: CEIC Data Company; Asian Development Bank estimates.

inflow moderated to $9.7 billion from $21.6 billion. The narrowing current account deficit and improving capital flows led to a balance of payment surplus. This outcome and the central bank's net purchase of $17.5 billion in foreign exchange, reversing net sales of dollars in FY2022, strengthened foreign exchange reserves from $578 billion in March 2023 to $626 billion as of February 2024 (Figure 2.17.9). The Indian rupee depreciated against the dollar by 1.1% in the first 11 months of FY2023 (Figure 2.17.10).

Figure 2.17.9 Foreign Exchange Reserves

Foreign exchange reserves remained higher than before the pandemic.

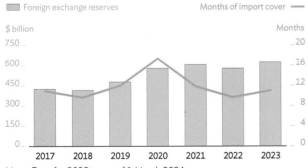

- Foreign exchange reserves
- Months of import cover ——

Note: Data for 2023 are as of 1 March 2024.
Sources: Haver Data Analytics; Asian Development Bank estimates.

Figure 2.17.10 Equity and Debt Flows and the Exchange Rate

Higher debt inflow supported the Indian rupee.

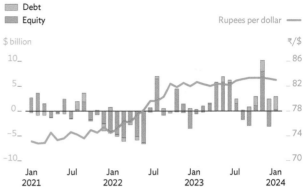

- Debt
- Equity
- Rupees per dollar ——

Sources: CEIC Data Company; Securities and Exchange Board of India.

Economic Prospects

Growth will be robust despite moderating in FY2024 and FY2025. It will be driven by public and private sector investment demand and by gradual improvement in consumer demand as the rural economy improves. Exports are likely to be relatively muted in FY2024 as growth in major advanced economies slows down but will improve in FY2025. Monetary policy is expected to remain supportive of growth as inflation abates, while fiscal policy aims for consolidation but retains support for capital investment. On balance, growth is forecast to slow to 7.0% in FY2024 but improve to 7.2% in FY2025 (Table 2.17.1).

Table 2.17.1 Selected Economic Indicators, %

Growth will dip in fiscal 2024 but remain robust this year and next.

	2022	2023	2024	2025
GDP growth	7.0	7.6	7.0	7.2
Inflation	6.7	5.5	4.6	4.5

GDP = gross domestic product.
Note: Years are fiscal years ending on 31 March of the next year.
Sources: Ministry of Statistics and Programme Implementation, Government of India; Reserve Bank of India; Asian Development Bank estimates.

Investment prospects are brightened by public capital expenditure and improving private investments. The central government allocation for capital expenditure is higher by 17% in FY2024 over the previous year. Capital expenditure by state governments will also remain strong, helped by central government transfers to state governments for infrastructure investment. On the private sector side, investment in housing will remain strong, driven by stable interest rates and higher income growth for high-income households. A new government initiative to support urban housing for middle-income households is expected to spur housing growth. Private corporate investment is also likely to grow. As per data collected by the Centre for Monitoring of Indian Economy, private sector projects announced and under implementation have grown rapidly since FY2021, indicating a strong project pipeline, though this has not yet translated into a meaningful increase in project completions (Figure 2.17.11).

Figure 2.17.11 Investment Projects under Implementation and Completed

Robust private sector project planning will drive investment higher.

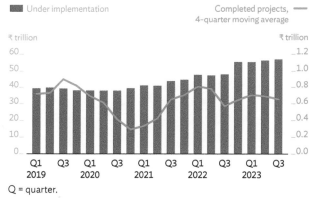

Q = quarter.
Note: Years are fiscal years ending on 31 March of the next year.
Source: Centre for Monitoring of Indian Economy.

Consumption demand will improve with higher incomes. Consumer confidence has improved in urban areas, with the current situation index that gauges consumer confidence improving to 95 in January 2024 from 85 in January 2023 (Figure 2.17.12). Urban consumption is expected to rise in FY2024, helped by falling inflation and gradual improvement in the urban labor market. The urban worker population ratio rose from 44.7% in the third quarter of FY2022 to 46.6% a year later, and the urban unemployment rate fell from 7.2% to 6.5% (Figure 2.17.13). Rural consumption was

Figure 2.17.12 Consumer Confidence Survey

Consumers are optimistic about the future economic situation.

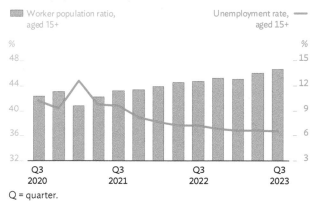

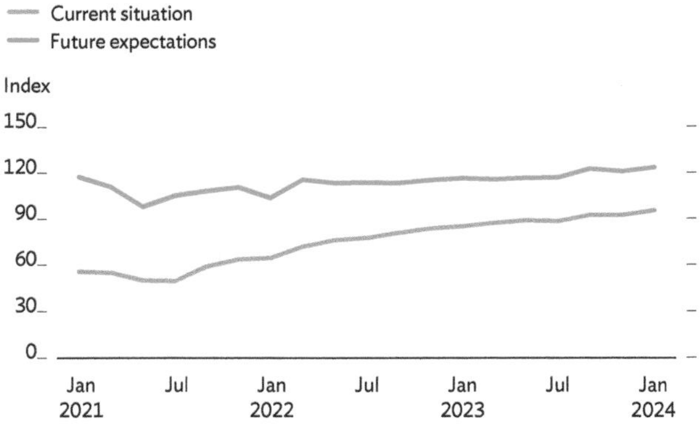

Note: Years are fiscal years ending on 31 March of the next year.
Source: Reserve Bank of India.

Figure 2.17.13 Labor Market Indicators

The unemployment rate has fallen.

Q = quarter.
Notes: Years are fiscal years ending on 31 March of the next year. Estimates use current weekly status.
Source: Periodic Labor Force Survey Report, Ministry of Statistics and Program Implementation.

muted in FY2023 as rural incomes suffered from erratic rainfall affecting agriculture, as indicated by greater demand for work under the Mahatma Gandhi National Rural Employment Guarantee Act (Figure 2.17.14). Assuming normal monsoon rainfall, rural consumption will improve in FY2024.

Net exports will continue to subtract from growth in FY2024 but improve in FY2025. In recent years, India's share in global goods exports has remained stable. In FY2024, goods exports will be depressed as advanced economies slow down, but they will improve somewhat in FY2025 as global growth improves. The export performance of electronics continues to be

Figure 2.17.14 Work Applications under the Mahatma Gandhi National Rural Employment Guarantee Act

Demand for work under the act rose due to lower agricultural income in FY2023.

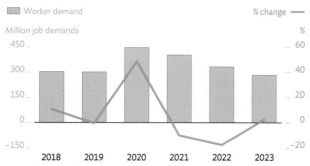

Notes: Years are fiscal years ending on 31 March of the next year; 2023 is to January 2024.
Source: CEIC Data Company.

Figure 2.17.15 Purchasing Managers' Indexes

The services and manufacturing indexes have remained in the expansionary zone.

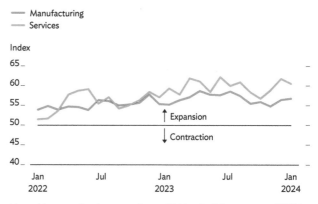

Notes: Years are fiscal years ending on 31 March of the next year. 2023 is to January 2024.
Source: CEIC Data Company.

strong, driven by increasing foreign investment in the industry. India's exports will be helped by continued strength in services, particularly information technology and digital business services. India continues to benefit from improved competitiveness in digital services featuring higher value added, including through Indian global capability centers set up by multinational corporations. Imports will outgrow exports in FY2024, driven by strong domestic demand especially for capital goods and intermediate goods.

On the supply side, service growth momentum is strong. The purchasing managers' index for services reached 60.6 in February 2024, painting an optimistic picture for services (Figure 2.17.15). Higher demand for financial, real estate, and professional services will be key contributors to growth. Manufacturing will benefit from relatively muted input cost pressures, which has boosted industry sentiments (Figure 2.17.16). Government efforts to simplify regulations and improve infrastructure will raise productivity and lead to greater competitiveness, thus helping growth in FY2025. Agriculture will benefit from a recovery in winter crops, as indicated by current agriculture sowing patterns and an expected normal monsoon. Relatively favorable terms of trade for agriculture due to higher food prices are also expected to boost output in FY2025. The contribution to growth from net indirect taxes will be lower in FY2024, after being boosted in FY2023 due to withdrawal of subsidies.

Figure 2.17.16 Industrial Business Outlook

The business outlook has recovered after sagging in Q4 of fiscal 2022.

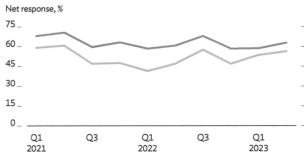

Q = quarter.
Notes: Years are fiscal years ending on 31 March of the next year, so Q1 is April–June. Net response is the share of respondents who gave a positive response minus those who gave a negative response.
Source: CEIC Data Company.

Inflation is expected to ease to 4.6% in FY2024 and 4.5% in FY2025. Food inflation has been persistent but is expected to moderate to 5.7% as agricultural production returns to trend in FY2024. According to a central bank survey, households' inflation expectations have continued to decline in line with core inflation. The latter is expected to decline from 4.4% in FY2023 to 3.8% in FY2024 on the lagged effect of tighter monetary policy, before rising to 5.0% in FY2025 because of higher demand. The inflation outlook will be helped by moderation in global inflation and a stable global crude oil market.

The government's focus on fiscal consolidation will continue, creating space for private borrowing. The FY2024 central government budget set an aggressive deficit target of 5.1% of GDP and reiterated the fiscal deficit target of 4.5% for FY2025. Revenue growth in FY2024 will be in line with the previous year, up by 11.0% over FY2023. However, driven by lower subsidy spending, FY2024 budgeted expenditure growth will be, at 6.0%, the lowest in the last 7 years, though capital spending will rise by 17.0% to $134 billion. Aggressive fiscal consolidation will enable the central government to reduce its gross market borrowing by 0.9% of GDP in FY2024. As domestic financial institutions are the primary buyers of government securities, reduced government borrowing will create room for greater private sector credit. Further, India's inclusion in the JP Morgan's Government Bond Emerging Markets Fund is expected to give a one-time boost to foreign purchases of rupee-denominated Indian government securities in FY2024, likely amounting to 10.0% of the central government's gross borrowing. The general government fiscal deficit, which includes the central and state governments, is expected to decline from 9.2% of GDP in FY2022 to 8.9% in FY2023 and 8.1% in FY2024. This assumes that state governments' fiscal deficits remain at 3.0% of GDP.

Monetary policy will become less restrictive this year as inflation nears the policy target of 4%, facilitating credit expansion. Less restrictive monetary policy and continued fiscal consolidation will pave the way for the rapid rate of increase in bank credit seen last year to continue in FY2024 and FY2025, notwithstanding regulatory tightening on unsecured personal loans. Credit growth will be driven mainly by loans to services, housing, and industry.

The current account deficit will widen moderately, but external financial conditions will be favorable over the forecast period. The current account deficit will widen to 1.7% of GDP in FY2024 and FY2025 on rising imports to meet domestic demand. However, portfolio capital inflow will remain strong, attracted by the performance of India's equity and debt markets. FDI inflow will likely remain muted in the near term due to tight global financial conditions but will pick up in FY2025 with higher industry and infrastructure investment.

Both upside and downside risks to the outlook arise from external and domestic sources. The economic outlook for India depends on price and financial market stability, which are crucial for consumer and business confidence. The outlook could thus be affected by negative global shocks, such as a supply shock in crude oil markets that spikes energy costs and raises global inflation, which could lead central banks to tighten financial conditions globally and in India. On the domestic side, there is a risk of underperformance in agriculture due to weather shocks that can affect demand and inflation. On the upside is a possibility of faster-than-expected FDI inflow, particularly into manufacturing, where many pipeline projects have been announced by corporations. Besides boosting output, FDI inflow would improve productivity. Better-than-expected global growth could boost exports and thus growth.

Policy Challenge—Boosting Trade by Integrating into Global Value Chains

India's growth strategy is predicated on substantial export growth. It can be achieved through integration into global value chains. A target of $2 trillion in exports of goods and services has been set by the government to be achieved by 2030. In FY2023, combined exports of goods and services reached an estimated $770 billion. Thus, considerable growth will be needed to reach the government's targets. Increasing goods exports requires India to integrate into global value chains (GVCs), which must entail India specializing in stages of production where it has a comparative advantage, as opposed to necessarily looking to be present in the entire value chain.

India participation in GVCs has been limited. Historically, India has been little engaged in highly integrated GVCs such as those that manufacture transport equipment, electrical and optical equipment, chemicals and chemical products, basic and fabricated metal, textiles, and textile products. As a result, India's share of global merchandise exports has remained relatively stable at about 1.8%–2.1% of GDP (Figure 2.17.17). Meanwhile, India has remained only a small player in the sizeable global GVC market. Its share of GVC exports rose by 0.9% from 2010 to 2017, as

Figure 2.17.17 India's Share of Global Exports
of Selected Goods

India's share of global exports did not improve significantly in recent years to 2022.

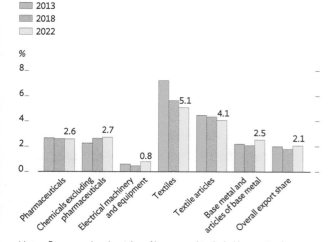

Notes: Base metal and articles of base metal include Harmonized System of Nomenclature chapters 72–83, textiles 50–60, textile articles 61–63; pharmaceuticals 30, chemicals 28–38 excluding chapter 30, and electrical machinery and equipment 85. Overall export share includes all two-digit system entries. Years are calendar years.
Source: World Integrated Trade Solution.

compared to over 10% for other emerging economies, accounting for only $241 billion, or 1.5% of global GVC exports in 2017.

On the other hand, India has been a global leader in service trade. Its share of global service exports increased from 3.5% in FY2017 to 4.6% in FY2022, driven by success in information technology and the services enabled by it. Service exports have emerged as a crucial driver of economic growth, their share accounting for 10% of GDP in FY2023. This success has led to consideration of a development model that is predicated primarily on services.

However, evidence suggests that goods exports have a larger impact on employment and growth than do service exports. First, goods exports and their indirect effects are found to be more employment-intensive than services exports. A study based on the inter-linkages between exports and employment in India using a supply-use table estimates

that in 2017, 143 jobs were generated per $1 million of goods exported, as compared to 55 jobs per $1 million of service exports (Veeramani et al. 2023). Second, export manufacturing jobs align better with educational attainment in India's labor force, as service exports generally require higher education. Third, participation in GVCs encourages FDI, which can generate spillover benefits in terms of productivity improvement and technology upgrades.

Infrastructure and business regulatory reform has helped trade growth in selected sectors, but additional measures are needed. Over the past few years, India has increased public spending on infrastructure, as discussed above. There has been a significant focus on improving logistics through the National Master Plan for Multi-modal Connectivity. In addition to infrastructure, the business regulatory environment has been streamlined with a simplified corporate tax regime and the simplification and digitization of administrative clearances. These measures have, along with the production-linked incentives for private companies to invest in selected sectors, led to greater trade in selected sectors. Notwithstanding slow global trade, electronic goods exports increased by 20.8% from April 2023 to January 2024 compared to the same period a year earlier. Imports of electronic goods also increased by 16.7% during this period, indicating that India is deepening its integration into the electronics GVC.

Further policy action is needed to improve India's trade competitiveness and integration into GVCs. A simplified tariff policy is needed along with continued efforts to improve trade and logistics infrastructure. Regionally, a few large-scale economic zones that provide a competitive ecosystem, the required infrastructure, and a streamlined regulatory environment should be developed. Further, infrastructure upgrades can be made to industrial parks and special economic zones already established. Improved spatial planning to provide logistics and infrastructure connectivity, and development around the economic zones, will help develop a thriving competitive ecosystem for businesses.

MALDIVES

Economic growth softened in 2023 along with tourism earnings despite increased tourist arrivals. Inflation rose with a hike in the goods and services tax rate, and the current account deficit widened as the service surplus shrank. With construction growth and tourism expansion, the outlook is for an economic upturn in 2024 and 2025, with inflation rising in 2024 but remaining low. Scant agricultural production and extreme import dependence threaten food security, especially as risks intensify from climate change and require steps to increase crop yields, including through the adoption of new agricultural techniques.

Economic Performance

Preliminary estimates show that the economy grew by 2.7% year on year in the first 3 quarters of 2023 (Figure 2.18.1). Fisheries, transportation and communication, construction, and real estate performed strongly in the period despite a dip in construction in the third quarter (Q3). However, tourism grew by just 0.01%, and its value added contracted in Q2 and Q3. All sectors, especially tourism, are estimated to have grown solidly in Q4, resulting in 4.4% GDP growth in 2023.

Tourist arrivals in Maldives grew by 12.1% in 2023 but without translating into higher tourism receipts. The increase in arrivals surpassed the pre-pandemic level by 10.3%, boosted by resumed flights from the People's Republic of China (PRC) in January 2023. The PRC accounted for 84.9% of the increase in tourist arrivals. Its share of the tourism market in 2023 was 10.00%, placing it behind India at 11.14% and Russia at 11.13%. Initial estimates indicate that travel receipts contracted by 6.0% year on year as advance travel sales for 2023 were booked in Q4 2022 to avoid a planned hike in 2023 of the goods and services tax (GST) rate. The average stay shortened to 7.6 days from 8.0 days in 2022 (Figure 2.18.2).

On the demand side, indications are that government investment expanded and fish exports recovered. Public infrastructure spending, largely on

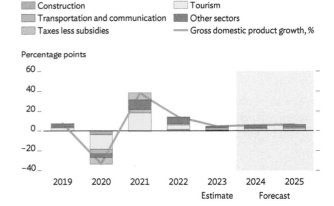

Figure 2.18.1 Supply-Side Contributions to Growth

Growth came from tourism and associated sectors, such as transportation and communication, and construction.

Construction · Tourism
Transportation and communication · Other sectors
Taxes less subsidies · —— Gross domestic product growth, %

Percentage points

Source: Maldives Monetary Authority. 2024. Monthly Statistics. February.

transport and road infrastructure and land reclamation, grew by 36.2% in 2023, exceeding the approved 2023 budget by 17.7%. Fisheries grew with the volume of fish exports rising by 3.5% in 2023 following a decline of 1.0% in 2022, though export value moderated on lower prices. Lack of data precludes further analysis.

Average inflation edged up to 2.9% in 2023 from 2.3% in 2022. The increase in the GST rate by 40.0% for the general sector and 33.3% for the tourism

---

This chapter was written by Elisabetta Gentile of the South Asia Department (SARD), ADB, Manila, and Macrina Mallari, SARD consultant.

Figure 2.18.2 Tourism Indicators

Travel receipts contracted as the average stay shortened, but tourist arrival growth remained strong in 2023.

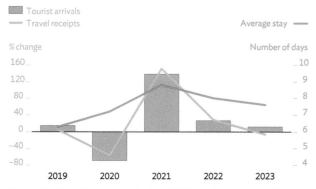

Source: Maldives Monetary Authority. 2024. Monthly Statistics. February.

Figure 2.18.3 Inflation

Inflationary pressure markedly rose during the first quarter of 2023 due to an increased GST rate.

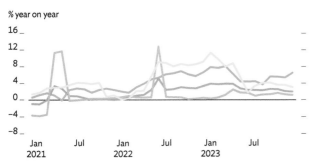

GST = goods and services tax.
Source: Maldives Monetary Authority. 2024. Monthly Statistics. February.

Figure 2.18.4 Balance of Payments

The current account deficit-to-GDP ratio deteriorated in 2023 due to a smaller service surplus as travel receipts declined.

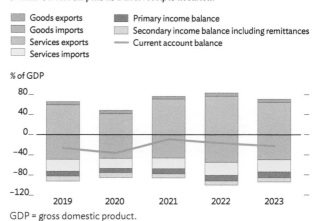

GDP = gross domestic product.
Source: Maldives Monetary Authority. 2024. Monthly Statistics. February.

Figure 2.18.5 Gross International Reserves

Foreign reserves substantially dropped in 2023 to just over a month of import cover by the end of 2023.

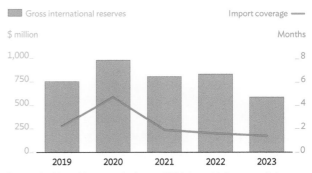

Source: Maldives Monetary Authority. 2024. Monthly Statistics. February.

sector from 1 January 2023 pushed up prices for most commodities (Figure 2.18.3). The increase was tempered by fiscal subsidies.

The current account deficit widened to equal 22.4% of GDP in 2023, from 16.3% in 2022. The larger deficit was mainly due to the service surplus contracting by an estimated 10.6% with lower travel receipts (Figure 2.18.4). With lower foreign exchange earnings from tourism, gross reserves declined by 29.3% to $588.6 million. This provided only 1.4 months of cover for imports of goods and services (Figure 2.18.5).

The GST hike boosted fiscal revenue growth in 2023 but not enough to keep pace with higher fiscal expenditure, which widened the fiscal deficit to 14.1% of GDP. This was slightly higher than the government's initial forecast of 13.8% of GDP and 39.0% larger than the previous year. Total revenue including grants expanded by 9.8% to 29.9% of GDP. Government expenditure grew by 17.7% to equal 44.0% of GDP including a Rf6.5 billion supplementary budget that was approved in November 2023 to cover additional current and capital spending and capital contributions to state-owned companies (Figure 2.18.6). The budget deficit was 57.9% externally funded, including a €50 million non-concessional budget-support loan from the Hungarian Export–Import Bank Private Limited.

Figure 2.18.6 Fiscal Indicators

The fiscal deficit is projected to stay elevated in 2024 and 2025.

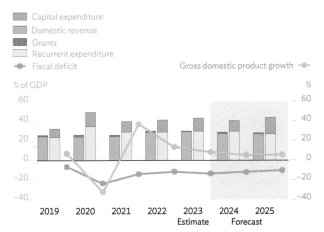

GDP = gross domestic product.

Sources: Maldives Monetary Authority. 2024. Monthly Statistics. February; Ministry of Finance. Maldives Budget 2024.

Total public and publicly guaranteed debt rose to 116.8% of GDP at the end of 2023, 14.5% higher than at the end of 2022 (Figure 2.18.7). External borrowing grew to 48.1% of GDP and was mainly used to finance the fiscal deficit. Domestic public debt climbed to 68.7% of GDP owing to higher central government borrowing, though guaranteed domestic debt dropped by 50.8%. Moody's Investors Service and Fitch Ratings kept Maldives' sovereign ratings at Caa1 stable and B– negative, respectively. However, both agencies underscored rising liquidity risks owing to the widening fiscal deficit and large debt repayment obligations. The International Monetary Fund's 2024

Figure 2.18.7 Public Debt including Guarantees

Total public and publicly guaranteed debt grew in 2023.

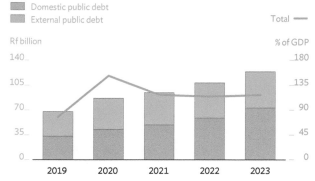

GDP = gross domestic product.

Source: Maldives Monetary Authority. 2024. Monthly Statistics. February.

Article IV Mission press release noted that, without significant policy changes, public debt is projected to stay elevated, and Maldives will remain at high risk of external and overall debt distress.

Economic Prospects

The economy will expand by 5.4% in 2024 and 6.0% in 2025 on continued tourism and construction growth (Table 2.18.1). Tourism and related transportation and communication services will account for half of the increase in GDP in both years, while construction will contribute around 5.0%. Receipts from tourism are forecast to rise by an average of 9.0% per year in 2024 and 2025. This is based on an expected average of around 2 million arrivals in 2024 and 2025, assuming a continuation of the trend in tourist arrivals, which rose by 16.9% in the first 2 months of 2024 compared to the same period last year. The government projects a 40.0% increase in tourist arrivals from the PRC as it embarks on massive promotional activites specifically targeting PRC visitors and negotiates additional direct flights from the PRC. It has set the promotion and expansion of tourism as a high priority and is aiming to open 20 new resorts this year and complete the Velana International Airport passenger terminal by Q4 2024 to accommodate higher tourist arrivals. With robust tourism, sectors directly related to travel and tourism, such as transportation and communication and wholesale and retail trade, are expected to expand, which will also strengthen private consumption.

Construction is projected to slow in 2024, given the tight fiscal position, before gradually picking up in 2025. The government has cut down Public Sector Investment Program financing by almost 24.0% this

Table 2.18.1 Selected Economic Indicators, %

Modest economic growth is projected in the next 2 years, with inflation edging up in 2024 before easing in 2025.

	2022	2023	2024	2025
GDP growth	13.9	4.4	5.4	6.0
Inflation	2.3	2.9	3.2	2.5

GDP = gross domestic product.

Note: 2023 inflation is a government estimate.

Sources: Maldives Monetary Authority. 2024. Monthly Statistics. February; Asian Development Bank estimates.

year as compared to 2023, but the program allocation is once again expected to increase by 30.7% in 2025 to support several mega projects. Private infrastructure investments, particularly in tourism and real estate, are also seen to prop up construction activity.

Growth in fisheries will likely be sustained as the new government embarks on the diversification and promotion of the sector. Maldives Fisheries and Ocean Resources Marketing and Promotion Limited is planning to introduce fish products and related services in foreign markets to boost revenues. The government is negotiating with European markets the reduction of taxes levied on its fish exports.

Inflation is expected to rise to 3.2% in 2024 with the removal of blanket subsidies, before gradually easing to 2.5% in 2025. A shift from blanket to targeted subsidies for fuel, electricity, staple food, and sewerage services, aiming to benefit just half of Maldivian households from July 2024, will drive overall inflation up this year, though it will be tempered by easing global commodity prices. Inflation is expected to decline in 2025 on continued moderation of food and energy prices and a high base effect.

Planned subsidy reforms and lower capital expenditure in 2024 will narrow the budget deficit. However, the deficit will remain large at 12.3% of GDP as total revenue is expected to grow by a mere 3.4%. The deficit is projected to decline further in 2025 as higher revenue growth offsets a rise in total expenditure but to stay above 10.0% of GDP. Maldives also faces heightened fiscal pressures, notably from huge debt service obligations combined with large and pesistent primary fiscal deficits, and high refinancing risk. At present, Maldives' external debt service payment is around $300 million per year. The refinancing requirement will climb from 2025 as repayment to Cargill Financial Service International Inc. of a $100 million private placement will fall due, and repayment of a line of credit facility with Exim Bank of India will commence. By 2026, Maldives also needs to settle a $500 million Islamic bond and another $100 million private placement with the Abu Dhabi Fund.

The current account deficit will stay elevated but narrow on higher tourism receipts and easing import prices. The surplus in services is expected to recover on higher travel receipts and improved collection of tax on tourism goods and services. Projected moderation of global commodity prices, particularly oil, will also contribute to tapering the merchandise trade gap. On balance, the current account deficit-to-GDP ratio in 2024 will decline to 16.0% before rising to 17.0% in 2025 on construction-related imports for the government's massive infrastructure investments.

The risks to the outlook are tilted to the downside. Extreme weather conditions from El Niño and geopolitical events may result in higher commodity prices that will worsen both the current account and the fiscal deficits as they could trigger higher subsidies. If realized, these risks could further imperil fiscal and debt sustainability, given Maldives' very high public debt and meager foreign exchange buffers. There is also a risk that tourism earnings will be lower than expected and that the implementation of government projects is delayed, hurting economic growth.

Policy Challenge—Enhancing Food Security

Maldives imports almost 100% of its food staples, leaving it vulnerable to exogenous shocks and food insecurity. Global events such as El Niño, the COVID-19 pandemic, and the Russian invasion of Ukraine raised the cost of food and oil imports and prices for consumer goods. Economic or agricultural output volatility in Maldives' main trade partners also affects domestic price movements and food supply sufficiency. Reflecting its dependence on imports, Maldives suffered a large gap in imported food staples during the Sri Lankan economic crisis, and, when onion supplies from India significantly dropped in 2023, the cost of onions skyrocketed. Estimates in 2021 found 13.4% of the population experiencing moderate or severe food insecurity. Therefore, food security needs to be improved urgently.

Dependence on imports is mainly due to geographical factors affecting the country. Lack of cultivable land, poor soil quality, limited water resources, and frequent extreme weather events like storm surges and flooding make agricultural production difficult in the country. Agriculture is mainly subsistence, while commercial farming remains confined to high-value crops that mostly go to tourist resorts. Livestock production is also limited, restricted to small pockets of poultry and egg production.

Despite inherent geographical constraints, agriculture still has potential to contribute to food security. Maldives has approximately 5,900 hectares of agricultural land but produces only 10% of the country's overall food requirement. Agriculture's average share of GDP was a paltry 1.5% from 2005 to 2022 (Figure 2.18.8). This suggests that there may be scope to expand agricultural production, but a number of challenges confronting the sector must be addressed. These include containing a drop in the number of farmers—which has fallen by 23.7% since 2013, necessitating reliance on foreign workers—and increasing crop yields. To this end, a lack of access to finance, and the high cost of basic farm inputs such as imported fertilizers and seeds, should be mitigated as they inhibit farmers' ability to increase their crop yields. As per Maldives Monetary Authority data, agriculture accounts for less than 1.0%

Figure 2.18.8 Agriculture Contribution to GDP

Agriculture's share in GDP has declined, averaging 1.5% during 2005-2022.

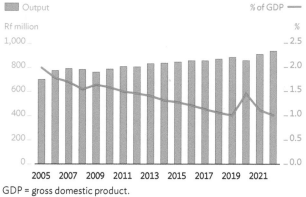

GDP = gross domestic product.
Source: Maldives Bureau of Statistics. 2023. *GDP Production*. Malé.

of total loans to small and medium-sized enterprises. Basic postharvest infrastructure for storage and transportation needs strengthening to enable farmers to bring their goods to market. This is particularly crucial, especially if farmers are to tap and supply the big tourist markets. Similarly, the sector needs better infrastructure to protect farmlands from natural hazards and climate risks.

It is also essential to enhance agriculture-related technical know-how and introduce modern techniques. As highlighted by the National Fisheries and Agricultural Policy, 2019–2029, Maldives' agriculture-related technical know-how is low. Beyond traditional agriculture, Maldives should invest more in alternative farming technologies to make local agriculture more resilient. Sustainable techniques such as vertical farming, aeroponics, and hydroponics allow large-scale production while minimizing land and water usage. Unfortunately, given the technical knowledge required and high initial financial investments, only a few producers employ these modern methods in Maldives—mostly on agricultural land leased to private businesses—and open field cultivation remains the chief farming technique in the country. The new government has pledged to introduce modern agricultural techniques as part of its efforts to improve food security. Tapping the private sector, the Ministry of Agriculture and Animal Welfare signed an agreement with VC Group Private Limited in January 2024 for a pilot project on vertical farming at the Hanimaadhoo Agriculture Center to identify the most feasible model for wider application across the country. This is in parallel with the planned and ongoing projects with development partners to increase agricultural produce through sustainable and innovative practices and contribute to food security. These measures will help move the country toward food security, but their implementation and further deepening will require political will and commitment.

NEPAL

Growth slid in fiscal 2023 as tight financial conditions replaced pandemic stimulus, and inflation flared as prices for oil and other commodities spiked. The current account deficit narrowed with a smaller trade deficit. Growth will pick up this year and in fiscal 2025 as domestic demand gradually revives, hydroelectric output increases, and recovery in tourism continues. Inflation will subside as oil prices moderate, and the current account deficit will substantially narrow on further reduction of the trade deficit and buoyant remittance inflow. As Nepal approaches graduation from the least-developed-country group, it must intensify its trade facilitation efforts.

Economic Performance

Preliminary official estimates show GDP expanded by 1.9% in fiscal year 2023 (FY2023, ended mid-July 2023) after rising by 5.6% in FY2022 (Figure 2.19.1). Agriculture grew by 2.7% in FY2023, improving on 2.2% a year earlier as cereal output increased on a favorable monsoon and the use of improved crop varieties. Industry grew by only 0.6% as manufacturing and construction contracted—affected by higher interest rates, import restrictions in the first 5 months of FY2023, and slackened external and domestic demand—and despite the energy subsector expanding by 19.4% as electricity generation increased. Service growth fell by nearly half to 2.3% in FY2023 as wholesale and retail trade contracted under dampened domestic demand, and as transportation and storage expanded only slightly. Accommodation and food services, however, registered robust growth of 18.6% on increased international tourist arrivals.

On the demand side, lower investment slowed growth in FY2023. Both public and private investment stalled (Figure 2.19.2). Fixed investment slumped by 10.9%, mainly from higher interest rates that dampened credit growth to the private sector, and on lower imports of both intermediate and capital goods, subtracting 3.9 percentage points from GDP growth. Despite sizeable remittance inflows, private consumption growth slowed to 4.1% from 6.8% a year earlier as purchasing power dipped. The merchandise trade deficit contracted

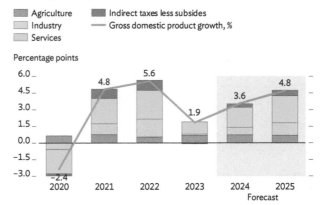

Figure 2.19.1 Supply-Side Contributions to Growth

Economic growth slowed in FY2023 but will trend upward this year and next, driven by services.

Legend:
- Agriculture
- Industry
- Services
- Indirect taxes less subsides
- Gross domestic product growth, %

Percentage points

Note: Years are fiscal years ending in mid-July of that year.
Sources: National Statistics Office. 2023. *National Accounts of Nepal 2021/22*; Asian Development Bank estimates.

by 21.7%, in real terms, on import and credit control measures. Services deficit also contracted by 11.6% as services' export growth surpassed import growth on higher tourist arrivals, pushing the contribution of net exports to GDP to 8.9 percentage points.

Inflation increased in FY2023 on higher oil and commodity prices, somewhat tempered by the tightening of monetary policy. Average annual inflation rose to 7.7% from 6.3% a year earlier

This chapter was written by Manbar Singh Khadka and Neelina Nakarmi of the Nepal Resident Mission, ADB, Kathmandu.

Figure 2.19.2 Demand-Side Contributions to Growth

Lower investment stalled growth in 2023.

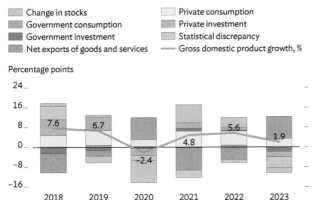

Note: Years are fiscal years ending in mid-July of that year.
Sources: National Statistics Office. 2023. *National Accounts of Nepal 2022/23*; Asian Development Bank estimates.

Figure 2.19.3 Monthly Inflation

Tightened monetary policy moderated an increase in average annual inflation in FY2023.

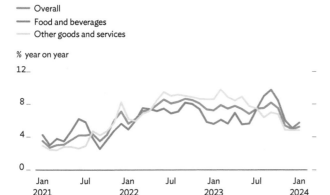

Source: Nepal Rastra Bank. 2024. *Recent Macroeconomic Situation.*

(Figure 2.19.3). Food inflation averaged 6.6% with prices up for cereals owing to supply-side shocks, particularly from India's wheat and rice export restrictions and Nepal's removal of value-added tax exemptions and price support for select food items. Nonfood inflation averaged 8.6% as prices rose for transportation, health care, education, housing, and utilities on rising oil prices and growing demand for these services. Average inflation decelerated to 6.4% in the first 6 months of FY2024 in line with subdued oil and commodity prices.

Nepal Rastra Bank, the central bank, tightened monetary policy in FY2023 to curb rising inflation and pressure on foreign exchange reserves. It raised

the policy rate and rolled back its lending to banks, which had increased fivefold during the COVID-19 pandemic, leading to a surge in market interest rates. Consequently, private sector credit growth slowed to 4.6% in FY2023 from 13.3% a year earlier. Nevertheless, broad money (M2) growth increased to 11.2% on increased borrowing by the government and more net foreign assets held by banks (Figure 2.19.4). As inflation moderated and foreign exchange reserves increased, the central bank lowered the policy rate by 100 basis points to 5.5% from December 2023. This has marginally softened commercial interest rates (Figure 2.19.5).

Figure 2.19.4 Credit and Broad Money Growth

Growth in credit to the private sector slowed in FY2023 as credit to the government increased.

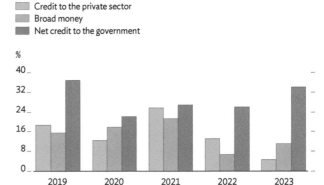

Note: Years are fiscal years ending in mid-July of that year.
Source: Nepal Rastra Bank. 2023. *Recent Macroeconomic Situation.*

Figure 2.19.5 Weighted Average Commercial Bank Interest Rates

Interest rates have trended downward so far in fiscal 2024.

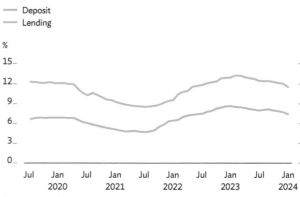

Source: Nepal Rastra Bank. 2024. *Recent Macroeconomic Situation.*

The FY2023 fiscal deficit widened to 6.1% of GDP from 3.2% a year earlier on sharp revenue shortfalls (Figure 2.19.6). Central government revenue fell to 16.6% of GDP as both direct and indirect tax collection weakened, mainly because of lower imports. Recurrent expenditures decreased marginally, largely owing to reduced fiscal transfers from the federal government to subnational governments.

Figure 2.19.6 Fiscal Indicators

The FY2023 deficit widened as revenues declined sharply.

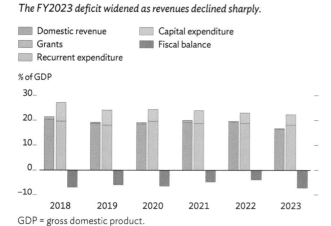

GDP = gross domestic product.
Note: Years are fiscal years ending in mid-July of that year.
Source: Ministry of Finance. Budget Speech 2023.

The current account deficit narrowed to 1.4% of GDP in FY2023, reflecting both an easing trade deficit and buoyant remittance inflows. Imports of goods declined because of credit controls and a ban on imports of some nonessential and luxury items. Exports of goods also decreased as India lowered its tariffs on refined edible oil imports, eroding Nepal's advantage from its tax-exempt export of edible oil to that country. Nevertheless, the merchandise trade deficit narrowed by 22.2%. Imports of services rose on an increased number of students traveling abroad for education, but this was outweighed by rising remittances, which grew by 12.1% in FY2023 as more workers migrated for employment overseas. Consequently, the current account deficit narrowed massively by 89.2% (Figure 2.19.7). Coupled with broadly stable net financial inflows, foreign exchange reserves increased to $11.7 billion, providing 10.0 months of import cover—a marked improvement from 6.9 months a year earlier (Figure 2.19.8). Reserves rose to $13.7 billion, or 12.1 months of import cover, in the first 6 months of FY2024 on stable financial inflows.

Figure 2.19.7 Current Account Indicators

The balance of payments improved with lower imports, higher remittances, and stable financial inflows.

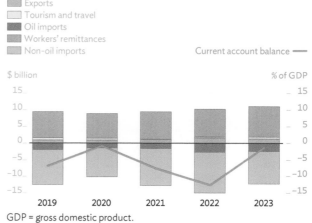

GDP = gross domestic product.
Note: Years are fiscal years ending in mid-July of that year.
Source: Nepal Rastra Bank. 2023. *Recent Macroeconomic Situation.*

Figure 2.19.8 Gross International Reserves and Foreign Exchange Adequacy

Foreign exchange reserves rose markedly in FY2023.

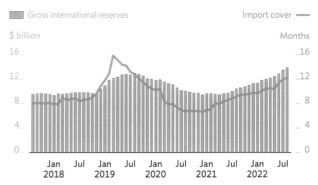

Note: Years are fiscal years ending in mid-July of that year.
Source: Nepal Rastra Bank. 2024. *Recent Macroeconomic Situation.*

Public debt increased to 41.3% of GDP in FY2023. Growth in total public debt has moderated since 2021 with the tapering of one-off COVID-19 expenses (Figure 2.19.9). However, domestic debt increased by 14.3% in FY2023 as the government ramped up borrowing to finance its burgeoning expenditures. External debt rose by 6.6%, and external debt service averaged 7.7% of exports during FY2019–FY2023. Despite the rise in public debt, Nepal's risk of debt distress is low, as the ratio of external debt to GDP remains low, as does that of external debt service to exports.

Figure 2.19.9 Public Debt

Relative to GDP, external public debt has stabilized but domestic public debt has risen.

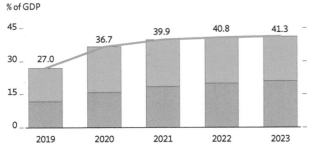

GDP = gross domestic product.
Sources: National Statistics Office; Financial Comptroller General Office; Public Debt Management Office.

Economic Prospects

GDP growth is forecast to accelerate to 3.6% in FY2024 (Table 2.19.1). The lingering weakness in domestic demand that continued in the first quarter of FY2024 will gradually dissipate in the remainder of the fiscal year as government investment outlays accelerate. Private consumption expenditure will rise as remittance inflow strengthens and prices moderate, while private investment expenditure will expand on monetary easing and financial sector reforms encouraging term loans. After contracting by 20.2% in FY2023 and a slow start in FY2024, public investment is expected to expand by 1.5% under the FY2024 budget as development projects are implemented. Overall fiscal policy will support growth despite the deficit being slated to decline to about 3.0% of GDP from 6.1% in FY2023. Exports will rise on higher electricity exports as Nepal continues to expand its

production and transmission infrastructure. However, merchandise imports, particularly of capital goods, will rise as capital expenditure ramps up, and service imports will rise on higher transport payments and travel costs for Nepalis going abroad. On balance, net exports will subtract from growth.

Gradual relaxation of monetary policy in FY2024 and improving consumer and investor confidence will stimulate economic activity. Key areas of the economy that contracted in FY2023, notably manufacturing and construction, have begun to expand, and all production sectors are expected to grow in FY2024. Industry will grow more rapidly than in FY2023 as capital spending by the government is ramped up in the second half of the fiscal year, and as an additional 900 megawatts of hydroelectricity comes online by the end of FY2024. Service sector growth will also likely accelerate as credit controls ease, interest rates further decrease, and tourism revenues expand. Agriculture growth may increase marginally from 2.7% in FY2023 to 2.8% as a record rice harvest is tempered by a shortfall in winter crops and other agricultural production, given the expectation of deficient rainfall this season.

GDP growth is expected to pick up to 4.8% in FY2025. Increased capital expenditure and continued progress in tourism and related services will push growth higher, assuming a favorable harvest. The successful conclusion of the International Monetary Fund's third review of the Extended Credit Facility on 14 December 2023 showed Nepal's medium-term outlook to be still favorable as strategic investments in infrastructure, especially in the energy sector, will support growth.

Inflation is forecast to moderate in FY2024 and FY2025. Given expected moderation in both international oil prices and inflation in India, the deceleration of inflation that began in the first half of FY2024 is expected to continue in the rest of the year. Inflation will average 6.5% in this fiscal year and decelerate to 6.0% in FY2025, assuming that the harvest is normal and oil prices are subdued.

The current account balance is forecast to fall into deficit in FY2024 after registering a surplus in the first half of the year. As the trade deficit contracted by 4.7% year on year in the first 6 months of FY2024,

Table 2.19.1 Selected Economic Indicators, %

Growth will accelerate in 2024 and 2025 as inflation declines.

	2022	2023	2024	2025
GDP growth	5.6	1.9	3.6	4.8
Inflation	6.3	7.7	6.5	6.0

GDP = gross domestic product.
Note: Years are fiscal years ending in mid-July of that year.
Sources: Government and Asian Development Bank estimates.

and as workers' remittances expanded by 22.6% year on year, the current account recorded a surplus of $1.2 billion. However, amid stable remittance inflows and higher imports in the remainder of the fiscal year, the FY2024 current account deficit is forecast at 0.7% of GDP. It will widen to 1.9% of GDP in FY2025 as imports increase, pushing up the deficit in goods trade, and net service payments expand on higher transport and outbound travel.

The economic outlook faces several downside risks. A downturn in the global economy would affect Nepal's tourism and remittance receipts. Any intensified geopolitical turmoil causing supply disruptions that push up global inflation and tighten global financial conditions could lead to a tightening of domestic monetary policy, undermining investment and consumption, and dragging down growth. Delays in the implementation of public projects could weigh heavily on growth as well. As Nepal is always at high risk from natural hazards, catastrophes can substantially reduce economic growth.

Policy Challenge—Trade Facilitation through Customs Reform and Modernization

Nepal needs to ramp up its trade facilitation efforts as it graduates from least-developed-country (LDC) status in 2026. Graduation will likely affect access to its traditional exports market, as Nepal will no longer enjoy preferential tariffs for LDCs. A 2022 International Trade Centre report titled *Nepal after LDC Graduation: New Avenues for Exports* indicates that graduation could result in the loss of export revenue but suggests that customs reform may offset some of these losses.

Some reforms have already been implemented since 2003. These reforms have helped align customs policies and legal documents with international best practices, automate some customs procedures, and build capacity in the customs administration. The government now plans to move toward paperless customs operations to facilitate foreign trade and make cross-border trade more cost effective and predictable, but further steps are needed.

The government should further automate customs processes and improve customs officials' productivity and the quality of physical infrastructure at border points. First, as suggested by the World Customs Organization's Framework of Standards to Secure and Facilitate Global Trade, the government should facilitate trade by strengthening automated risk-management systems to identify risky consignments even while reducing the physical inspection of goods. This requires installing equipment like scanners and sophisticated X-ray machines at customs offices. The framework recommends that the images thus generated should be tallied with customs declarations through an automated system of customs data. This will help Nepal avert risks, map new risks in key customs operations, and gather intelligence to further strengthen risk management. Second, Nepal must prioritize its training of Department of Customs (DOC) employees. The training program has already helped DOC to execute behind-the-border functions more effectively, but DOC still lacks well-trained people who can make maximum use of modern information and communications technology. Third, Nepal needs high-quality infrastructure at borders to facilitate trade. It has built dry ports in major customs points and integrated check posts, and it plans to build more check posts at major custom points. It should link these facilities with high-quality access roads to remove bottlenecks constraining cargo movement. It should also build logistics facilities such as accredited plant quarantine laboratories at appropriate locations to facilitate exports of herbs, food products, and other agricultural produce.

In sum, Nepal must pursue customs reform that includes hard infrastructure as well as soft reforms. DOC's ongoing customs reform modernization plan, 2022–2026 should be accelerated and strengthened. Requisite resources for these reforms are limited, but several development partners have provided financial and technical support with continued and renewed support to simplify, harmonize, and modernize customs procedures. Nonetheless, Nepal faces challenges to implement reforms smoothly because procurement contracts are poorly executed and DOC management changes frequently. The government should address these systemic issues to facilitate the implementation of reforms, which not only facilitate foreign trade but also help generate more financial resources for development.

PAKISTAN

The economy shrank as floods, uncertainty, and disrupted external support caused public investment to plunge and private investment and industry to contract. Inflation reached a 5-decade high as supply disruption and currency depreciation propelled increases in food and energy prices. If reforms are implemented, growth is forecast to restart gradually this fiscal year and improve slightly next year. Inflation is projected to moderate somewhat this year, and more next year, under stabilization policies. Improving women's financial inclusion is critical to strengthen growth.

Economic Performance

The economy contracted as devastating floods, political unrest, and policy slippage curbed investment, consumption, and production. Real GDP declined by 0.2% in fiscal year 2023 (FY2023, ended 30 June 2023) following 6.2% expansion in FY2022. On the demand side, private consumption growth slipped to 2.4% from 7.1% in FY2022 (Figure 2.20.1), reflecting higher living costs and slower nominal income growth amid a weakening of employment. Limited fiscal resources led to a 31.6% drop in public investment, while private investment fell by 14.6%, in line with the pessimistic outlook. A steep decline in imports from ad hoc import controls allowed net exports to contribute positively to growth.

On the supply side, growth slowed or contracted in all main sectors. Growth in agriculture was halved to 2.3% from 4.3% in FY2022 as cotton and rice output declined (Figure 2.20.2). Less cotton production, scarcity of inputs due to import controls, and political instability and economic uncertainty led industry to contract by 3.8%, reversing expansion by 7.0% in FY2022. Large-scale manufacturing, accounting for nearly half of industry, shrank by 9.9%, while construction declined by 9.2%. With imports, crops, and industry all declining, services stagnated, with growth falling to 0.1% from 6.7% in FY2022.

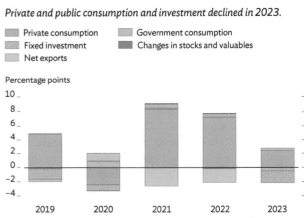

Figure 2.20.1 Demand-Side Contributions to Growth

Private and public consumption and investment declined in 2023.

- Private consumption
- Fixed investment
- Net exports
- Government consumption
- Changes in stocks and valuables

GDP = gross domestic product.
Note: Years are fiscal years ending on 30 June of that year.
Source: Pakistan Bureau of Statistics. National Accounts Tables Base FY2016: Table 9.

Currency depreciation, increases to administered prices, and supply disruptions from floods and import controls caused inflation to soar. Average inflation jumped from 12.2% in FY2022 to a 5-decade high of 29.2%, as increases in food prices, representing more than half of the overall price index, rose from about 13% to nearly 40% (Figure 2.20.3). Core inflation increased to 16.2% in urban areas and 20.6% in rural areas.

This chapter was written by Khadija Ali, Farzana Noshab, and Maleeha Rizwan of the Pakistan Resident Mission, ADB, Islamabad.

Figure 2.20.2 Supply-Side Contributions to Growth

In 2023, growth slowed significantly in agriculture and services while industry contracted.

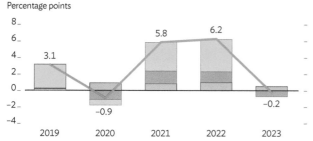

GDP = gross domestic product.

Note: Years are fiscal years ending on 30 June of that year.

Source: Pakistan Bureau of Statistics. National Accounts Tables Base FY2016: Table 6 and 7a.

Figure 2.20.3 Monthly Inflation

Inflation jumped to a 5-decade high in 2023 due to high food and energy price increases.

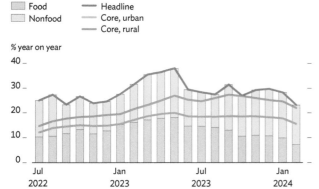

Source: Pakistan Bureau of Statistics. Monthly Review on Price Indices: February 2024.

Monetary policy was tightened to curb inflationary expectations and contain external imbalances. The State Bank of Pakistan, the central bank, raised its policy rate by a cumulative 700 basis points to 22.0% (Figure 2.20.4) and linked interest rates for subsidized credit schemes to the policy rate to strengthen monetary policy transmission. Credit to the private sector declined by 0.8% in FY2023, reversing a rise of 21.1% in FY2022.

The budget deficit showed little change as the government missed major fiscal targets. The fiscal deficit declined slightly from 7.9% of GDP in FY2022 to

Figure 2.20.4 Interest Rates and Inflation

The central bank raised its policy rate sharply as inflation accelerated.

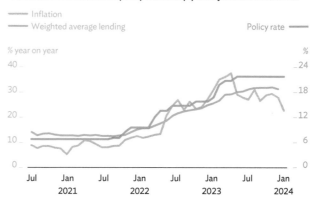

Sources: State Bank of Pakistan. Economic Data; Pakistan Bureau of Statistics. Monthly Review on Price Indices: February 2024.

7.7%, still exceeding both the budget target of 4.9% and the revised target of 6.9% for the supplementary budget passed in February 2023, which included provisions for flood relief and rehabilitation. The primary balance recorded a deficit of 1.0% of GDP, improving on a 3.1% deficit in FY2022 but well short of the targeted 0.2% surplus. Fiscal targets were missed in FY2023 because the economic slowdown and import controls limited revenue to about 11.4% of GDP. Although nontax revenue rose from 1.9% of GDP to 2.1% as the petroleum levy was raised to its statutory limit, a weak economy caused tax revenue to fall from 10.1% of GDP in FY2022 to 9.2%, despite measures implemented in February 2023 raising direct tax revenue by 0.4% of GDP. Despite cuts in noninterest expenditure, mounting interest payments from higher interest rates, a growing stock of public debt, and significant currency depreciation undermined fiscal consolidation efforts and limited the drop in total expenditure to 0.9 percentage points, from 20.0% of GDP in FY2022 to 19.1%.

Stringent import controls aimed at preventing the depletion of foreign exchange reserves slashed the current account deficit. The deficit fell by 87%, from 4.7% of GDP in FY2022 to 0.7% (Figure 2.20.5), despite declines in exports and workers' remittances. Imports of goods and services fell by 29.0% in FY2023 to $60 billion, as the central bank imposed restrictions on foreign exchange to curb rapid depletion of foreign reserves. Administrative restrictions on imports resulted in a scarcity of raw materials and intermediate inputs that, coupled with flood-related crop damage,

Figure 2.20.5 Current Account Components

The current account deficit shrank in 2023 following the imposition of strict import controls.

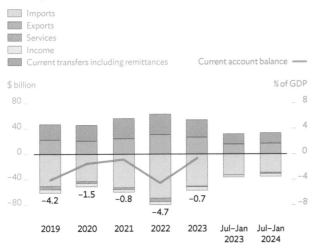

GDP = gross domestic product.
Note: Years are fiscal years ending on 30 June of that year.
Source: State Bank of Pakistan. Economic Data: External Sector. Summary Balance of Payments as per BPM6 - January 2024.

reduced exports. Efforts to manage the exchange rate led to the emergence of a parallel foreign exchange market with a substantial premium over the official exchange rate, prompting some inward remittances and proceeds from service exports to shift to the parallel market. Increased pressure on the currency from tightened foreign currency liquidity in the interbank market led to downgrades by credit rating agencies. Recorded workers' remittances fell by $4.0 billion to $27.3 billion in FY2023 (Figure 2.20.6).

Figure 2.20.6 Remittances

Remittances declined in 2023 as a parallel foreign exchange market emerged.

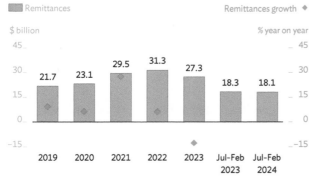

Note: Years are fiscal years ending on 30 June of that year.
Source: State Bank of Pakistan. Economic Data: External Sector. Worker's Remittances.

Foreign reserves declined to critically low levels as suspension of the ongoing International Monetary Fund (IMF) Extended Fund Facility (EFF) slowed official inflows. Despite the cut in the current account deficit, Pakistan's external financing requirements remained high because of large debt repayments. Securing adequate inflows to cover financing needs became a major challenge, as bilateral and multilateral inflows slowed with the suspension of the IMF EFF, requiring debt repayments to be financed largely by drawing down official reserves. Pakistan's access to world financial markets was further constrained by tight global financial conditions and rapid deterioration in its external position. Thus, gross foreign exchange reserves declined by more than half, from $9.8 billion at the end of FY2022 to $4.4 billion a year later. Reserves were restored in July 2023 with the start of a new short-term IMF Stand-By Arrangement (SBA) (Figure 2.20.7).

Figure 2.20.7 Gross Official Reserves and Exchange Rate

International reserves were restored with a short-term International Monetary Fund program in July 2023.

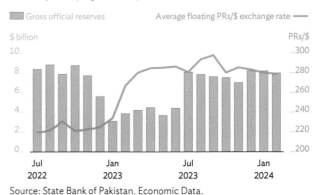

Source: State Bank of Pakistan. Economic Data.

Economic Prospects

Growth is projected to remain subdued in FY2024 and pick up in FY2025, provided economic reforms take effect. Real GDP is projected to grow by 1.9% in FY2024 (Figure 2.20.8), driven by a rebound in private sector investment linked to progress on reform measures and transition to a new and more stable government. An expansion in private consumption and a rise in workers' remittances from a move toward a market-determined exchange rate should buttress growth. However, low confidence,

Figure 2.20.8 Gross Domestic Product Growth

Growth is forecast to restart gradually in 2024 and improve slightly in 2025.

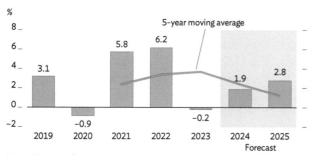

Note: Years are fiscal years ending on 30 June of that year.

Sources: Pakistan Bureau of Statistics. National Accounts Tables Base FY2016: Table 5; Asian Development Bank estimates.

a surge in living costs, and the implementation of tighter macroeconomic policies under the IMF SBA will restrain domestic demand. In FY2025, growth is projected to reach 2.8% (Table 2.20.1), driven by higher confidence, reduced macroeconomic imbalances, adequate progress on structural reforms, greater political stability, and improved external conditions.

Table 2.20.1 Selected Economic Indicators, %

Growth will revive this year and accelerate next year, with inflation declining.

	2022	2023	2024	2025
GDP growth	6.2	−0.2	1.9	2.8
Inflation	12.2	29.2	25.0	15.0

GDP = gross domestic product.

Note: Years are fiscal years ending on 30 June of that year.

Sources: Pakistan Bureau of Statistics, National Accounts Tables (Base FY2016), Table 6; Pakistan Bureau of Statistics, Price Statistics, Monthly Price Indices (Base FY2016); Asian Development Bank estimates.

On the supply side, growth will be led by post-flood recovery in agriculture. Output will rise from a low base on improved weather conditions and a government package of subsidized credit and farm inputs that will support expanded area under cultivation and improved yields. Higher farm output will help expand manufacturing, which will also benefit from the increased availability of critical imported inputs. Large-scale manufacturing expanded in 3 of the first 6 months of FY2024. Higher crop output and some improvement in global growth are expected

to support recovery in industrial output in the latter half of the year. Construction will remain weak due to elevated construction costs, higher tax rates on property transfers implemented in the FY2024 budget, and rationalization of public investment to consolidate the fiscal position. Growth in services is projected to strengthen in FY2024 as recovery in agriculture and industry benefit services.

Inflation will remain elevated at about 25.0% in FY2024, driven by higher energy prices, but is expected to ease in FY2025 (Figure 2.20.9). While improvement in food supplies and moderation of inflation expectations will likely ease inflationary pressures, further increases in energy prices envisaged under the IMF SBA are projected to keep inflation high. Headline consumer inflation increased to 28.0% in the first 8 months of FY2024, mainly from hikes in administered energy prices. Although improved supplies have tempered food inflation, it remains high, driven largely by rising prices for energy and inputs to agriculture. Core inflation also remains elevated, reflecting domestic recovery and the pass-through of upward adjustments in energy prices.

Figure 2.20.9 Inflation Outlook

Inflation is projected to decline this year and next.

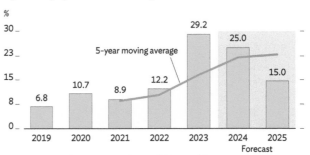

Note: Years are fiscal years ending on 30 June of that year.

Sources: Pakistan Bureau of Statistics, Price Statistics: Monthly Review on Price Indices - February 2024; Asian Development Bank estimates.

Headline inflation is expected to decrease to 15.0% in FY2025 as progress on macroeconomic stabilization restores confidence. The central bank has maintained a tightened monetary policy, keeping the policy interest rate at 22.0% in response to persistent inflationary pressures and external imbalances. The central bank has committed to keeping an appropriately tight policy to lower inflation to its medium-term target range of 5%–7%.

The government projects significant fiscal consolidation in the medium term, supported by increased revenues and rationalized spending. The goal is to achieve a primary surplus of 0.4% of GDP and an overall deficit of 7.5% of GDP in FY2024, with both declining gradually in subsequent years. Considerable progress toward the goal occurred during the first half of the fiscal year, with a primary surplus of 1.7% of GDP and an overall deficit of 2.3% (Figure 2.20.10). Total revenue increased to 6.5% of GDP in the first half of FY2024 from 5.6% in the same period in FY2023, mainly from higher petroleum levy receipts and increased profit transfers from the central bank. Tax collection increased by 29.5%, as reforms in the personal income tax, higher taxes on property transfers, and the reintroduction of taxes on cash withdrawals from banks and the issuance of bonus shares raised direct tax collections. Revenue mobilization is expected to strengthen in the medium term, reflecting planned reforms to broaden the tax base. A rise in interest payments equal to 1.0% of GDP from higher interest rates boosted expenditure to 8.8% of GDP in the first half of FY2024 from 7.6% a year earlier. Fiscal consolidation will also benefit from plans to rationalize current expenditure.

The relaxation of import restrictions, coupled with economic recovery, is expected to widen the current account deficit. The current account deficit fell to $1.1 billion in the first 7 months of FY2024 from $3.8 billion in the same period in FY2023, as the merchandise trade deficit narrowed by 30.8% (Figure 2.20.11). Merchandise imports declined by 11.1% from weak demand growth, lower global food and fuel prices, and higher domestic production of cotton and wheat. Merchandise exports rose by 9.3%. However, imports are expected to expand during the year as domestic demand strengthens and stabilization of the currency market makes it easier for firms to import inputs. Thus, the current account deficit is projected to widen to 1.5% of GDP in FY2024. A transition toward a market-determined exchange rate is expected to encourage remittance inflows through official channels, thus enhancing the economy's resilience under future external shocks. However, Pakistan will continue to face challenges from substantial new external financing requirements and the rollover of old debt, exacerbated by tight global financial conditions.

Figure 2.20.10 Fiscal Indicators

Total revenue increased in H1 FY2024 due to higher tax and nontax revenue collections.

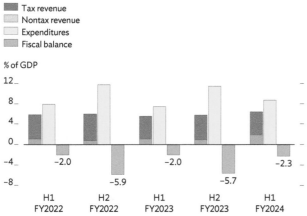

GDP = gross domestic product, H = half.
Note: Years are fiscal years ending on 30 June of that year.
Source: Ministry of Finance. Pakistan Summary of Consolidated Federal and Provincial Fiscal Operations 2022–23 and 2023–24.

Figure 2.20.11 Trade Balance

The merchandise trade deficit shrank in 2024 as exports increased while imports declined.

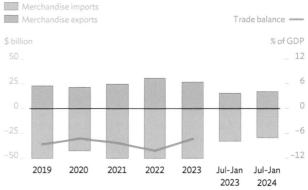

GDP = gross domestic product.
Note: Years are fiscal years ending on 30 June of that year.
Source: State Bank of Pakistan. Economic Data: External Sector. Summary Balance of Payments as per BPM6 - January 2024.

The outlook is uncertain, with high risks on the downside. Political uncertainty that affects macroeconomic policy making will remain a key risk to the sustainability of stabilization and reform efforts. On the external front, potential supply chain disruptions from escalation of the conflict in the Middle East would weigh on the economy. With Pakistan's large external financing requirements and weak external buffers, disbursement from multilateral and bilateral partners remains crucial. However, these inflows could be hampered by lapses in policy implementation. Further IMF support for a medium-term reform agenda would considerably improve market sentiment and catalyze affordable external financing from other sources.

Policy Challenge—Closing a Financial Inclusion Gender Gap

Pakistan has one of the lowest financial inclusion rates for women in the world. While Pakistan's overall financial inclusion has improved, the gender gap in account ownership more than doubled over the past decade, reaching 32% in 2021. The World Data Lab estimates that, without immediate action, this gap will widen to over 42% by 2030. In a World Bank survey encompassing 135 economies, Pakistan ranked fourth lowest overall, and third lowest in Asia, on female financial inclusion. More than three out of every five Pakistani women remain unbanked.

Pakistani women face multiple barriers when accessing finance. On the demand side, low female labor force participation means that most women lack a steady income stream and are largely dependent on male family members for their financial needs. Social and religious traditions influence gender roles, with women viewed as homemakers rather than breadwinners. The absence of formal income and proper documentation makes it difficult for women to open and maintain standard bank accounts, as banks consider them high risk. Moreover, low literacy levels and insufficient financial education undermine women's ability to utilize formal banking channels and render them more susceptible to fraud. Rural women are further marginalized, as their access to banks is even more limited due to long distances and commute times.

On the supply side, expanding women's financial inclusion requires strong will and a prioritized push for legal and regulatory change. New rules must support gender-inclusive finance while easing persistent liquidity constraints in the sector. The central bank's Banking on Equality Policy is a monumental step in advancing women's financial inclusion. The Securities and Exchange Commission of Pakistan has also initiated significant steps toward refining the regulatory framework for nonbank finance companies, including microfinance institutions that traditionally target women in Pakistan.

Regulators should continue to play a critical role in providing an enabling regulatory environment. They should continue to influence action by financial service providers to promote gender-inclusive finance and incentivize the country's financial institutions to integrate a gender focus into the national financial services industry and widen access to digital financial services, including mobile banking, digital wallets, and banks on wheels. Financial institutions can also promote greater gender diversity at their access points and mandate more robust gender-disaggregated data collection and target setting. Commercial banks and fintech enterprises should continue to dedicate time and resources to better understand the needs of women customers and the strategic value of women's market, organize gender-sensitivity training for their staff, and design women-centric products and services.

Gender-inclusive opportunities for smaller enterprises and microfinance should be expanded further. This can involve credit guarantee schemes, export financing facilities, business development and financial literacy training, tax incentives to banks, and digitalized business registration processes. In addition, the sector would benefit from the continued growth of a gender bonds market to channel much-needed finance to women-owned businesses.

SRI LANKA

GDP contracted in 2023, but green shoots of recovery are emerging. Growth revived in the second half of 2023 and is expected to continue in 2024 and 2025. Inflation decelerated to single digits last year following a peak in 2022 and will remain below 10% in 2024 and 2025. Challenges remain, and the upcoming electoral cycle must not delay the reforms required to address the recent economic crisis. Sri Lanka needs to address vulnerability to poverty to ensure inclusive growth.

Economic Performance

Signs of recovery are emerging with stronger reserves and currency appreciation. Agriculture, industry, and services recorded growth year on year in the second half of 2023, and inflation decelerated. Official reserves excluding a People's Bank of China currency swap strengthened from $500 million at the end of 2022 to $3.0 billion at the end of December 2023 on multilateral funding and Central Bank of Sri Lanka net purchases of $1.75 billion (Figure 2.21.1). Foreign exchange inflow improved, and continuing suspensions of debt service on commercial and official

bilateral public debt helped reduce outflow, easing pressure on the balance of payments. After depreciating sharply in 2022, the Sri Lankan rupee appreciated by 12.1% against the dollar in 2023 as the country moved to a flexible exchange rate (Figure 2.21.2).

An International Monetary Fund (IMF) Extended Fund Facility program approved in March 2023 is making progress. Following approval by the IMF executive board of the 48-month, $3.0 billion Extended Fund Facility arrangement, a total of

Figure 2.21.1 Gross Official Reserves

Usable reserves inched up in 2023 and reached $3.0 billion by year end.

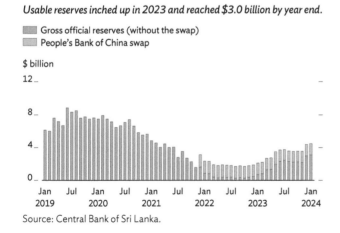

Source: Central Bank of Sri Lanka.

Figure 2.21.2 Central Bank Net Foreign Exchange Purchases and the Exchange Rate

The central bank recorded net monthly dollar purchases in most of 2023.

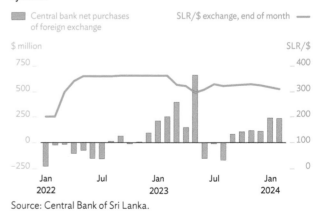

Source: Central Bank of Sri Lanka.

This chapter was written by Lakshini Fernando, Nirukthi P. Kariyawasam, and Dinuk de Silva of the Sri Lanka Resident Mission, ADB, Colombo.

$670 million was disbursed in two tranches in March and December 2023. In September 2023, the IMF released a governance diagnostic report on Sri Lanka, its first in Asia, highlighting systemic and severe governance weaknesses and vulnerability to corruption across state functions. In February 2024, the government issued an action plan to address these vulnerabilities.

The economy contracted in the first half of 2023 but grew by 3.0% in the second half. The agriculture and services sectors grew 2.5% and 7.0%, respectively, compared with the first half of 2023 while the industry sector contracted 0.1%. With improved harvests of rice, fruit, vegetables, and spices, agriculture grew by 2.6% in 2023 despite inclement weather dampening the sector's performance. Industry shrank by 9.2% as manufacturing contracted by 3.2% and construction by 20.8%, constrained by higher taxes and low demand. Despite accommodation and food and beverage services increasing by 26.0% as tourist arrivals improved, the whole service sector declined by 0.2%, buffeted by higher direct and indirect taxes and dampened consumer and investor sentiment (Figure 2.21.3).

Weak domestic demand dragged down economic performance. Consumption fell by 2.2% in 2023, with private consumption declining by 1.6%, constrained by higher prices, and government consumption declining by 5.4%, constrained by tight fiscal space. Gross capital formation also declined by 7.9%, as gross fixed capital formation declined by 9.3%. Growth in net exports of goods and services remained positive because of import restrictions in the first half of 2023 (Figure 2.21.4).

Headline inflation measured by the Colombo consumer price index dropped to an average of 17.4% in 2023, compared to 46.4% in 2022. Primary contributors were lower fuel prices, subdued demand, better supply, and tight monetary policy measures until mid-2023, including high policy rates and low liquidity injections. Food inflation eased to an average of 12.1% compared to 64.7% in 2022 and a peak of 94.9% in September 2022 (Figure 2.21.5). Core inflation declined from its peak of 50.2% in September 2022 to an average of 14.5% in 2023. As inflation eased, the central bank reduced its policy rates by 700 basis points from June 2023 to March 2024. The statutory reserve ratio was also reduced for the first time in almost 2 years, by 2.0 percentage points. With market

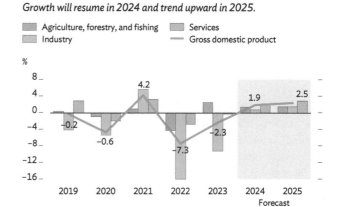

Figure 2.21.3 Gross Domestic Product Growth by Sector

Growth will resume in 2024 and trend upward in 2025.

Sources: Department of Census and Statistics of Sri Lanka; Asian Development Bank estimates.

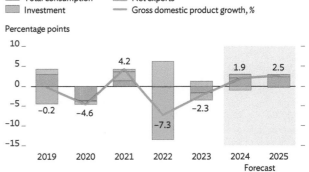

Figure 2.21.4 Demand-Side Contributions to Growth

Domestic demand contracted in 2023 as total consumption declined.

Sources: Department of Census and Statistics of Sri Lanka; Asian Development Bank estimates.

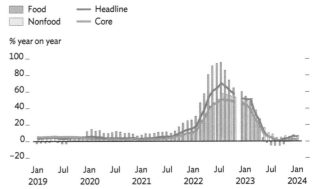

Figure 2.21.5 Inflation

Inflation moderated toward the central bank target range.

Note: In January 2023, the Department of Census and Statistics revised the inflation base measured by the Colombo consumer price index from 2013 to 2021, as indicated by a disconnect in the figure.

Source: Department of Census and Statistics of Sri Lanka.

interest rates falling below 15% and early signs of an economic recovery, the contraction in credit demand eased (Figure 2.21.6).

The finance sector has stabilized, but vulnerabilities remain. Banks have maintained capital buffers in line with regulatory requirements under Basel III, resulting in a core equity Tier 1 ratio of 13.5% and capital adequacy ratio of 16.3% in the third quarter (Q3) of 2023. However, the stage 3 loan ratio, which allows early recognition of nonperforming loans, was high at 11.6% in Q4 2022, compared with 8.4% in Q1 2022,

and even higher at 13.4% in Q3 2023 (Figure 2.21.7). Although adequate provision for impairment has been made for international sovereign bonds held by banks, any rise in impaired loans that would require additional provisioning, and any unexpected economic shock, could further stress the sector.

Revenue-based fiscal consolidation under the IMF Extended Fund Facility was a central area of focus in 2023. Following tax increases implemented in 2022, the authorities raised personal income tax rates and introduced narrower brackets at the start of 2023. As a result, the IMF estimates government revenue and grants to have reached 10.2% of GDP, improving from 8.3% in 2022. Expenditure is expected to reach 19.0% of GDP, marginally higher than 18.5% in 2022. Expenditure remained high because of interest paid on domestic refinancing. Higher revenue coupled with higher nominal GDP lowered the budget deficit to 8.8% of GDP in 2023 from 10.2% in 2022 (Figure 2.21.8). Official data indicates a primary surplus of SLRs124 billion from January to September 2023, amounting to 0.6% of GDP. This greatly improved compared to an IMF program primary deficit target of SLRs160 billion and was a key indicator of the progress in reforms thus far.

Total public debt increased as debt restructuring negotiations continued. Domestic public debt reached 63.4% of GDP in Q3 2023 from 60.8% in 2022. The total public debt-to-GDP ratio increased

Figure 2.21.6 Private Sector Credit Growth versus the Prime Lending Rate

The contraction in credit demand eased as interest rates declined.

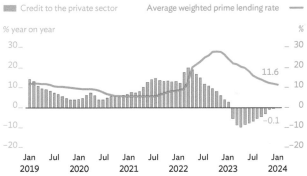

Note: The average weighted prime lending rate is compiled weekly by the Central Bank of Sri Lanka using weekly lending rates commercial banks offered to their prime customers.

Source: Central Bank of Sri Lanka.

Figure 2.21.7 Impaired Loan Ratio

A rising impaired loan ratio is a cause for concern.

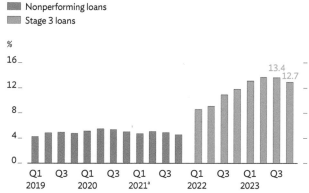

Note: The average weighted prime lending rate is compiled weekly by the Central Bank of Sri Lanka using weekly lending rates commercial banks offered to their prime customers.

a The central bank discontinued in 2022 its calculation of nonperforming loans and introduced instead stage 3 loan classification, which gives banks more discretion to provide against high-risk assets even before default.

Source: Central Bank of Sri Lanka. Financial sector statistics.

Figure 2.21.8 Central Government Finances

Both the primary and the overall fiscal balance improved in 2023.

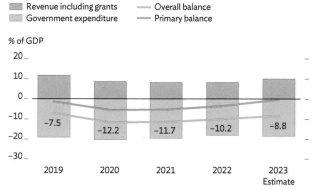

GDP = gross domestic product, IMF = International Monetary Fund.

Note: IMF forecasts used for 2023. Data on government expenditure for 2019 and 2020 are from the October 2021 edition of the IMF World Economic Outlook Database and adjusted for the new GDP base, 2015 =100.

Sources: Central Bank of Sri Lanka; IMF. World Economic Outlook Database, October 2021; Ministry of Finance; IMF estimates.

from 89.0% at the end of 2019 to 125.7% by the end of 2022, at which point central government debt reached 115.5% of GDP. Public debt declined to 115.7% at the end of 2023, as growth in debt was outpaced by that of nominal GDP due to inflation. An agreement in principle was reached with the official creditor committee in November 2023, and a preliminary agreement was reached in October 2023 with the Export–Import Bank of China regarding restructuring public external debt held by them. Domestic debt optimization was completed in 2023. An agreement in principle with commercial creditors has yet to be reached.

Sri Lanka's current account surplus in 2023, the first surplus since 1977, is estimated equal to 1.4% of GDP (Figure 2.21.9). It came as imports fell and tourism and migrant remittances grew. Merchandise exports recorded a 9.1% decline in 2023 because of subdued global demand for garments, but tourism earnings rose sharply to $2.1 billion, up by 82.0% from 2022, as tourist arrivals rebounded by 107%, albeit remaining below the 2017–2018 average of 2.2 million arrivals (Figure 2.21.10). In the first 9 months of 2023, export earnings from transport services also increased by 140%. Remittance inflow rose by 57.5% to reach $6.0 billion, still below the pre-pandemic average of $7.0 billion in 2017–2019 (Figure 2.21.11). Imports fell by 8.1% as import restrictions were imposed for most of the first half of 2023 and as lower purchasing power and higher taxes dampened import demand.

Figure 2.21.9 Key Balance of Payments Indicators

The current account improved in 2023 as the trade deficit narrowed.

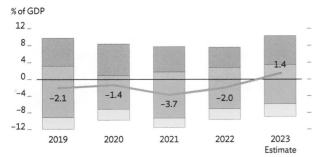

GDP = gross domestic product.
Sources: Central Bank of Sri Lanka; Department of Census and Statistics of Sri Lanka; Asian Development Bank estimates for 2023.

Figure 2.21.10 Tourist Arrivals

Tourist arrivals sharply improved in 2023.

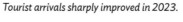

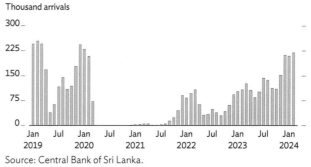

Source: Central Bank of Sri Lanka.

Figure 2.21.11 Monthly Remittance Inflow

Remittance inflow improved in 2023 but remained below the recent yearly average.

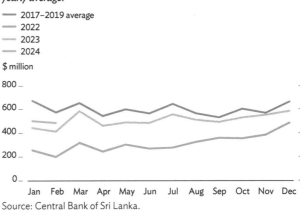

Source: Central Bank of Sri Lanka.

Economic Prospects

The economy will recover gradually in 2024 and 2025. Key forward-looking indicators like the purchasing managers' index and the industrial, index of production, are improving. Construction, stalled during the height of the crisis, is resuming but will be tempered by an increase in the value-added tax, which will raise raw material prices and dampen housing construction. The service sector will be supported by higher tourist arrivals and receipts, and the finance sector by lower interest rates and consequently higher demand for credit. Industry will see a resumption in construction projects and higher manufacturing, and agriculture will be supported by cheaper fertilizer. However, the higher costs of raw materials, higher taxes, and unpredictable weather will likely weigh on growth across sectors. With gradual economic stabilization, consumer and business sentiment will improve, leading to a cautious recovery in private consumption and investment, but this is likely to be dampened by the higher prices following the value-added tax increase and uncertainty from the electoral cycle. Limited fiscal space will likely restrain government expenditure. With the removal of most import restrictions in the second half of 2023, net exports of goods and services are likely to turn negative in 2024.

Against this background and with the low base effect from 2023, economic growth is forecast at 1.9% in 2024 and 2.5% in 2025 (Table 2.21.1). The resumption of growth hinges on the assumed continuation of reforms and better supply conditions. Crucial reforms include the expected enactment in 2024 of a public financial management act, which will strengthen fiscal discipline, and a debt management law to mitigate medium-term refinancing risks, as well as the completion of external debt restructuring.

Table 2.21.1 Selected Economic Indicators, %

Growth will resume and accelerate, and inflation will moderate.

	2022	2023	2024	2025
GDP growth	−7.3	−2.3	1.9	2.5
Inflation	46.4	17.4	7.5	5.5

GDP = gross domestic product.
Note: In January 2023, the Department of Census and Statistics revised the inflation base measured by the Colombo consumer price index from 2013 to 2021.
Sources: Department of Census of Statistics of Sri Lanka; Asian Development Bank estimates.

Inflation is expected to average 7.5% in 2024 and fall within the central bank target range in 2025. Weak transmission to market interest rates and higher taxes will dampen growth in domestic demand, pushing inflation down substantially in 2024 and into the central bank's target range of 4%–6% in 2025. Consumer demand will see a gradual pickup as credit demand improves, adding inflationary pressure.

High recurrent expenditure will add pressure on the fiscal balance. The IMF projects total revenue to increase to 13.0% of GDP in 2024 from an estimated 10.2% of GDP in 2023 through higher direct and indirect taxes and efforts to widen the taxpayer base. However, the domestic debt burden

will increase interest costs to 8.4% of GDP in 2024, resulting in total expenditure increasing to 20.3% of GDP in 2024 despite lower capital expenditure. The recapitalization of banks will add another 1.4% of GDP in expenditure. Public sector salaries and interest costs are expected to account for 54.1% of expenditure in 2024. Commitment to maintaining a primary surplus is expected to continue, but the fiscal deficit is likely to widen because the government expects recurrent expenditure to increase from 15.8% of GDP in 2023 to 16.8% in 2024. Any divestment of state-owned assets under consideration should improve the fiscal balance.

The current account surplus will narrow in 2024 due to an increasing trade deficit. Despite improving business sentiment, exports are expected to remain flat due to subdued global demand. The loosening of import restrictions in 2023 and possibly those on vehicle imports in 2024 will push imports higher, though limited purchasing power will continue to curtail significant import demand. The service and transfer balance will improve with a rebound in tourism, growth in other export services from improved business confidence, and strong remittance inflow, but will be tempered by a growing deficit in goods trade, narrowing the current account surplus. External debt servicing may resume in 2024 if the external debt restructuring is completed which may exert pressure on the Sri Lankan rupee that has thus far appreciated in 2024.

Risks to the outlook tend to the downside. Among them, the most important is uncertainty associated with the upcoming elections, including any possible impact on fiscal policy and reform implementation. Commitment to the reform program will also be tested by efforts to balance public sentiment with the implementation of the IMF program. Delays in the completion of a debt restructuring agreement and any barriers to passing key legislation could dampen sentiment and derail growth. Sri Lanka is reeling from high outmigration, particularly by the young, leading to higher skills mismatch, which could impact forecasts if prolonged. Weakness in the finance sector may prolong a full recovery. Additionally, weather vagaries could adversely impact agriculture and food security. Weaker-than-expected growth in key export markets could lead to increasingly tepid demand for exports, and geopolitical uncertainty could impinge on growth.

Policy Challenge—Addressing Poverty Vulnerability as the Economy Recovers

The pandemic and the subsequent socioeconomic crisis reversed more than a decade of gains against poverty. The World Bank estimates that the $3.65/day poverty rate rose to 25.0% in 2022 from 11.3% in 2019 and 23.8% in 2009/10 and forecasts the rate to reach 27.5% in 2024 (Figure 2.21.12). The multidimensional vulnerability index developed by the United Nations Development Programme estimates that over half of the population faces overlapping vulnerabilities beyond income that lead them into poverty traps; 82% of such vulnerable people live in rural areas. Rural residents, in particular workers on large plantations, suffered from loss of economic opportunity, and the urban poor faced the dual vulnerability of inconsistent earnings with limited private coping mechanisms and restricted access to social protection. The impact of severe supply shortages and elevated inflation had disproportionate effects on households headed by women, the elderly, children, the disabled, and other vulnerable groups. While inflation has subsided to single digits, prices continued to be elevated, with the average index 91.8% higher in 2023 than in 2021. Wages have failed to keep up with rising prices, prolonging the squeeze on purchasing power and pushing more people into poverty. Rising maternal and child malnutrition poses a serious threat to human capital development and growth.

The near-term priority during economic recovery is to lay institutional and structural frameworks for an inclusive social protection system. In the absence of a cohesive social protection strategy and governance mechanism, programs in the past have been fragmented, with low coverage, poor targeting, high inclusion and exclusion errors, and low payments. In 2023, however, the government introduced the Aswesuma program to consolidate over 25 state-sponsored cash-transfer programs that were previously managed by several government agencies. The new social protection program covers nearly 40% of the population at various income levels and includes a self-registry database for a more objective and streamlined selection process aimed at minimizing leakage. This program can be further strengthened with increased individual support, better forward planning and an effective graduation mechanism with technical and life skills training, better financial literacy education, and enhanced social and financial inclusion. The government must establish a comprehensive long-term strategy for poverty eradication that monitors progress and incorporates regular social dialogue to ensure the representation and participation of all stakeholders.

Addressing gender inequality is a key priority. In an economically active population of 8.5 million in 2022, female labor force participation was only 32.1%, down from 33.6% in 2018 prior to the economic crisis. Key reasons for this include a lack of safe and affordable childcare facilities, inadequate provision for flexible working hours, onerous household responsibilities and care duties socially imposed on women, and public transport inadequacies for women. While the private sector has addressed these shortcomings to some extent, the government can tackle gender inequality through a more supportive framework for female labor participation by introducing flexible work hours and mandating equal pay. Reforming labor laws is also essential to formalize informal employment and protect workers from exploitation. Given the absence of an employment-linked support system, a contributory unemployment insurance scheme and related laws may be considered.

The government should enhance access to public services to mitigate inequalities and better target poverty alleviation efforts. The integration of social protection programs with other public services such as education and health care would ensure universal

Figure 2.21.12 Poverty Rate

Back-to-back shocks to the economy since 2020 have eroded a decade of gains against poverty.

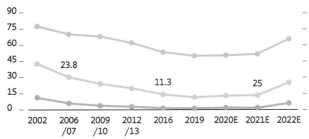

E = estimate, PPP = purchasing power parity.
Source: World Bank. Poverty and Inequality Platform.

access to essential services, improve targeting and coverage, and expand social inclusion. In this regard, government efforts to revamp education policy with updated curricula, improved teacher training, and digitalization are welcome. While the state-sponsored universal health-care coverage and subsidized medicine provide considerable support to the poor, the government can better leverage the health-care system for more targeted measures and promote health insurance programs to protect the poor and vulnerable. The government should intensify efforts to train and retain health and care staff, particularly considering significant outmigration by professionals. Given fiscal constraints, expanding access to services could be achieved by enabling greater private sector participation in essential services. Investments in infrastructure for water supply, road connectivity, and energy are needed to address inequality in income and opportunity, and in access to resources.

Creating jobs and fostering sustainable livelihoods would go a long way toward alleviating poverty. This can begin by improving workforce productivity, particularly in agriculture, which employs 27% of the labor force but contributes little to GDP. The government must prioritize modernizing agriculture by resolving issues regarding farmland, investing to improve land productivity, and promoting greater value addition and diversification in agricultural exports. Policies targeting structural economic transformation—by promoting investment in manufacturing and technology, digital inclusion, the adoption of global best practices in industry, and skill enhancement—would ensure increased job creation outside of agriculture with high productivity and thus bolster worker earning capacity across the economy. To catalyze economic expansion, development, and job creation, the government should promote private sector participation through consistent policies and the regulatory, legal, and institutional support necessary for private sector development. Embracing pro-poor tourism policies by providing the necessary regulatory support and capacity building would ensure optimal transfers of benefits to local communities.

OUTHEAST ASIA

Brunei Darussalam
Cambodia
Indonesia
Lao PDR
Malaysia
Myanmar
Philippines
Singapore
Thailand
Timor-Leste
Viet Nam

BRUNEI DARUSSALAM

Growth is forecast to accelerate in 2024, partly due to a pickup that started in the second half of 2023. A rebound in services underpinned the economic recovery over the last 3 years, but the outlook for the next 2 years depends on recovery in the oil and gas sector. Headline inflation has been subdued recently, but food prices remain high. Fiscal consolidation and revenue diversification are needed in the medium term to ensure fiscal equity.

Economic Performance

The economy had robust growth in the fourth quarter of 2023. The long-subdued oil and gas sector recorded its first growth in the past 3 years, pushing GDP growth up by 6.8% (Figures 2.22.1 and 2.22.2). Meanwhile, growth in services, which has remained strong since the second half of 2022, slowed somewhat. This was partly due to normalization in food and beverage services, which had exceptionally strong sales growth in the second half of 2022 and the first half of 2023 (Figure 2.22.3).

On the demand side, private consumption continued to support growth. Despite signs of a slowdown in consumption in supply-side data, private consumption on the demand-side grew by 4.8% in the fourth quarter. Fixed investment, by contrast, continued to decline. Weaker domestic demand dragged down imports by 8.3% on weak machinery and transport equipment imports, contributing to GDP growth for the fourth consecutive quarter. However, exports continued to decline for the fourth straight quarter, as exports of minerals, including oil and gas, fell compared to the same period last year (Figure 2.22.4).

Figure 2.22.1 Supply-Side Contributions to Growth

In 2021–2023, growth came mostly from services.

Percentage points

Q = quarter.
Source: CEIC Data Company.

Figure 2.22.2 Gas and Oil Production

Oil and gas production remained at record lows in 2023 before rebounding in the fourth quarter.

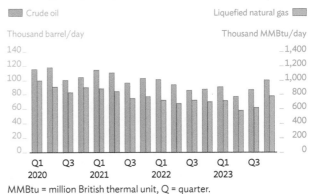

MMBtu = million British thermal unit, Q = quarter.
Source: Department of Economic Planning and Statistics.

This chapter was written by Yuho Myoda and Nedelyn Magtibay-Ramos of the Economic Research and Development Impact Department, ADB, Manila.

Figure 2.22.3 Retail Sales

Food and beverage sales have normalized from the rebound in growth.

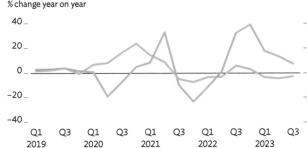

— Food and beverage services
— Retail sales

% change year on year

Q = quarter.
Note: Sales index is not seasonally adjusted, 2019 = 100.
Source: Haver Analytics.

Figure 2.22.4 Goods Exports

Mineral fuels exports declined in 2023 from the 2022 recovery.

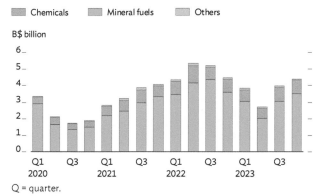

☐ Chemicals   ☐ Mineral fuels   ☐ Others

B$ billion

Q = quarter.
Source: CEIC Data Company.

Figure 2.22.5 Sources of Inflation

Declining communications and transport prices dragged down inflation.

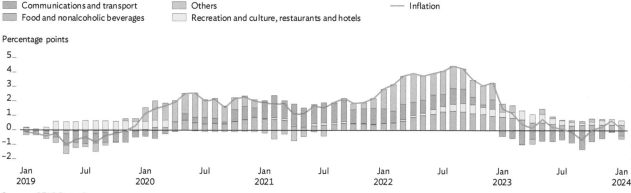

☐ Communications and transport   ☐ Others   — Inflation
☐ Food and nonalcoholic beverages   ☐ Recreation and culture, restaurants and hotels

Percentage points

Source: CEIC Data Company.

Inflation remained close to zero in the second half of 2023. Nevertheless, headline inflation rebounded to 0.7% in December 2023, the highest since May. Food and non-alcoholic beverages remained at 2.1%, driving inflation since October (Figure 2.22.5). Elevated international food prices kept rice and cereals inflation at 1.6% despite the country's price cap on specific foods. Non-alcoholic beverage prices remained high at 11.1% in December since their spike in July 2023, partly due to an increase in the sugar beverage tax. Meanwhile, significant deflation in communications and transport, which account for more than a quarter of the total consumption basket, continued to offset inflationary pressures from food and services in 2023.

Economic Prospects

Growth is forecast to accelerate to 3.7% in 2024. Growth is expected to remain more robust than the historical trend as the economy continues to recover from the aftereffects of the pandemic (Table 2.22.1). Previously deferred investment in the oil and gas sector will boost fixed investment over the forecast period. Supported by the replacement of production equipment and the opening of the Salman oilfield, daily oil production is expected to recover from 89,000 barrels per day to 95,000 barrels per day. Liquefied natural gas production is expected to recover from 678 billion British thermal units per day to more than 700 British thermal units per day. The recovery in oil and gas production will boost growth through higher exports. As production is expected to normalize in 2024, growth will moderate to 2.8% in 2025.

Table 2.22.1 Selected Economic Indicators, %

Growth will accelerate in 2024 before moderating in 2025.

	2022	2023	2024	2025
GDP growth	−1.6	1.4	3.7	2.8
Inflation	3.7	0.4	1.1	1.0

GDP = gross domestic product.

Sources: CEIC Data Company; Asian Development Bank estimates.

Inflation is expected to remain above 1% for the outlook period as temporary downward pressures fade. The average annual inflation rate is expected to be 1.1% in 2024 and 1.0% in 2025, reflecting higher prices of food, including sugar beverages, while negative short-term pressures, such as falling prices of imported cars and airline tickets, are expected to dissipate in 2024. The depreciation of the Brunei dollar against major trading partner currencies through mid-2023 may also push up inflation through a delayed transfer to retail prices.

Economic diversification will continue under the Vision of Brunei 2035 plan. Brunei Darussalam's long-standing efforts at economic diversification showed some progress in 2023. In agricultural product exports, leveraging its reliable halal certification system, the country signed a trade facilitation agreement with Sabah, Malaysia for halal food products. Also, the country shipped its first local food exports to Singapore in September. Brunei Darussalam is also investing to take advantage of its proximity to many offshore oil fields to become a ship dismantling and repair center. Demand for repair and disposal of related facilities in Southeast Asia is expected to grow in the coming years. Investment in the yard at Pulau Muara Besar through a public-private partnership began in 2022, with construction expected to be completed in 2025. If successful, the integrated yard project is expected to bring more employment and income opportunities. That should help decrease the ratio of the oil and gas sector to GDP, which is currently around 50%.

The growth outlook relies heavily on the recovery in oil and gas production. Risks are tilted to the downside. Limited private investment for maintenance and renewal in prior years may lower the operating rate of production facilities and, thus, future output in the oil and gas sector. The government recognizes that rising geopolitical tension is a downside risk on growth

and an upside risk for inflation as it may dampen oil prices via weaker global demand and increase production costs through supply chain disruptions. Yet elevated international energy prices, if more persistent than currently expected, will be a tailwind for the country's trade and fiscal balances over the forecast period.

Policy Challenge—Revenue Diversification and Fiscal Consolidation

Fiscal consolidation is required in the medium term for inter-generational equity. The government has been mostly running a fiscal deficit since fiscal year (FY) 2015 (ended 31 March 2015), following the drop in oil prices in the middle of 2014 (Figure 2.22.6). With an abundant sovereign wealth fund from past mineral revenues—as of October 2023, the $73 billion in assets under management is equivalent to four times nominal GDP—the country has low short-term fiscal risk. However, according to an International Monetary Fund (IMF) analysis based on the permanent income hypothesis, the current fiscal deficit is well above the preferred standard in the medium to long term. Moreover, the acceleration in the global transition to net-zero by 2035 is further clouding the long-term outlook for oil and gas demand and prices, making revenues increasingly uncertain for the country.

Figure 2.22.6 Fiscal Balance

The fiscal accounts have been mostly in deficit since FY2015.

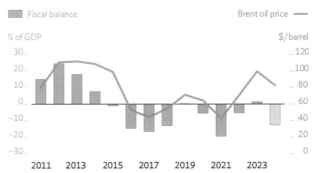

FY = fiscal year, GDP = gross domestic product.

Notes: Years are fiscal years ending on 31 March of that year. The fiscal balance for fiscal year 2024 is the government's estimate. Corresponding oil prices are from calendar years 2010 to 2023, as each fiscal year covers 3 quarters of the previous year.

Source: CEIC Data Company.

Brunei Darussalam needs both expenditure rationalization and domestic resource mobilization.
The government has been controlling a variety of food and fuel prices over the long term at a significant fiscal cost through government purchases, distribution, and price caps. Reviewing and rationalizing these broad-based subsidies into targeted transfers to vulnerable groups is recommended. According to the IMF, energy subsidies amounted to about 6% of GDP in 2022. On the revenue side, over 70% of total revenue derives from oil- and gas-related sources. Currently, Brunei Darussalam is the only country without a general consumption tax among ASEAN members. Introducing goods and services taxes with properly targeted transfers to cushion the adverse effect on vulnerable groups will strengthen and diversify revenue sources. The country also lacks a personal income tax. In the long term, introducing an income tax with a relatively high exemption threshold could help cushion the regressivity of the general consumption tax. Alternatively, the government could gradually raise the employers' and introduce an employees' contribution to the Employees Trust Fund to cover broader social security expenses in the future.

CAMBODIA

Tourism and non-garment manufacturing led economic growth in 2023. Falling imported fuel costs contributed to reduced inflationary pressures. Economic recovery is expected to continue this year and next, with continued tourism recovery and strong manufacturing growth. In contrast, agriculture, construction, and real estate are expected to grow moderately. Inflation should remain subdued amid stabilized global fuel prices. As Cambodia is poised to graduate out of the United Nations least-developed-country category in 2027, it is imperative to plan strategically for a smooth transition.

Economic Performance

Economic recovery continued amid mixed industrial performance. Real GDP grew but slightly slower from 5.2% in 2022 to an estimated 5.0% in 2023 led by a recovery in tourism and robust non-garment manufacturing. Industrial output contracted by an estimated 0.2% due to reduced international demand for garments, footwear, and travel goods (GFT) (Figure 2.23.1). Notwithstanding a 12.1% decline in GFT exports in 2023, exports of non-GFT manufactures, including vehicle parts, solar panels, and auto tires, surged by 28.4%. Construction had tepid growth, with a marginal 1.4% increase in construction material and equipment imports.

Services had robust growth, while agriculture expanded moderately. Services showed a robust recovery, growing by an estimated 12.0% in 2023. International tourist arrivals rose to 5.5 million in 2023 from 2.3 million in 2022, reaching 82.5% of the 2019 pre-pandemic levels (Figure 2.23.2). The strong recovery in tourism contributed significantly to food and accommodations, domestic trade, transport, and telecommunications services. However, the real estate sector's recovery remained muted due to low levels of foreign investment. Agricultural output grew by an estimated 1.1% in 2023, fueled by external demand for Cambodian produce. Agriculture exports grew by 8.5%, with notable increases in cassava, milled rice, cashew nuts, and rubber.

Figure 2.23.1 Supply-Side Contributions to Growth

Growth continued in 2023, led by tourism recovery and robust non-garment manufacturing.

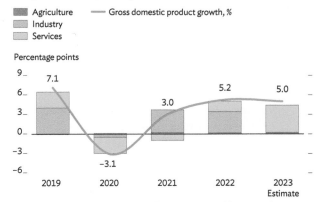

Sources: Ministry of Economy and Finance; National Institute of Statistics; Asian Development Bank estimates.

Inflation moderated in 2023 mainly on falling global fuel and food prices. Inflation decelerated in the first half before edging up in the second half, settling at 2.7% year on year at year-end. The annual average inflation rate stood at 2.1%, down from 5.3% in 2022. The exchange rate remained stable, averaging KR4,110 per US dollar. Money supply (M2) growth accelerated to 12.5% from 8.2% in 2022, but credit growth to the private sector slowed to 3.9% from 18.6% amid tighter global financial conditions.

This chapter was written by Poullang Doung and Duong Nguyen of the Cambodia Resident Mission, ADB, Phnom Penh.

Figure 2.23.2 Tourist Arrivals

Tourist arrivals rebounded led by visitors from neighboring economies.

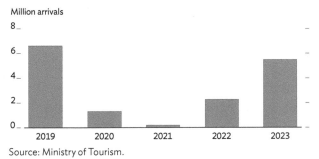

Source: Ministry of Tourism.

An expansionary fiscal policy was implemented in 2023. The government sustained its strategic economic recovery plan, prioritizing socio-economic measures in 2023. The government budget deficit is preliminarily estimated at 3.1% of GDP in 2023, lower than the planned 5.1% under the 2023 Budget Law (Figure 2.23.3). Revenue fell short of the planned 22.0% of GDP, settling at 21.2%, while expenditure, at 24.2% of GDP, remained lower than the budgeted 27.1%. The government issued the equivalent of $58.3 million in sovereign bonds in 2023 to diversify its financing sources. Public external debt rose from $10.0 billion in 2022, the equivalent of 33.9% of GDP, to $11.2 billion in 2023, or 35.0% of GDP.

Large tourism receipts and falling goods trade deficit led the current account into surplus. Imports contracted by 17.0% in 2023 due to a drop in gold, garment material, fuel, and vehicle imports. Exports increased by an estimated 1.7%, led by robust growth in non-GFT manufactures and gold exports. The tourism

Figure 2.23.3 Fiscal Indicators

Tax revenue and capital spending were lower than budgeted, leading to a smaller budget deficit than targeted.

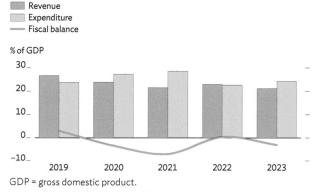

GDP = gross domestic product.
Source: Ministry of Economy and Finance; Asian Development Bank estimates.

Figure 2.23.4 International Reserves

International reserves picked up, partly contributed by buoyant foreign investment inflows.

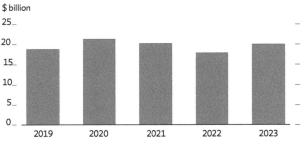

Source: National Bank of Cambodia.

recovery turned service trade into surplus. Foreign direct investment (FDI) rose by 10.6% to $4.0 billion, and contributed to an increase in international reserves to $20.0 billion, the equivalent of 8.2 months of imports (Figure 2.23.4).

Economic Prospects

Stronger industrial exports will drive faster growth. The economy is set to grow by 5.8% in 2024 and 6.0% in 2025. The expansion is partly attributed to positive outlook for GFT exports, which have gained momentum since the last quarter of 2023 (Table 2.23.1 and Figure 2.23.5). Robust demand for Cambodia's non-GFT manufactured goods should sustain their export growth over the forecast period. Industrial output growth should accelerate to 8.0% in 2024 and 8.4% in 2025. Construction, however, may see only modest growth, largely because of the prolonged property sector downturn in the People's Republic of China (PRC).

Further recovery in tourism will fuel economic growth. Services are projected to grow by 5.4% in 2024 before tapering slightly to 5.2% in 2025, as

Table 2.23.1 Selected Economic Indicators, %

Growth is projected to accelerate in 2024 and 2025, with inflation remaining low in both years.

	2022	2023	2024	2025
GDP growth	5.2	5.0	5.8	6.0
Inflation	5.3	2.1	2.0	2.0

GDP = gross domestic product.
Sources: Ministry of Economy and Finance; National Institute of Statistics; Asian Development Bank estimates.

Figure 2.23.5 Gross Domestic Product Growth

Growth will accelerate in 2024 and 2025, staying above the 5-year moving average.

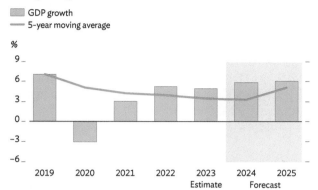

GDP = gross domestic product.
Sources: National Institute of Statistics; Asian Development Bank estimates.

Figure 2.23.6 Inflation

Inflation should remain low in 2024 and 2025 on expected lower energy prices.

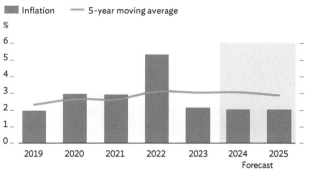

Sources: National Institute of Statistics; Asian Development Bank estimates.

tourism continues to recover. Tourist arrivals, especially from fellow Association of Southeast Asian Nations members, will likely increase, supported by the region's positive economic prospects. The recent inauguration of the Siem Reap International Airport will also likely attract more tourists. However, the recovery in real estate is expected to be gradual, constrained by reduced investment from the PRC.

Agriculture will likely continue its moderate growth. Agriculture is forecast to grow by 1.3% in 2024 and 1.4% in 2025, buoyed by rising export demand and domestic consumption. The positive trajectory is further supported by recent bilateral free trade agreements with the PRC, the Republic of Korea, and the United Arab Emirates, and Cambodia's participation in the Regional Comprehensive Economic Partnership.

Low and stable inflation is expected to continue. Headline inflation will average around 2.0% in 2024 and 2025 if global fuel prices remain stable (Figure 2.23.6). The National Bank of Cambodia, committed to maintaining a stable exchange rate against the US dollar to preserve price stability and public confidence in the riel, plans to set a policy rate to anchor market interest rates while actively promoting broader use of the riel.

Gradual fiscal consolidation should begin this year. Following years of fiscal expansion to stimulate the economy, the government will embark on a gradual fiscal consolidation from 2024 to restore the fiscal buffers diminished during the pandemic. The new

revenue mobilization strategy 2024–2028, under preparation, envisages a focus on enhancing revenue collection through greater tax administration efficiency rather than introducing new taxes. Spending will align with the government's Pentagonal Strategy, which prioritizes education and skills development along with expanding health-care coverage and social assistance for the poor and vulnerable. With external public debt forecast at 36.3% of GDP in 2024 and 37.3% in 2025, the risk of public debt distress remains low (Figure 2.23.7). The government plans to issue the equivalent of $108 million in sovereign bonds in 2024 to finance revenue-generating investment projects.

An expected rise in demand for imported goods will drive the current account balance back into deficit. Since the pandemic, gold trade has been volatile and unpredictable, with gold exports spiking in 2020, followed by a surge in imports in 2021 and 2022. This trend reversed again in 2023 when gold exports surged, turning the current account into surplus. Exports of

Figure 2.23.7 Public External Debt

Public external debt remains sustainable with low risk of debt distress.

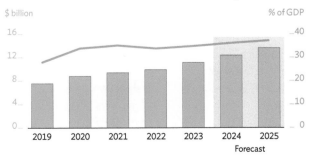

GDP = gross domestic product.
Sources: Ministry of Economy and Finance; Asian Development Bank estimates.

goods are expected to account for 76.3% of GDP in 2024 and 77.7% in 2025, while imports are expected to reach 96.6% of GDP this year and 97.5% in 2025. As a result, the goods trade deficit is projected to be 20.3% of GDP in 2024 and 19.8% in 2025. With a services trade surplus expected at 5.1% of GDP in 2024 and 5.5% in 2025, the current account deficit is projected at 8.6% of GDP in 2024 and 7.6% in 2025, assuming more stabilized gold trade. The deficit will be financed by FDI and aid inflows, bolstering gross international reserves to approximately $25.0 billion by the end of 2025, covering over 7.6 months of imports of goods and services.

Risks to the outlook tilt to the downside. Risks include potential slower growth in major economies like the US, Europe, and the PRC; the high level of private debt impacting financial sector growth and the broader economy; a renewed rise in energy prices; and effects from extreme weather events.

Policy Challenge—Ensuring a Smooth Transition from Least-Developed-Country Category

Cambodia is on track to graduate from the least-developed-country (LDC) category. Two decades after being included in the United Nations LDC category, the country met the graduation criteria for the first time in 2021. According to the UN 2024 triennial review, gross national income per capita is currently $1,590, crossing the threshold of $1,306; human assets index is 77.8, above the 66 threshold level; and the economic and environmental index is 24.1, below the 32 threshold level. Thus, Cambodia is well-positioned to pass its second consecutive triennial review this year, potentially graduating out of the LDC category in 2027.

Graduation offers long-term benefits. By sending positive signals on the country's development and stability, it will likely attract higher FDI and stimulate faster economic growth. Graduation may also accelerate economic diversification, reducing reliance on a few products and markets. Preparing for graduation often involves strengthening institutions and capacity, leading to more effective governance, policy implementation, and resilience to external shocks.

Graduation, however, will bring immediate challenges. Loss of trade benefits, such as duty-free privileges and lenient rules of origin, will impact several key exports, most notably GFT exports to the European Union (EU), which accounted for 12.7% of all exports in 2023 (Figure 2.23.8). The World Trade Organization projects that graduation could lead to a 6.0% drop in exports by LDCs, particularly affecting GFT. Graduation will also reduce official development assistance (ODA), an important factor contributing to the past decade of high growth and development.

Figure 2.23.8 Export Markets in 2023

Garments accounted for most exports to the EU.

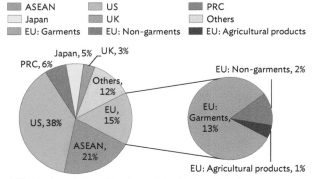

ASEAN = Association of Southeast Asian Nations, EU = European Union, PRC = People's Republic of China, UK = United Kingdom, US = United States.
Source: Ministry of Economy and Finance.

Cambodia must start preparing for a smooth transition. The country should continue expanding its participation in free trade agreements, including those with the EU, to secure market access post-graduation. It should also intensify commitment to economic diversification into new markets and higher value-added products. It should also explore the Generalized System of Preferences Plus (GSP+)—which extends zero-tariff benefits to newly graduated countries—by ratifying the remaining environmental protection and good governance conventions. Strengthening human capital development, supporting climate-resilient infrastructure, and fostering a conducive business environment for micro, small and medium-sized enterprises should remain cornerstones of long-term growth. Finally, it is imperative to strengthen domestic resource mobilization to diversify funding sources and reduce reliance on ODA for public investment in infrastructure and social development projects.

INDONESIA

As the commodity boom faded in 2023, GDP growth slowed. Domestic demand is playing a larger role in driving economic growth and will likely continue to do so over the forecast period. Inflation is expected to soften further, while the current account deficit will expand gradually. Reaching the government's medium- to long-term growth targets requires improved productivity, which implies continued efforts to improve human capital through adequate education, healthcare, and social protection.

Economic Performance

Domestic demand played a stronger role as a source of growth as the commodity boom waned. GDP grew by 5.0% in 2023, down from 5.3% in 2022 when the economy rebounded after pandemic restrictions eased and activity resumed. Growth in 2023 was driven primarily by robust private consumption and stronger public investment. Domestic demand contributed 4.8 percentage points to growth, slightly higher than its pre-COVID-19 average of 4.7 percentage points 2015–2019 (Figure 2.24.1).

Consumption remained robust as the economy returned to normal, inflation eased, and pre-election spending rose. Private consumption, accounting for 54% of GDP, grew by 4.9% in 2023, slightly lower than the 5.0% in 2022, as spending growth on leisure, travel, accommodation, and restaurants slowed due to the high 2022 base. Spending on durable goods grew slightly higher than in 2022, supported by improved purchasing power and a boost from pre-election buying. Growth in services was significantly above the 2019 level, while the increase in durable goods purchases remained lower, suggesting a shift in post-pandemic spending. Consumption by non-profit institutions grew by a strong 18.1% as activity ramped up ahead of the 2024 elections. Government consumption increased by 2.9% in 2023, coming from a low base following the 2022 contraction.

Figure 2.24.1 Demand-Side Contributions to Growth

Domestic demand played a larger role as a source of growth as the commodity boom waned.

Legend:
- Domestic demand
- Imports of goods and services
- Exports of goods and services
- Statistical discrepancy
- Gross domestic product growth, %

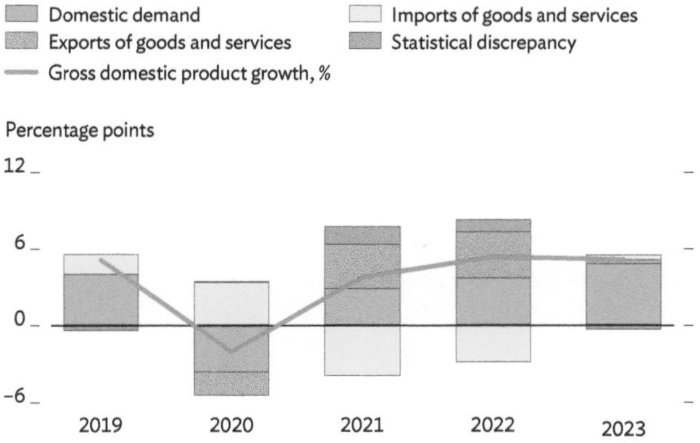

Source: Haver Analytics.

Higher spending on public infrastructure boosted investment in 2023. Fixed capital formation increased by 5.8% in 2023, much stronger than the 4.0% growth in 2022. Construction rebounded and contributed about half of investment growth as the government accelerated priority infrastructure projects and the New Capital City development to meet its targets by the end of the government's term in 2024. In contrast, investment in machinery and equipment grew much slower, from 22.4% in 2022 to 3.1% in 2023, partly due to businesses' wait-and-see stance before the 2024

This chapter was written by Arief Ramayandi of the Economic Research and Development Impact Department, ADB, Manila, and Priasto Aji of the Indonesia Resident Mission, ADB, Jakarta.

elections. Aggregate investment, including inventories, contributed a substantial 1.9 percentage points to GDP growth.

Net exports contributed to GDP growth as real imports fell. Real export growth of goods and services slowed to 1.1% in 2023 due to weak global demand, down from double-digit growth rates the previous 2 years. This occurred despite the revival in foreign tourism, which raised real services exports by almost 40%. However, the declining appetite for imports also led to a fall in real imports by 1.6%, which allowed net exports to contribute 0.7 percentage points to GDP growth.

A shrinking merchandise trade surplus drove the current account into a slight deficit. The volume of merchandise exports expanded by 8.4% in 2023, but weak global demand substantially lowered global commodity prices and offset the growth in volume (Figure 2.24.2). Goods exports declined by 11.3% in US dollar terms, and the value of shipments to major trading partners dropped in 2023. Goods imports fell by 7.3% in US dollar terms. The decline was mainly attributed to lower intermediate goods imports, which account for 72.6% of total imports, due to softening exports (Figure 2.24.3). Given these, the full-year merchandise trade surplus fell by 26% to $46.4 billion. Adding the deficits in services trade ($17.9 billion) and the income account ($30 billion), the 2023 current account balance fell into a small deficit of $1.6 billion, equivalent to 0.1% of GDP.

Figure 2.24.3 Contributions to Growth of Merchandise Imports, by Type

As exports fell, so did intermediate goods imports.

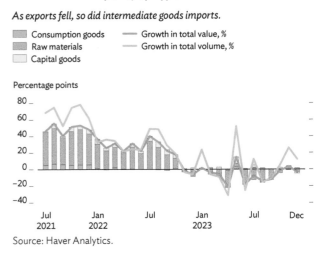

Source: Haver Analytics.

The capital and financial account surplus more than offset the current account deficit. The balance of payments recorded a surplus after the capital and financial accounts rebounded from a 2022 deficit with a $8.7 billion surplus in 2023 (Figure 2.24.4). Portfolio investment showed a net inflow of $2.3 billion for the year despite net outflows in the second and third quarters, due to rising external pressures from the tight global financial conditions. Net direct investment fell by 19.4% but remained a still substantial $14.6 billion. The capital and financial account surplus more than offset the current account deficit, resulting in a balance of payments surplus of $6.3 billion.

Figure 2.24.2 Merchandise Exports

Weak global demand lowered global commodity prices and offset higher export volumes.

Source: Haver Analytics.

Figure 2.24.4 Balance of Payments

The capital and financial account surplus more than offset the current account deficit.

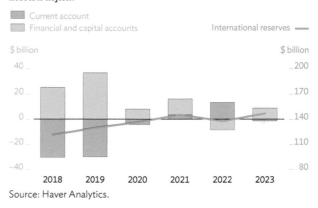

Source: Haver Analytics.

Growth slowed across all production sectors except mining and construction. High base effect from 2022 slowed growth slightly in most sectors, but mining and construction were boosted by the government's initiated industrial down-streaming program and accelerated priority infrastructure projects. Services' contribution to growth fell from 2.9 percentage points in 2022 to 2.7 percentage points in 2023, still more than half of total growth, led by wholesale and retail trade, transport, and information and communications. The contribution from manufacturing declined from 1.0 percentage points in 2022 to 0.9 in 2023. Other industries' contribution jumped to about 1.0 percentage points in 2023 from 0.6 percentage points a year earlier, mainly due to strong growth in mining and construction.

Inflation eased back into Bank Indonesia's target range, but volatile food prices pose new challenges. Inflation averaged 3.7% over 2023. Inflation fell from 5.1% year on year in January 2023 to 2.8% in December as the impact of the fuel price increase on administered prices in 2022 faded in September (Figure 2.24.5). Inflation fell back within Bank Indonesia's target band of 3% ±1% by the end of the year, with core inflation falling by about half to 1.7% given well-anchored inflation expectations and normalized domestic demand. However, prices of basic food commodities, including rice, sugar, and chicken, have risen lately due to supply constraints, prolonged El Niño weather, and trade disruptions caused by export restrictions from key food producers. To address these issues, the government implemented price stabilization and food

assistance programs for the poor. Entering 2024, core inflation remained stable at 1.7%, but headline inflation rose to 2.8% in February from 2.6% in January due to higher food prices.

The monetary policy stance remained largely unchanged and used more to manage the exchange rate. Given stable inflation, the policy rate in 2023 remained mostly constant except for a 25 basis points increase to 6.0% in October to help stabilize the rupiah. Bank Indonesia also conducted regular central bank auctions of derivatives and government securities to help further stabilize the exchange rate. The rupiah depreciated slightly by 2.0% in the year to December 2023, or by 2.5% on average against the US dollar (Figure 2.24.6). Despite a $12 billion dip in gross international reserves between March and October 2023 due to foreign debt repayments and central bank support of the rupiah, reserves increased by $8 billion to $147 billion in 2023, covering 6.7 months of imports. Increasing external pressures led the central bank to adopt capital flow measures. Aside from raising the interest rate in October, Bank Indonesia mandated 30% of commodity export earnings to be held in local banks starting in August and introduced new foreign exchange-denominated instruments in September to attract liquidity.

Figure 2.24.6 Reserves and the Exchange Rate

Overall, the rupiah depreciated slightly in 2023, while gross international reserves grew.

Source: Haver Analytics.

External debt remains manageable. External debt as a share of GDP was 29.7% in December 2023, steady since 2022 but down from 39.0% in March 2021, in line with the debt repayment schedule (Figure 2.24.7). Public debt was 15.3% of GDP with private debt equivalent to 14.4% of GDP in 2023. The international

Figure 2.24.5 Monthly Inflation

Inflation eased, but volatile food prices posed new challenges.

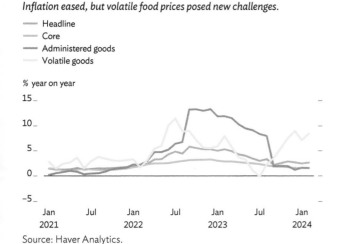

Source: Haver Analytics.

Figure 2.24.7 External Debt Indicators

External debt as a share of GDP has remained steady since early 2022.

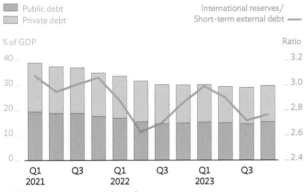

GDP = gross domestic product, Q = quarter.
Source: Haver Analytics.

reserves to short-term external debt ratio declined from 3.1 in 2021 to 2.8 in 2023. Sovereign credit ratings are all stable and remain above investment grade.

Fiscal policy remains prudent, with tax collection accelerating and spending on target. The government targeted a budget deficit equal to 2.9% of GDP for 2023, but it ended up at 1.7% as revenue exceeded the budget target by 13% after a percentage point increase in the value-added tax rate in April 2022 (Figure 2.24.8). Spending nearly missed its target due to persistent spending challenges but was compensated for in the last 2 weeks of 2023 when 15% of the targeted budget was disbursed. Capital spending increased markedly by 27.7% as the government

Figure 2.24.8 Fiscal Indicators

The budget deficit was lower than planned as revenue exceeded its target.

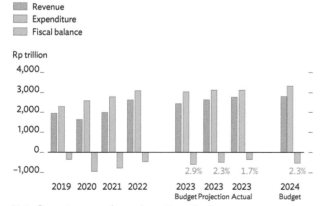

Note: Percentages are of gross domestic product.
Source: Ministry of Finance.

boosted investment, while social spending contracted by 2.9%. Total central government debt as a share of GDP was about 39.0% in 2023, declining slightly from 39.4% in 2020, but rising from 30.2% in 2019.

Regulations to implement the recently introduced landmark legislation on essential reforms are underway. These include supporting regulations to the Omnibus Job Creation Law which aims to encourage trade and investment while improving business operations; a tax harmonization law that increases tax ratios and improves tax compliance; and a financial sector omnibus law that provides comprehensive regulations for Indonesia's financial sector. These measures aim to alleviate structural barriers that restrict competitiveness and productivity growth.

Economic Prospects

The new administration will likely continue the progress of the current government. The February 2024 nationwide presidential, legislative, and regional head elections held across 37 provinces, 415 districts, and 93 cities went smoothly overall. The presidential election was concluded in one round and the new administration is expected to continue to help improve the investment climate and public financial management.

Fiscal policy will stimulate growth in 2024. The administration increased its 2024 budget deficit target to 2.3% of GDP from 1.7% of GDP in 2023. Civil servant salaries will be raised. Social spending is expected to increase by 12.0%. Total public investment in 2024, including investment finance such as capital injections to state-owned enterprises, will remain at 1.9% of GDP (Figure 2.24.9). Government revenue is expected to increase by 1.0% in 2024, and spending will increase by 6.1%. Because of the government's cautious projections, revenue may surpass expectations and lower the deficit.

Monetary policy will continue targeting price stability, focusing on managing capital flows and the exchange rate. The policy interest rate within the forecast horizon will be influenced by US Federal Reserve interest rate adjustments. Given well-anchored inflation expectations, Bank Indonesia will likely continue focusing on managing excessive

Figure 2.24.9 Public Investment

Public investment in 2024 will remain at 2023 levels.

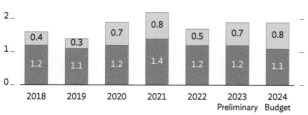

GDP = gross domestic product.
Source: Ministry of Finance.

Figure 2.24.10 Consumer Demand Indicators

Consumer demand indicators are broadly at pre-pandemic levels.

Source: Haver Analytics.

capital outflows and exchange rate movements. However, the bank's decision to lower its inflation targets to 2.5% ±1% in 2024 from 3.0% ±1% in 2023 may limit the headroom for policy flexibility. Bank Indonesia introduced liquidity instruments to limit the impact of higher interest rates on domestic economic activity. These include reducing the minimum reserve requirement for banks that lend to priority sectors and micro-, small, and medium-sized enterprises, loosening mortgage and vehicle loan rules, and lowering banks' macroprudential liquidity buffer on rupiah-denominated assets to reverse the slowdown in private credit growth. Growth in credit to the private sector edged up from 9.5% in October 2023 to 10.3% in January 2024.

Consumption is forecast to remain robust, while investment will likely remain stable. The trends in consumer confidence and retail sales are broadly in line with pre-pandemic levels (Figure 2.24.10). Election-related spending, the government's social assistance programs, the planned civil servant salary increase in 2024, and lower expected inflation over the forecast period will boost consumption. Investment will likely remain stable this year and increase next year, boosted by government projects and prior reforms. The current administration will likely speed up priority infrastructure and Capital City projects until the new government takes office in October. Private investment is expected to pick up in 2025 as the new administration defines its plans and businesses' wait-and-see attitude toward investment fades. Manufacturing is expected to continue to grow in line with the continuous expansion of the manufacturing purchasing managers' index over

the past 30 months. The gradual implementation of the Omnibus Job Creation Law should also help promote investment in 2025.

Weak commodity prices and global growth will hamper goods exports, widening the current account deficit. While global demand and commodity prices will likely remain soft, rupiah depreciation will support the incomes of commodity exporters. Services exports will still benefit from a continued recovery in tourism. The pickup in imports, especially related to stronger investment prospects, will tend to widen the current account deficit. Portfolio and direct investment inflows are expected to keep the overall balance of payments in surplus through the forecast period. Due to the widening current account deficit, the rupiah could soften this year against the US dollar. Nonetheless, real net foreign trade in the national accounts is still expected to add somewhat to GDP growth. Metal export volumes will continue to grow, having contributed to significant growth in manufacturing output in recent years.

On balance, domestic demand will continue to promote growth and offset the weaker contribution from net exports. Robust private consumption, public infrastructure spending, and gradually improving investment should help sustain GDP growth during the forecast horizon. GDP is projected to expand at 5.0% in 2024 and 2025 (Table 2.24.1).

Inflation is projected to decline further from a 3.7% average in 2023 to 2.8% in 2024 and 2025. Improved supply-side management and well-anchored

Table 2.24.1 Selected Economic Indicators, %

Growth will remain solid, supported by investment and private consumption.

	2022	2023	2024	2025
GDP growth	5.3	5.0	5.0	5.0
Inflation	4.1	3.7	2.8	2.8

GDP = gross domestic product.
Sources: Central Bureau of Statistics; Asian Development Bank estimates.

inflation expectations will help keep inflation within the lower inflation target range. The country's official regional inflation task force will continue playing an essential role in managing domestic cost-push inflation. Although healthy, the growth forecasts for this year and next will not overheat the economy and thus will continue to anchor domestic price stability. Softer prospects for global oil prices and the relatively ample fiscal space projected will help stabilize movements in administered components of domestic prices.

Risks to the forecast are just about evenly balanced for 2024 and will likely be on the upside for 2025. For 2024, the smooth February elections may improve business confidence, resulting in stronger and faster tailwinds on investment. It is also unlikely the Fed will increase its policy rate further and will possibly start easing this year, thus inducing stability in global demand, potentially reducing borrowing costs, and easing access to external financing. However, the possibility that the Fed rate will stay higher for longer than expected, continuing geopolitical uncertainty, and further climate change related shocks—may disrupt global value chains and induce sharper declines in the terms of trade. For 2025, risks are on the upside because of hopes that the global environment will settle down.

Policy Challenge—Improving Productivity Through Human Capital Development

Improving human capital productivity is needed to ensure a prosperous Indonesia by 2045. To transform Indonesia into a prosperous nation as envisaged by the National Vision 2045, the country needs to overcome

substantial obstacles in human capital development. Labor productivity growth has fallen below average economic growth in the past decade and even declined before the COVID-19 pandemic hit (Figure 2.24.11). To ensure more productive labor, it is critical the country attains a state of inclusive and sustainable human development by addressing issues such as the skills mismatch, access to health and social protection, and provide a healthier environment for workers.

Figure 2.24.11 Labor Productivity

Labor productivity has been growing slower than average economic growth over the past decade.

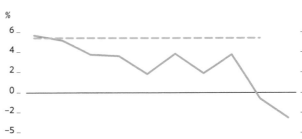

GDP = gross domestic product.
Source: Asian Productivity Organization.

Addressing skills mismatches and secondary and tertiary education enrollment are major concerns. Indonesia's workforce is comprised primarily of elementary and middle school graduates (Figure 2.24.12). Many secondary school graduates lack marketable skills, with the unemployment rate highest for workers at this level of education. The government has developed schemes to ensure more

Figure 2.24.12 Overall Labor Composition by Education

Indonesia's workforce is mostly elementary and middle school graduates.

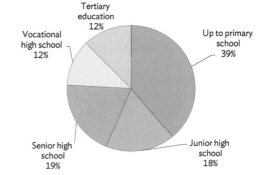

Source: Statistics Indonesia.

equitable access to learning opportunities, such as the Indonesia Smart Program and other financing programs to access education. At the same time, ministries under the Coordinating Ministry of Economic Affairs have also launched initiatives to improve Indonesia's Technical and Vocational Education and Training output and enhance skills matching in the labor market. These include labor market information, funding schemes, curriculum alignment, learning quality enhancement, and monitoring and evaluation.

Universal health coverage is essential to ensure physical well-being. Equitable health system coverage remains a challenge, and the country needs to improve health system availability. For example, Indonesia had only 0.7 physicians per 1,000 people in 2021, less than the World Health Organization's minimum requirement of 1 physician. The country has also worked to promote Indonesia's National Health Insurance (JKN) and regional health-care services. Despite its broad coverage, the survival of the JKN system remains a challenge. In 2019, JKN served 83.6% of the population, with only 39.6% paying premiums, with the remainder receiving government subsidies. JKN's deficits are projected to continue to widen as the number of participants increase. Payment compliance and preventative and promotional health initiatives must be improved to lessen JKN's future burden.

Access to social protection for the striving middle class and a responsive system are crucial. Indonesia has established poverty-related social protection programs. However, existing schemes do not adequately cover around half of Indonesia's population, who spend approximately twice or less the national poverty line each month, leaving them particularly vulnerable to shocks. More extensive and efficient social protection is needed to enable aspiring Indonesians to enter and remain in the middle class. The government needs flexible finance and dynamic, regularly updated targeting data to quickly identify and reach potential program beneficiaries to increase coverage to the vulnerable middle class and create a responsive social security system.

LAO PEOPLE'S DEMOCRATIC REPUBLIC

The economy continued its moderate recovery in 2023, backed by services, including tourism, transport, and logistics. However, macroeconomic pressures from an unsustainable debt burden persisted, dragging down growth. In addition, a late monsoon season and low rainfall suppressed agriculture and electricity output. External demand will continue to support moderate growth in 2024 and 2025. Continuing macroeconomic imbalances pose risks to refinancing, price stability, and food security.

Economic Performance

The economy grew by 3.7% in 2023, supported by services, including tourism, transport, and logistics. As mobility improved across Southeast Asia, regional tourism helped to stimulate spending in domestic services such as hotels, trade, and transport (Figure 2.25.1). Tourist arrivals reached 3.4 million in 2023, up from 1.3 million in 2022, but remained below pre-pandemic levels (Figure 2.25.2). The railway service between the Lao People's Democratic Republic (Lao PDR) and the People's Republic of China (PRC) carried more than 1.8 million passengers in 2023, up from 1.0 million passengers in 2022, and transported

4.2 million tons of freight, up from 2.2 million tons in 2022. Wholesale and retail trade also expanded as international and local retailers opened new franchises.

However, macroeconomic challenges, including high external debt service, low revenues, and exchange rate depreciation, continued to hamper growth. In the official market, the Lao kip lost half its value against the US dollar in 2022 and a further 16.3% in 2023. It also fell against regional currencies in 2023, including 21.3% against the baht and 15.6% against the yuan, contributing to high domestic inflation (Figure 2.25.3). As the kip lost its value against other currencies, the ratio of foreign currency deposits to broad money—or "dollarization"—increased to 68.7% in 2023 (Figure 2.25.4).

Figure 2.25.1 Supply-Side Contributions to Growth

Continued improvement in services supported economic recovery.

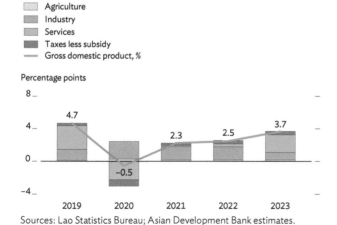

- Agriculture
- Industry
- Services
- Taxes less subsidy
- Gross domestic product, %

Percentage points

Figure 2.25.2 Tourist Arrivals

Tourist arrivals more than doubled in 2023.

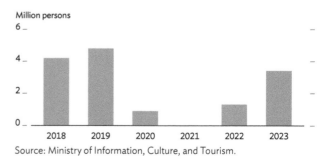

Million persons

Sources: Lao Statistics Bureau; Asian Development Bank estimates.

Source: Ministry of Information, Culture, and Tourism.

This chapter was written by Emma Allen and Soulinthone Leuangkhamsing of the Lao Resident Mission, ADB, Vientiane.

Figure 2.25.3 Lao Kip Exchange Rate Index

The kip continued to fall against the US dollar and regional currencies.

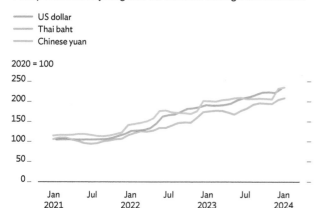

US = United States.
Sources: Bank of the Lao PDR; Asian Development Bank estimates.

Figure 2.25.4 Foreign Currency Deposits

Foreign currency deposits increased as the kip depreciated.

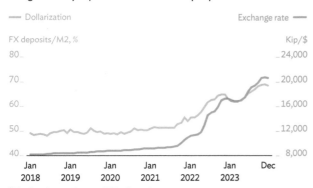

FX = foreign exchange, M2 = broad money.
Sources: Bank of the Lao PDR; Asian Development Bank estimates.

Figure 2.25.5 Monthly Inflation

Inflation was in double digits during 2023.

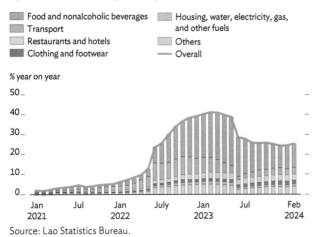

Source: Lao Statistics Bureau.

Consumer prices rose more than wages, causing real incomes and purchasing power to fall in many households. Average inflation jumped from 23% in 2022 to 31.2% in 2023, with lags in imported price adjustments and higher domestic prices driving the increase. Prices for rice, sugar, oil, and chicken doubled over the course of 2023. Rising prices for food, hotels, and restaurants coupled with a weak kip pushed the inflation rate to a high of 41.3% in February 2023 before moderating to 24.4% in December (Figure 2.25.5). With household purchasing power declining, school dropouts increased, with as many as one in three children of lower secondary school age not attending school—twice as many as the average lower-middle-income economy. With the kip depreciation, differentials between the statutory monthly minimum wage in the Lao PDR and Thailand have widened, now equivalent to $71 and $225, respectively. As a result, as many as one in eight Lao PDR workers have migrated across the border for work, creating skills and labor shortages in the domestic labor market.

The late start of the 2023 monsoon season delayed cultivation while low rainfall reduced hydropower output. The growing season was delayed due to below-average rainfall, as indicated by the Normalized Difference Vegetation Index (Figure 2.25.6). Other factors affecting agriculture production were labor shortages and rising input costs. Despite poor weather, the country benefited from strong external demand for cash crops, with exports of cassava and sugar rising from $616.9 million in 2022 to $707.7 million in 2023. However, the benefits were partially offset by high prices for agricultural inputs. Hydropower generation suffered from low rainfall, with electricity output contracting by 4.1% to 46.8 million kilowatt-hour compared to 2022 (Figure 2.25.7). Electricity exports reached $2.4 billion, while imports were $117 million, up from $40 million in 2022.

The private sector recovery remained subdued. Total domestic credit, particularly to the private sector, decelerated in 2023, largely due to lower kip lending (Figure 2.25.8). Businesses across the economy reported difficulty in timely access foreign currencies to support operations. Nonetheless, mining continued to be strong, with mineral output increasing in 2023—especially gold bullion, gold ore, iron ore, and potassium. Gold ore and bullion exports earned $703 million, with iron ore exports at $410.6 million

Figure 2.25.6 Normalized Difference Vegetation Index

Crop planting was delayed in 2023 by the late monsoon.

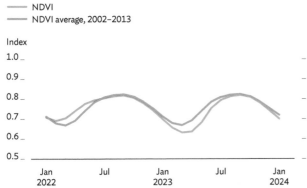

NDVI = Normalized Difference Vegetation Index.
Sources: World Food Programme; Asian Development Bank estimates.

Figure 2.25.7 Rainfall

Rainfall fell below the 20-year average in 2023.

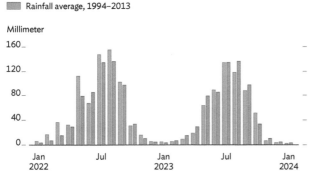

Sources: World Food Programme; Asian Development Bank estimates.

Figure 2.25.8 Credit to the Economy

Credit growth decelerated.

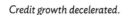
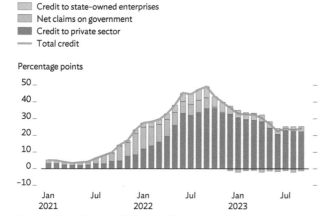

Sources: Bank of the Lao PDR; Asian Development Bank estimates.

and potassium salt at $400.9 million. This helped to create a small trade surplus of $112 million. Overall export of goods reached $9.6 billion in 2023, an increase of 0.3% from 2022, while goods imports cost $9.5 billion, an increase of 7.4% from 2022. Imports included $1.2 billion for diesel and gasoline.

High debt and debt servicing persisted amid low foreign reserves. As the Lao PDR's ability to service its debt deteriorated, the Thai Rating and Information Services lowered its rating for the sovereign from BBB– to BB+—which closed Thailand's bond market for the Lao PDR government and its state-owned enterprises. Public and publicly guaranteed debt to GDP was estimated above 120% in 2023, with liquidity pressure mounting from scheduled debt servicing requirements averaging more than 10% of GDP annually during 2024–2029 (Figure 2.25.9). Gross official reserves, including a $0.8 billion currency swap with the People's Bank of China, were reported at $1.8 billion as of end-September 2023, equivalent to 2.3 months of imports (Figure 2.25.10). The IMF Article IV 2023 report assessed the Lao PDR as being in debt distress with an unsustainable debt burden.

Expenditure control kept the fiscal deficit from rising further. The fiscal deficit expanded to 2.0% of GDP in 2023 from 0.2% in 2022 as allowances for civil servants increased to offset the rising cost of living and government debt servicing. Overall expenditure was restrained in the first 10 months of 2023, with capital spending reaching only KN27.8 trillion or 62% of the annual plan. Revenue collection

Figure 2.25.9 Public Debt

Public debt reached a critical level.

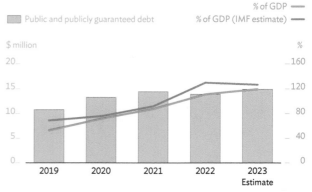

GDP = gross domestic product, IMF = International Monetary Fund.
Sources: IMF; Ministry of Finance; Asian Development Bank estimates.

Figure 2.25.10 Reserves and Imports

Reserve coverage is inadequate.

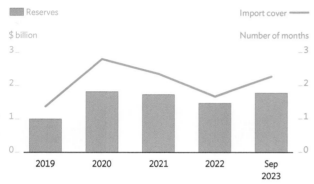

Sources: Bank of the Lao PDR; Asian Development Bank estimates.

reached KN32.5 trillion or 85% of the plan. The fuel exemption cost the budget KN3.5 trillion or 9.2% of the budget. Deficit financing was supported by bond issuance and central and commercial bank lending to the government.

Economic Prospects

A moderate recovery is projected, with GDP growth at 4% in 2024 and 2025, supported by external demand (Table 2.25.1). Growth in services, including trade, transportation, and logistics, is set to continue with increasing tourist arrivals. Foreign investment will continue to finance logistics and renewable energy projects. However, domestic consumption and investment will continue to be affected by macroeconomic pressures stemming from unsustainable debt, with inflation high and fiscal policy tight, which will constrain the overall economic recovery.

Table 2.25.1 Selected Economic Indicators, %

The outlook is for a moderate growth recovery amid continuing high inflation.

	2022	2023	2024	2025
GDP growth	2.5	3.7	4.0	4.0
Inflation	23.0	31.2	20.0	7.0

GDP = gross domestic product.
Sources: Lao Statistics Bureau; Asian Development Bank estimates.

External demand from tourism and logistics will support services. With open borders and major connectivity infrastructure upgrades complete, particularly the Lao PDR–PRC Railway, international tourist arrivals are projected to increase from 3.4 million to 4.2 million in 2024. With the Lao PDR the Association of Southeast Asian Nations Chairman in 2024, tourism and other hospitality-related businesses should benefit. The Thanaleng dry port, part of an integrated logistics park in the capital, Vientiane, closed a 10-year $67 million loan facility in January 2024, which will boost trade.

Foreign investment in renewable energy will help drive moderate industrial growth. The Lao PDR continues to attract new investment for clean energy exports. In 2023, the $4.0 billion Pak Lay and Pak Beng Hydropower projects totaling 1.7 gigawatt (GW) were signed. Investments for 2GW in wind power are expected for 2024 and 2025. The direct and indirect effects of these investments will support moderate growth in construction, including the expected completion of the Monsoon Wind Power Project by 2025.

Climate risk remains a concern for agriculture. El Niño weather conditions weakened in the first quarter of 2024, but lingering effects will likely lead to above-normal temperatures, influencing rainfall patterns in 2024. There is a chance of a shift to a La Niña weather pattern toward the end of 2024, adding the risk of flooding in 2025. High input costs, labor shortages, and disaster risk weigh on prospects for improved agricultural production. However, external demand for agriculture commodities should remain robust, especially for cassava, banana, and livestock, which have received higher import quotas under bilateral trade agreements with the PRC, Thailand, and Viet Nam.

Regional demand for goods and services will allow a small trade surplus. Regional tourism and export demand for electricity, minerals, and crops are expected to offset import demand to put the overall trade balance in surplus. Imports will likely be subdued by a weaker kip and higher excise charges.

Inflationary pressures will persist due to continuing macroeconomic imbalances. Consumer prices are projected to rise an average of 20% in 2024 before moderating to 7.0% in 2025. Prices are expected to continue to rise as businesses pass on costs linked to currency depreciation from imported goods and wage adjustments. Inflation is projected to gradually return to single digits by 2025, assuming continued tight monetary and fiscal policy as well as effective implementation of Prime Minister's Order No. 10 (2023) that introduced reforms on foreign currency use and export earnings repatriation.

Fiscal and monetary policy will remain tight amid debt stress. The government has reduced external borrowing to improve its debt sustainability and fiscal position. The return of the value added tax rate to 10% in March this year will help reach the target of a primary surplus over the next 2 years. However, despite compressed capital spending, the overall fiscal deficit will be around 2.5% of GDP this year and next due to high debt service payments.

Liquidity constraints due to unsustainable debt remain a key risk. Macroeconomic instability—from debt stress, inadequate foreign exchange reserves, and incomplete reforms—are key risks to economic recovery. In addition, state-owned enterprises face increased refinancing risks, and banking liquidity constraints may hinder private sector recovery. A slower-than-expected recovery in neighboring economies and higher-than-expected commodity prices remain key external risks to the outlook.

Policy Challenge—Addressing Macroeconomic Imbalances Key to Tackling Food Security

Food insecurity persists. As many as one in seven of the population had to deal with food insecurity in 2023, with rural dwellers twice as likely as urban dwellers to face shortages (Figure 2.25.11). About two-thirds of the population live in rural areas, with many working in agriculture. Yet agriculture contributes only 15% to GDP. Therefore, earnings and farm incomes remain low, and many lack access to enough safe and nutritious food to meet their dietary needs.

Worsening macroeconomic imbalances have affected food security. While household location and livelihood are important determinants of food insecurity, the country's worsening macroeconomic

Figure 2.25.11 Share of Population that are Food Insecure, 2022–2023

One in seven are food insecure.

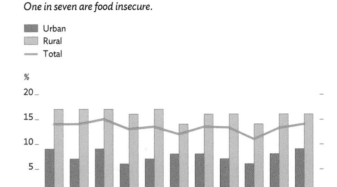

Source: World Food Programme. 2023. Lao PDR: Food Security Monitoring—Remote Household Food Security Survey Brief. Vientiane.

imbalances—notably rising public debt, steep currency depreciation, and elevated inflation—have contributed to persistent food and nutrition challenges. High food inflation is of particular concern, averaging 39.5% in 2023 (Figure 2.25.12). This has reduced purchasing power, affecting almost all households, with half forced to devise food-coping strategies, such as reducing food consumption and meal frequency to bridge their nutritional needs.

Food insecurity and poor nutrition come at a high cost. There are serious long-term consequences associated with households responding to current

Figure 2.25.12 Inflation

High food inflation has contributed to persistent food and nutrition challenges.

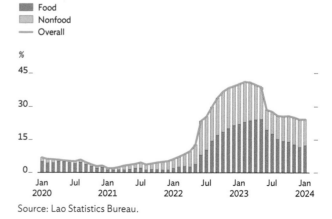

Source: Lao Statistics Bureau.

stress by reducing food quality and quantity, including malnutrition-related issues—such as stunting—that can reduce the lifetime productivity of a child. With a children-under-five stunting rate of 32.8%, among the highest globally, malnutrition is estimated to cost the Lao PDR 2.6% of GDP annually.

Measures have been taken to respond to recent household stress. To help address worsening food and nutrition security linked to inflationary pressures, the Ministry of Agriculture and Forestry raised grant financing from the Global Agriculture and Food Security Program to bring down the cost of essential farm inputs, such as pesticides and fertilizers, and promote climate resilient farming by providing grants. The government is also working with development partners using multisectoral approaches to help improve food security and nutrition. These include expanding social assistance, improving health services, and investing in clean water and sanitation.

Moving forward, longer-term sustainable financing mechanisms are needed to address the multidimensional nature of food insecurity within the context of macroeconomic instability. This includes reforms to address the country's economic and financial challenges and continuing to upscale nutrition-sensitive and climate-resilient social assistance. The multisectoral response program must also include strategies to improve rural livelihoods, including solutions for low agricultural productivity and insufficient access to agriculture credit. Improving farmers' access to financial services—including microfinance, microinsurance and adapting financial products to meet agriculture cashflow needs—are part of a broader suite of solutions to address these systemic issues.

MALAYSIA

Growth slowed in 2023 on softer external demand and lower commodity prices. Inflation trended downwards as government subsidies and price controls continued from 2022. Stronger growth is expected in 2024 and 2025 as global trade and the technology sector recovers. Inflation is projected to increase slightly from an increase in taxes and lower fuel subsidies. To support Malaysia's green transition, the government needs to craft a comprehensive and holistic approach to a greener economy.

Economic Performance

The challenging external environment hampered growth. Malaysia's GDP growth slowed to 3.7% in 2023 from 8.7% in 2022. The normalization of global goods demand led to the weaker performance, which affected manufacturing. At the same time, exports fell by 7.9% amid flat growth of global trade, weaker commodity prices, and a delayed rebound of the global technology sector. Meanwhile, higher investment and solid domestic consumption underpinned economic growth in 2023 (Figure 2.26.1).

Exports contracted by 7.9% in 2023 after expanding by 14.5% in 2022. Lower demand from major trading partners and tempering of commodity prices led to the decline. All major exports contracted, including palm oil-based commodities and palm oil, petroleum, and electrical and electronic products (Figure 2.26.2). As the export contraction outpaced the decline in imports, the trade balance decreased by 11.3% in 2023.

Resilient domestic consumption kept overall growth positive. As demand for goods normalized, private consumption continued to support growth, albeit at a more moderate 4.7% pace in 2023 compared to 11.2% in 2022. Lower inflation and improved labor market conditions continued to sustain household spending in 2023. The unemployment rate fell to 3.4%

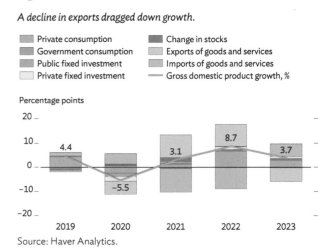

Figure 2.26.1 Demand-Side Contributions to Growth

A decline in exports dragged down growth.

- Private consumption
- Government consumption
- Public fixed investment
- Private fixed investment
- Change in stocks
- Exports of goods and services
- Imports of goods and services
- —— Gross domestic product growth, %

Percentage points

Source: Haver Analytics.

in 2023 from 3.8% the previous year (Figure 2.26.3). Household spending also benefitted from several policy measures, such as continuing fuel, food, and electricity subsidies and minimum wage increases for micro-enterprises. However, as the government rationalized electricity subsidies and price controls, public consumption growth decelerated from 4.5% in 2022 to 3.9% in 2023.

This chapter was written by James Villafuerte of the Southeast Asia Department (SERD), ADB, Manila, and Mae Hyacinth Kiocho and Joyce Marie Lagac, SERD consultants.

Figure 2.26.2 Exports of Key Commodities

Exports deteriorated amid a slowdown in external demand and a downtrend in the technology sector.

— Total exports
— Palm oil and palm-oil based products
— Electrical products
— Petroleum products

% change year on year, 3-month moving average

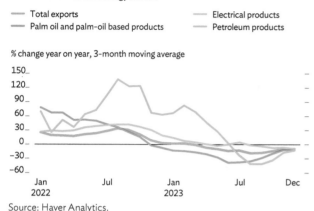

Source: Haver Analytics.

Figure 2.26.3 Labor Market Indicators

Labor market conditions improved as the unemployment rate declined further and wages increased.

— Manufacturing nominal wage
— Services nominal wage
Unemployment rate ▨

% change year on year | % of labor force

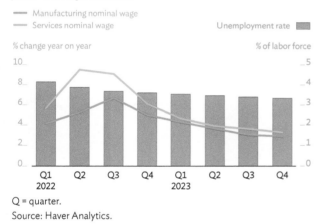

Q = quarter.
Source: Haver Analytics.

Figure 2.26.4 Investments

Investment remained positive, although the pace of implementation was moderate.

▨ Approved Investments   Foreign Direct Investment —

RM billion   RM billion

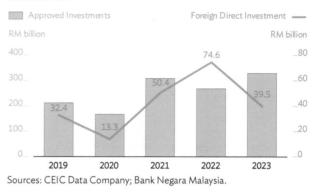

Sources: CEIC Data Company; Bank Negara Malaysia.

Figure 2.26.5 Supply-Side Contributions to Growth

Industry's contribution was minimal, given the weak manufacturing performance, while services remained a key driver of growth.

▨ Agriculture
▨ Import duties
▨ Industry
▨ Services
— Gross domestic product growth, %

Percentage points

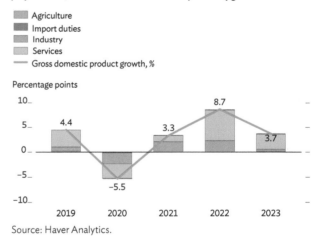

Source: Haver Analytics.

Public investment rose by 8.6% in 2023 from 5.3% in 2022. The increase was driven primarily by higher capital outlays of public corporations and a spike in federal government development expenditures. The substantial increase in development expenditure was supported by capital spending on the Pan Borneo Highway and the East Coast Rail Line (ECRL) projects. Private investment expanded by 4.6% in 2023, lower than the 7.2% growth in 2022. Approved investments increased by 23.0% from RM267.8 billion in 2022 to RM329.5 billion in 2023. However, realized investment for the year might be lower given reduced foreign direct investment (Figure 2.26.4).

Weak external demand and a delayed recovery in the technology sector weighed down manufacturing. Manufacturing was stagnant, posting only 0.7% growth in 2023, substantially lower than the 8.1% growth in 2022 (Figure 2.26.5). After growing in 2022 by 14.2%, manufactured electrical and electronic products contracted by 1.6% in 2023.

Accelerated infrastructure projects and vibrant tourism buoyed expansion in construction and services. Construction posted the highest growth, increasing by 6.1% in 2023 compared to 5.0% in 2022. Meanwhile, resilient domestic demand for goods, expenditures on local travel, and large tourist arrivals supported the increase in consumer- and tourism-related services.

Inflation eased to 2.5% in 2023 from 3.4% in 2022. Food inflation declined from 5.9% to 4.9% and transport from 4.7% in 2022 to 1.1% in 2023 (Figure 2.26.6). Policy measures such as fuel and electricity subsidies and price controls for chicken and eggs brought down inflation.

There was less monetary tightening in 2023 compared to 2022. Bank Negara Malaysia (BNM) tightened the monetary policy rate from 2.75% to 3.0% in May 2023 to manage persistent core inflation (Figure 2.26.7). The increase brought the monetary policy rate back to its pre-pandemic level. Despite the sharp fall in the ringgit against the US dollar, BNM maintained its policy rate until the end of 2023.

External factors weakened the Malaysian ringgit. The ringgit depreciated against the US dollar by 4.0% (Figure 2.26.8) by the end of 2023. It was lowest in October 2023, averaging RM4.75 per US dollar. The US Federal Reserve's hawkish stance and the weaker-than-expected recovery of the People's Republic of China (PRC) drove the ringgit downward.

The fiscal position remained stable despite weaker economic growth. The fiscal deficit narrowed to 5.0% of GDP in 2023 from 5.5% in 2022. Government revenues expanded at a slower pace of 7.0%, following the 25.9% increase in 2022. Government expenditures also increased by a more moderate 3.2% in 2023 from 18.4% in 2022 due to the removal of COVID-19 funds and lower growth in operating expenditures.

The external current account balance continued to be in surplus in 2023. The surplus fell to 1.2% of GDP in 2023 from 3.2% in 2022, due to a nearly 30.0% decline in the goods account. However, the services deficit continued to shrink on increased tourism receipts.

External debt edged higher to 68.2% of GDP in 2023 from 63.9% in 2022. The rise came partly from increased interbank borrowings, loans, non-resident deposits and holdings of domestic debt securities, and partly from the ringgit's depreciation against the US dollar—foreign currency-denominated debt

Figure 2.26.6 Monthly Inflation

Inflation trended downward as price increases for most commodities decelerated.

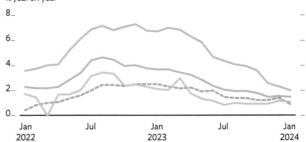

Source: Haver Analytics.

Figure 2.26.7 Policy Rate

The policy rate increased once in 2023 compared to 2022's series of increases.

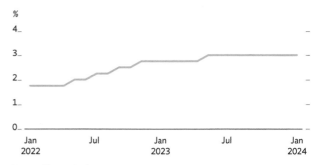

Source: Haver Analytics.

Figure 2.26.8 Exchange Rate

The ringgit weakened against the US dollar, driven by external factors.

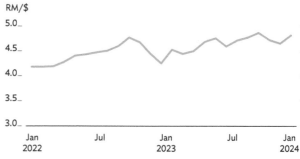

Source: CEIC Data Company.

comprises 66.9% of total external debt. As of the end of 2023, international reserves totaled $113.5 billion, covering 5.4 months of goods and services imports.

Economic Prospects

Solid domestic spending, moderate inflation, and improved trade will drive economic prospects for 2024. Firm private consumption, lower inflation, a supportive monetary policy stance, along with the recovery of external demand, global trade, and the global technology sector support the year's economic prospects. GDP is projected to rise by a faster 4.5% in 2024 and 4.6% in 2025 (Table 2.26.1 and Figure 2.26.9).

Domestic consumption, both private and public, will continue to support growth. Growth in private consumption is expected to revert to its long-term trend of approximately 5.0%. Stable prices, continued improvements in the labor market, and supportive policy measures will prop up consumer sentiment and spending.

Table 2.26.1 Selected Economic Indicators, %

Stronger growth and relatively stable inflation are expected in 2024 and 2025.

	2022	2023	2024	2025
GDP growth	8.7	3.7	4.5	4.6
Inflation	3.4	2.5	2.6	2.6

GDP = gross domestic product.
Sources: Department of Statistics Malaysia; Asian Development Bank estimates.

Figure 2.26.9 Gross Domestic Product Growth

The economy is projected to thrive in 2024 and 2025.

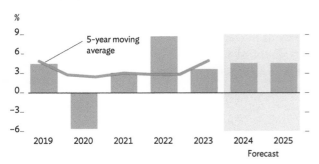

Source: *Asian Development Outlook* database.

The fiscal outlook leans towards budgetary consolidation in the coming years. The 2024 budget emphasizes reforming the fiscal position to become more sustainable. In line with the Public Finance and Fiscal Responsibility Act, the government is committed to reducing the fiscal deficit to 3.0% of GDP and ensuring that debt reaches 60.0% of GDP or below within 3 to 5 years. In 2024, the aim is to reduce the fiscal deficit further to 4.3% of GDP from 5.0% in 2023. The government plans to enact fiscal reforms that strengthen the management and mobilization of revenues and reduce spending leakages.

An expanded revenue base and shift to targeted subsidies may lead to a rise in inflation. Inflation is expected to remain manageable as oil and commodity prices moderate. Nevertheless, upward pressure on prices may come from changes in tax and subsidy policies. Several measures to increase tax revenues include expanding the scope of taxable services, introducing a capital gains tax on unlisted shares and implementing a high-value goods tax. Meanwhile, temporary price controls will be lifted, and a targeted subsidy on fuel will be rolled out in the second half of 2024.

Large infrastructure investments and initiatives to restructure the economy are needed to increase growth. The continuation and acceleration of infrastructure projects, such as ongoing transport-related projects and renovations of dilapidated rural schools and clinics, will promote public investment. Other projects expected to start in 2024 include flood mitigation projects and the expansion of the Samajaya High-Tech Park in Sarawak and Tok Bali Industrial Park in Kelantan. Meanwhile, the government's strategic initiatives require substantial investment in the private sector. These initiatives include restructuring the economy's growth by focusing on high-value-added activities under the New Industrial Master Plan 2030, the transition to a green economy as laid out in the National Energy Transition Roadmap, and the expansion of the digital economy as presented in the MyDIGITAL initiative.

A more optimistic outlook on global trade and upcycle in the technology sector indicate a recovery in exports and a more robust manufacturing performance. After contracting from March to December 2023, exports have started to show signs of recovery, growing by 8.7% in January 2024. Manufacturing has also improved, with the manufacturing purchasing managers' index (PMI) increasing to 49.0 in January 2024. Although still below 50.0, the index was higher at the start of 2024 compared with the 47.8 average Manufacturing PMI in 2023 (Figure 2.26.10).

Figure 2.26.10 Manufacturing Purchasing Managers' Index

The manufacturing index contracted throughout 2023, but started to improve in January 2024.

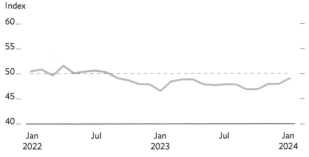

Note: A purchasing managers' index reading <50 signals deterioration, >50 improvement.
Source: CEIC Data Company.

Services will remain a key contributor to growth with innovations in the retail trade and the rebound in tourism. Wholesale and retail trade growth, particularly retail, is poised to strengthen from wider use of digital transactions. Based on the Business and Economics Survey, the income of establishments from e-commerce transactions reached RM1,153.5 billion in 2023, an increase of 4.9% from 2022. Under the MyDIGITAL initiative, the government has taken steps to harness investments to develop the digital economy, aiming to expand the digital economy by 25.5% of GDP in 2025. This will increase retail digital transactions. Also, introducing environmentally friendly motor vehicle models at lower prices should expand the segment. Meanwhile, tourism arrivals are projected to increase to 27 million in 2024, higher than the pre-pandemic level (Figure 2.26.11).

New external developments and their impact on the economy's trajectory can lead to changes in monetary policy. So far, the monetary policy rate supports economic growth and manages inflation. On managing the ringgit, the government and BNM

Figure 2.26.11 Tourist Arrivals

The rise in tourist arrivals continued to support services.

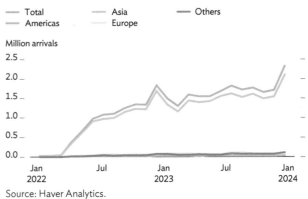

Source: Haver Analytics.

are looking into measures aside from using the monetary policy rate to strengthen the ringgit. These include examining export proceeds, encouraging government-linked companies and investment companies to constantly revert and convert foreign investment income into ringgit, controlling overseas investments, and encouraging Malaysians to support local products and investments.

Although the prospects appear optimistic, growth remains subject to downside risks. Particularly notable are a lower-than-expected recovery of external demand, especially from the PRC, and worsening geopolitical tensions that can lead to a rise in commodity prices. On the other hand, the upsides to growth include better-than-expected consumption and tourism activities, higher spillovers of the uptrend in the technology sector, and accelerating implementation of new and existing projects.

Policy Challenge—Advancing Green Growth

Malaysia is committed to advancing growth sustainability and conserving natural resources. Malaysia is focused on advancing green growth, enhancing energy sustainability, and transforming its water sector. It has adopted a whole-of-nation approach to pursue green growth, an inclusive way for all stakeholders to share responsibility and accountability in implementing a clean, green, and resilient agenda. Energy sustainability will be supported by an adequate supply of energy resources, infrastructure, and renewable energy as alternative energy sources to complement energy efficiency measures. Adopting Integrated Water Resource Management (IWRM) is key to achieving Malaysia's long-term goal to increase water management efficiency and generate greater employment in the water sector.

In energy, the government has pledged to phase out coal-fired power plants and increase the share of renewable energy to 70% of installed capacity by 2050 to achieve net-zero. In 2020, the total national installed capacity from renewables increased to 23%. Numerous initiatives support the shift to renewables. The Green Investment Tax Allowance grants companies allowances to adopt renewable energy in their operations and upgrade their energy efficiency. The Green Income Tax Exemption offers generous tax cuts for companies providing services related to green technology activities. The Green Electricity Tariff allows consumers to reduce their carbon footprint by using electricity from renewable energy. Institutional and financing capacities were also strengthened to support the green agenda.

To improve the coordination between stakeholders, the Climate Governance Malaysia was set up in 2019 and the Malaysia Climate Action Council was established in 2020. In 2019, BNM and the Securities Commission coordinated a collective financial sector response to climate risks and improve climate-related financing opportunities in capital and financial markets. Malaysia also established the Sustainable Development Financing Fund and Public Transport Fund to support sustainable development initiatives. In addition, the *Amanah Lestari Alam* was established in 2020 to increase awareness and change behavior concerning the environment through long-term, inter-generational and education-focused initiatives.

Despite ongoing progress, several challenges remain to accelerate Malaysia's transition to a green economy. The unsustainable consumption and production practices of Malaysia's economy use resources inefficiently. The large volume of waste generated from economic activities damages the environment and results in expensive clean-up and mitigation measures. To support and finance the transition, Malaysia requires considerable investment. According to the National Energy Transition Roadmap, an estimated RM1.3 trillion ($280 billion) of investments is needed for Malaysia's energy transition.

Malaysia must increase access to sustainability-related education and public awareness on green issues. In a recent survey conducted by The Economist magazine (2023), only 15% of employees in Malaysia consider green skills to be important. Employees have also reported that a lack of time and the high cost of courses are key barriers to acquiring green skills. The fragmentation, inaccessibility, and insufficient data quality have hindered comprehensive data analysis to support evidenced-based risk-informed decision-making processes.

Malaysia is committed to fostering the development of a clean and efficient economy. However, governance-related issues need to be addressed, including limited enforcement capacity, inadequate monitoring, reporting, and evaluation. These are key barriers to accelerate Malaysia's transition toward a green economy. It is imperative to create an enabling environment for the circular economy and more sustainable and responsible businesses, particularly micro, small, and medium-sized enterprises.

MYANMAR

The economy has suffered from prolonged instability and conflict, leading to a decline in GDP growth. Exchange rate volatility, inflation, and disruptions in trade and logistics have worsened the impact. Continuing uncertainty makes it difficult to respond to basic human needs and address climate risks. It is crucial to address these issues promptly.

Economic Performance

Growth declined significantly due to instability and conflict. GDP growth for fiscal year 2023 (FY2023, ended 31 March 2024) is estimated to drop to 0.8% from 2.4% in FY2022 due to broad-based declines across key sectors (Figure 2.27.1). Agriculture contracted by 1.8%, mainly due to increased costs along with conflict-induced supply chain and logistic disruptions. Industrial activity grew by a marginal 2.2%, affected by a power deficit, exchange rate fluctuations, an uncertain business environment, and weak global demand. Services grew by 1.0%, supported by modest growth in domestic travel and tourism, finance, and health. By the end of FY2023, international tourist arrivals increased to 83,606, almost seven times higher than the previous year. Despite this growth, instability remains a barrier for tourism to reach its full potential.

Inflation remained in double digits. Average annual inflation in FY2023 remained high at 22% due to several factors, such as supply chain disruptions, shortages, currency depreciation, and increasing transportation costs. In June 2023 (latest available data), food prices saw a surge in inflation, reaching 33.2%, while nonfood products increased by 15% during the same month. Increasing instability across the country has hindered food production and trade flows, worsening inflationary pressures, particularly in conflict-affected areas.

Internal and external challenges constrained trade. Trade has declined significantly since March 2023 due to weaker global demand and increased

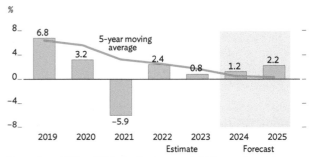

Figure 2.27.1 Gross Domestic Product Growth

Instability and conflict are hampering growth.

Notes: From 2019 to 2021, the fiscal year ends 31 September of that year; 2022 onward years are fiscal years ending 31 March of the following year.
Sources: Central Bank of Myanmar. 2023. *Quarterly Financial Statistics Bulletin 2023 Volume I*; Asian Development Bank estimates.

internal political unrest. Merchandise exports dropped by 13.9% in the last quarter of FY2023, with a sharp decline in livestock (65.4%), forestry products (56.1%), manufactured goods (20.0%), and mineral products (19.2%). An unfavorable business environment, international sanctions, and exchange rate volatility hindered investment demand for public and private projects. As a result, imports decelerated by 7.9% in the last quarter of FY2023, primarily driven by a drastic slowdown in capital and intermediate imports, including Cut-Make-Pack imports for garment manufacturing. The current account deficit widened to 5.5% in FY2023 from 3.4% in FY2022, as the decline in exports outpaced the deceleration in imports. Foreign

---

This chapter was written by Joel Mangahas and Eve Cherry Lynn of the Myanmar Resident Mission, ADB, Manila.
Effective 1 February 2021, ADB placed a temporary hold on sovereign project disbursements and new contracts in Myanmar.

direct investment commitments remained muted and, as of the third quarter FY2023, were 48.3% below the levels recorded before the onset of COVID-19 pandemic in 2020.

The FY2023 fiscal deficit remained high due to lower revenue collection. Revenue decreased due to subdued public and private sector economic activity and lower export revenue. The fiscal deficit in FY2023 is estimated to be around 6.0% of GDP, down from 6.5% in FY2022.

Economic Prospects

Due to persistent uncertainty and instability, the economy is expected to weaken further. Increased armed conflict in several regions has negatively affected economic activity. As a result, real GDP growth is predicted to remain low, at 1.2% in FY2024 and 2.2% in FY2025 (Table 2.27.1). This is significantly less than the average growth rate of 6%–7% between FY2016 and FY2019. Agriculture will likely see a further decline of 1% in FY2024 due to higher production costs, conflict, and trade disruptions. Disruptions along border areas, especially with the People's Republic of China, have significantly lowered exports and imports. In January 2024, agricultural exports decreased by 10.7%, which will likely continue unless the situation improves.

Table 2.27.1 Selected Economic Indicators, %

Growth is expected to remain low, but inflation will improve.

	2022	2023	2024	2025
GDP growth	2.4	0.8	1.2	2.2
Inflation	27.2	22.0	15.5	10.2

GDP = gross domestic product.
Note: Years are fiscal years ending 31 March of the following year (covering 1 April–31 March).
Sources: Central Bank of Myanmar. 2023. *Quarterly Statistics Bulletin Volume I*; Asian Development Bank estimates.

Growth in industry and services will be moderate. The unfavorable business environment, power shortages, weak global demand, and supply constraints create downward pressures on industrial growth. In addition, conflict escalation in northern Myanmar further stifles an already fragile demand and supply environment. Therefore, industry is expected to grow by only 2.5% in FY2024 and 3.0% in FY2025. In January 2024, imports declined by 7.9%, with a significant drop in capital, intermediate, and Cut-Make-Pack imports, indicating a decline in public and private investment, garment production, among other industries. Despite international tourism remaining subdued, domestic tourism has picked up, especially in conflict-free zones. Thus, services is expected to grow by 1.2% in FY2024 and 2.2% in FY2025, driven by slight improvements in telecommunications, travel and tourism, and transportation. However, growth is limited by rising transportation costs and security issues. Persistent macroeconomic instability poses risks to the banking and finance sector, constraining its stability and growth.

Inflation will continue to remain elevated. The decrease in food production and supply, coupled with a contraction in agriculture, worsened inflationary pressures. In addition, the Kyat has persistently depreciated as the Central Bank of Myanmar continues to monetize the fiscal deficit. As a result, inflation is expected to remain high at 15.5% in FY2024 before easing to 10.2% in FY2025.

The current account and fiscal deficits are expected to remain high. Ongoing conflicts at the border are expected to impact trade negatively, as border trade accounts for almost 40% of the total (Figure 2.27.2). The trade deficit rose to $1.2 billion in January 2024, nearly three times more than the previous year. As a result, the current account deficit is projected to reach 5.8% of GDP in FY2024 and 5.0% in FY2025 (Figure 2.27.3). Due to sluggish economic growth and the unfavorable trade position, revenue collection is expected to be low throughout FY2024. Therefore, the fiscal deficit is expected to remain high at 5.7% of GDP in FY2024 and 5.5% in FY2025 (Figure 2.27.4).

Myanmar's economy faces multiple risks and pressing challenges. Continuing tensions in the country have impeded reforms to support economic and sustainable development, making the country more vulnerable and increasing poverty. There are other risks as well, such as a global slowdown that is worse than anticipated, international sanctions, and weaker external assistance, which could negatively affect trade and investment. Additionally, there is a limited fiscal headroom against potential shocks.

Figure 2.27.2 Merchandise Trade Indicators

Border conflicts are harming trade.

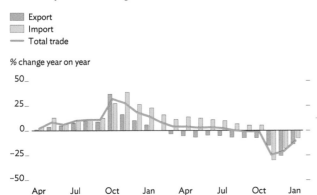

Source: Ministry of Commerce.

Figure 2.27.3 Current Account Balance

The current account deficit remains high.

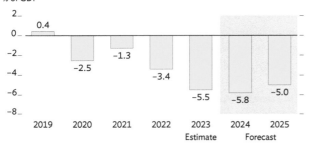

GDP = gross domestic product.

Notes: From 2019 to 2021, the fiscal year ends 31 September of that year; 2022 onward years are fiscal years ending 31 March of the following year.

Sources: Central Bank of Myanmar. *Balance of Payment Statistics*; Asian Development Bank estimates.

Figure 2.27.4 Fiscal Balance

The fiscal deficit is expected to remain wide.

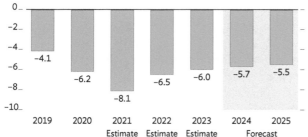

GDP = gross domestic product.

Notes: From 2019 to 2021, the fiscal year ends 31 September of that year; 2022 onward years are fiscal years ending 31 March of the following year.

Sources: Central Bank of Myanmar. 2023. *Quarterly Financial Statistics Bulletin 2023 Volume I*; Asian Development Bank estimates.

Policy Challenge—Responding to Basic Human Needs and Strengthening Climate Resilience

Living conditions are deteriorating sharply.

The country faces heightened conflict, economic difficulties, food insecurity, and rapidly rising poverty, reversing the socioeconomic progress made over the past decade. The United Nations Humanitarian Response Plan estimates that 18.6 million people, or 33% of the country's population, will need humanitarian assistance in 2024, up from 17.7 million in 2023. Aid workers aim to reach 5.3 million people in critical need, requiring $994 million for lifesaving support. As of 27 January 2024, 97% of the required funding was lacking. Repeating the severe underfunding in 2023, when just 29% of the requirements were met, would be catastrophic for those affected this year. This dire humanitarian situation demands immediate global attention and a substantial increase in funding.

Myanmar's high exposure to natural hazards and climate-related risks worsens economic and humanitarian crises.

The country is highly vulnerable to natural hazards. It scores 9.2 out of 10 on the INFORM Index and ranks 160th out of 185 countries on the Notre Dame Global Adaptation Initiative Index (Figure 2.27.5). It shows that Myanmar is simply unprepared to deal with the physical impact of natural

Figure 2.27.5 INFORM Risk Index

Myanmar is highly vulnerable to natural hazards.

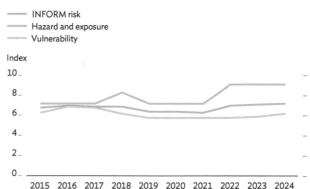

Notes: The INFORM Risk Index measures hazards and people's exposure to them, vulnerability, and available resources to manage these risks. It generates a risk profile for each economy, assigning a rating between 0 and 10 for overall risk as well as its individual components.

Source: DRMKC—Disaster Risk Management Knowledge Centre. Myanmar Risk Profile.

hazards and climate change, given its weak institutional capacity and lack of fiscal space. It remains highly susceptible to climate-related risks, with frequent extreme weather events that damage infrastructure, disrupt agriculture, displace people, and cause loss of life and livelihoods.

These events also strain fiscal resources, hinder economic development, and exacerbate poverty and food insecurity, particularly among the vulnerable. Climate change has also been called a "threat multiplier" in conflict-affected countries, intensifying violence when combined with socio-political issues such as poverty, state fragility, and inequality. Flooding is a frequent annual threat, especially during the monsoon season, and has worsened since 1990. On average, natural hazards reduce annual GDP by 0.9%. After Cyclone Mocha, damage to infrastructure and agriculture was estimated at $2.24 billion, equivalent to approximately 3.4% of Myanmar's 2021 GDP. Building resilience against natural hazards and climate change is crucial to bolster the economy and improve humanitarian conditions.

Overcoming significant constraints is key to deliver timely humanitarian aid to the poor and vulnerable groups. Myanmar's complex operational environment, characterized by conflict and restrictions on humanitarian access, makes it difficult to deliver aid efficiently and effectively. Insecurity in conflict-affected areas significantly constrains humanitarian organizations from delivering needed aid to vulnerable populations. In regions with ongoing conflict and violence, aid workers face numerous risks to their safety and well-being. Security threats make it difficult and risky to provide humanitarian assistance. In some cases, access may be restricted entirely, preventing aid from reaching the neediest. Insecurity also poses challenges in ensuring the safety of aid deliveries. Organizations must establish strong security measures to address these challenges, provide staff training on risk reduction, and build relationships with local partners to enhance safety and security. Limited infrastructure, particularly in rural areas, hinders aid delivery. Poor transportation networks and communication systems make it difficult for aid organizations to reach needy communities, especially during emergencies.

PHILIPPINES

Growth eased in 2023, though still strong, supported by domestic demand. The outlook is for growth to pick up in 2024 and 2025 amid moderating inflation and monetary easing. The current account deficit will narrow, supported in part by strengthening services exports. Promoting higher levels of private sector participation in the economy will be vital to further raise growth and productivity. Building on structural reforms and further measures to enhance the investment climate will support this agenda.

Economic Performance

The economy showed solid growth in 2023 although it eased from 2022 as high inflation and interest rates tempered demand. GDP rose 5.6% in 2023, down from 7.6% in 2022, supported by household consumption and investment (Figure 2.28.1). Household consumption, which comprises three-fourths of GDP, rose by 5.6% after an 8.3% increase in 2022. Overall, however, household consumption remained robust amid low unemployment and steady remittances from overseas workers. The unemployment rate slid to 3.1% in December 2023 from 4.3% in December 2022, with 1.5 million new jobs created. Worker remittances expanded by 3.0%

in 2023, equivalent to 8.5% of GDP. Government consumption rose only 0.4% in 2023 after a 4.9% increase in 2022 during national elections. Difficulties in procurement were among the factors that led to the slowdown in government consumption.

Fixed investment remained strong on higher outlays for industrial machinery and brisk construction. Fixed investment rose 8.1% after 9.7% growth in 2022 (Figure 2.28.2). Public construction grew by 9.7% with large public infrastructure projects underway. Higher private investment was driven by industrial machinery and equipment purchases and

Figure 2.28.1 Demand-Side Contributions to Growth

Domestic demand continued to drive growth.

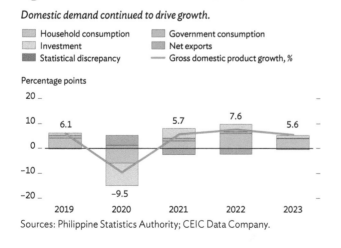

Sources: Philippine Statistics Authority; CEIC Data Company.

Figure 2.28.2 Contributions to Fixed Investment Growth

Brisk public and private construction spurred investment.

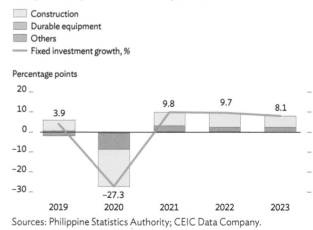

Sources: Philippine Statistics Authority; CEIC Data Company.

This chapter was written by Cristina Lozano and Teresa Mendoza of the Philippines Country Office, ADB, Manila.

an 8.6% rise in private construction. Net exports held back GDP growth. Merchandise exports fell on weak external demand. These were partly cushioned by sustained growth in services exports driven by tourism and business process outsourcing.

Services largely drove GDP growth, led by retail trade and tourism. On the production side, services, providing over half of GDP and employment, expanded by 7.2% and contributed nearly 80% of the GDP expansion (Figure 2.28.3). Transport, accommodation and food services grew in the double digits on buoyant tourism. Growth in retail trade, which comprises one-fourth of services, remained strong at 6%, along with finance (8.9%) and professional and business services (6.7%).

Figure 2.28.3 Supply-Side Contributions to Growth

Broad-based expansion in services largely fueled growth.

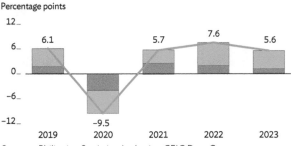

Sources: Philippine Statistics Authority; CEIC Data Company.

Industry's growth slowed on subdued manufacturing. Industry grew by 3.6% in 2023, down from 6.5% in 2022, contributing nearly a fifth to GDP growth. Construction generated nearly 60% of this growth. Manufacturing, while nearly two-thirds of industrial output, contributed less as its growth slowed to 1.3% from 4.9% in 2022. Food manufacturing, about half of total manufacturing, rose along with increased production of electrical and transport equipment. These were partially offset by a decline in electronic products due to sluggish external demand. Agriculture rose modestly by 1.2% as weather-related disturbances affected output. Structural impediments such as underinvestment in irrigation have limited productivity growth.

Inflation slowed in the fourth quarter of 2023 as food prices moderated. Headline inflation moderated to 3.9% in December (6.0% 2023 average) and core inflation to 4.4% (6.6% 2023 average). Lower prices of vegetables and other food items contained overall food inflation, though rice inflation remained elevated at 19.6% from 15.8% in November.

The fiscal deficit narrowed as revenue grew faster than expenditure. The fiscal deficit equaled 6.2% of GDP in 2023, down from 7.3% in 2022, in line with fiscal consolidation goals. Revenue grew by 7.9%, outpacing the 3.4% growth in expenditure. Expenditure included increases in funding for infrastructure, health and education programs, and social assistance. Revenue was supported by increased tax collection (6.5% growth year on year) and higher remittances from government-owned and controlled corporations. The national government debt stood at 60.2% of GDP as of the end of December 2023 from 60.9% a year earlier (Figure 2.28.4). It remains on track with the government goal of reducing debt to below 60% of GDP by 2025. Domestic debt is 68.5% of total debt, with long-term debt about three-fourths of the total. The higher share of domestic borrowing helps reduce vulnerability to foreign exchange shocks. The country's investment-grade sovereign credit ratings were affirmed in 2023.

Figure 2.28.4 National Government Debt

The higher share of domestic debt reduces vulnerability to external shocks.

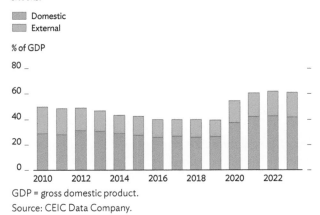

GDP = gross domestic product.
Source: CEIC Data Company.

The balance of payments shifted into surplus as the current account deficit narrowed. The current account deficit slid to 2.6% of GDP in 2023 from a 4.5% deficit in 2022 (Figure 2.28.5). Merchandise exports declined, but imports slid even more. Lower imports

Figure 2.28.5 Current Account Components

Higher services exports and remittances support the current account.

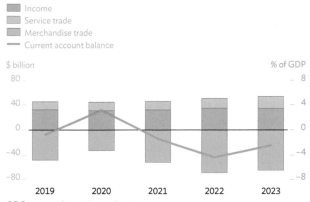

- Income
- Service trade
- Merchandise trade
- Current account balance

GDP = gross domestic product.
Source: CEIC Data Company.

were due to moderating domestic demand, lower imports of raw materials and manufacturing inputs, and the decline in prices of imported commodities. The merchandise trade deficit fell to 15.1% of GDP from 17.2%. Rising remittances and services exports partly cushioned the merchandise trade deficit. In the financial account, higher net inflows came from increased foreign borrowing by resident banks, other sectors and the national government. These offset lower foreign direct investment and portfolio investment net outflows. The overall balance of payments shifted into surplus, equal to 0.8% of GDP, after a 1.7% deficit in 2022. The external debt-to-GDP ratio was 28.7% at the end of December 2023 from 27.5% at end-2022. The Philippine peso appreciated marginally through the end of 2023. Official reserves were $102 billion at the end of February 2024, covering 7.5 months of imports along with service and income payments.

Economic Prospects

Broad-based domestic demand will lift economic growth. The economy is projected to grow by 6.0% in 2024 and 6.2% in 2025 as domestic demand picks up (Table 2.28.1). Moderating inflation and monetary easing bode well for investment and household consumption. Government consumption will rebound as ongoing measures improve budget execution and tackle procurement delays.

Table 2.28.1 Selected Economic Indicators, %

Growth will remain solid, supported by investment and private consumption.

	2022	2023	2024	2025
GDP growth	7.6	5.6	6.0	6.2
Inflation	5.8	6.0	3.8	3.4

GDP = gross domestic product.
Source: Asian Development Bank estimates.

The unemployment rate has stayed low, supporting household consumption. The unemployment rate was 4.5% in January 2024, down from 4.8% in January 2023, below the pre-pandemic average. Meanwhile, the labor force participation rate was at 61.1%, lower than 64.5% in January 2023, with the drop mostly due to women workers. The return to onsite work has been cited as among the factors which reduced women's labor force participation rate to 49.3% from 53.7%. Wage and salaried jobs in private firms increased by 1.5 million over the year. While vulnerable jobs (own-account and unpaid family workers) have declined, they still account for a third of total employment. Other challenges include the increase in share of elementary and low-skill jobs from the pre-pandemic level (Figure 2.28.6). In 2023, the government approved the "Trabaho para sa Bayan" Act (National Employment Master Plan), a comprehensive plan supporting workers and business. It covers industry-relevant upskilling and reskilling programs, active labor market programs including employment facilitation, and support to micro, small and medium enterprises (MSMEs) such as increasing their access to finance, among others.

Figure 2.28.6 Employment by Type

Training is essential for workers to move into technical and higher skilled positions.

- Elementary occupations, clerical support
- Skilled agricultural
- Managers, professionals, technical
- Service and sales workers
- Machine operators, assemblers
- Others

% of total employed

	January 2019	January 2024
	10	8
	22	14
	6	9
	11	11
	17	23
	33	35

Sources: Philippine Statistics Authority; CEIC Data Company.

Large public infrastructure projects will continue to boost investment. Under the government's infrastructure program, there are 67 flagship projects underway, with 30 more projects approved as of March 2024. The infrastructure program includes projects such as bridges, expressways, ports, and railways. Other projects involve agriculture, power, health, digital connectivity, and water management.

Robust expansion in services will continue to drive growth. Retail trade, food services and accommodation, and travel will benefit from strong household consumption and growing tourism. The government targets 7.7 million international visitor arrivals this year from 5.4 million in 2023. Tourism provided 11.4% of total employment in 2022, with its share to GDP rising to 6.2% from 5.2% in 2021. Industry's prospects are also good. The manufacturing purchasing managers' index (PMI) rose from 50.9 in January to 51.0 in February, the sixth consecutive month of expansion (Figure 2.28.7). The upturn came from a rise in new factory orders, partly on a rebound in export sales. Manufacturers increased hiring in line with improved demand. Construction will continue to benefit from public infrastructure projects and buoyant private construction for residential, commercial, and office buildings. Bank lending to businesses expanded by 5.9% in January 2024 from 5.6% in December 2023.

The 2024 budget raises expenditure by 9.5%, with a third allocated to social services. This includes funding for conditional cash transfers to about

4.4 million poor families, national health insurance, food stamp and livelihood programs, and free tertiary education tuition in state universities and colleges. Infrastructure spending is planned to equal 5.0%–6.0% of GDP this year and over the medium term, after 5.8% of GDP in 2023.

New revenue measures will support higher investment while pursuing fiscal consolidation. Under the government's medium-term fiscal framework, the fiscal deficit is programmed to narrow further to 5.6% of GDP in 2024 and reach 3.7% by 2028. Additional revenue measures proposed include new taxes on digital service providers and single-use plastics, and reforms to existing motor vehicle user charges. Carbon-pricing instruments through a carbon tax are being studied. Digitalization is improving tax administration and taxpayer compliance, including electronic filing of returns and invoicing.

Programs aim to make spending more efficient. Bills pending in Congress seek to right-size the government bureaucracy to enhance public service delivery by streamlining, restructuring, and further digitalizing government operations and systems. Additional public financial management reform is being institutionalized to ensure timely program implementation.

Inflation is expected to moderate to 3.8% in 2024 and 3.4% in 2025. Inflation averaged 3.1% in the first 2 months of 2024 as easing global oil prices curbed transport costs (Figure 2.28.8). Food inflation has slowed from last year though it remains high for some

Figure 2.28.7 Manufacturing Purchasing Managers' Index

The PMI continues to indicate that manufacturing will expand.

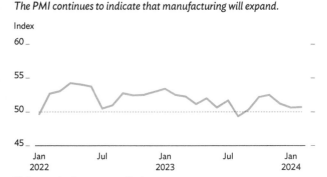

PMI = purchasing managers' index.
Note: A purchasing managers' index reading <50 signals deterioration, >50 improvement.
Source: CEIC Data Company.

Figure 2.28.8 Monthly Inflation

Inflationary pressures stemmed mainly from food prices.

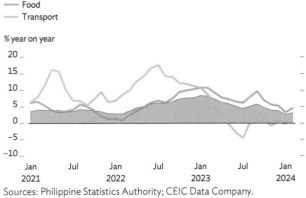

Sources: Philippine Statistics Authority; CEIC Data Company.

commodities, particularly rice. Reduced tariffs on some food items, including rice, corn, and pork were extended to December 2024 to help contain food inflation. This will help reduce inflationary pressures due to El Niño and cases of African swine fever. Core inflation, which excludes volatile food and energy prices, has declined since April last year to 3.6% in February 2024, suggesting easing underlying pressures (Figure 2.28.9). Should inflation continue to stay within the central bank's 2% to 4% target for the year, monetary authorities may cut policy rates in the second half of 2024. The central bank has kept policy rates steady after a cumulative 450 basis points hike from May 2022 to October 2023. The higher policy rate reined in growth in broad money (M3) to 6.0% year on year in January 2024, lowest pace in a year.

Figure 2.28.9 Inflation

Inflation has moved within the central bank's 2% to 4% target.

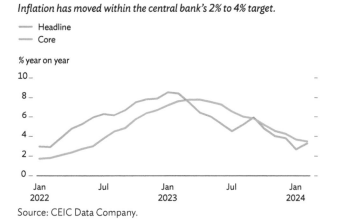

Source: CEIC Data Company.

The current account deficit will narrow in 2024 and 2025, supported by services exports. Tourism and business process outsourcing should remain buoyant, while merchandise exports will improve moderately in 2025. The steady increase in remittances from overseas workers will continue to help lift the current account. Lower global oil prices will also ease import costs.

The growth outlook is subject to downside risks. Severe weather events could increase inflationary pressure. Other risks include a sharper slowdown in major advanced economies, heightened geopolitical tensions, and higher global commodity prices than expected.

Policy Challenge—Promoting Greater Private Sector Participation

The private sector is an important engine of growth and productivity. It generates jobs, contributes to government revenues, drives innovation and improves efficiency through technology adoption. The Philippine Development Plan 2023–2028 underscores the need for greater private sector participation through stronger public–private collaboration along with the structural and regulatory reforms needed to enhance the policy environment.

Despite relatively strong GDP growth, investment in the Philippines lags behind its neighbors. While fixed investment has been over 20% of GDP since 2013, it remains lower than the 30% of GDP in neighbors such as Indonesia and Viet Nam. Similarly, foreign direct investment inflows remain lower than its neighbors, partly reflecting the country's low global ranking as an investment destination. The Philippines ranked 52 out of 64 countries in the 2023 World Competitiveness Report by the International Institute for Management Development. It ranked 13 out of 14 countries included from the Asia and Pacific region. Infrastructure gaps remain among its key challenges, including in energy, transportation, and logistics. Poor connectivity limits access to factor and product markets, raises costs, and undermines the competitiveness of private firms.

A proactive reform agenda is making the country more attractive as an investment destination. Recent reforms have opened the country to more foreign investment and trade. Restrictions on foreign participation were eased in 2022, allowing full foreign ownership in sectors such as renewable energy, telecommunications, airports, shipping, railways, and expressways. Capitalization requirements for foreign investors in retail trade have also been lowered. The Corporate Recovery and Tax Incentives for Enterprises (CREATE) law, which reduced the corporate income tax rate from 30% to 25% (20% for MSMEs), is being refined to match incentives with investors and encourage investment in strategically important sectors. These reforms complement the country's 2023 ratification of the Regional Comprehensive Economic Partnership.

The enhanced public–private partnership (PPP) regulatory framework will help further mobilize private investment for infrastructure development. The PPP Code of the Philippines enacted in 2023 consolidates all legal frameworks and creates a unified system for investors involved in PPPs. Private sector participation in infrastructure helps reduce pressure on public finances and encourages greater expertise in designing and managing infrastructure projects, particularly complex projects such as long-span bridges and subways. The government's infrastructure flagship program featured 185 big-ticket projects as of March 2024 worth ₱9.1 trillion (about $163 billion), 45 to be financed through PPPs. In February 2024, the rehabilitation, operation and maintenance of the Ninoy Aquino International Airport, the country's main gateway, was awarded to the private sector—the largest solicited PPP project in nearly 25 years.

Further measures can enhance the investment climate. The private sector is dominated by a few large conglomerates. MSMEs constitute 99.5% of all enterprises and 63% of total employment. Yet they continue to face challenges in accessing finance and navigating red tape. High administrative burdens on startups, such as numerous permits and licenses, prevent ease of entry of small players. High trade costs also restrict competition and reduce opportunities for domestic firms to access larger markets. It is critical to strengthen market competition, including efforts across government to implement competition policy and deter anti-competitive practices. The Anti-Red Tape Authority has spearheaded efforts to streamline and automate government-related procedures to reduce the regulatory burden at both national and local government levels. Continuing capacity-building measures for local government units (LGUs) to make their localities more investor-friendly are vital. While LGUs are mandated to implement electronic one-stop shops for business, some face capacity constraints. About 40% of LGUs as of February 2024 have adopted the system.

Accelerating private investment in key sectors, including green and resilient energy, is critical for a better business environment. Coal and oil continue to dominate the energy mix, and the Philippines remains a net importer of fossil fuels. High energy costs are often cited as a key barrier to economic competitiveness. If current trends continue, energy self-sufficiency is expected to worsen as natural gas supplies from the Malampaya gas field dwindle. The government

has sought to mobilize investment in renewable power generation to meet its 50% target share in the mix by 2040 (from a 22% share in 2022). The clean energy transition will require planning to replace and decommission fossil fuel-based power plants, and explore opportunities to develop geothermal, offshore wind, and floating solar capabilities. This also requires investment in energy storage, transmission, and grid resilience to accommodate the planned increase in renewable supply. The government has established the Energy Virtual One-Stop Shop System to streamline permits for new energy investments and assisting LGUs to adopt the system.

The private sector can also play a greater role in expanding digital infrastructure. Telecommunications face critical infrastructure gaps. In 2020, only 56.1% of households had internet access at home, with access largely concentrated in the capital, Metro Manila, nearby provinces, and in central Luzon. Most regions in the Visayas and Mindanao reported less than 50% access. Structural challenges of the local telecommunication industry and the archipelagic nature of the country have left poor tower coverage, the lowest among Association of Southeast Asian Nations members. Growing domestic demand cannot be met due to an industry dominated by only a few major players. To help attract private investment, the government issued a common telecommunications tower policy in 2020, with the initial wave of operator licensing and construction already underway. There is an accompanying need for more backhaul capacity and universal coverage which the National Broadband Plan seeks to address, with significant scope for private sector participation. The Open Access in Data Transmission Bill pending in Congress removes the legislative franchise requirement for telecommunications service providers and simplifies the licensing process to promote more competition.

A more inclusive and robust financial system is also vital. Relative to its peers, the Philippines must further deepen its capital markets, strengthen competition and technology adoption in banking, increase insurance penetration, and grow its mutual and pension fund ecosystem. These changes can potentially improve access to capital and the productivity of MSMEs. It will also facilitate more investment in productivity-enhancing innovation and entrepreneurship, disaster resilience projects including in agriculture, and enhance social protection.

SINGAPORE

GDP growth moderated in 2023 dragged by weaker performance of the manufacturing sector amid softer external demand. Growth should accelerate this year supported by the turnaround in manufacturing, robust domestic demand, and stronger external trade, and will further improve in 2025. Inflation moderated in 2023 as energy prices eased and will continue its downward momentum over the forecast horizon. Population aging remains a challenge to Singapore's medium to long-term development.

Economic Performance

Singapore's GDP growth accelerated in the last quarter of 2023. After sluggish growth in the first half of 2023, GDP growth in the fourth quarter accelerated to 2.2%, improving on the 1.0% growth in the third quarter. The pickup came from a recovery in manufacturing and robust growth in services and construction (Figure 2.29.1). Manufacturing expanded by 1.4% in the last quarter, a reversal from four consecutive quarters of contraction. Services grew broadly, positively contributing to growth in the fourth quarter. Construction increased further due to higher demand in both public and private sectors. For the full year, Singapore's economy grew by 1.1%, down from 3.8% in 2022. Growth in services and construction outweighed the overall contraction in manufacturing.

Subdued domestic demand dragged down growth in 2023 (Figure 2.29.2). Domestic demand contracted by 2.5% in 2023, driven by a decline in investment and private consumption. Investment contracted by 11.4% due to depleted inventories and lower private spending. Consumer spending slowed by 3.8% from 8.2% in 2022, partly because of moderating but still elevated prices of goods and services. Meanwhile, government consumption rebounded by 2.6% from the previous year's 1.9% contraction as the government spent more on economic and social development. Despite softer external demand, net exports of goods and

Figure 2.29.1 Supply-Side Contributions to Growth

Manufacturing pushed up growth in the last quarter of 2023.

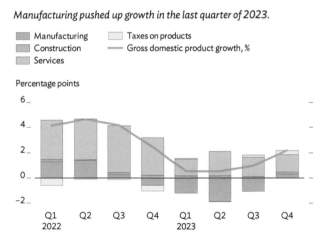

Q = quarter.
Source: Ministry of Trade and Industry. Economic Survey Singapore 2023.

services contributed positively to growth, as exports grew by 2.4% in real terms, more than the 1.0% growth in imports.

Headline inflation moderated largely due to lower oil prices and private transport costs. Consumer price index inflation eased to 4.8% year on year in 2023 from 6.1% in 2022. The increase in private transport costs fell to 8.2% compared with 19.2% in 2022

This chapter was written by Shu Tian and Mai Lin Villaruel of the Economic Research and Development Impact Department, ADB, Manila.

Figure 2.29.2 Demand-Side Contributions to Growth

Growth was dragged down by a big drop in investment.

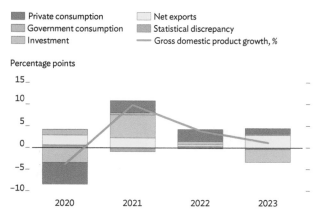

Source: Ministry of Trade and Industry. Economic Survey Singapore 2023.

Figure 2.29.3 Inflation

Headline inflation edged downward while core inflation increased marginally.

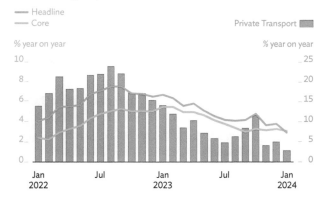

Source: CEIC Data Company.

because of easing prices for automobiles and a steeper decline in petrol costs (Figure 2.29.3). In contrast, core inflation, which excludes accommodation and private transport costs, increased slightly to 4.2% year on year in 2023 from 4.1% in 2022, mainly due to higher price increases for food, recreation and culture, and health care.

Monetary policy remained unchanged while fiscal policy remained accommodative. After monetary tightening to contain inflationary pressures, the Monetary Authority of Singapore (MAS) maintained its rate of currency appreciation beginning October 2022 as inflation continued to moderate. Meanwhile, the

fiscal deficit will reach 1.0% of GDP in FY2023 (ended 31 March 2024), higher than the expected 0.5% due to expenditures outpacing the revenue increase.

The current account surplus widened, led by a strong goods surplus. Merchandise exports fell 7.4% in US dollar terms in 2023 while imports contracted by 10.9%, resulting in a higher goods surplus. However, net service exports narrowed to 6.5% of GDP from 8.3%, driven by lower net receipts for transport services. Thus, the current account surplus widened to 19.8% of GDP, as the higher goods balance and lower net primary income deficit outweighed the drop in trade services balance (Figure 2.29.4).

Figure 2.29.4 Current Account Balance Indicators

The current account balance remained resilient despite softer external demand.

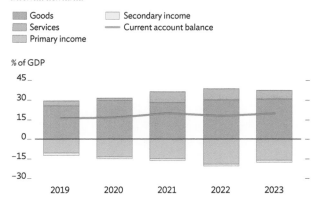

GDP = gross domestic product.
Source: CEIC Data Company.

Economic Prospects

GDP is forecast to grow by 2.4% in 2024, up from 1.1% in 2023, supported by a continuing recovery in manufacturing and external trade (Table 2.29.1). The manufacturing Purchasing Managers' Index (PMI) has been expansionary since the last quarter of 2023, driven by higher output, new orders, and external demand (Figure 2.29.5). The electronics PMI has signaled expansion, rising from 49.9 in October to 50.6 in January 2024 and 50.4 in February 2024, indicating more stabilized expansion. Growth in manufacturing is expected to gradually pick up in tandem with the turnaround in global electronics demand. Growth in services will remain resilient, supported by trade-related sectors. Finance will improve as global monetary

Table 2.29.1 Selected Economic Indicators, %

Growth accelerates and inflation slows over the next 2 years.

	2022	2023	2024	2025
GDP growth	3.8	1.1	2.4	2.6
Inflation	6.1	4.8	3.0	2.2

GDP = gross domestic product.
Sources: Ministry of Trade and Industry. Economic Survey Singapore 2023; Asian Development Bank estimates.

Figure 2.29.5 Purchasing Managers' Index

The overall manufacturing and electronics PMIs show strong expansion.

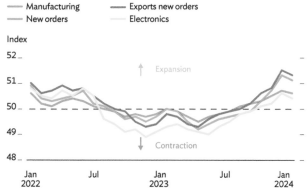

PMI = purchasing managers' index.
Source: CEIC Data Company.

Figure 2.29.6 Trade Indicators

Both exports and imports grew strongly in January after contracting in December

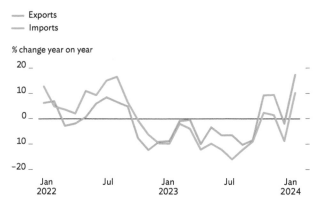

Source: Asian Development Bank calculations.

tightening is expected to end in 2024, creating favorable financial conditions. Domestic- and tourist-related activities will moderate as demand normalizes. Construction will continue to benefit from contracts awarded in 2023, which increased in value by 13.4%.

Domestic demand will remain resilient, and stronger exports should boost GDP growth.
A recovery in investment and stable consumption will support domestic demand. Higher domestic taxes will dampen private consumption—the goods and services tax (GST) increased from 8% to 9% from 1 January 2024. This will be balanced by improving economic conditions and resilient wage growth. Public spending will continue to support growth as the government maintains its accommodative fiscal stance, with the budget deficit at 0.4% of GDP in FY2024, narrower than FY 2023. The outlook for investment is positive, supported by investment committed in 2023 and robust public projects. The anticipated monetary

easing will also encourage more investments in the near term. External demand is also showing signs of recovery. Exports increased by 16.1% in January 2024, supported by strong growth in non-oil and oil exports. Imports grew by 9.4% with trend continuing throughout the year (Figure 2.29.6). Hence, GDP will grow by 2.4% in 2024 as manufacturing and external trade continue to recover. GDP will grow by 2.6% in 2025.

Headline inflation is expected to moderate to 3.0% in 2024 and 2.2% in 2025. While the hike in GST, increase in water prices, and planned wage increases (especially to lower-wage earners) could add price pressure, headline inflation will nonetheless moderate gradually. Factors contributing to easing inflation include lower cost of accommodation on higher unit supply, reduced private transport costs on lower oil prices, and normalizing food prices and the cost of services. These factors, along with the appreciating nominal effective rate, should keep Singapore's imported inflation low in the coming months. MAS expects both headline and core inflation to be in the range of 2.5%–3.5% in 2024.

Risks to the outlook remain tilted to the downside amid uncertainty. Notable risks include the US monetary policy stance, possible disruptions in disinflationary momentum, and spillover effects from the economic slowdown and deflation in the People's Republic of China (PRC). Longer-than-expected geopolitical tensions and adverse weather events could disrupt global supply chains and commodity markets, disrupting disinflation momentum. Uncertainty on the timing of US monetary easing may also lower sentiment over investment and financial conditions.

Policy Challenge—Aging Well in Singapore

Singapore's population is aging rapidly compared to many economies. Individuals aged 65 years and older comprise nearly 20% of the population, according to the government's 2023 population report, an increase of 116.0% from 2013 to 2023 (Figure 2.29.7). Singapore will also become a super-aged society by 2026, only 27 years after it became an aged society in 1999. This is faster than the PRC (32 years), Japan (36 years), Germany (76 years), and the US (86 years).

Figure 2.29.7 Population Growth of Age: 65+, 2013 to 2023

Singapore's old-age population rose faster than the world average.

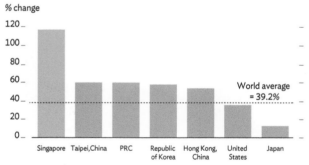

PRC = People's Republic of China.
Source: Asian Development Bank calculations using data from the United Nations, World Population Prospects (2022) and Our World in Data.

Rapid aging has profound economic impact. In the 2023 budget, the finance minister said that demographic aging will be a key economic issue over the medium to long term. With the rapid expansion of the older population, health care, elderly care, and social welfare will all create a heavy fiscal burden. Meanwhile, aging also challenges long-term GDP growth as workforce supply and productivity fall due to age-related factors. The working-age population is projected to decrease by

approximately 16% by 2050, resulting in a decline in the proportion of individuals aged 15 to 64 from 72% to 56%. This demographic shift is expected to reduce Singapore's growth potential by 0.5 percentage points.

Singapore has implemented various policies to address aging. To broaden sources to support health care, the government has introduced initiatives like mandatory long-term care insurance (CareShield Life) and promoted proactive health management and preventative health care through initiatives such as Healthier SG. To support elderly care, Singapore set up a Home Caregiving Grant and established Active Aging Centers and Care Hubs to provide more services and social connections. To bolster the workforce, the 2023 Action Plan for Successful Ageing provides a credit scheme to support hiring older workers. Singapore has also raised the retirement age from 62 to 63 and re-employment age from 67 to 68. Various upskilling programs, such as the National Silver Academy and the Seniors Go Digital program, have enhanced seniors' employability and productivity.

More measures are needed to address the remaining aging challenges. First, as a regional innovation hub, Singapore may further advance innovation and digital technology to deliver health care and elderly care services with better efficiency, greater accessibility, and enhanced effectiveness. Innovative models and technology solutions such as health technology and smart caring devices both cost-effectively improve elderly services and contribute to economic growth when there is sufficient demand. Second, to further promote workforce and productivity, Singapore may continue to explore calibrated immigration policies. Strategic immigration reforms can supplement the workforce by attracting professionals and workers with skills better aligned to Singapore's development. Households, especially with young children, can also offset demographic imbalances and sustain economic growth. Finally, to bolster the sustainability and resilience of the retirement finance system, Singapore may consider additional saving and investment options to the current retirement financing system anchored by the Central Provident Fund. For example, Singapore may develop an independent investment advisory and ecosystem to promote individuals' retirement savings.

THAILAND

Economic growth decelerated in 2023 due to a government budget delay and external headwinds. A stronger recovery in tourism, higher public spending, and a rebound in merchandise exports should support growth in 2024 and 2025. Risks remain tilted to the downside because of heightened geopolitical tensions and climate change issues. The government's digital wallet scheme could help on the upside. Developing a good ecosystem for a green transition is challenging over the medium-term but crucial for a successful outcome.

Economic Performance

In 2023, the Thai economy expanded by 1.9%, slowed down from 2.5% growth in 2022, dampened by a contraction of government spending and weak goods exports (Figure 2.30.1). Goods exports contracted by 2.8%. Lower exports of computer parts and accessories were due to the growing popularity of solid-state drives replacing hard disk drives. Other manufacturing exports such as air conditioners, metal and steel, and chemicals and petrochemical products declined due to subdued global demand. By contrast, agricultural exports expanded due to concerns over food security in several countries. In addition, Thailand's rice exports benefited from India's export ban.

Thanks to the continued recovery in tourism, services exports were the main contributor to overall exports in 2023. International tourists reached 28.2 million, significantly up from 11.1 million in 2022 (Figure 2.30.2). The top five sources were Malaysia followed by the People's Republic of China (PRC), the Republic of Korea, India, and Russian Federation. Tourist arrivals from these economies returned to pre-pandemic levels, except from the PRC. However, those from the PRC returned slowly and were just 32% of the 2019 pre-pandemic level. Overall, the export value of goods and services expanded by 2.1%.

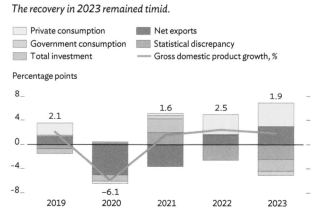

Figure 2.30.1 Demand-Side Contributions to Growth

The recovery in 2023 remained timid.

- Private consumption
- Government consumption
- Total investment
- Net exports
- Statistical discrepancy
- Gross domestic product growth, %

Percentage points

Source: Office of the National Economic and Social Development Council.

Private consumption recorded robust growth in 2023, expanding by 7.1% on the back of rising tourism-related activities. The labor market improved, especially in services. As a result, the unemployment rate declined from 1% at the end of 2022 to 0.8% in 2023. In addition, government measures to reduce household energy bills supported private consumption, particularly of non-durable goods. Private investment grew moderately, by 3.2%, primarily driven by the expansion in industrial plant construction and investment in services.

This chapter was written by Chitchanok Annonjarn of the Thailand Resident Mission, ADB, Bangkok.

Figure 2.30.2 Monthly International Tourists

Tourism continued its strong recovery in 2023.

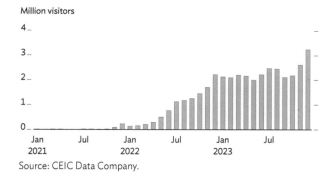

Source: CEIC Data Company.

Figure 2.30.3 Public Debt

Public debt remained below the legal debt ceiling.

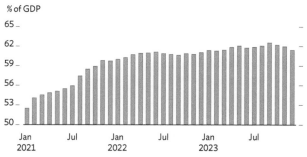

GDP = gross dometic product.
Source: Public Debt Management Office.

Public consumption fell by 4.6% mainly due to the phasing out of COVID-related social transfers.
Public investment, likewise, fell by 4.6% from a decline in the maintenance of roads and bridges, a delay in the 2024 fiscal budget (starting October 2023), and a lower disbursement in state-owned enterprises' energy and utility projects. As a result, the fiscal deficit slightly narrowed from 3.5% in fiscal year (FY) 2022 (ending September 2022) to 3.4% in FY2023. Fiscal stability remained sound. At the end of FY2023, public debt stood at 62.4% of GDP, below the 70% ceiling (Figure 2.30.3).

Imports dropped by 2.2% in line with the fall in goods exports. Raw material and intermediate goods imports, particularly for electronic parts and integrated circuits, declined in line with lower production and exports of electronics, computers, peripheral equipment, and data storage devices. In contrast, imports of capital and consumer goods expanded, especially electric vehicle imports.

On the supply side, services contributed the most to growth. Several tourism-related industries continued to grow. Services output expanded by 4.3% led by accommodations and food service as well as transportation and storage, mostly due to the rising number of domestic and foreign tourists (Figure 2.30.4).

Meanwhile, agriculture output expanded by 1.9% due to favorable weather in the first half of 2023 but industry contracted. Major agricultural crops, namely paddy rice, palm oil, cassava, and pineapple, suffered in the latter half of 2023 due to

Figure 2.30.4 Supply-Side Contributions to Growth

Services was the main driver of growth.

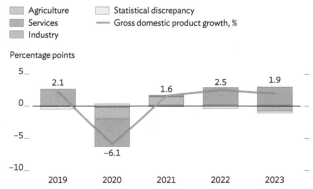

Source: Office of the National Economic and Social Development Council.

El Niño phenomenon. Agricultural products saw a high de-stocking because the drought lowered output, so production was less than sales. Manufacturing output contracted by 3.2% in line with the goods export contraction. Various industrial products, such as petrochemical and computer products, saw a substantial stock rundown because of weak export orders.

Headline inflation was 1.2% in 2023, mainly due to higher costs in producing fresh food and unfavorable weather conditions for some crops, while core inflation reached 1.3%. Headline inflation in 2023 declined sharply from 6.1% in 2022, due to government measures to ease the cost of living, such as electricity price cuts, cooking gas price caps, and reduced excise taxes on fuel. Monetary policy remained supportive of growth. The policy interest rate by the end of 2023 was 2.5%, up from 1.5% at the beginning of the year as the economy continued to recover (Figure 2.30.5). On the monetary policy target, the Ministry of Finance and the Bank of Thailand (the central bank) mutually agreed to set the inflation target at 1.0%–3.0% for 2024. The Thai baht strengthened marginally against the US dollar in 2023 as the market expected the US Federal Reserve to end its rate-hike cycle.

Table 2.30.1 Selected Economic Indicators, %

Moderate growth is expected in 2023–2024.

	2022	2023	2024	2025
GDP growth	2.5	1.9	2.6	3.0
Inflation	6.1	1.2	1.0	1.5

GDP = gross domestic product.
Source: Asian Development Bank estimates.

Figure 2.30.5 Inflation and Policy Interest Rate

Inflation fell due to lower energy prices; the policy rate was raised as the economy recovered.

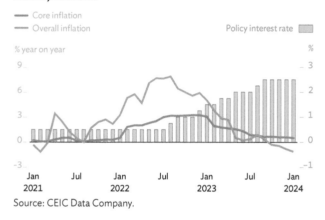

Source: CEIC Data Company.

Figure 2.30.6 Gross Domestic Product Growth

Private investment and exports will likely play a greater role in supporting economic growth.

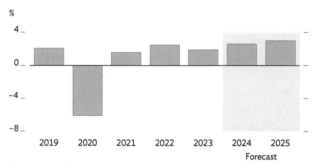

Source: *Asian Development Outlook* database.

Economic Prospects

Economic growth should pick up in 2024 and 2025 primarily from strong domestic demand, underpinned by a continued recovery in tourism and a rebound in merchandise exports. Real GDP is projected to expand by 2.6% in 2024 and 3.0% in 2025 (Table 2.30.1; Figure 2.30.6).

Exports of goods and services are forecast to grow by 5.4% this year and 4.1% in 2025. A gradual upturn in goods exports is expected over the forecast period. Key goods exports such as food and beverages, agricultural products, automotive and parts, electronics, and electrical appliances should improve on the back of improving global trade volume and higher agricultural prices due to supply constraints following El Niño. Services exports are expected to continue to grow in 2024 and 2025. Imports are forecast to expand by 4.0% this year and 2.6% next year, driven mainly by imported capital goods and raw materials for increased investment and export production. Further recovery in tourism should return services exports close to

pre-pandemic levels. International tourist arrivals are forecast to reach 34 million in 2024 and 38 million in 2025.

Private consumption should continue to benefit from recovering tourism activity, an improving labor market, and rising consumer confidence. Private consumption is expected to grow by 3.5% in 2024 and 3.4% in 2025, remaining the main contributor to economic growth. Short-term government measures such as the Easy-E-Receipt program—personal income tax deduction for spending up to B50,000 on eligible goods or services from 1 January to 15 February 2024—and measures to reduce electricity and fuel prices in the first half should also help boost private spending.

Private investment is projected to increase by 3.3% this year and 3.5% in 2025. Supporting investment will be growth in tourism and private consumption, government initiatives to boost investment in targeted industries (such as the electric vehicle industry [Phase II] in 2024–2027), and crowd-in effects from new infrastructure investment in late FY2024.

Investment in export-oriented sectors should gradually increase in the latter half of 2024 in line with the outlook for goods exports. In addition, foreign direct investment is expected to rise this year and next, as reflected by a 5-year high in applications for investment promotion in 2023. Significant contributions came from the PRC; Singapore; Japan; and Taipei,China in electric vehicles and smart electronics.

Following the election in May 2023, the FY2024 budget was delayed, and the government is now expected to begin disbursements in the second half of FY2024. The expenditure budget for FY2024 at B3.48 trillion shows spending rising by 9.3% and the budget deficit dropping to B693 billion, or 3.6% of GDP. Public consumption is forecast to increase by 1.5% in 2024 and 2.5% in 2025. Meanwhile, a few new infrastructure projects, including electric train extension, rail, expressway, and intercity motorway projects, are expected to start construction in 2024. On the revenue side, a new tax on foreign-sourced income has been in effect since the start of 2024. Any income earned overseas from employment, business, or property, regardless of when it enters Thailand, must be declared and taxed in the year the income is earned; this will help raise government revenue and narrow the budget deficit. Public investment is expected to grow by 1.0% in 2024 and 3.2% in 2025.

El Niño will largely affect major crop cultivation. The government has taken several measures to address the water shortage, focusing on reducing water use in agriculture, promoting cultivation of water-saving crops, and strengthening water storage capacity. It is also reallocating funds from investment projects that have not shown short-term returns to swiftly address the ongoing drought crisis. Rice, cassava, sugarcane, rubber, and palm oil are more sensitive to water shortages, so crop output is expected to decline this year. Agricultural output this year is projected to grow by just 2.0%, gradually rising to 2.2% next year. The industry outlook is forecast to improve in line with the export recovery. Thailand's international and domestic tourism should remain strong in volume and receipts. Thus, services should grow by 4.8% in 2024 and 4.3% in 2025.

Headline inflation is forecast to remain low as government measures to ease the cost of living will likely be extended, lowering energy prices. Headline

inflation is projected to rise to 1.0% this year and 1.5% next year. Nonetheless, strengthening domestic consumption and higher food prices due to lower agricultural output could exert upward pressure on core inflation (Figure 2.30.7).

Figure 2.30.7 Inflation

Inflation is forecast to remain low.

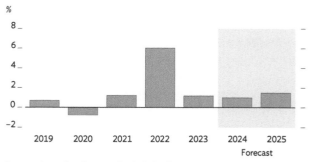

Source: *Asian Development Outlook* database.

Risks to the outlook are tilted to the downside. The Thai economy faces rising uncertainties stemming from external factors, including climate change and geopolitical issues. Domestically, the digital wallet scheme—a B10,000 digital cash handout to Thai nationals aged 16 and older who earn less than B70,000 per month or have less than B500,000 in bank deposits—could be an upside to the outlook, as it provides a short-term boost for private consumption. However, the program will cost the government a massive B500 billion (2.6% of GDP).

Policy Challenge—Developing the Ecosystem for a Green Transition

Thailand is at a crossroads in its climate strategy, urgently needing tangible action plans to revolutionize and green its economy. A transition is already underway. Thailand is in the process of enacting its first Climate Change Act to regulate greenhouse gas emissions and enhance capacity for climate change adaptation in every sector. It revised the National Adaptation Plan, aiming to build adaptive capacity and enhance climate resilience in six priority sectors, including water resource management, agriculture and food security, tourism, public health, natural resources management, and human settlements and security.

Thailand is also implementing several emission reduction policies across the economy, such as tax incentives for renewable energy investments, the Environmentally Sustainable Transport System Plan, and a Waste Management Roadmap. On financing, the first phase of Thailand Taxonomy was launched last year as a crucial step toward a sustainable finance landscape. It provides guidance, frameworks, and standards for investors and stakeholders to define "green" projects and avoid "greenwashing."

New institutions are being created. To improve climate change management, Thailand established a new department within the Ministry of Natural Resources and Environment to coordinate efforts to address climate change issues. In late 2023, Thailand launched the Thai Climate Initiative Fund (ThaiCI) as a financial mechanism to support climate change operations in reducing greenhouse gas emissions, adapting to climate change, and achieving the goal of Carbon Neutrality by 2050 and Net Zero by 2065.

Carbon pricing is an essential mechanism for businesses to achieve carbon neutrality and net zero targets. A carbon tax will come into force in the next few years. A voluntary carbon credits market already operates, but market size remains small (Figure 2.30.8). There is no stringent emission cap and carbon prices are relatively low under the emissions trading system. However, they fluctuate significantly as the various carbon standards are not yet fixed. The market is not determined by demand and supply, implying that prices under this system are ineffective in reducing greenhouse gases. The initial costs of some projects are high and have long repayment horizons, which create a significant financial burden for businesses that want to develop their own carbon credit projects. Also, carbon credits may not suit small and medium enterprises (SMEs), which are

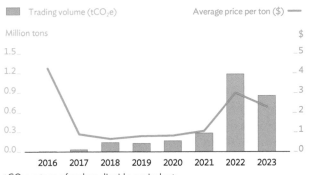

Figure 2.30.8 Carbon Credits Market in Thailand

The volume and price of trading carbon credits in Thailand are relatively low compared to the global market.

tCO$_2$e = tons of carbon dioxide equivalent.
Sources: https://carbonmarket.tgo.or.th; World Bank State and Trends of Carbon Pricing 2023.

the majority of businesses in Thailand. Moreover, SMEs usually face constraints in accessing credit and financial products, making them vulnerable in the transition toward a green economy. Thus, scaling up the carbon pricing market and addressing SME financial issues is crucial for policymakers to pursue a strong and inclusive green transition.

Strengthening capacity-building in green skills is also required to support new technologies and green initiatives. As brown industries that emit high levels of greenhouse gases are set to decline, it could cause significant job losses, especially for low-skilled workers. According to a Thailand Development Research Institute study, at least 8 million low-skilled workers in brown industries will have to shift to green jobs that require higher professional skillsets. Also, Thailand lacks qualified workers for green jobs, such as environmental engineers and renewable energy technicians. Thus, the government should invest more in education and green skill training programs for a smooth transition.

TIMOR-LESTE

Economic growth decelerated in 2023 as budget expenditure fell. Inflation accelerated further to its highest level since 2013, and the current account balance weakened. Growth will accelerate in 2024 and 2025 as capital investment increases and consumption remains robust. Inflation will moderate due to eased pressure on prices of imported goods and services, and the current account deficit will expand as imports increase. Timor-Leste needs a multi-sectoral food and nutrition security approach that will provide a productive labor force to sustain growth.

Economic Performance

Economic growth slowed in 2023, driven by declining budget expenditure. Following modest growth of 2.9% in 2021 and a strong 4.0% economic rebound in 2022, estimated GDP (nonpetroleum) growth slowed to 1.9% last year mainly due to lower budget expenditure and high inflation. Despite the considerable expenditure initially budgeted, actual spending decreased due to an underperforming budget during an election year. Following the May 2023 elections and formation of the new government in July, public spending was curtailed by the new government's expenditure cuts. Regaining consumer confidence since 2022, government transfers, worker remittances, and a steady recovery in household income have supported private consumption. Government consumption is estimated to have increased by 2.9% in 2023. Net exports dragged growth down by 3.2 percentage points as the current account deficit deteriorated by an equivalent 36.4% of estimated GDP (Figure 2.31.1).

On the supply side, growth slowed across key sectors. The estimated GDP growth in services and agriculture slowed, decreasing their contribution to growth by 3.0 percentage points to 1.6 points in line with the drop in domestic demand. Manufacturing growth normalized after a strong rebound in 2022, contributing only 0.2 percentage points to growth. However, construction recovered slightly after 4 years of deep contractions, contributing a mere 0.1 percentage points to growth (Figure 2.31.2).

Figure 2.31.1 Demand-Side Contributions to Growth

Consumption was a major factor driving growth.

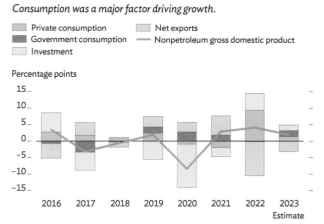

Sources: National Institute of Statistics of Timor-Leste; Asian Development Bank estimates.

Inflation hit a 10-year high despite targeted subsidies. Average consumer price inflation accelerated from 7.0% in 2022 to 8.4% in 2023, with prices 8.7% higher in December 2023 than a year earlier. Elevated food and non-alcoholic beverage prices, and high alcohol and tobacco prices were significant drivers of the surge. Despite subsidies to rice importers, average annual rice prices jumped by 9.4 percentage points to 15.9% in 2023 (Figure 2.31.3).

The fiscal deficit decreased in 2023 due to lower spending. A 14.1% drop in expenditure outpaced a 5.9% revenue decline, resulting in a 22.1% decrease

This chapter was written by Bold Sandagdorj of the Timor-Leste Resident Mission, ADB, Dili.

Figure 2.31.2 Supply-Side Contributions to Growth

Growth slowed across key economic sectors.

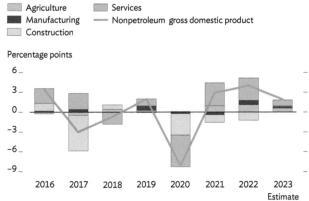

Note: Supply-side contributions to growth were adjusted by net taxes on products.

Sources: National Institute of Statistics of Timor-Leste; Asian Development Bank estimates.

Figure 2.31.3 Inflation

Consumer price inflation hit a 10-year high in 2023.

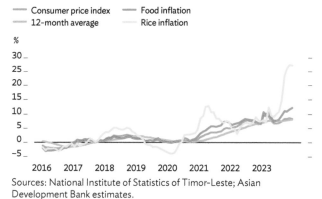

Sources: National Institute of Statistics of Timor-Leste; Asian Development Bank estimates.

Figure 2.31.4 Government Budget

Spending cuts narrowed the fiscal deficit in 2023.

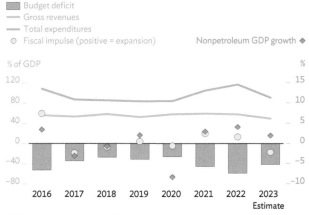

GDP = gross domestic product.

Sources: National Institute of Statistics of Timor-Leste; Ministry of Finance; International Monetary Fund; Asian Development Bank estimates.

Figure 2.31.5 Current Account Balance

The external balance weakened due to the persistent trade deficit and lower primary income.

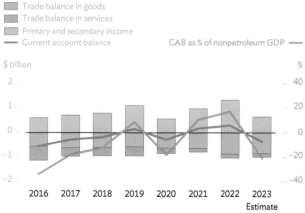

CAB = current account balance, GDP = gross domestic product.

Sources: National Institute of Statistics of Timor-Leste; International Monetary Fund; Asian Development Bank estimates.

in the estimated budget deficit in 2023 to the equivalent of 41% of GDP. The estimated tax ratio stayed low at 8.3% because of the low tax base and underdeveloped private sector. Government debt remained flat, and the estimated debt-to-GDP ratio decreased slightly from 15.2% in 2022 to 14.0%, only 2.5 percentage points higher than the pre-pandemic ratio (Figure 2.31.4).

The external account balance weakened largely due to lower petroleum income. Despite the goods and services deficit marginally narrowing by 2.6% in 2023, the estimated current account balance fell into a deficit equal to 20.1% of GDP. Combined

primary and secondary income declined by 52.4% due to a 63% reduction in income from the petroleum sector as reserves ran out at the *Bayu-Undan* field (Figure 2.31.5).

The Petroleum Fund balance grew by 5.7% to $18.2 billion in 2023 as investment income increased. Lower receipts and increased pressure on drawdowns highlight the need to better leverage development financing opportunities for productive and long-term investments in human capital, infrastructure, public services, and private sector development (Figure 2.31.6).

Figure 2.31.6 The Petroleum Fund

A reversal in net investment income raised the sovereign wealth fund balance.

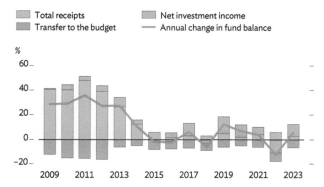

Sources: Central Bank of Timor-Leste. 2009–2023. The Annual and Quarterly Reports of the Petroleum Fund; Asian Development Bank estimates.

Remittances, the second largest source of capital inflows, recovered strongly over the past 4 years. Worker remittances have been increasing as more workers migrate due to limited domestic employment opportunities, the impact of seasonal worker programs, and improved money transfer services. Coffee is a strategically significant agricultural export, accounting for over 95% of nonpetroleum merchandise exports, though it remains small and volatile. The combined ratio of coffee exports and personal remittances to GDP averaged 12% over the past 4 years but remains 5.4 percentage points lower than its 2010 peak (Figure 2.31.7).

Broad money growth moderated to 2.7% in 2023 (Figure 2.31.8). With a contractionary government budget, the central bank maintained its accommodative policy stance to support private credit. Despite credit growth rising an average 26.7% per year in 2022–2023 due to rising consumer lending, estimated bank credit-to-GDP remained low at 26.3% in 2023 (Figure 2.31.9).

Figure 2.31.7 Coffee Exports and Personal Remittances

Remittances have grown steadily, while coffee exports remain modest.

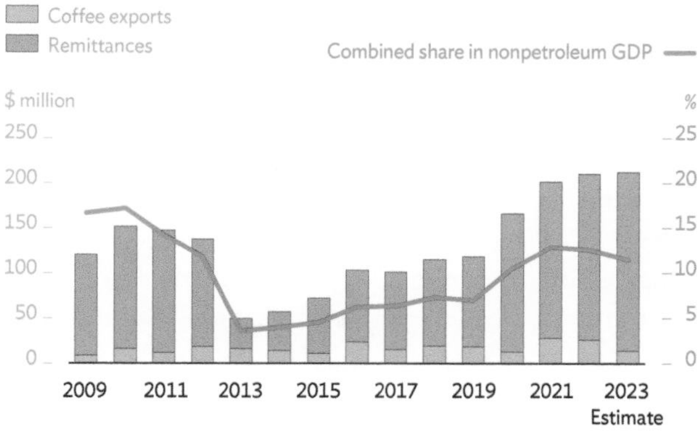

GDP = gross domestic product.
Sources: National Institute of Statistics of Timor-Leste; World Bank; Asian Development Bank estimates.

Figure 2.31.8 Money Supply

Broad money growth moderated.

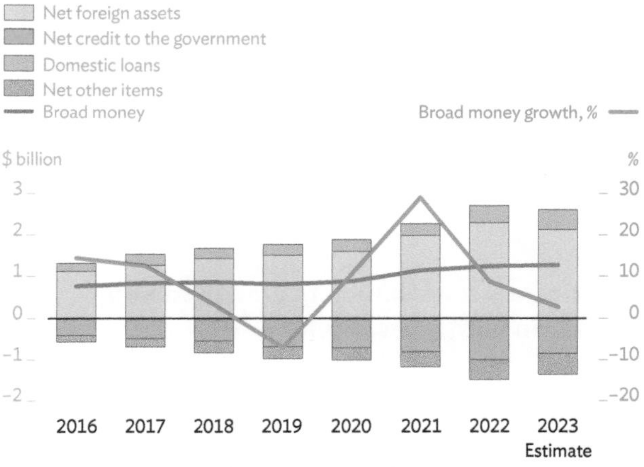

Sources: Central Bank of Timor-Leste; Asian Development Bank estimates.

Figure 2.31.9 Banking Sector Credit

Driven by retail lending, domestic credit grew by 20.8% in 2023.

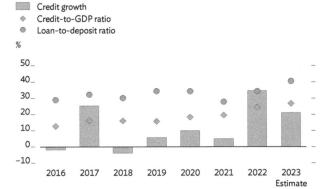

GDP = gross domestic product.
Sources: Central Bank of Timor-Leste; National Institute of Statistics of Timor-Leste; Asian Development Bank estimates.

Economic Prospects

The near-term economic outlook has improved with growth forecast to rise by 3.4% in 2024 and 4.1% in 2025 (Table 2.31.1). Expansionary fiscal policy will be the main growth driver for 2024–2025 along with steady consumption, keeping GDP growth above the average 3% annual growth rate between 2003–2022. The 2024 budget calls for 14.5% higher spending than in 2023, driven by the new government's medium-term prioritization of public investment with a specific focus on the *Greater Sunrise* gas and condensate field and related South Coast infrastructure development.

Table 2.31.1 Selected Economic Indicators, %

Growth will rise, and inflation will moderate.

	2022	2023	2024	2025
GDP growth	4.0	1.9	3.4	4.1
Inflation	7.0	8.4	3.5	2.9

GDP = gross domestic product.
Sources: National Institute of Statistics of Timor-Leste; Asian Development Bank estimates.

Investment's contribution to growth should increase in both years. Capital expenditure is planned to increase by over 52% year on year, representing more than four-fifths of total budget expenditure in 2024. Investment's contribution to growth will accelerate in 2025, assuming the government concludes its review of investment projects financed by international financial institutions soon. This will enable disbursements to resume for these projects beginning the second half of this year. Investment will also grow in 2025 as new projects aimed at narrowing the country's large infrastructure gap begin and capital investments related to the *Greater Sunrise* field start flowing.

Consumption will remain the main contributor to growth. A continued increase in current transfers, salaries and wages, consumer loans issued by local banks, and robust personal remittances amid a lower inflationary environment will support private consumption. The contribution of government consumption to growth will remain steady on recurrent government spending for goods and services.

Inflation will moderate over the forecast period, with the current account deficit expected to widen. Average inflation will moderate from its 2023 peak to 3.5% in 2024 and 2.9% in 2025 as price pressure from trading partners eases and global commodity price risks wane. Despite their impact on domestic revenue mobilization, reversed import duties, including excise taxes on tobacco, sugar, and sugary beverages, will contribute to lower inflation. The current account deficit is projected to widen in 2024 and 2025 as primary income declines further due to a rundown of reserves in the *Bayu-Undan* petroleum field, and imports of goods and services increase with greater domestic demand, supported by an expansionary budget.

There are downside risks to the outlook. These include climate-related disaster risk and extreme weather conditions associated with El Niño, terms-of-trade shocks, rising food and energy prices caused primarily by geopolitical tensions, trade and supply chain disruptions, and risks associated with public service delivery and lower spending on investment projects.

Policy Challenge—Ensuring Food Security

Food insecurity remains high for about 63% of the population. Ensuring adequate food supply remains a priority. The risk of a food supply shock persists due to high dependency on food imports, climate risks, and disasters caused by natural hazards. An estimated 27% of the population face high acute levels of food insecurity. About 47% of children under 5 years old are stunted, 9% of children suffer from acute malnutrition, and 23% of women of reproductive age are anemic. The maternal and child prevalence of undernourishment is high at 40%.

Ensuring food security is a fundamental and immediate policy challenge in Timor-Leste. Past government measures to improve food security included subsidies to rice importers to stabilize domestic prices, a School Meals initiative, and improving livestock disease control. Using a more holistic approach, Timor-Leste has great potential to improve its food security.

First, a multi-sectoral approach should be implemented. The recent establishment of the nutrition and food security working group as part of the inter-ministerial task force led by the Vice Prime Minister for Social Affairs is a welcoming step to monitor the implementation progress of multi-sectoral nutrition and food security action plans and achieve key policy targets.

Second, a more conducive environment for domestic food production and agricultural productivity should be supported. More than 70% of the population depends on rain-fed subsistence agriculture as their main source of income. Promoting climate-resilient agriculture and diversifying agriculture products will boost agriculture production and increase farmers' income. This also requires risk mitigation and prevention, which include (i) reducing climate and disaster risk caused by natural hazards and El Niño by strengthening climate resilience; (ii) improving access to water, hygiene, sanitation, and waste management for disease control; and (iii) developing essential infrastructure for food and agriculture production, providing producer-and-consumer connectivity through properly maintained roads, market access, and value chains.

Third, access to finance should be increased for food producers and other key stakeholders, including related micro, small and medium-sized enterprises. This includes investments and financing for food production, warehousing, and trade and supply chain financing. It can be provided by local banks, development finance, on-lending, and public-private partnerships to help integrate farmers into food supply chains and markets, increase agricultural productivity, and promote rural employment.

VIET NAM

Slowing global demand and high international interest rates hampered Viet Nam's growth in 2023. A timely switch to an accommodative monetary policy to support growth was among the key measures taken for the economy to move back on the path to recovery. Sizeable public investment this year should further restore growth. Inflation is expected to edge up in tandem with the economic revival. A key policy challenge is enhancing public investment effectiveness for short-term stimulus and as a foundation for longer-term development.

Economic Performance

Growth decelerated sharply to 5.0% in 2023 from 8.0% in 2022. The slow global recovery, prolonged Russian invasion of Ukraine, and recent conflicts in the Middle East reduced global demand, significantly dampening Viet Nam's export-led manufacturing—its primary growth driver—slashing its growth by almost half to 3.6%. The sharp decline in manufacturing reduced industry's growth to 3.7%, just half the 7.5% a year earlier. The troubled real-estate sector led construction down to 7.1% from 7.9% in 2022 (Figure 2.32.1).

Other sectors remained healthy. Agriculture sustained its 3.8% growth as a pickup in commodity prices encouraged farming. A steady increase in international visitor arrivals—estimated at 12.6 million or 3.4 times more than in 2022—remained nonetheless below pre-pandemic levels. It still helped services grow by 6.8% in 2023.

Domestic demand recovered, but slower than expected. Fiscal measures to support growth such as a 2% reduction in value-added tax and public investment aided consumption. Retail sales grew by 9.6% compared with 2022, though far less than the 20% increase in 2022. Despite stable disbursement of foreign direct investment (FDI), rising by 3.5%, turbulence in the corporate bond market and a real-estate downturn lowered private investor confidence, driving private

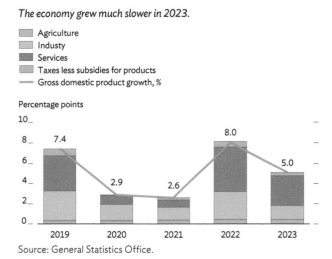

Figure 2.32.1 Supply-Side Contributions to Growth

The economy grew much slower in 2023.

- Agriculture
- Industy
- Services
- Taxes less subsidies for products
- Gross domestic product growth, %

Percentage points

Source: General Statistics Office.

investment down to 2.7% in 2023, its lowest level in 10 years. The downturn led total investment to contract by 6.2%, a reversal from the 11.3% increase in 2022. Weak external demand lowered trade.

Average inflation reached 3.3% in 2023, slightly higher than 3.2% in 2022 (Figure 2.32.2). A broad-based global economic slowdown tamed global oil prices and helped ease inflationary pressure. Price controls for electricity, healthcare, and education also restrained inflation.

This chapter was written by Nguyen Ba Hung, Nguyen Luu Thuc Phuong, and Chu Hong Minh of the Viet Nam Resident Mission, ADB, Ha Noi.

Figure 2.32.2 Monthly Inflation

Inflationary pressure eased.

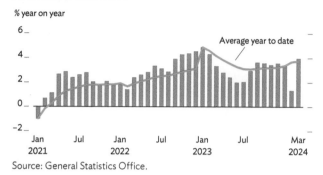

Source: General Statistics Office.

The State Bank of Viet Nam (SBV), the central bank, shifted to an accommodative monetary stance amid the growth deceleration. Decreasing growth in the last quarter of 2022 prompted the SBV to slash its key policy interest rate four times in 2023, cutting rates by 1.5%. The cuts widened the gap between the US Federal Funds rate and SBV policy rates, increasing pressure on the dong, causing a decline of indirect portfolio investment and heightening the risk of imported inflation. The dong depreciated 1.2% against the US dollar in 2023.

Following policy rate cuts, commercial banks lowered deposit rates on average by 3%–5% to boost credit. The SBV also encourages banks to use other credit schemes to spur growth. Bank credit growth reached an estimated 13.5%, while total liquidity growth shot up to 10.3% by the end of 2023 from 6.2% a year earlier (Figure 2.32.3).

Financial fraud rattled capital markets in 2022 and 2023. Timely regulatory changes including bond restructuring, among other measures, helped stabilize market sentiment in early 2023. New issuance value rose by 19.6% year on year, largely due to low base effects. However, delayed payments of principal and/or interest on restructured corporate bonds outstanding—estimated an equivalent of $40 billion—will continue to fuel market pressure in 2024.

The trade surplus was a record $28 billion in 2023 as imports declined faster than exports. Exports receipts totaled $355.5 billion (83% of GDP), down 4.4% from 2022, while imports fell to $327.5 billion (76% of GDP), an 8.9% drop. Shipments of mobile phones, computers, and electronic products, accounting for 30% of total exports, decreased by 3.6%. Meanwhile, machinery and equipment, accounting for 12% of total exports, fell by 5%.

The sizable trade balance supported the current account surplus estimated at 5.9% of GDP from a modest surplus of 0.3% a year ago. Higher remittances also supported the current account balance. The wide differentials with global interest rates led to a capital and financial account deficit estimated at 0.7% of GDP in 2023. However, the substantial current account surplus turned the overall balance of payments to an estimated surplus of 1.3% of GDP in 2023 from a deficit of 5.6% of GDP in 2022 (Figure 2.32.4). By the end of 2023, foreign reserves had improved to 3.3 months of imports from 2.8 months at the end of 2022.

Figure 2.32.3 Credit and Money Supply Growth

Credit growth slowed but total liquidity improved in 2023.

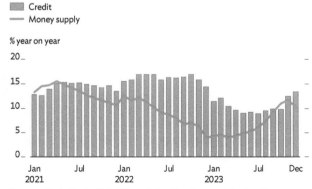

Sources: State Bank of Viet Nam; Asian Development Bank estimates.

Figure 2.32.4 Balance of Payments

A current account surplus lifted the overall balance.

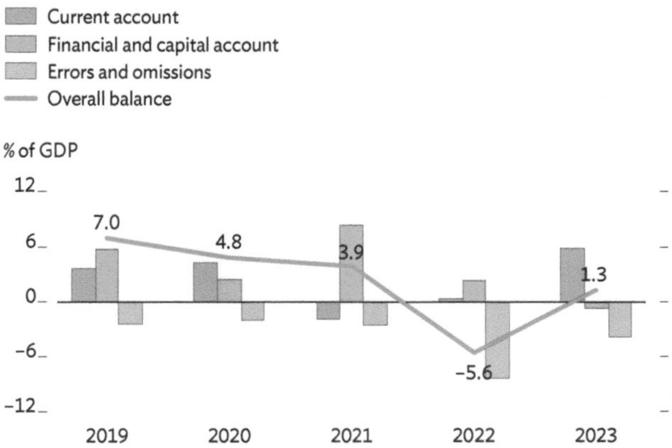

Current account
Financial and capital account
Errors and omissions
Overall balance

% of GDP

GDP = gross domestic product.

Sources: State Bank of Viet Nam; Asian Development Bank estimates.

Fiscal policy in 2023 remained expansionary. A 22.4% reduction in export and import earnings in 2023 reduced revenue by 5.4%, while increased capital expenditure pushed up total spending by 10.9%. However, well-controlled public debt repayments and contained current expenditures helped maintain a relatively balanced budget with a mild estimated deficit of 0.14% of GDP.

Economic Prospects

The economy is expected to grow 6.0% in 2024 and 6.2% in 2025 (Table 2.32.1). A relatively broad-based growth restoration in export-led manufacturing, services, and stable agriculture would make the gradual recovery possible. Positive inflows of FDI and remittances, a sustained trade surplus, continued fiscal support, and a substantial public investment program would also stimulate growth. For the first quarter of 2024, the economic growth accelerated to 5.7% from 3.4% a year ago. However, downside risks from global geopolitical uncertainties and exposed domestic structural fragilities could impede growth.

Table 2.32.1 Selected Economic Indicators, %

Growth will improve in 2024 and 2025, with inflation rising this year.

	2022	2023	2024	2025
GDP growth	8.0	5.0	6.0	6.2
Inflation	3.2	3.3	4.0	4.0

GDP = gross domestic product.
Sources: General Statistics Office; Asian Development Bank estimates.

The gradual return of new orders and consumption revived manufacturing growth at the end of 2023, with the trend gaining further momentum in 2024. Manufacturing expanded at 6.8% in the first quarter of 2024, compared with the contraction of 0.5% a year ago, contributing to industrial growth of 6.3% (Figure 2.32.5). Lower interest rates, fiscal measures supporting growth, and the recently improved land-related legal framework should support construction. However, slow global growth and still high global policy rates could weigh down export-led manufacturing growth.

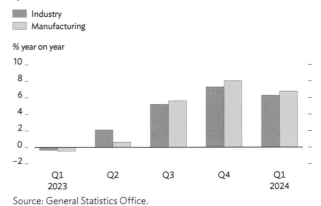

Figure 2.32.5 Industry and Manufacturing Growth

Manufacturing and industrial production improved in the first quarter of 2024.

Source: General Statistics Office.

Low domestic interest rates, fiscal policy measures, and wage increases will spur consumption-led services in 2024. Retail sales in the first quarter of 2024 were 8.2% higher than the same period in 2022 (Figure 2.32.6). Revived economic activity, though slow, will elevate logistic services, while liberalized visa policy will likely boost tourism. Overall, services are forecast to expand by 7.7% in 2024. Global demand for agricultural commodities and free trade agreements will continue supporting agricultural exports.

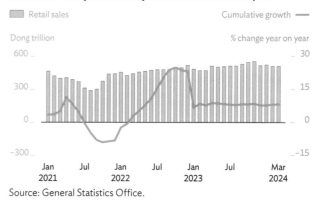

Figure 2.32.6 Retail Sales

Retail sales in the first months of 2024 increased over last year.

Source: General Statistics Office.

Monetary policy will pursue the dual objectives of price stability and growth, even as policy space is limited. The expected slowdown in the global economy in 2024 could tame global oil prices and consequently ease inflationary pressure. Average inflation for the first quarter of 2024 slowed to 3.8%

from the high level of 4.2% in the same period last year. Inflation is forecast to rise slightly to 4.0% in 2024 and 2025. Though the inflation forecast remains below the 4%–4.5% target, near-term pressure may persist from geopolitical tensions and disruptions of global supply chains.

The Fed expects to cut interest rates in 2024 and external inflation will continue to cool, though more gradually than expected. The Fed rate cuts in 2024 would help relieve the pressure on the dong. However, the heightened risk of nonperforming loans—which peaked at an estimated 4.6% of loans outstanding at the end of 2023 compared with 2.0% in 2022—would reduce the prospect for additional monetary easing. The newly amended Law on Credit institutions effective 1 July 2024 will also better monitor lending activities.

Given limited monetary policy space, fiscal and investment spending will be key for growth in 2024. A comfortable fiscal position with a mild budget deficit and a low public debt-to-GDP ratio provides sufficient fiscal space to support growth. The ongoing value-added tax reduction program was extended until June 2024 and could be extended further to the end of 2024. A sizable amount of public investment, equivalent to $27.3 billion, has been programmed for disbursement this year. Together with disbursements from 2023, this additional public investment would significantly stimulate growth. A gradual revival of export-led manufacturing would support FDI. Registered FDI increased by 13.4%,

and disbursed FDI went up 7.1% in the first quarter of 2024 compared with the same period last year (Figure 2.32.7). Accelerated public investment and improved business conditions can spur private investment in 2024.

Softening global demand will limit the trade recovery in 2024. Global growth is expected to bounce back slower than expected, which could also slow Viet Nam's export recovery. Exports in the first quarter of 2024 grew by 17%, while imports increased by 13.9% (Figure 2.32.8). Imports and exports will grow modestly by 4%–4.5% this year and next as external demand gradually recovers. Renewed manufacturing activity would push up imports of production inputs. As a result, the current account surplus is projected to be 1.5% of GDP in 2024.

Figure 2.32.8 Trade Indicators

Exports are showing some signs of recovery.

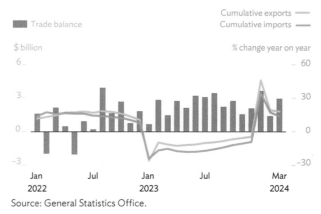

Source: General Statistics Office.

The economy will likely grow slightly faster in 2024 than in 2023, although risks are tilted toward the downside. Softened global demand caused by slow economic recovery and continued geopolitical tensions would slow the full recovery of Viet Nam's export-led growth. Delayed normalization of interest rates in the US and other advanced economies would also impede the monetary policy shift to one supporting growth. As a result, fiscal measures for supporting growth and public investment would ultimately become the key policy options to reignite growth. More importantly, the growth slowdown has heightened the risks of structural fragilities, especially excessive reliance on FDI-led export manufacturing, weak linkages between manufacturing and the rest of the economy, the

Figure 2.32.7 Foreign Direct Investment

Foreign direct investment remained strong in the first months of 2024.

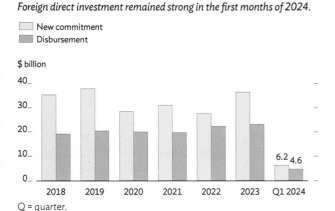

Q = quarter.
Source: General Statistics Office.

incipient capital markets, overreliance on bank credit, and regulatory barriers to business. Policy measures in 2024 would therefore need to combine short-term growth support measures with long-term structural remedies to promote sustainable growth.

Policy Challenge—Accelerating Disbursement of Public Investment

Public investment is a critical engine of economic growth, but plans must be implemented for this engine to provide power. According to the Ministry of Planning and Investment, an increase of 1% in public investment disbursement corresponds to a 0.058% increase in GDP growth. In addition, every 1 dong of disbursed public investment capital stimulates 1.61 dong of investment capital from the non-state sector. However, the execution rate compared to planned investment has been consistently low, hovering around 80% for the year (Figure 2.32.9). While the government has tried to address this problem, progress has been insufficient.

Figure 2.32.9 Public Investment

The disbursement rate has shown little change over 2022–2024.

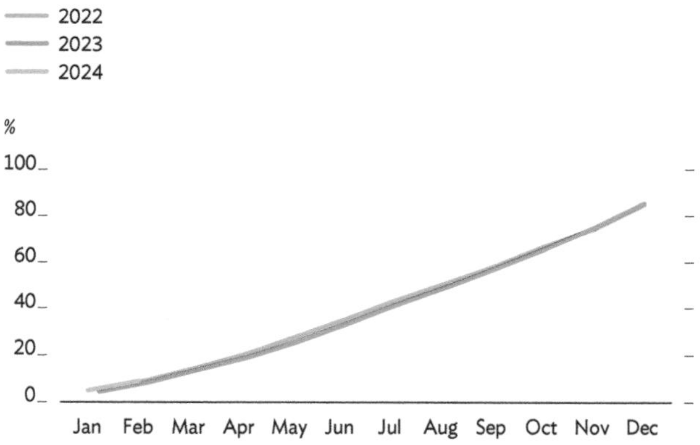

— 2022
— 2023
— 2024

Sources: General Statistics Office; Asian Development Bank estimates.

First, projects approved with allocated budgets sometimes are not ready to move forward, causing extensive delays. A systematic approach to improve project readiness can significantly enhance effective implementation. Many projects require preparatory groundwork, such as feasibility studies, land clearance arrangements, and preparatory procurement in parallel with project approval procedures. Better readiness to expedite project implementation will help minimize cost overruns.

Second, projects sometimes require design or budget changes even after approval and budget allocation. This can cause long interruptions before project work can start. One major obstacle to timely and quality project preparation is the complexity of regulations, particularly land use planning, land acquisition, and site clearance. This rigidity is a crucial challenge in situations of market fluctuations. Soaring prices due to shortages of materials and inputs for production, driven by regulatory constraints, lead to higher costs, forcing contract renegotiations or the need for additional funding and approvals. As part of improving project cycle procedures, regulations should be revised to allow for principle-based flexibility and fit-for-purpose adjustments. This will help facilitate efficient project approval and management that can be adapted to various circumstances without repeating the approval process. It is also important to strengthen the capacity of provincial and local public investment staff to improve the quality of project preparation.

Third, weak coordination between public investment and budget processes has resulted in slow and insufficient budget allocation. In recent years, it has been reported that central agencies received higher allocations than what they can initiate, while provinces received too little to meet their needs. The pressing challenge of the mismatch between allocated budgets and investment mandates often leads to inefficiencies and delays in project implementation—funds may not be optimally directed toward identified priority areas, resulting in suboptimal resource utilization. This limits project progress and capital utilization efficiency.

The government has adopted measures to enhance transparency, efficiency, and accountability in budget allocation and disbursement. This promotes better coordination between central and local authorities, prioritizing projects based on impact and readiness, and implementing rigorous monitoring mechanisms to ensure funds are utilized effectively and efficiently. However, their effectiveness seems to be limited. Disparities among the execution capabilities at different government levels highlight the need to strengthen the allocation process and build the capacity of local governments. The ongoing decentralization of public investment mandates and fiscal responsibilities has exposed weaknesses in addressing inter-provincial or regional challenges. The budget processes could be adjusted to allow for flexibility, which would be more efficient at any level (central or provincial) to contribute resources to a regionally coordinated project.

In 2024, public investment will continue to play a vital role in supporting the economy. Following budget approval by the National Assembly, the Prime Minister approved the capital allocation plan of D688.5 trillion to continue building infrastructure and driving economic development. The government has implemented various policy measures to expedite disbursement of public investment and enhance effective execution. These measures include a series of resolutions and directives focusing on different aspects of public investment disbursement. However, to sustain progress, more systematic measures are required to improve the legal and regulatory processes for successful implementation. By proactively addressing these obstacles in an integrated manner throughout the project cycle, Viet Nam can unlock the full potential of its public investment initiatives, driving sustainable economic growth and development.

THE PACIFIC

FIJI

Continued recovery in tourism boosted economic growth in 2023. Pent-up demand led to record visitor arrivals despite high global inflation and tight monetary policies in key tourism markets. Tax reforms and increased demand supported robust government revenue despite tight labor market conditions from worker migration. The primary sector's contribution declined while industry rose moderately. The economic outlook is sluggish due to a projected slowdown in travel demand and significant capacity limits in tourism. Major government-led reforms are likely to generate new private sector investment, but their full impact may not be felt for several years.

Economic Performance

GDP grew by 7.8% in 2023 on continued strong growth in tourism. Services, buoyed by a boost in tourist arrivals, continued as the main driver of economic activity, adding 6.9 percentage points. This had positive spillover effects on wholesale and retail trade, transportation, construction, and finance (Figure 2.33.1). Lower agricultural production led

to its smaller contribution to GDP. Sugar and timber production fell significantly in 2023 due to adverse weather conditions and factory disruptions.

Visitor arrivals in 2023 exceeded pre-pandemic levels. Total arrivals were 4% higher than in 2019 (Figure 2.33.2). Arrivals from Australia (47% of the

Figure 2.33.1 Supply-Side Contributions to Growth

Tourism's recovery led economic growth in 2023.

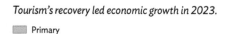

- Primary
- Industry
- Services
- Gross domestic product growth, %

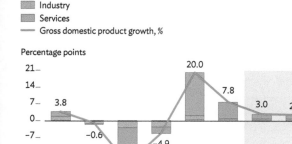

Sources: Fiji Bureau of Statistics; Asian Development Bank estimates.

Figure 2.33.2 Visitor Arrivals

Arrivals reached record levels.

- Australia
- New Zealand
- North America
- Europe
- Asia
- Pacific Islands
- Others

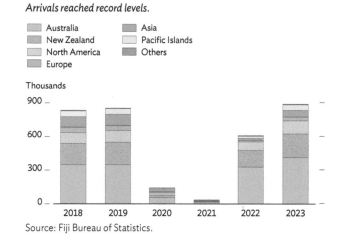

Source: Fiji Bureau of Statistics.

This chapter was written by Isoa Wainiqolo of the South Pacific Subregional Office, ADB, Suva, and Anna Jennifer L. Umlas, consultant, Pacific Department, ADB, Manila.

total), New Zealand (24%), the United States (11%), and Canada (2%) all exceeded 2019 levels. During the peak tourism season from June to September, major hotel occupancy rates were between 84% and 87%.

Consumption spending remained upbeat, supported by increases in personal income. Increased wages, a 15.6% surge in commercial bank lending, and record inward remittances (up 20.4%) helped finance high consumption in 2023. While new investment lending rose, actual investment was suppressed by high building material costs, as domestic cement sales fell by 5% during the year.

The fiscal deficit narrowed in 2023 due to high revenue collection. In line with general improvement in economic conditions, revenue rose by 22.6% in fiscal year 2023 (FY2023, ended 31 July 2023), largely due to increases in indirect tax revenues. Conversely, expenditure increased by only 0.6%, reflecting delays in capital project implementation and general government fiscal consolidation. This reduced the fiscal deficit to the equivalent of 6.9% of GDP, down from 11.9% the previous year (Figure 2.33.3).

As the deficit declined the debt-to-GDP ratio also fell. The debt-to-GDP ratio declined from 88.8% at the end of FY2022 to 80.0% at the end of FY2023. While the share of external debt to total debt has increased over time, much of it is concessional financing from multilateral and bilateral partners with low interest

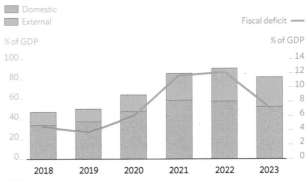

Figure 2.33.3 Public Debt

Improved revenue collection and tight control on expenditure reduced the fiscal deficit.

GDP = gross domestic product.
Note: Years are fiscal years ending 31 July of that year.
Sources: Fiji Ministry of Finance; Reserve Bank of Fiji.

rates and extended maturity periods. Apart from FY2021 when Fiji repaid its global bonds, external loan repayments have stayed under 8% of government revenues (Figure 2.33.4).

Financial developments reflected the overall economic improvement in 2023. The weighted average lending rate of commercial banks fell to 4.77% in 2023 from 5.20% in 2022, indicative of stable liquidity positions. Private sector credit expanded by 7.6%, driven by increased lending for consumption and investment in real estate, housing, and tourism-related sectors.

Figure 2.33.4 Debt Service

A better lending mix helped repayments.

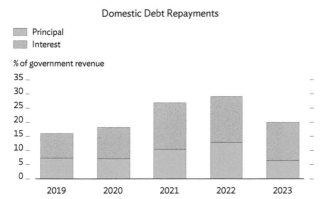

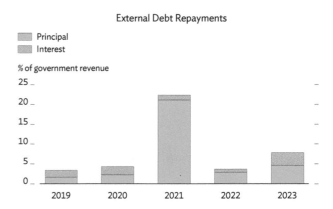

Note: Years are fiscal years ending on 31 July of that year.
Sources: Fiji Ministry of Finance; Reserve Bank of Fiji.

Annual average inflation fell to 2.4% in 2023 due to lower commodity prices and trading partner inflation (Figure 2.33.5). With the tax rate hike towards the latter half of the year, inflation rose to 5.0% in the last quarter of 2023 from just 1.5% in the first 3 quarters. Essential food items, which make up a significant share of household expenditure, were not affected by the VAT rate change.

Figure 2.33.5 Inflation

Low import prices helped reduce inflation in 2023.

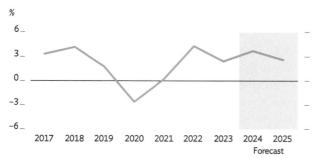

Sources: Fiji Bureau of Statistics; Asian Development Bank estimates.

The current account deficit narrowed significantly to 9.5% of GDP from 17.2% in 2022. The trade deficit widened by 8.3% due to increased imports of machinery, food items and mineral fuels. However, this was substantially offset by strong inflows from tourism and remittances.

Economic Prospects

Growth is projected to slow to 3.0% in 2024 and 2.7% in 2025 (Table 2.33.1). Tourism remains the main driver of economic activity despite an expansion in other sectors, notably agriculture and business process outsourcing. However, the growth rate in visitor

arrivals is projected to decelerate in 2024 and 2025 due largely to capacity constraints, such as hotel room inventory and migrating workers. High occupancy rates in key areas are pushing up hotel prices. This may make it difficult for Fiji to compete with other destinations such as Indonesia and Thailand.

Inflation is projected to rise to 3.7% in 2024 consistent with high inflation observed so far and the trend in commodity prices. Price increases resulting from the change in value-added tax (VAT) rate in August 2023 may persist in the first half of 2024, but inflation is expected to fall back to 2.6% in 2025.

The fiscal position is expected to improve over the forecast period. Recent tax reforms should add essential government revenues as the economy recovers. Government revenue is projected to increase to 27.9% of GDP in FY2024 from 22.1% of GDP in FY2023, mainly due to an increase in VAT rates from 9% to 15% for most goods and services. The government plans to slow expenditure growth in the medium term to reduce the debt-to-GDP ratio to pre-pandemic levels. Constraints in capacity and delays in implementing capital projects may further reduce the fiscal deficit. This trend is projected to continue into FY2025. Consequently, the debt-to-GDP ratio is projected to drop below 78% by the end of 2025.

Policy Challenge—Boosting Tourism Capacity for Sustained Recovery

Over the next few years, limited tourist accommodation might slow sustainable economic growth. Currently, there are 13,000 hotel rooms available from 421 licensed accommodation providers. There is also a growing number of unlicensed short-term accommodation providers on platforms such as Airbnb.

The government should act to sustain tourism growth and keep hotel pricing competitive. The government can help in three ways. It needs to ease impediments to domestic and foreign tourism investment; improve tourist infrastructure, particularly in outer islands; and consider alternative forms of tourism.

Table 2.33.1 Selected Economic Indicators, %

Growth is expected to moderate as the economy stabilizes following a post-pandemic rebound.

	2022	2023	2024	2025
GDP growth	20.0	7.8	3.0	2.7
Inflation	4.3	2.4	3.7	2.6

GDP = gross domestic product.

Source: Asian Development Bank estimates.

Fiji should act quickly to attract more investment in tourism. Potential investors, particularly foreign investors, likely see the government's complex foreign investment procedures as a barrier to investment in tourism. The government should accelerate efforts to streamline and expedite investment processes while simultaneously prioritizing environmental protection and promoting sustainable tourism. Stakeholders see delays in finalizing and obtaining approval for an Environmental Impact Assessment as a critical obstacle to realizing investments. To address this, the government has established an interministerial body to help streamline investment-related processes.

Fiji can also work on spreading tourism activity and benefits to more areas. Currently, 75% of hotel rooms are concentrated in the Coral Coast-Nadi corridor on the country's largest island, Viti Levu. Fiji could spread tourism benefits by improving transportation connections to outer islands like Vanua Levu, Fiji's second-largest island. The government, with support from development partners, is upgrading airports in Savusavu and Labasa, the two primary tourism hubs on Vanua Levu. In addition, there is an ongoing feasibility study for constructing a new airport capable of accommodating larger aircraft. While sea transportation remains viable, the initial focus should be on enhancing key connecting jetties to Vanua Levu. Other potential areas such as Taveuni and Sun Coast could also benefit from increased marketing, contributing to a more widespread distribution of tourism benefits. Spreading tourists out to more areas may help relieve the strain on hotel room availability and hotel prices around Viti Levu.

The government can further explore alternative forms of tourism such as sports, retirement and medical tourism. In 2022, a Fiji rugby team joined the Super Rugby Pacific competition, which includes teams from Australia and New Zealand. It is estimated that the six games Fiji hosted during the following season resulted in 40,328 nights of overseas visitor stays that would not have happened otherwise. The positive effects of these events can be effectively utilized during Fiji's tourism offseason. Fiji also has the potential to attract medical tourists from neighboring Pacific countries who travel as far as Asia for medical treatment. For this to happen, Fiji requires additional privately operated hospitals to enhance its healthcare infrastructure. A study by the International Finance Corporation indicates opportunities for private sector investment in advanced diagnostic facilities and specialist care hospitals. Fiji can build on its two recent public-private partnerships for its Lautoka and Ba hospitals.

PAPUA NEW GUINEA

Growth slowed in 2023 on lower resource output, while foreign exchange restrictions and frequent power supply disruptions stifled other economic activity. The resumption of full production at the Porgera gold mine should accelerate growth in 2024 and 2025, but civil unrest in January this year and a poor business environment cloud the outlook. Energy reforms such as tariff adjustments are urgently needed to improve economic prospects.

Economic Performance

Growth slowed to an estimated 2.0% in 2023 as resource output weakened (Figure 2.34.1). Production of gold and liquefied natural gas (LNG) fell below 2022 levels, resulting in a 2.0% contraction in the resource sector. A combination of maintenance and bad weather affected gold production, while scheduled maintenance lowered output at the LNG plant.

The non-resource sector expanded moderately by an estimated 3.4%. Easing global supply chain disruptions supported growth in manufacturing along with information and communications. Increased government spending provided stimulus to education, health, and public administration. However, after a spike in 2022, the fall in global commodity prices—including those for the country's key agricultural exports—weakened economic activity. Low palm oil production also slowed growth in agriculture.

Several business impediments, including a lack of foreign exchange, stifled non-resource economic activity. Despite the central bank's increased interventions in 2023 to provide foreign exchange to the market, businesses continued to struggle with timely access, hindering restocking and investment. The protracted and unresolved dispute between Puma Energy, the country's near-monopoly fuel supplier, and the central bank over forex and regulatory issues affected transport. Other setbacks to business operations last year included disruptions

Figure 2.34.1 Supply-Side Contributions to Growth

Growth slowed in 2023 as resource output contracted.

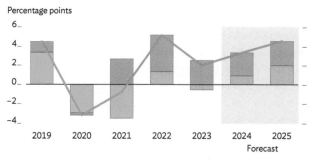

- Mining and petroleum
- Non-resource
- Gross domestic product growth, %

Source: Asian Development Bank estimates using data from Papua New Guinea National Statistical Office.

to power and water supply, frequent cancellations and delays in domestic flights due to technical issues with Air Niugini's aging fleet, and glitches in banking transactions. Sales in various sectors were reported to have dropped substantially during the year.

Headline inflation slowed, but prices of essential consumer items continued to surge. The consumer price index (CPI) rose by 2.3% in 2023, down from 5.3% in 2022 (Figure 2.34.2). This was mostly driven by a one-off decrease of 22.9% in education costs as the government implemented its Tuition Fee Free

This chapter was written by Marcel Schroder and Magdelyn Kuari of the Papua New Guinea Resident Mission, ADB, Port Moresby.

Figure 2.34.2 Inflation

A one-off drop in education costs brought down inflation, but prices rose for many consumer goods and services.

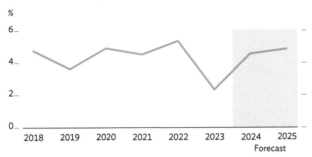

Sources: Papua New Guinea National Statistical Office; Asian Development Bank estimates.

Table 2.34.1 Selected Economic Indicators, %

Strong mining performance will drive growth in 2024 and 2025.

	2022	2023	2024	2025
GDP growth	5.2	2.0	3.3	4.6
Inflation	5.3	2.3	4.5	4.8

GDP = gross domestic product.
Source: Asian Development Bank estimates.

Education Policy. Inflation decelerated for several CPI components, including housing, communications, recreation, and alcoholic beverages, tobacco, and betelnut. However, costs for many essential consumer goods and services soared. Prices for food and non-alcoholic beverages rose by 7.0%, household equipment by 9.0%, and clothing and footwear by 7.0%.

A supplementary budget in November 2023 estimated the fiscal deficit at 4.4% of GDP. The government's fiscal consolidation plan continued to reduce the fiscal deficit from 5.3% of GDP in 2022. Although total expenditure increased through the operational budget, it was offset by additional revenue from taxes on salaries and wages. Public debt rose to the equivalent of 52.6% of GDP. An IMF program approved in March 2023 supports further fiscal consolidation to promote both external and overall debt sustainability. The IMF's first review report in December found that the government was meeting all end-June 2023 criteria and implementing its structural benchmarks.

Economic Prospects

Growth is projected to accelerate to 3.3% in 2024 and 4.6% in 2025 on strong mining output (Table 2.34.1). Following the conclusion of the Porgera Project Commencement Agreement, the Porgera gold mine resumed operation on 22 December 2023, ending almost 4 years of closure. The mine produced its first gold in February and full production is expected

to resume in the third quarter. Along with increased output from Ok Tedi and Lihir in 2025—the other two major mines—the sector is expected to grow by 10.0% in 2024 and 23.4% in 2025. In the petroleum and gas sector, production at newly drilled wells will likely support growth in 2024, before flattening afterward.

Porgera's reopening should generate growth spillovers to the rest of the economy. The mine's reopening should create additional operation-related spending on goods and services, employment, and provide foreign exchange inflows. A boost in cocoa and copra oil production, while somewhat offset by slight decreases in coffee and copra output, is expected to support growth in agriculture, forestry, and fisheries. Continued government spending should boost growth in construction. Several favorable developments should help transport's prospects. Air Niugini, the national airline, has temporarily leased a Boeing 737, reducing flight delays and cancellations. The airline will purchase six new aircraft and lease five more to replace its ageing fleet. The first plane is scheduled to join Air Niugini's fleet in 2025. Further stimulus will be provided by a new airport terminal in Lae and a roundtrip flight connection between Port Moresby and Guangzhou in the People's Republic of China that began in late December 2023.

Forex restrictions, the foremost business constraint, could ease under the IMF program this year. The central bank has allowed the Kina to depreciate gradually, bringing it closer to a market rate. To promote a steady transition to greater exchange rate flexibility under the IMF program, a limit on unmet import-related forex orders has been established. Set initially at $150 million in January 2024, the ceiling will be reduced each quarter, reaching $75 million in December.

Civil unrest in January and ongoing challenges such as power supply disruptions cloud the outlook. Strikes by law enforcers over a pay cut resulted in looting and damaging retail shops throughout the capital Port Moresby. The unrest spread to other provinces but was swiftly contained. In total, 53 businesses were affected with an estimated damage of about K1.2 billion (1.2% of GDP) and 2,000 jobs lost. These losses, combined with shaken investor and consumer confidence, will decrease spending. Persisting forex restrictions will cause delays and higher costs for businesses in rebuilding lost capacity, replenishing stocks, and expanding operations. Disruptions to power and water supply in the main urban centers will also affect business operations in key sectors. Especially in Lae, the country's manufacturing and logistics hub, businesses face frequent blackouts and power fluctuations, forcing them to rely on generators to maintain operations, escalating operational costs and affecting competitiveness. In February and March, Puma Energy again limited fuel supplies over forex issues, affecting mobility across the country.

Headline inflation is expected to rise because of base effects, exchange rate depreciation, and civil unrest. Education subsidies will continue, but their disinflationary effect will dissipate throughout the year. While slowing global inflation lowers imported inflation, it is counterbalanced by further exchange rate depreciation as the central bank moves to a market-determined exchange rate. Domestic inflation could rise because of supply issues caused by the civil unrest. To assist businesses affected by the looting and the wider economy generally, the central bank lowered the Kina Facility Rate, its main monetary policy instrument, from 2.5% to 2.0% in February, where it will likely remain. Overall, inflation is projected to accelerate to 4.5% in 2024 and 4.8% in 2025. However, El Niño could disrupt agriculture and lead to higher commodity prices.

The government's fiscal consolidation aims to balance the budget by 2027. The consolidation strategy involves domestic revenue mobilization while restraining and rationalizing spending. The government plans to further reduce the fiscal deficit to 3.3% of GDP in 2024 and 2.0% of GDP in 2025 (Figure 2.34.3). As a result, public debt is projected to decrease to 51.1% of GDP in 2024 and 49.2% of GDP

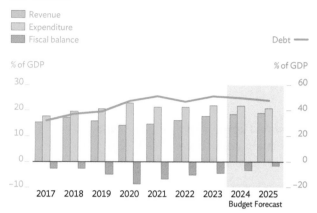

Figure 2.34.3 Fiscal Balance and Debt

Under the national budget, the fiscal deficit will be reduced to 2.0% of GDP in 2025.

GDP = gross domestic product.
Source: Papua New Guinea Department of Treasury.

in 2025. Under the IMF program, the country must limit the present value of new external borrowing to $1,072 million in 2024 and keep the fiscal deficit at or below K4,810 million (3.9% of GDP).

Revenue growth is projected to outweigh expenditure growth, subject to risk. Revenue excluding development partner grants is projected to increase in 2024 by K2.8 billion (2.6% of GDP) mainly from taxes on profits, salaries, and wages, and non-tax revenue. Expenditure will grow less, by K1.86 billion (1.8% of GDP). The capital budget allocation is projected to increase by 9.0%, the operations budget by 8.0%, and the payroll bill by 1.3%. These projections are, however, at risk because they do not consider the damage from the social unrest and potential government assistance to affected businesses. Executing the budget will continue to depend on support from bilateral and multilateral development partners.

Risks to the outlook are predominantly on the downside. A key threat is any delay to resumption of full production at Porgera. Other downside risks include worsening law and order conditions and forex access, and an escalation in a dispute on fuel supply that could severely affect mobility. Disaster and weather-related events such as El Niño are threats to agricultural output. A major upside risk, subject to increasing uncertainty, is the start of Papua LNG, a multibillion-dollar gas project. After progressing to the front-end engineering and design phase in March 2023, several related factors have delayed a final investment decision. These include regulatory approvals, environmental issues, gas marketing, and securing financing.

Policy Challenge—Reforming the Energy Sector

Unreliable power supply limits economic growth in the main urban areas. The electricity supply is generally poor and blackouts are frequent because of inadequate generation capacity and aging networks. Self-generation and backup generation (entirely diesel-based) are common for business and residential areas and have increased over recent years due to repeated blackouts. Operation and maintenance costs of power generation are high, but efficiencies low. The power utility, PNG Power Limited (PPL), has deprioritized maintenance on its network and generation assets because of the utility's deteriorating financial condition. This is driven by low tariffs, last adjusted in 2013, which barely recover PPL costs, and high technical and commercial losses. Aging network infrastructure leads to high losses, while electricity theft, illegal connections, and a low bill collection rate leave PPL with revenues well below expenses.

PNG lacks a national government-led plan for energy sector development. PPL instead conducts internal generation and grid planning that is neither backed nor aligned with the national regulator or the government's national budget financing plan. Since 2013, private sector participation has been allowed in power generation. As a result, independent power producers (IPPs) have made ad hoc investments that are not coordinated with grid development. Although the government set a target in 2010 to achieve 70% electrification by 2030, less than 20% of the population can currently access electricity.

The transition from diesel generation to cheaper and cleaner renewable energy resources is limited. Although PNG has abundant renewable energy resources—hydropower, solar, wind, biomass, and geothermal energy—these have not been fully explored or utilized. Hydropower has been the backbone of the country's power supply, but its role has diminished over the years, with limited new capacity added. Despite excellent solar potential and high returns on investments for many locations in the country and good alignment with peak power demand during the day, photovoltaics have not been deployed at a utility scale. Legal barriers and restrictions on behind-the-meter renewable energy installations block the development of private firms' solar photovoltaic. Hence, rooftop photovoltaic panels have been limited to small off-grid applications.

Reforms in three key areas are needed to improve power generation and promote growth. The first is to restore the financial sustainability of the power sector by adjusting tariffs and improving the utility's operations. The regulator needs to establish a process and methodology for independent annual tariff adjustments, while considering the effects on poor and vulnerable households. PPL also needs to develop a comprehensive revenue strategy to reduce commercial losses and public sector payment arrears, and to connect more commercial customers. Second, there is a need to create a national transition plan to a low-carbon power sector, including guidelines to prioritize and fund power sector infrastructure. The government further needs to issue national regulations related to planning, implementation, and monitoring. This includes removing legal barriers and restrictions to renewable energy installations. And third, reforms are needed to enable efficient private sector involvement in the power sector. This requires issuing regulations on the process of competitive bidding for IPP investment. Open, transparent, and competitive tenders with bankable power purchase agreements will attract private sector investment, while promoting technical efficiency and cost-competitiveness.

SOLOMON ISLANDS

Growth rebounded in 2023 as economic activity normalized after the COVID-19 pandemic while construction for the Pacific Games also provided a boost. In 2024 and 2025, growth is expected to moderate slightly, but continue to be led by industry and services. The budget deficit should narrow as the government focuses on fiscal recovery. Public debt is projected to increase to finance infrastructure and budget deficits, while inflation is expected to decelerate in line with global trends. Balancing fiscal sustainability with long-term investment needs is an ongoing challenge.

Economic Performance

Growth rebounded in 2023 as the country recovered from the COVID-19 pandemic and hosted the Pacific Games. The economy grew by 2.5% in 2023 after an average 2.7% contraction in 2020–2022, due to the pandemic and the November 2021 civil unrest. Economic activity rebounded as COVID-19 restrictions were lifted and the Pacific Games spurred a construction boom to build new stadiums and sports facilities. The country welcomed 26,030 international visitors, 255% more than in 2022, providing stimulus for local businesses.

Logging output was higher than anticipated, while fish exports increased. The three major export categories in 2023 were logs and timber (41%), minerals (26%), and fish (17%). After 4 years of decline, log production rose by 3% and the value of log and timber exports increased by 9% (Figure 2.35.1), facilitated by the lifting of COVID-19 restrictions. Vessel maintenance issues and poor weather conditions in the second half of the year contributed to a 17% drop in the fish catch, 22,093 metric tons in 2023. However, because of a significant increase in fish prices, the value of exports increased by 46%.

The minerals sector performed well as the Gold Ridge Mine had its first full year of operations since 2014. Gold production in 2023 increased by

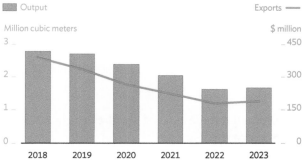

Figure 2.35.1 Log Output and Exports

After declining for 4 consecutive years, log output and exports increased slightly in 2023.

Sources: Central Bank of Solomon Islands; Asian Development Bank estimates.

268% to 64,712 ounces compared with 17,565 in 2022. Export of minerals increased by 270%, making it the second largest export category, behind logs and timber (Figure 2.35.2). Overall merchandise exports increased by 32% in 2023, while imports increased by 13%, largely for the Pacific Games. Import growth came mostly from machinery and transport equipment (31% growth), and food and live animals (22% growth).

The fiscal deficit expanded in 2023 largely due to spending for the Pacific Games. Expenditure increased by 5% from 2022, while revenue and grants

---

This chapter was written by Katherine Passmore of the Pacific Liaison and Coordination Office, ADB, Sydney, and Prince Cruz, consultant, Pacific Department, ADB, Manila.

Figure 2.35.2 Exports

As the contribution of logs and timber to exports declines, full-year operations of Gold Ridge Mine pushed mineral exports into second place in 2023.

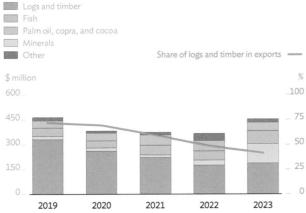

Sources: Central Bank of Solomon Islands; Asian Development Bank estimates.

dropped by 4%. Export duties on logs contributed 11% of government revenue, a substantial decline from their 2018 peak of 21%. Capital expenditure—27% of total expenditure—increased by 67% to help fund infrastructure for the games, while wages and salaries rose by 4%. The wage bill contributed 36% to overall expenditure. The fiscal deficit expanded from 4.0% of GDP in 2022 to 6.5% in 2023.

Government debt increased significantly in 2023 to help finance the fiscal deficit. Total debt increased from 14.5% of GDP in 2022 to 19.2% in 2023. Domestic debt increased by 46% mainly through the sale of government development bonds to the National Provident Fund and state-owned enterprises. External debt rose by 32%.

Overall inflation decelerated in 2023 in line with global trends. Inflation decelerated from 5.4% in 2022 to 4.6% in 2023. Food price inflation slowed from 7.4% to 5.0%, while transport inflation went down from 14.1% to 7.4%. In March 2023, the Central Bank of Solomon Islands (CBSI) tightened monetary policy by raising the cash reserve ratio from 5% to 6% to help ease inflation.

Economic Prospects

Growth in 2024 and 2025 is expected to moderate as activity related to the Pacific Games winds down. Following the one-off surge in construction and tourism in 2023, growth is expected to moderate to 2.2% in 2024 and 2025 largely driven by construction, wholesale and retail trade, communications, and mining (Table 2.35.1 and Figure 2.35.3). Several projects, including some delayed by the pandemic, are expected to proceed within the forecast period and boost growth. These include airport upgrades and power plant construction, along with initiatives to support crop production and fisheries. A general election in April 2024 is likely to temporarily dampen economic activity in the capital as voters return to their home province to vote, while local businesses are expected to defer stock purchases to mitigate against any potential election-related unrest.

Table 2.35.1 Selected Economic Indicators, %

Economic growth will moderate in 2024 and 2025 as the boost from Pacific Games construction dissipates, while inflation slows.

	2022	2023	2024	2025
GDP growth	−4.2	2.5	2.2	2.2
Inflation	5.4	4.6	3.2	2.7

GDP = gross domestic product.
Sources: Central Bank of Solomon Islands; Asian Development Bank estimates.

Figure 2.35.3 Supply-side Contributions to Growth

After 3 years of contraction, the economy recovered in 2023 with a strong boost from the Pacific Games.

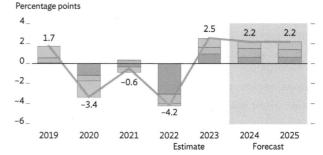

Sources: Solomon Islands National Statistics Office; Asian Development Bank estimates.

The budget deficit in 2024 is expected to narrow as the government focuses on fiscal recovery.
Expenditure is budgeted to fall by 8% compared with 2023. The 2024 budget focuses on delivering essential services and existing contractual arrangements, lowering development expenditure by 44% compared with 2023. However, payroll expenditure is expected to rise by 19%. Additional costs for maintenance of new infrastructure from the Pacific Games and higher input costs for existing projects will add pressure to the budget. In the first quarter lead up to the 2024 election, infrastructure spending will likely be delayed due to caretaker government arrangements, a convention under which no important decisions or new initiatives are undertaken until a new government is confirmed. Expenses to run the general election are expected to be covered by development partners. Revenue is forecast to increase by less than 1%, and budget support from development partners is projected to drop by 24%. Despite the reduced deficit, the budget still faces a significant financing gap.

Constituency development funds (CDFs)— intended to support rural development—will continue to play a significant expenditure role amid reforms. While there will be a reduced government contribution to CDFs in 2024, they are typically provided with additional funding from the People's Republic of China. The CDF Act of 2023 was enacted in December 2023, shifting much of the decision-making and administration from members of parliament to civil servants and constituency committees. These reforms are expected to improve governance, transparency, and expenditure quality.

Public debt is projected to increase to finance infrastructure and recurring budget deficits. Overall debt is expected to rise to 26.7% of GDP in 2025, still within the government's debt ceiling of 35%. Domestic debt is projected to increase from 8.5% of GDP in 2023 to 12.4% in 2025, while external debt will rise from 11.5% in 2023 to 13.0% in 2025 (Figure 2.35.4). The government has doubled its treasury bill ceiling to SI$200 million to help finance the budget and provide flexibility. This aligns with a reform introduced through the CBSI (Amendment) Act 2023, which raised the ceiling of central bank advances, credit facilities or guarantees to the government from 5% to 15% of average government revenue over the 3 preceding years. The shift to domestic financing may

Figure 2.35.4 Public Sector Debt

Despite a massive increase from 2022 to 2025, public debt should remain below the 35% of GDP ceiling set by the government.

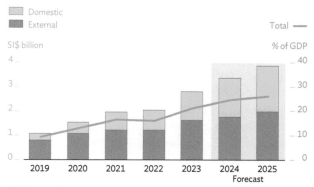

GDP = gross domestic product.
Sources: Central Bank of Solomon Islands; Asian Development Bank estimates.

increase debt servicing obligations, but the depth of the local debt market is limited as domestic buyers of government debt are few and may be subject to internal ceilings.

Remittances will continue to grow as seasonal work programs expand. The government expects the number of workers availing of seasonal work programs in Australia and New Zealand to rise from 6,800 at end-2023 to as many as 16,000 by 2028. Remittances have jumped from an average $20 million per year from 2010–2020 to $51 million in 2021 and $85 million in 2023 (equivalent to 5% of GDP). These payments provide an important boost to household income and consumption.

Inflation is expected to decelerate further in 2024 and 2025, in line with global trends. Poor weather conditions in early 2024 and the increased global rice price will put temporary pressure on prices, but overall inflation is expected to decline to 3.2% in 2024 and 2.7% in 2025. The CBSI may adopt an accommodative monetary policy in late-2024 as inflationary pressures ease. Risks to the outlook include climate change impact, civil unrest, geopolitical tensions, weak external demand, international financial and price volatility, and ongoing international conflicts.

Policy Challenge—Restoring Fiscal Sustainability

With persistent budget deficits and rising public debt, fiscal discipline must be a priority for the incoming government. After 5 consecutive years of deficits and a series of events with significant economic and fiscal impacts—the pandemic, civil unrest in November 2021, and the 2023 Pacific Games—the government must focus on restoring fiscal discipline (Figure 2.35.5). Cash reserves were significantly drawn down in 2023, and some invoices for the Pacific Games remained outstanding in the first quarter of 2024.

Introducing carefully designed fiscal anchors could guide fiscal policy and the budget cycle and help achieve fiscal sustainability. The government has already adopted some important measures to maintain fiscal discipline. These include debt limits and the Public Financial Management Act 2013, which prohibits the government from borrowing to fund recurrent expenditure when there is a budget deficit. While the government aims to hold cash reserves sufficient to cover at least 2 months of spending, it has proven a challenging target. Examples of fiscal anchors include a ceiling on wages as a portion of total expenditure or a limit on the budget deficit. In 2018, the IMF proposed a budget deficit limit of 1.5% of GDP, but this proposal has not progressed. Fiscal anchors would complement ongoing government efforts to diversify revenue and mobilize domestic resources, including extensive tax reform.

Figure 2.35.5 Fiscal Balance

Surpluses averaged 2.8% of GDP from 2011 to 2015 before turning to deficits in 2016–2017 and 2019–2023.

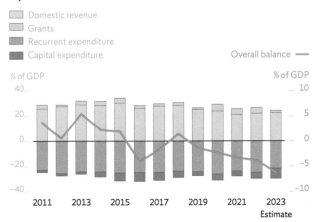

GDP = gross domestic product.
Sources: Central Bank of Solomon Islands; Asian Development Bank estimates.

Restoring fiscal sustainability must be balanced with continued investment in development priorities. At times of fiscal deficit, the development budget becomes most at risk, as it funds initiatives beyond maintenance of essential services such as longer-term investments in health and education. The 2024 budget shows expenditure restraint, but the revenue trend is weak. With the focus on maintaining essential services, investment in key development priorities may suffer. Balancing these priorities will continue to be a challenge for the government in the medium-term.

VANUATU

Economic growth slowed in 2023 as the impact of three cyclones damaged agriculture and infrastructure, and also pushed up inflation. Recovery in 2024 and 2025 is expected to depend mainly on tourism growth and construction, as the government tries to finance the huge reconstruction needs. With rising intensity and frequency of climate-induced disasters, the government must find alternative ways to finance disaster preparedness and response.

Economic Performance

Growth decelerated to 1.0% in 2023 as the country was pummeled by two cyclones in March and another in October (Table 2.36.1). Twin tropical cyclones (TC) Judy and Kevin affected 66% of the population. Total damage and loss was estimated at Vt51.3 billion, equivalent to 43.3% of GDP. For agriculture alone, the impact on crops and fisheries was around Vt15.1 billion. In October, category 5 TC Lola affected 37% of the population. Around 6,384 houses were destroyed and 12,768 damaged in March, while 5,750 were destroyed and 15,700 damaged in October.

Widespread damage forced the government to prioritize infrastructure recovery. A TC Judy and Kevin post-disaster needs assessment cited total recovery needs of Vt91.6 billion (77.4% of GDP). The TC Lola recovery plan placed recovery needs at Vt43.3 billion (36.7% of GDP), with Vt40.8 billion for infrastructure. The government passed supplementary budgets to allot funding for relief and reconstruction needs, with capital spending raised by 33%. Relief allocations from subsidies, grants, and transfers were increased by 48%.

Despite the increased budget, government spending contracted. Government expenditure fell 8% in 2023 compared with the previous year. Although capital spending was up by 7%, current spending was down, largely because of delays in approving the budget

Table 2.36.1 Selected Economic Indicators, %

Cyclone damage pulled down growth in 2023 and pushed up inflation.

	2022	2023	2024	2025
GDP growth	2.0	1.0	3.1	3.6
Inflation	6.7	13.5	4.8	2.9

GDP = gross domestic product.
Sources: Vanuatu National Statistics Office; Asian Development Bank estimates.

due to political instability and cyclone-related delays to implementation of planned activities. The largest decline was in subsidies, grants, and transfers which fell by 25%. Conversely, tax revenue increased by 20% and nontax revenue by 15%. The fiscal balance therefore moved from a deficit equivalent to 5.8% of GDP in 2022 to a surplus of 1.5% in 2023 (Figure 2.36.1). This was in lieu of a deficit of 9.0% projected in the December supplementary budget.

Tourism and remittances provided relief to the economy. Tourism receipts jumped to $193 million (19.6% of GDP) in 2023. Although arrivals by air increased from 30,000 in 2022 to 82,000 in 2023, they slowed in the aftermath of the cyclones (Figure 2.36.2). Air arrivals for the year remained just 70% of the pre-pandemic average of 2018 and 2019. On the other

---

This chapter was written by Katherine Passmore of the Pacific Liaison and Coordination Office, ADB, Sydney, and Prince Cruz, consultant, Pacific Department, ADB, Manila.

Figure 2.36.1 Fiscal Indicators

Disaster impact hampered program and project implementation leading to lower current spending and a fiscal surplus in 2023.

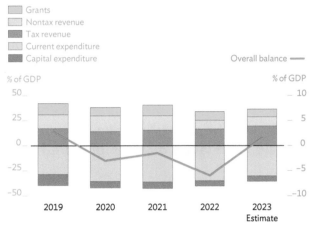

GDP = gross domestic product.
Sources: Vanuatu Department of Finance and Treasury; Asian Development Bank estimates.

Figure 2.36.2 Tourism Receipts and Visitor Arrivals, by Mode of Travel

While cruise ship arrivals exceeded pre-pandemic levels, the recovery of air arrivals slowed after the cyclones in 2023.

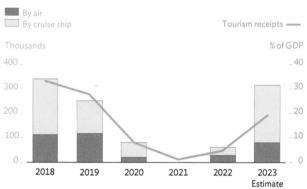

GDP = gross domestic product.
Sources: Vanuatu National Statistics Office; Reserve Bank of Vanuatu; Asian Development Bank estimates.

hand, cruise ship arrivals exceeded 240,000 in 2023. Remittances, mainly from seasonal workers in Australia and New Zealand, continued to grow—although at a slower pace—by 4% to $177 million in 2023 (equivalent to 17.9% of GDP).

Damage to supply networks and crops pushed inflation to its highest level in decades. From 6.7% in 2022, inflation increased to 13.5% in 2023, the highest since 1987, although based on a new price basket (Box). Aside from cyclone damage and the

Box New Consumer Price Index Weights for Vanuatu

Incorporating the results of the 2019–2020 Household Income and Expenditure Survey, new weights for the basket of goods in the consumer price index were implemented in the first quarter of 2023. The weight for food and nonalcoholic beverages increased from 38.4% to 44.5%, transport rose from 6.8% to 14.2%, alcoholic beverages, tobacco, and narcotics rose from 7.1% to 11.2%. In contrast, the weight for housing and utilities declined from 20.9% to 11.6%. When an item has a greater weight in the basket of goods, price fluctuations of that item have a larger impact on overall reported inflation. Reported inflation for previous years was also adjusted (e.g., from 11.9% in the old series to 6.7% in the new series for 2022).

Source: Vanuatu National Statistics Office.

lingering impact of the Russian invasion of Ukraine on fuel prices, a 36.0% increase in the minimum wage in June increased inflationary pressures. With inflation significantly above the 0%–4% target range, the Reserve Bank of Vanuatu (RBV) tightened monetary policy in late 2023.

Economic Prospects

The economy is expected to recover with growth of 3.1% in 2024 and 3.6% in 2025, boosted by tourism and reconstruction. Spending by tourists and domestic households will likely boost services including retail trade, accommodation and restaurants, and transportation (Figure 2.36.3). Reconstruction is expected to be led by development partners, tourism-related businesses, and families of seasonal workers. Agriculture will also likely grow after contracting in 2023.

Although remittances are expected to slow, they will remain significant. Various proposals are being considered to balance the benefits of outmigration for seasonal work programs with the needs of domestic industries, especially tourism and public services. Several issues need to be addressed. These include ensuring that workers outside the main urban areas also gain access to seasonal worker opportunities,

Figure 2.36.3 Supply-Side Contributions to Growth

Growth in tourism and reconstruction drives economic recovery as services and industry expand.

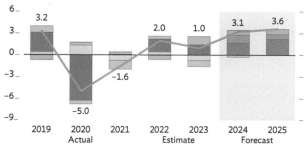

Sources: Vanuatu National Statistics Office; Asian Development Bank estimates.

protecting the welfare of seasonal workers at their workplace, minimizing absconding, and improving reintegration after workers return.

Despite problems hounding Air Vanuatu, the tourism outlook remains bright. The state-owned carrier continued to experience maintenance woes leading to flight cancellations and delays. The slack was picked up by other regional carriers. Opening more routes to these carriers could support the tourism revival. For instance, arrivals from New Zealand have exceeded the pre-pandemic average since the reopening of Honiara-Port Vila-Auckland flights by Solomon Airlines in July 2023.

Cruise ship visitors will continue leading the tourism revival in 2024 and 2025. A significant dip in arrivals by air was seen after the cyclones in March 2023, but cruise ship arrivals remained resilient and are expected to continue growing in the forecast period. With frequent disasters, developing more areas for cruise ship tourism and climate-proofing tourism infrastructure will consolidate the sector's growth potential. Demand from cruise ship visitors can provide immediate support to communities in cyclone-hit areas. Although the average expenditure per visitor arriving by plane is around five times that of a cruise ship visitor, the infrastructure needed for cruise ships is also relatively lower.

Although overall revenues are expected to increase, they will not cover extensive reconstruction needs. The delay in the passage of the 2024 budget means that spending in the first quarter was likely restrained once again. This means that government-led reconstruction and other major recovery support measures will likely be delayed. While tax revenue is expected to increase significantly with increased tourism activity, nontax revenues—mainly from Honorary Citizenship Programs (HCPs)—are expected to continue to decline. HCP revenues fell from Vt14.4 billion in 2020 to Vt8.1 billion in 2023. With lingering issues on visa-free access to the European Union and United Kingdom, HCP revenues are projected to decline to around Vt6.0 billion in 2024 (equivalent to 4.8% of GDP).

Inflation is expected to ease as supply chains are restored and agriculture recovers. Along with lower global commodity prices, the normalization of supply chains, especially for food, should lead to lower inflation at 4.8% in 2024 and 2.9% in 2025 (Figure 2.36.4). The impact of monetary policy tightening in late 2023 is expected to be felt fully in 2024. Although the key policy rate was kept at 2.25%, the RBV doubled the volume of RBV notes to Vt200 million per month effective October 2023. In January 2024, the commercial bank statutory reserves deposit ratio was raised to 5.50% from 5.25%.

Figure 2.36.4 Inflation

Massive damage to agriculture and infrastructure pushed up food prices in 2023.

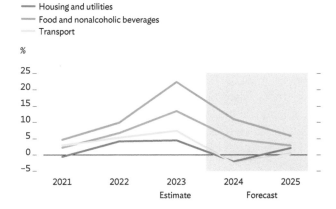

Sources: Vanuatu National Statistics Office; Reserve Bank of Vanuatu; Asian Development Bank estimates.

Political instability is a risk to growth. Political instability contributed to the slow disbursement of government funds in 2023 and delayed the resolution of key policy issues. The ruling coalition was replaced in September 2023 but returned to power in October under a different prime minister. To address political instability, several laws, including one requiring political party registration, will be subject to a referendum in May 2024.

Policy Challenge—Financing Immediate Disaster Response

The disasters that struck in 2023 highlight the need to scale-up disaster response financing and implementation support. The government can use up to 1.5% of approved appropriations during a state of emergency after a disaster or financial crisis. After the cyclones in March, the Vt813 million in emergency funds was clearly insufficient. This necessitated supplementary budgets of Vt1.4 billion in May 2023 and Vt3.2 billion in December. There are also constraints in implementing projects using available resources.

In past disasters, Vanuatu benefitted from contingent disaster financing, but it remains insufficient to meet recovery needs. Contingent disaster financing gives economies rapid access to disaster response finance. After TC Pam in 2015, Vanuatu received $1.9 million from the Pacific Catastrophe Risk Assessment and Financing Initiative (PCRAFI)—a regional market-based parametric disaster insurance pool. However, after a cyclone in 2018 and volcanic eruptions in 2017–2018, Vanuatu was not deemed eligible for payouts. With perceived low returns amid high costs, Vanuatu opted out of the insurance in 2018. Nevertheless, Vanuatu has access to contingency financing from development partners. For example, under the World Bank's contingency financing program, Vanuatu received a $10 million grant in 2020 for TC Harold and COVID-19, and a $9.5 million grant in March 2023.

Options for borrowing to finance recovery and reconstruction remain limited. Reconstruction after TC Pam in 2015 led to a sharp increase in external debt

from 14% of GDP in 2014 to 39% in 2020. Despite a decline to 36% in 2023, external debt remains close to the 40% external debt ceiling with limited scope for further domestic borrowing (Figure 2.36.5). Yet, additional financing will likely be needed to complete some existing loan-funded projects due to higher input costs.

Figure 2.36.5 Public Debt

Massive reconstruction needs after Tropical Cyclone Pam in 2015 pushed external debt near the 40% debt-to-GDP ceiling.

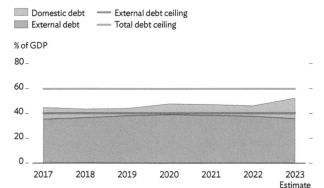

GDP = gross domestic product.
Sources: Vanuatu Department of Finance and Treasury; Asian Development Bank estimates.

More options for disaster response financing and climate resilience are needed. Analysis is ongoing on disaster-responsive budgeting and financial instruments. The TC Lola Recovery Plan calls for establishing trust funds for disaster relief and response to reduce post-disaster food insecurity. It also stresses the key role development partners have to play. More broadly, the importance of accessing international climate funds cannot be overstated, as they can be used to enhance climate resilience and reduce vulnerability of communities and infrastructure to disasters triggered by natural hazards. Reduced vulnerability will have a direct flow-on effect to future requirements for disaster response financing. Vanuatu has long advocated compensation for countries most affected by climate change. It is now leading on the international stage for climate change accountability through the International Court of Justice. A loss and damage fund was agreed upon at COP28 in December 2023—a fund first proposed by Vanuatu in 1991. As the frequency and intensity of disasters rise, both disaster response and climate resilience financing must increase complemented by increased implementation support.

CENTRAL PACIFIC ECONOMIES

The resumption of infrastructure projects pushed growth higher in Kiribati and Tuvalu, but in Nauru growth slowed as the Australian-funded Regional Processing Centre scaled down operations. Growth is expected to continue in the three economies although for different reasons. Inflation is projected to moderate in Kiribati and Tuvalu, but will shoot up in Nauru due to higher communication costs. As rising sea levels threaten livelihoods and food security, immediate and concerted efforts to mitigate the threat and associated risks are needed.

Kiribati

The economy expanded in 2023 supported by infrastructure projects and social protection spending. The recovery gained momentum in 2023 from the resumption of large infrastructure projects. GDP grew by 4.2%, up from 3.9% in 2022 (Figure 2.37.1). Social protection programs, notably the copra subsidy and unemployment benefits, supported household incomes and domestic consumption.

Economic growth is forecast to accelerate to 5.3% in 2024 before falling back to 3.5% in 2025. The roll-out of energy, water, transport, and health projects in 2024, sustained social protection spending, and increased wages for civil servants are expected to drive growth over the forecast period. Downside risks remain focused on commodity price volatility, general elections, and natural hazards, which could jeopardize the smooth implementation of infrastructure projects.

Kiribati's fiscal deficit narrowed in 2023, but will likely widen again in 2024. The fiscal deficit narrowed to the equivalent of 2.3% of GDP in 2023 from 2.7% in 2022. Revenue increased by 18.7%, as income from fishing licenses increased by 41.8% and tax revenues by 27.4% (Figure 2.37.2). During the same period, current expenditure jumped by 5.3%, with higher spending on social protection. In 2024, the fiscal deficit is projected

Figure 2.37.1 Gross Domestic Product Growth

Economic growth in 2023 was driven by the resumption of infrastructure projects, although it slowed slightly in Nauru.

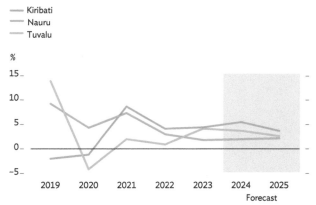

— Kiribati
— Nauru
— Tuvalu

Note: Years are fiscal years ending on 30 June of that year in Nauru and coinciding with the calendar year in Kiribati and Tuvalu.

Sources: Kiribati, Nauru, and Tuvalu budget documents; International Monetary Fund Article IV reports; Asian Development Bank estimates.

to widen to 9.7% of GDP from a wage increase for government employees and a decline in budget support from development partners.

Inflation accelerated in 2023 but will likely moderate over the next 2 years. Inflation accelerated from 5.3% in 2022 to 9.7% in 2023 driven by

This chapter was written by Lily-Anne Homasi and Isoa Wainiqolo of the South Pacific Subregional Office, ADB, Suva; Katherine Passmore of the Pacific Liaison and Coordination Office, ADB, Sydney; and Prince Cruz, Ana Isabel Jimenez, and Anna Jennifer Umlas, consultants, Pacific Department, ADB, Manila.

Figure 2.37.2 Kiribati Fiscal Components

The fiscal deficit slighlty fell in 2023 as fishing license revenue recovered.

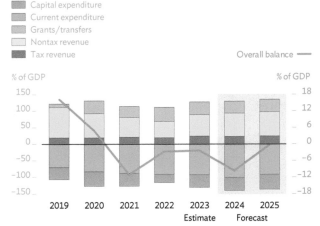

- Capital expenditure
- Current expenditure
- Grants/transfers
- Nontax revenue
- Tax revenue

Overall balance ——

GDP = gross domestic product.

Source: Asian Development Bank estimates using Kiribati budget documents.

Table 2.37.1 Selected Economic Indicators, %

Growth is expected to accelerate in Kiribati and Nauru in 2024, but slow in Tuvalu.

	2022	2023	2024	2025
Kiribati				
GDP growth	3.9	4.2	5.3	3.5
Inflation	5.3	9.7	4.0	3.0
Nauru				
GDP growth	2.8	1.6	1.8	2.0
Inflation	1.5	5.2	10.3	3.5
Tuvalu				
GDP growth	0.7	3.9	3.5	2.4
Inflation	12.2	7.2	3.0	3.0

GDP = gross domestic product.

Note: Years are fiscal years ending on 30 June of that year in Nauru and coinciding with the calendar year in Kiribati and Tuvalu.

Source: Asian Development Bank estimates.

transportation and food prices (Table 2.37.1). Lower inflation is projected over the forecast period from moderating global commodity prices, improved supply-side conditions, and base effects.

A rebound in fishing license fees sustained the current account surplus in 2023 and will continue to do so through 2025. The current account surplus

in 2023 was estimated to be 10.2% of GDP, bolstered by the resurgence in fishing license fees (Figure 2.37.3), which offset higher deficits on goods and services. The balance of Kiribati's sovereign wealth fund—the Revenue Equalization Reserve Fund—reached 33% of GDP at the end of 2023 after posting an annual return of 16.4%. Fishing revenues and remittances are expected to continue supporting the surplus as Kiribati's infrastructure projects resume, despite being dependent on imported materials and equipment.

Figure 2.37.3 Fishing License Revenue

Fishing license revenue rebounded in Kiribati but declined in Nauru and Tuvalu in 2023.

—— Kiribati
—— Nauru
—— Tuvalu

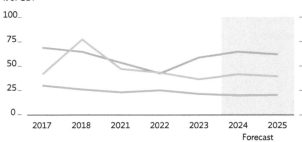

GDP = gross domestic product.

Notes: Years are fiscal years ending on 30 June of that year in Nauru and coinciding with the calendar year in Kiribati and Tuvalu.

Sources: Kiribati, Nauru, and Tuvalu budget documents; International Monetary Fund Article IV reports; Asian Development Bank estimates.

Nauru

Growth slowed to 1.6% in FY2023 (ended 30 June 2023), as activities in the Australia-funded Regional Processing Centre (RPC) were downscaled. With the shift to an "enduring capability" mode in July 2023, Nauru agreed to maintain RPC facilities regardless of the number of transferees, with the possibility of scaling up operations. The number of RPC employees fell from approximately 575 in December 2021 to less than 50 in December 2022.

Revenues related to RPC operations fell. Overall RPC-related revenue fell from 64% of total revenue in FY2022 to 53% in FY2023. Personal and corporate income taxes fell by 7%, while visa fees—largely for transferees—declined by 4%. With grants also falling by

13%, the fiscal surplus shrank from the equivalent of 24.7% of GDP in FY2022 to 19.1% in FY2023, despite a 6% decline in overall expenditure (Figure 2.37.4).

Figure 2.37.4 Nauru Fiscal Components

Fiscal surplus shrinks as Regional Processing Centre revenues decline.

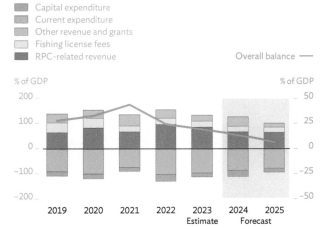

GDP = gross domestic product, RPC = Regional Processing Centre.
Note: Years are fiscal years ending on 30 June of that year.
Source: Asian Development Bank estimates using International Monetary Fund and Nauru budget documents.

Inflation accelerated from 1.5% in FY2022 to 5.2% in FY2023 on higher global commodity prices (Figure 2.37.5). As most goods are imported, international price pressures were felt strongly in the domestic market. Transport prices jumped 21.7%, as oil prices increased due to the Russian invasion of Ukraine. Furnishings and household maintenance rose 5.2% in FY2023 and food prices by 3.7%.

Economic growth is expected to remain stable in FY2024 and FY2025, driven by infrastructure and services. Growth is projected at 1.8% in FY2024 and 2.0% in FY2025. As the economy adjusts to reduced RPC activity, construction of Nauru port will continue to drive economic activity, with the potential to enhance trade, transportation, and fishing. Increased exports, particularly through the Australian government-guaranteed Pacific Flights Program, will also support growth. The program provides air links from Brisbane to the North Pacific, with Nauru Airlines servicing Palau since November 2023. Nauru Airlines received its seventh aircraft in February 2024, with four used for passenger flights and three for freight.

Figure 2.37.5 Inflation

Easing global prices for fuel, food, and other commodities will lower inflation.

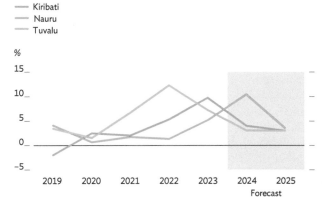

Note: Years are fiscal years ending on 30 June of that year in Nauru and coinciding with the calendar year in Kiribati and Tuvalu.
Sources: Kiribati, Nauru, and Tuvalu budget documents; International Monetary Fund Article IV reports; Asian Development Bank estimates.

The fiscal surplus is expected to decline as fiscal uncertainty clouds the outlook. Total revenue and grants are expected to increase by 4% in FY2024, largely due to a 98% increase in grants from development partners offsetting an expected 9% decline in revenue. This includes a projected 58% drop in revenues related to the RPC. Expenditure is projected to increase by 8% with capital expenditure rising 82%. The fiscal surplus is therefore projected to fall to the equivalent of 13.6% of GDP in FY2024.

Inflation is projected to peak in FY2024 before decelerating in FY2025. Inflation is expected to increase to 10.3% in FY2024. Food inflation is expected to increase by 13% reflecting a higher price of rice, while communications is projected to soar by 85% due to repricing by the sole service provider at the end of 2023. Inflation is expected to decelerate to 3.5% in FY2025 in line with global prices.

A shift in diplomatic relations will impact development assistance. In January 2024, Nauru established diplomatic relations with the People's Republic of China (PRC). It is expected that budget support from Taipei,China intended to service loans from the Taipei,China EXIM Bank will stop, and alternative support from the PRC will materialize. This will likely have fiscal implications.

Box Rebasing Nauru's National Accounts

Using results from the 2012–2013 Household Income and Expenditure Survey (HIES), the national accounts of Nauru have been updated. The base year has been changed to FY2013 from FY2007. This resulted in an increased weight for manufacturing from 4% to 9% (mainly based on phosphate mining), and reduced weights for financial and business services from 17% to 12%, and public services from 24% to 20%. The resulting changes in GDP growth rates are significant. For instance, GDP growth in FY2019 was adjusted from 1% to 9% (box figure). Real GDP in FY2020 based on the new series is higher by 40% compared to the old series, while nominal GDP is higher by 9%. Further, GDP per capita in FY2020 in the new series is 17% higher than in the old series, which may have consequences on Nauru's access to overseas development assistance.

Nauru Gross Domestic Product Growth

—— Old series
—— New series

Sources: International Monetary Fund. World Economic Outlook Database. October 2022 and October 2023; International Monetary Fund. 2023. 2023 Article IV Consultation—Press Release: Staff Report; and Statement by the Executive Director for the Republic of Nauru.

Tuvalu

The economy expanded by 3.9% in 2023. The lifting of COVID-19 restrictions in late-2022 revived economic activity, particularly in construction, as infrastructure projects resume, trade, and hospitality. Capital projects funded by development partners are projected to contribute to 3.5% growth in 2024 and 2.4% in 2025.

Consumer prices rose by 7.2% in 2023. This was led by higher prices for telephone calls, internet services, various food items, and fuel due to the Russian invasion of Ukraine. Inflation is projected to moderate to 3.0% in 2024 and 2025 in line with trends in global commodity prices and trading partner inflation.

The government recorded a fiscal surplus equivalent to 1.1% of GDP in 2023. Revenue increased by 1.5% with development partner grants rising by 52.8% (Figure 2.37.6). Expenditure increased by 8.4% in 2023 due to increases in both operating and capital expenditures. In 2025, the fiscal balance is likely to move into deficit, as the domestic revenue base narrows and current expenditure remains high.

The trade deficit widened by 33% in 2023 as infrastructure projects resumed. Imports increased by 32.9% mostly due to high imports of fuel and capital

Figure 2.37.6 Tuvalu Fiscal Components

Increase in grants helped maintain a fiscal surplus in 2023.

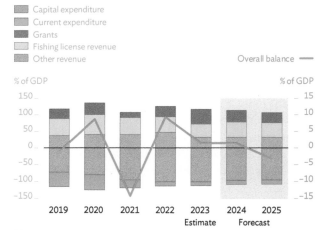

GDP = gross domestic product.
Source: International Monetary Fund. 2023. Tuvalu 2023 Article IV Consultations.

machinery, with the latter in line with the resumption of infrastructure projects. While import prices are projected to subside from their peak in 2022–2023, increased economic activity will likely result in higher imports of goods and services in 2024 and 2025.

Tuvalu continues to face persistent challenges to sustained growth. There remain downside risks, including fiscal revenue volatility and the adverse impact of climate change. Fishing license revenues are intricately tied to fish stocks and susceptible to the effects of climate.

Policy Challenge—Responding to Rising Sea Levels

Sea levels in the Pacific are rising faster than the global average. A 2022 World Meteorological Organization report showed that water levels were rising about 4.2 millimeters (mm) per year in the Pacific, above the global mean rate of 3.4mm. It has become clear that climate change impact is increasingly affecting Central Pacific economies, with more than 75% of their populations living in low coastal areas (Figure 2.37.7). For example, most of Kiribati's 33 islands sit less than two meters above sea level. Tuvalu's highest point is about 4.5 meters above sea level. Although Nauru's average elevation is 36 meters, about 80% of the population live in coastal areas less than 10 meters above sea level.

Figure 2.37.7 Vulnerability to Rising Sea Levels

Central Pacific economies are among the most at risk to sea-level rise with the majority of their people living near coastlines.

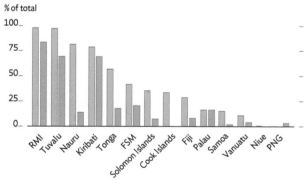

FSM = Federated States of Micronesia, PNG = Papua New Guinea, RMI = Republic of the Marshall Islands.
Note: Data on "land area where elevation is below 5 meters" is not available for the Cook Islands and Niue.
Sources: Pacific Data Hub; World Development Indicators.

Sea-level rise is a threat to livelihoods and food security. Rising sea levels in the Pacific have increased coastal erosion and inundation, contributing to the loss of productive agricultural lands and freshwater. They also affect marine and coastal environments that are essential sources of livelihood.

Urgent action and permanent solutions are needed. Building coral-rock seawalls is a short-term solution, but they are easily destroyed by high tides. Some communities have relocated inland, and efforts have been made to expand mangrove forests to reduce soil erosion and alleviate the impact of storm surges. Some people migrate to other countries. For instance, around 20% of Tuvalu's population have already relocated, many to New Zealand under the Pacific Access Category. In 2014, Kiribati purchased land in Fiji for possible relocation, but is now using it for food production. In 2023, the "Falepili Union" treaty was agreed between Australia and Tuvalu, providing an avenue for "migration with dignity."

As Central Pacific economies act, support from the global community is needed. Tuvalu's Future Now Project has launched three initiatives to help preserve the country's identity: (i) lobbying the global community to address climate change solutions; (ii) securing legal territorial and maritime boundaries; and (iii) creating a digital nation. In 2021, the Nauru government launched the Higher Ground Initiative (HGI)—a long-term plan to safeguard people's livelihoods. Supported by several development partners, the HGI intends to restore land at higher elevations (mostly former phosphate mining areas) and build new homes and key infrastructure for planned domestic migration. The government described HGI as their "single most important climate adaptation action." In Kiribati, initiatives have been discussed with development partners, including the development of integrated flood management plans as part of infrastructure development. Climate-proofing will be an essential feature of infrastructure projects to improve resilience and reduce risks associated with sea-level rise and other climate change impacts. Continuous monitoring and studies to enhance understanding of rising sea levels and their impact will support policy design to effectively address this pressing issue.

NORTH PACIFIC ECONOMIES

Economic performance improved as visitor arrivals to Palau picked up, and the Federated States of Micronesia and the Marshall Islands had their first full year without pandemic-related mobility restrictions. Growth in the North Pacific is expected to continue with inflation moderating in line with international price trends. Stronger public sector management and long-term fiscal planning will be key to harness the benefits from the renewed Compacts of Free Association (COFAs) with the United States (US), as well as to build resilience to future shocks.

Federated States of Micronesia

Growth returned as economic activity resumed in earnest. The economy expanded by 2.6% in fiscal year 2023 (FY2023, ended 30 September 2023 for all three North Pacific economies), reversing the 0.6% contraction in FY2022 (Figure 2.38.1). The removal of pandemic-related restrictions, notably border controls, enabled public infrastructure projects and general economic activity to resume. Construction, transportation, hotels and restaurants, and retail trade drove growth.

Inflation remained elevated. Revived domestic demand led to economic growth. However, the resulting rise in prices, boosted by global food and fuel prices, drove up inflation from 5.0% in FY2022 to 5.3% in FY2023.

The fiscal surplus fell despite higher revenues. The government realized a fiscal surplus equivalent to 3.0% of GDP in FY2023, down from 8.6% in FY2022. This was due to base effects from high corporate income tax revenues paid by foreign firms in FY2022, as well as higher national government wages and a resumption in capital spending that offset increased tax revenues from the economic recovery. External debt was equivalent to 12.5% of GDP at the end of FY2023, down from 14.0% a year earlier.

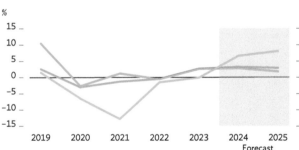

Figure 2.38.1 Gross Domestic Product Growth

The economies of the Federated States of Micronesia and Marshall Islands grew faster due to revived economic activity, while the contraction in Palau slowed as tourism continued to recover.

— Federated States of Micronesia
— Marshall Islands
— Palau

Note: Years are fiscal years ending on 30 September of that year.
Source: Asian Development Bank estimates; International Monetary Fund country reports.

Higher public investment should support continued growth. The economy is projected to grow by 3.1% in FY2024 and 2.8% in FY2025 (Table 2.38.1). The recovery of tourism and increased public investment—supported by the renewed COFA once it enters into force—will likely drive construction, expand output, and stimulate other economic sectors. Even

---

This chapter was written by Kaukab Naqvi and Cara Tinio of the Pacific Department, ADB, Manila.

Table 2.38.1 Selected Economic Indicators, %

Recoveries have commenced, and inflation is decreasing from its recent highs.

	2022	2023	2024	2025
Federated States of Micronesia				
GDP growth	−0.6	2.6	3.1	2.8
Inflation	5.0	5.3	4.1	3.5
Marshall Islands				
GDP growth	−0.7	2.5	2.7	1.7
Inflation	3.2	6.5	5.5	3.7
Palau				
GDP growth	−1.7	−0.2	6.5	8.0
Inflation	13.2	12.4	5.5	1.0

GDP = gross domestic product.
Note: Years are fiscal years ending on 30 September of that year.
Source: Asian Development Bank estimates.

with the new COFA providing much-needed fiscal space to expand investments, a declining workforce caused by out-migration poses a significant downside risk as it could jeopardize implementation of large public projects.

Inflation is expected to ease only gradually as domestic factors push up prices. Inflation is forecast at 4.1% in FY2024. An expected drop in international prices will moderate inflation, but upward price pressure will likely come from increased demand as the economy recovers, as well as water scarcity from El Niño and its subsequent impact on food production. Inflation is projected to decline to 3.5% in FY2025 as El Niño ends and international prices continue to soften.

Fiscal deficits are likely in the near term, though the renewed COFA, once approved, could lead to a surplus. The government is projected to incur fiscal deficits equivalent to 4.6% of GDP and 3.0% in FY2025. Higher expenditures, driven mainly by a larger public payroll and continued spending, will likely outpace increased revenues. However, the fiscal outlook in the medium and long term is expected to improve with the resumption of financial assistance under the renewed compact with the US. External debt is expected to rise to 15.9% of GDP in FY2024 before easing to 15.0% in FY2025.

The renewed compacts brighten North Pacific fiscal and growth prospects. On 9 March 2024, the US President signed into law the third COFA renewal agreements with all three North Pacific economies. Once their governments complete the approval process, the agreements will provide substantial financial support to the North Pacific for 20 years while the US retains access to their airspace and waters. Besides adding significant fiscal resources, the financial support should increase public investment and potentially deliver economic benefits. Enhanced public investment and quality infrastructure, by improving connectivity and the business environment, can attract private sector investment and raise potential growth.

Marshall Islands

The economy grew by 2.5% in FY2023 after contracting by 0.7% in FY2022. Revived fisheries and construction output contributed significantly to the rebound. The number of purse seine transshipment vessels calling at Majuro Port rose by 15.6% (year-on-year) during FY2023, with the related volume of tuna transshipped up by 4.8% (Figure 2.38.2). Public infrastructure projects funded by development partners and preparations for the June 2024 Micronesian Games drove construction output. Spending in the months leading to the November 2023 elections also contributed to the increased economic activity.

Figure 2.38.2 Tuna Transshipment in Majuro Port, Marshall Islands

Transshipments increased in 2023.

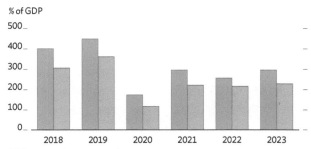

GDP = gross domestic product.
Note: Years are fiscal years ending on 30 September of that year.
Sources: Marshall Islands Marine Resources Authority. 2023. Annual Report FY2022. Majuro; *The Marshall Islands Journal*. 2024. Tuna operations strong in 2023. 18 January.

International price movements and domestic supply constraints pushed up prices. Inflation rose to 6.5% in FY2023 from 3.2% in FY2022 (Figure 2.38.3). The cost of imported fuel remained high especially in the early part of the fiscal year, affecting utility and transportation prices, while food costs mirrored international price trends. The suspension of the Marshall Islands' sole air cargo carrier between February and June 2023 disrupted local supply chains, adding to price pressures arising from revived domestic demand.

Figure 2.38.3 Inflation

Inflation has been elevated due to a combination of international price movements and domestic pressures.

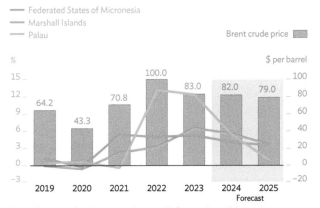

Note: Years are fiscal years ending on 30 September of that year.
Source: Asian Development Bank estimates; International Monetary Fund country reports.

The fiscal position was largely balanced in FY2023. Tax collection increased by 14% due to economic recovery, which helped sustain revenue levels despite small declines in grants from development partners and nontax revenues. However, capital spending grew by 67% due to public infrastructure projects and preparations for the Micronesian Games. As a result, the fiscal surplus declined from 0.7% of GDP in FY2022 to 0.1% of GDP in FY2023. External debt declined from 24.5% of GDP at the end of FY2022 to 21.1% at the end of FY2023, supported by continued access to grant financing.

Growth is projected at 2.7% in FY2024 and 1.7% in FY2025. The expansion in fisheries and construction output will likely continue in the near term, while hosting the Micronesian Games in June 2024 is expected to increase business activity and stimulate

growth in FY2024. However, the economy is projected to grow at a slower pace in FY2025 once the stimulus from the Micronesian Games fades.

Inflation will moderate, even as domestic demand exerts price pressures. Inflation is expected to slow to 5.5% in FY2024. However, as domestic demand will likely increase due to the hosting of the Micronesian Games, prices could remain elevated. In addition, the ongoing El Niño has led to water scarcity, affecting food prices. Nevertheless, as the El Niño subsides and domestic demand normalizes, inflation should decline to 3.7% in FY2025.

Power outages in Majuro pose a serious downside risk. In December 2023, the country's capital began experiencing prolonged power outages due to widespread breakdowns in its aging electricity infrastructure, causing the government to declare a state of emergency on 25 January 2024. If not resolved quickly, the situation will significantly affect connectivity, economic activity, and the availability of goods.

The fiscal position will likely slip into deficit in the near term, but renewed compact grants would brighten this outlook. A surplus equivalent to 0.2% of GDP is forecast for FY2024 as tax collections continue to rise, enabling revenues to just cover increased expenditures. The government has approved a withdrawal of $19.4 million from its Compact Trust Fund for education, health, and infrastructure management. A fiscal deficit equivalent to 1.0% of GDP is expected in FY2025 as expenditures grow faster than revenues, but there is a significant upside risk from the possible resumption of compact grants this year. External debt is projected to increase slightly from $59.7 million (equivalent to 21.2% of GDP) at the end of FY2023 to $62.3 million (19.4%) by the end of FY2025.

Palau

The economy contracted for the fourth consecutive year despite recovery in tourism. GDP contracted by 0.2% in FY2023. This was a substantial improvement on the contraction of 1.7% in FY2022 and largely reflected a 279.1% growth in tourist arrivals as flights from Taipei,China and Macau, China resumed. Despite this increase, the number of visitors remained substantially below pre-pandemic levels (Figure 2.38.4).

Figure 2.38.4 Visitor Arrivals in Palau, by Source

Visitor arrivals, though improving, remain well below pre-pandemic levels.

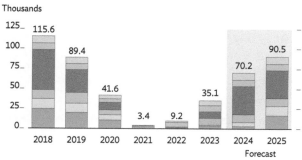

US = United States.

Note: Years are fiscal years ending on 30 September of that year.

Sources: Palau Bureau of Budget and Planning, Palau Bureau of Immigration, and Palau Visitors Authority.

International price movements and domestic factors kept inflation elevated. Prices grew by 12.4% in FY2023, driven by high international prices for food and fuel in late 2022 and the start of the Palau Goods and Services Tax (PGST). The largest price increases were for food (16.3%), housing and utilities (14.6%), and transport (13.1%).

The fiscal deficit narrowed despite the subdued economic recovery. Reforms starting in January 2023, including the PGST, lifted tax revenue to the equivalent of 20.8% of GDP in FY2023, higher than the average of 17.2% in FY2020–FY2022. Expenditure continued to decline as public infrastructure projects wound down. The fiscal deficit thus fell to the equivalent of 0.5% of GDP in FY2023 from 3.0% in FY2022. Public debt equaled 91.8% of GDP at the end of FY2023, slightly down from 92.7% a year earlier.

Growth is expected to resume as tourism and construction recover. The economy is forecast to grow by 6.5% in FY2024 and 8.0% in FY2025.

Tourism arrivals should continue to rise, reaching pre-pandemic levels only after FY2025. In addition, election-related spending should boost output in the latter half of FY2024. Construction is expected to rebound with the implementation of new public infrastructure projects.

Inflation is forecast to moderate to 5.5% in FY2024 and 1.0% in FY2025. Prices will likely fall as international food prices decline and the base effect from the PGST introduction fades.

Fiscal surpluses are expected to return. Recent reforms should maintain strong tax collection while keeping expenditures in check. A surplus equivalent to 3.4% of GDP is projected for FY2024, narrowing to 1.9% in FY2025 as spending rises (Figure 2.38.5). Once the renewed COFA enters into force, financial assistance under the agreement will boost the amount of grants. Higher growth, combined with the return of fiscal surplus, would ensure a sustainable and declining debt-to-GDP ratio. However, increasing subsidies to state-owned enterprises and grants to government entities—including the social security system—could become a significant fiscal drain if critical reforms are not implemented.

Figure 2.38.5 Fiscal Positions

Budget surpluses are narrowing and deficits returning, but the COFA renewals should brighten fiscal prospects.

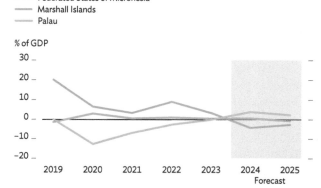

GDP = gross domestic product.

Note: Years are fiscal years ending on 30 September of that year.

Source: Asian Development Bank estimates; International Monetary Fund country reports.

Policy Challenge—Strengthening Public Sector Management and the Long-term Fiscal Framework to Harness the Benefits of Growth

Once the renewed COFAs enter into force, North Pacific governments will have additional fiscal space; thus, it is essential to enhance public sector management and develop a fiscal framework to increase public investment efficiency. The renewed compacts will channel $7.1 billion to the three North Pacific economies over 20 years to support government operations and capital investment. These resources will help upscale productive investments and support more broad-based, inclusive, and sustainable growth. To do this, it is critical to upgrade public investment management, enhance the quality of public investment, and manage risk. Addressing capacity constraints and improving expenditure efficiency would also help raise potential economic growth.

Developing a sustainable spending plan over the medium-term can also reduce economic volatility and improve the quality of public service. This will require a long-term reform agenda and additional capital resources to support complementary investments. The extra funds available through the renewed COFA should provide fiscal headroom to support large investments. However, this requires accompanying reforms to improve domestic resource mobilization (DRM) and ensure ample fiscal buffers to help mitigate external shocks—including those from disasters and public health emergencies. Higher quality infrastructure and an improved business environment supported by reforms can be instrumental in achieving private sector-led growth.

To this end, efforts are ongoing to strengthen tax systems. North Pacific economies began implementing DRM measures to help build fiscal self-sufficiency while the previous compact was in effect. Recent measures range from direct revenue-enhancing policies to administrative improvements:

- Pursuant to its Public Financial Management Reform Roadmap 2023–2026, the Federated States of Micronesia has begun training relevant government staff in audit and tax administration and use of the Automated Systems for Customs Data (ASYCUDA). It is preparing to implement a new financial management information system (FMIS) and it has introduced a set of standard operational budgetary procedures.

- The Marshall Islands is focusing on strengthening tax administration. It has begun implementing a new FMIS to improve monitoring revenue and debt. The government will also adopt ASYCUDA to help strengthen customs revenue collection.

- Palau implemented a package of tax reform measures including the PGST, a business profits tax, and a reduced wage tax for certain income levels. The package updates an inefficient, distortionary tax regime, broadens the revenue base, and promotes equity.

To further enhance DRM, a programmatic approach is needed, complemented by measures to build the capacity to manage and use these increased fiscal resources. North Pacific governments recognize the importance of prioritizing and phasing in DRM measures. This approach not only minimizes the burden on limited government staff but also ensures that measures taken build upon each other. The Federated States of Micronesia has drawn up a roadmap to guide its DRM efforts, while the Marshall Islands uses an approach that focuses on improving administrative efficiency before developing revenue-enhancing measures. Palau, on the other hand, is fine-tuning its tax reforms before modernizing supporting tax and customs systems. In addition, to ensure expanded fiscal resources are managed and utilized efficiently, the North Pacific governments need to address understaffing and skills gaps by improving education and training and creating career pathways to help attract workers into public service and strategic economic sectors.

SOUTH PACIFIC ECONOMIES

Growth resumed in Samoa and Tonga after borders reopened in fiscal year 2023 (FY2023, ended 30 June for all South Pacific economies), and the Cook Islands economy continued to expand as tourism remained strong. Tourism, as well as construction—mainly public infrastructure projects—will sustain growth in the near term. Inflation fell in FY2023 as international food and fuel prices continued to moderate. To maintain growth, targeted policies are needed to address local labor gaps and sustain remittance flows.

Cook Islands

Growth accelerated in FY2023 to 13.3% and, driven by strong tourism recovery, should remain positive in FY2024 and FY2025 (Figure 2.39.1). Tourist arrivals exceeded 70% of FY2019 levels, with 81.3% coming from New Zealand. Infrastructure projects, notably upgrades to the Rarotonga airstrip and health facilities on Rarotonga and the outer islands, also supported growth. Growth for FY2024 is projected to be 9.1% and 5.2% for FY2025, again driven by tourism and infrastructure investments. An acute labor shortage, delays in infrastructure projects, and natural hazards are downside risks to recovery.

Inflation peaked in FY2023 and is projected to fall as fuel and food prices stabilize. The Russian invasion of Ukraine disrupted supply and escalated global fuel prices and transportation costs. This caused inflation to increase from 3.6% in FY2022 to 13.2% in FY2023 (Table 2.39.1). Inflation is expected to fall in FY2024 and FY2025 to 2.3% as imported fuel and food prices stabilize.

The fiscal deficit is projected to narrow over the medium term. The government's fiscal deficit fell to the equivalent of 2.4% of GDP in FY2023 because of underspending on capital projects delayed by the pandemic. Their resumption is projected to bring the

Figure 2.39.1 Gross Domestic Product Growth

Growth in 2023 was driven by a recovery in tourism and resumption of construction projects.

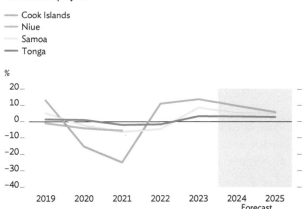

— Cook Islands
— Niue
— Samoa
— Tonga

Note: Years are fiscal years ending on 30 June of that year.

Sources: Cook Islands Ministry of Finance and Economic Management; Niue Statistics Office; Samoa Bureau of Statistics; Tonga Department of Statistics; and Asian Development Bank estimates.

deficit slightly higher, to 2.7% of GDP in FY2024, even if tax revenue is expected to rise. In FY2025, a 1.8% of GDP fiscal surplus is forecast, supported by a 5.6% growth in tax revenue. Public debt equaled 44.0% of GDP at the end of FY2023 but is projected to fall below 35.0% by the end of FY2025.

This chapter was written by Lily-Anne Homasi and Isoa Wainiqolo of the South Pacific Subregional Office, ADB, Suva; Cara Tinio of the Pacific Department (PARD), ADB, Manila; and Ana Isabel Jimenez and Anna Jennifer Umlas, PARD consultants.

Table 2.39.1 Selected Economic Indicators, %

Recoveries have commenced, but inflation was near record highs in 2023.

	2022	2023	2024	2025
Cook Islands				
GDP growth	10.5	13.3	9.1	5.2
Inflation	3.6	13.2	2.3	2.3
Samoa				
GDP growth	−5.3	8.0	4.2	4.0
Inflation	8.8	12.0	4.5	4.3
Tonga				
GDP growth	−2.2	2.8	2.6	2.3
Inflation	8.2	9.7	4.5	4.2

GDP = gross domestic product.

Note: Years are fiscal years ending on 30 June of that year.

Source: Asian Development Bank estimates.

Samoa

Growth resumed in FY2023 after 3 years of contraction. After contracting by 5.3% in FY2022, GDP grew by 8.0% as the reopened border revived tourism and infrastructure projects were implemented. However, GDP was still only 92.1% of the FY2019 level.

Tourism is catching up to pre-pandemic levels, while remittances continued strong growth. After 3 quarters of open borders, visitor arrivals in FY2023 were 76.1% of their FY2018–FY2019 levels (Figure 2.39.2) and tourism receipts reached 78.0% of their pre-pandemic value. These factors helped narrow the current account deficit from the equivalent of 13.5% of GDP in FY2022 to 4.9% in FY2023. Meanwhile, remittances continued their strong growth, increasing by 13.6% during the fiscal year.

Tourism and construction should continue to drive growth in the near term. GDP is projected to grow by 4.2% in FY2024, moderating slightly to 4.0% in FY2025. Besides continued implementation of public infrastructure projects, hosting international events—such as the Commonwealth Heads of Government Meeting (CHOGM) in October 2024—should boost economic activity and visitor arrivals. In addition, cruise ship tourism is increasing with 26 ships scheduled to visit Samoa through the end of 2024. However, accommodation and labor constraints may limit growth.

Figure 2.39.2 Visitor Arrivals, Relative to Pre-pandemic Levels

Visitor arrivals recovered significantly across the South Pacific.

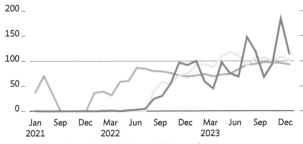

Note: Years are fiscal years ending on 30 June of that year.

Sources: Cook Islands Ministry of Finance and Economic Management; Samoa Bureau of Statistics; Tonga Department of Statistics.

Inflation will moderate from recent highs. Inflation spiked to 12.0% in FY2023, the highest in decades, from 8.8% in FY2022 (Figure 2.39.3). Moderating international commodity prices were slow to reach Samoa. Inflation is projected to decline to 4.5% in FY2024 and 4.3% in FY2025 as both international and local price pressures ease, although international price volatility remains a significant risk.

The fiscal position remains in surplus and external debt is decreasing. The government's fiscal surplus was equivalent to 3.8% of GDP in FY2023 compared with 6.4% in FY2022. Revenues rose by 10.0%, driven

Figure 2.39.3 Inflation

More moderate inflation is expected in 2024 and 2025 as lower international commodity prices pass through to consumers.

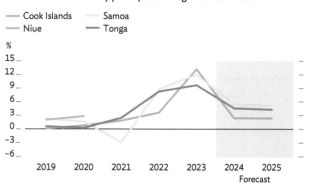

Note: Years are fiscal years ending on 30 June of that year.

Sources: Cook Islands Ministry of Finance and Economic Management; Samoa Bureau of Statistics; Tonga Department of Statistics; Asian Development Bank estimates.

by a 27.4% spike in value-added tax (VAT). Although some capital expenditures deferred in FY2022 were allotted in FY2023 and recurrent spending increased, expenditures rose by a modest 5.5%. Domestic revenues are expected to continue growing in the near term, while expenditures would peak in FY2024 because of preparations for CHOGM, before declining in FY2025. These should result in fiscal surpluses equivalent to 4.7% of GDP in FY2024 and 6.0% in FY2025. Public external debt continues to decline, falling to 42.2% of GDP at the end of FY2023 from a high of 56.5% in FY2021, and will likely fall further to 38.1% in FY2024 and 31.6% by the end of FY2025.

Tonga

The economy rebounded in FY2023. After 2 years of contraction, the economy grew by 2.8%. The August 2022 border reopening revived tourism and public investment projects. Remittances grew by 12.0% from FY2022 levels.

Construction is seen to support post-pandemic growth. The economy is projected to grow by 2.6% in FY2024 and 2.3% in FY2025, driven by continued construction activity as the government pursues major infrastructure projects and investments in climate resilience. Reconstruction and rehabilitation following the January 2022 volcanic eruption and tsunami are also continuing. Visitor arrivals—which in FY2023 were 62.9% of FY2018–FY2019 levels—should continue to grow but remain below pre-pandemic levels during the forecast period because of limited flight connections and tourist accommodations. Shortages of skilled labor may also constrain overall economic activity.

Inflation is expected to moderate, but price pressures remain. Inflation was 9.7% in FY2023, higher than 8.2% in FY2022, pushed up by a 12.2% increase in local prices arising from supply bottlenecks and higher local food costs. Inflation is forecast to moderate to 4.5% in FY2024 and 4.2% in FY2025 as international food and fuel prices decline.

Fiscal surpluses are expected to continue in the near term. The government had a fiscal surplus equivalent to 5.6% of GDP in FY2023, reversing the 0.9% deficit in FY2022 (Figure 2.39.4). Improved compliance, revived business activity, and higher VAT collections supported a 12.0% increase in internal

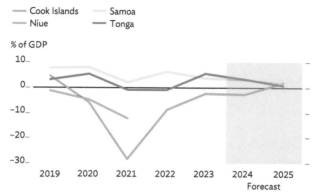

Figure 2.39.4 Fiscal Positions

Fiscal surpluses are expected to continue in Samoa and Tonga, with the Cook Islands rising out of deficit.

GDP = gross domestic product.
Note: Years are fiscal years ending on 30 June of that year.
Sources: Cook Islands Ministry of Finance and Economic Management; Samoa Bureau of Statistics; Tonga Department of Statistics; Asian Development Bank estimates.

revenue collections and increased budget support from development partners helped boost grant inflows. These offset a 1.5% rise in expenditures. Surpluses are projected to be equivalent to 3.3% of GDP in FY2024 and 0.9% of GDP in FY2025. This is despite planned fiscal expansion as revenue collections and grants are expected to remain strong. External debt should decline from the equivalent of 31.7% of GDP in FY2023 to 25.8% in FY2024 and 21.3% in FY2025.

Niue

The economy improved as borders reopened and tourism returned. Tourism picked up further in FY2024 as flights doubled to 2 per week starting November 2023. But visitor arrivals remained well below pre-pandemic levels.

The fiscal deficit in FY2023 widened to 26.4% of FY2021 GDP. Revenue increased by 20.0% in FY2023 consistent with improving economic activity but fell short of the 26.1% growth in expenditure. Capital expenditure increased significantly as the border reopened and trade resumed. Higher fuel prices raised government subsidy expenditure.

Inflation reached 8.6% in FY2023. Higher prices for frozen chicken, fuel, and imported beer were major contributors. Apart from cost increases in communications and education, there were increases averaging 8.2% across all other subcategories. High global inflation affected prices in most categories. Imported inflation increased by 9.6% in 2023, nearly four times faster than domestic price growth.

Policy Challenge—Charting Conducive Labor Market Conditions

South Pacific labor migration has increased.
Attracted by higher wages and seasonal work opportunities in Australia and New Zealand, increasing numbers of South Pacific islanders are seeking overseas employment. This is on top of liberal migration policies accorded to South Pacific citizens, such as those under the Cook Islands' and Niue's free association arrangements with New Zealand.

Although the rise in overseas workers has boosted remittances, it has also depleted local labor supply.
Remittances are a significant income source for many households in Samoa and Tonga, and strong inflows helped them weather the economic downturn during the pandemic (Figure 2.39.5). However, the Tongan government is having difficulties in filling vacancies in its civil service. The acute labor shortage in the Cook Islands is constraining output across many economic sectors.

Remittance dynamics may change dramatically if labor mobility policies expand, and without appropriate measures to shore up labor supply.
Migration flows would likely increase as it becomes more possible for migrant workers to become permanent residents and have their families join them. Entire families living abroad reduces the social issues associated with families living apart for long periods, but it also reduces the propensity to remit funds to the source country. With many residents abroad, governments and local businesses in the Cook Islands and Niue have turned to migrant labor to fill the gap. Niue is also piloting an intra-Pacific labor mobility program in its health sector to address labor shortages. The pilot is anticipated to help design a broader and longer-term labor mobility scheme with other Pacific islands. Remittance flows in these countries have also

Figure 2.39.5 Remittance Inflows

Remittances became more important as an income source during the pandemic, particularly in Samoa and Tonga.

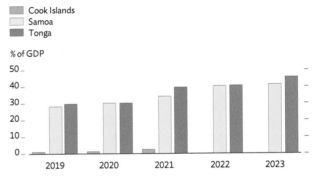

GDP = gross domestic product.
Notes: Years are fiscal years ending on 30 June of that year. Data not available for the Cook Islands, from 2022 onwards, and Niue.
Sources: Cook Islands Ministry of Finance and Economic Management; Central Bank of Samoa; Tonga Department of Statistics; Asian Development Bank estimates.

reversed, with local families supporting relatives living abroad (e.g., for school expenses) and migrant workers sending money to their home countries.

Policymakers need to balance the need to address domestic labor shortages with the economic benefits of overseas worker remittances.
Remittances support economic resilience in the worker's home country. Maintaining remittance inflows requires the continued deployment of new workers overseas to help preserve home-country ties and thus a worker's desire to send money home. To achieve this while ensuring an adequate supply of quality local labor, South Pacific economies should continue to invest in health and education to build a higher quality, skilled workforce. Aligning skills training with national development plans, meeting local business needs, and establishing clear employment pathways could encourage graduates to work in their home country. In addition, improving the business climate would encourage migrants and remittance recipients to develop and invest in local enterprises. It may still be necessary to maintain the flow of new migrant workers into South Pacific economies to help augment limited capacity—particularly in the Cook Islands and Niue where the workforce is small—and this may provide opportunities for knowledge transfer.

3

STATISTICAL APPENDIX

STATISTICAL NOTES AND TABLES

The statistical appendix presents in 18 tables selected economic indicators for the 46 developing member economies of the Asian Development Bank (ADB). The economies are grouped into five subregions: the Caucasus and Central Asia, East Asia, South Asia, Southeast Asia, and the Pacific. Most of the tables contain historical data from 2019 to 2023; some have forecasts for 2024 and 2025.

The data were standardized to the degree possible to allow comparability over time and across economies, but differences in statistical methodology, definitions, coverage, and practices make full comparability impossible. The national accounts section is based on the United Nations System of National Accounts, while the data on the balance of payments use International Monetary Fund (IMF) accounting standards. Historical data were obtained from official sources, statistical publications, and databases, as well as the documents of ADB, the IMF, and the World Bank. For some economies, data for 2023 were estimated from the latest available information. Projections for 2024 and 2025 are generally ADB estimates based on available quarterly or monthly data, though some projections are from governments.

Most economies report by calendar year. The following record their government finance data by fiscal year: Brunei Darussalam; Bhutan; Fiji; Hong Kong, China; Singapore; Tajikistan; and Thailand. Reporting all variables by fiscal year are South Asian economies (except for Bhutan, Maldives, and Sri Lanka), the Cook Islands, the Federated States of Micronesia, Myanmar, the Marshall Islands, Nauru, Niue, Palau, Samoa, and Tonga. In Afghanistan, 2019 and 2020 fiscal years ended 20 December of that year, but since 2021 the fiscal year is from 21 March of the previous year to 20 March of the current year.

Regional and subregional averages or totals are provided for seven tables: A1, A2, A6, A11, A12, A13, and A14. For tables A1, A2, A6, A11, A12, and A14, averages were weighted by purchasing power parity gross domestic product (GDP) in current international dollars. Purchasing power parity GDP data for 2019–2022 were obtained from the IMF World Economic Outlook Database, October 2023 edition. Weights for 2022 were carried over to 2025. For Table A13, regional and subregional totals were computed using a consistent sum, which means that if economy data were missing for a given year, the sum excluded that economy.

Tables A1, A2, A3, A4, and A5: National Accounts. These tables show data on output growth, production, and demand. Changes were made to the national accounts series for some economies to accommodate a change in source, methodology, and/or base year. Constant factor cost measures differ from market price measures in that they exclude taxes on production and include subsidies. Basic price valuation is the factor cost plus some taxes on production, such as property and payroll taxes, and less some subsidies, such as for labor but not for products. The series for Afghanistan, Bangladesh, the Cook Islands, the Federated States of Micronesia, India, the Marshall Islands, Myanmar, Nauru, Nepal, Niue, Pakistan, Palau, Samoa, and Tonga reflect fiscal year data, rather than calendar year data, and those for Timor-Leste reflect GDP excluding the offshore petroleum industry. Some historical data for Turkmenistan are not presented for lack of uniformity. A fluid situation permits no forecasts for Afghanistan in 2024–2025.

Table A1: Growth Rate of GDP, % per year. The table shows annual growth rates of GDP valued at constant market prices, factor costs, or basic prices. GDP at market prices is the aggregate value added by all resident producers at producers' prices including taxes less subsidies on imports plus all nondeductible value-added or similar taxes. Most economies use constant market price valuation. Pakistan uses constant factor costs, and Fiji basic prices.

Table A2: Growth Rate of GDP per Capita, % per year. The table provides the growth rates of real GDP per capita, which is defined as GDP at constant prices divided by population. Also shown are data on gross national income per capita in US dollar terms (Atlas method) for 2022 sourced from the World Bank's World Development Indicators online.

Table A3: Growth Rate of Value Added in Agriculture, % per year. The table shows the growth rates of value added in agriculture at constant prices and agriculture's share of GDP in 2022 at current prices. The agriculture sector comprises plant crops, livestock, poultry, fisheries, and forestry.

Table A4: Growth Rate of Value Added in Industry, % per year. The table provides the growth rates of value added in industry at constant prices and industry's share of GDP in 2022 at current prices. This sector comprises manufacturing, mining and quarrying, and, generally, construction and utilities.

Table A5: Growth Rate of Value Added in Services, % per year. The table gives the growth rates of value added in services at constant prices and services' share of GDP in 2022 at current prices. Services generally include trade, banking, finance, real estate, and similar businesses, as well as public administration. For Malaysia, electricity, gas, water supply, and waste management are included under services.

Table A6: Inflation, % per year. Data on inflation rates are period averages. Inflation rates are based on consumer price indexes. The consumer price indexes of the following economies are for a given city only: Cambodia is for Phnom Penh, the Marshall Islands for Majuro, and Sri Lanka for Colombo. A fluid situation permits no forecasts for Afghanistan in 2024–2025.

Table A7: Change in Money Supply, % per year. This table tracks annual percentage change in broad money supply at the end of the period, M2 for most economies. M2 is defined as the sum of currency in circulation plus demand deposits (M1) plus quasi-money, which consists of time and savings deposits including foreign currency deposits. For the Kyrgyz Republic broad money is M2X. For the Cook Islands; Georgia; Hong Kong, China; India; Kazakhstan; and Solomon Islands, broad money is M3 which adds longer-term time deposits. For Sri Lanka broad money is M2b, or M2 plus bond funds.

Tables A8, A9, and A10: Government Finance. These tables give central government revenue, expenditure, and fiscal balance expressed as percentages of GDP in nominal terms. Where full-year data are not yet available, GDP shares are estimated using available monthly or quarterly data. For Cambodia, Georgia, India, Kazakhstan, the Kyrgyz Republic, Mongolia, the People's Republic of China, and Tajikistan, transactions are those reported by the general government. A fluid situation permits no estimates for Afghanistan in 2022–2023.

Table A8: Central Government Revenue, % of GDP. Central government revenue comprises all nonrepayable receipts, both current and capital, plus grants. These amounts are computed as a percentage of GDP at current prices. For the Republic of Korea, revenue excludes social security contributions. For Azerbaijan and Kazakhstan, revenue includes transfers from the national fund. Grants are excluded for Malaysia and Thailand. Revenue from disinvestment is included for India. Only current revenue is included for Bangladesh.

Table A9: Central Government Expenditure, % of GDP. Central government expenditure comprises all nonrepayable payments to meet both current and capital expenses, plus net lending. These amounts are computed as shares of GDP at current prices. For Thailand, expenditure refers to budgetary expenditure excluding externally financed expenditure and borrowing. For Tajikistan, expenditure includes externally financed public investment programs. One-off expenditures are excluded for Pakistan.

Table A10: Fiscal Balance of the Central Government, % of GDP. Fiscal balance is the difference between central government revenue and expenditure. The difference is computed as a share of GDP at current prices. Data variation may arise from statistical discrepancy when, for example, balancing items for general governments (central plus selected subnational governments), and from differences between coverage used in individual revenue and expenditure calculations and fiscal balance calculations. For Fiji, the fiscal balance excludes loan repayment. For Georgia, the fiscal balance is calculated according to the IMF Government Finance Statistics Manual 2021 format, as is the Cambodia general government fiscal balance using the 2014 manual. For Solomon Islands, fiscal balance does not include balance of payment grants.

For Thailand, the fiscal balance is the cash balance of combined budgetary and nonbudgetary balances. For Turkmenistan and Viet Nam, the fiscal balance does not include off-budget accounts. For Singapore, fiscal balance includes special transfers (top-ups to endowment and trust funds) and contributions from net investment returns. For the Republic of Korea, it excludes funds related to social security.

Tables A11, A12, A13, and A14: Balance of Payments. These tables show the annual flows of selected international economic transactions of economies as recorded in their balance of payments. Some historical data for Turkmenistan are not presented for lack of uniformity.

Tables A11 and A12: Growth Rates of Merchandise Exports and Imports, % per year. These tables show the annual growth rates of exports and imports of goods. Data are in million US dollars, primarily obtained from the balance-of-payments accounts of each economy. Export data are reported free on board. Import data are reported free onboard except for the following economies, which value them based on cost insurance and freight: Afghanistan; Hong Kong, China; Georgia; India; the Lao People's Democratic Republic; Maldives; Myanmar; Singapore; and Thailand.

Table A13: Trade Balance, $ million. The trade balance is the difference between merchandise exports and imports. Figures in this table are based on the export and import amounts used to generate tables A11 and A12.

Table A14: Current Account Balance, % of GDP. The current account balance is the sum of the balance of trade in merchandise, net trade in services and factor income, and net transfers. The values reported are divided by GDP at current prices in US dollars. A fluid situation permits no estimates for Afghanistan in 2021–2023.

Table A15: Exchange Rates to the US Dollar, annual average. Annual average exchange rates are quoted as the local currency per US dollar.

Table A16: Gross International Reserves, $ million. Gross international reserves are defined as the US dollar value at the end of a given period of holdings in foreign exchange, gold, special drawing rights, and IMF reserve position. For Taipei,China, this heading refers to foreign exchange reserves only. In some economies, the rubric is foreign assets plus the reserves of national monetary authorities (the net foreign reserves of, for example, the State Bank of Pakistan) plus national funds for earnings from oil or other natural resources. A fluid situation permits no estimates for Afghanistan in 2022–2023.

Table A17: External Debt Outstanding, $ million. For most economies, external debt outstanding includes short-, medium-, and long-term debt, public and private, as well as IMF credit. For Armenia, Cambodia, and Maldives, only public external debt is reported. Intercompany lending is excluded for Georgia. Data for 2023 are as of the end of September for Singapore and Thailand. A fluid situation permits no estimates for Afghanistan in 2022–2023.

Table A18: Debt Service Ratio, % of exports of goods and services. This table generally presents the total debt service payments of each economy, which comprise principal repayment (excluding short-term debt) and interest payments on outstanding external debt, given as a percentage of exports of goods and services. For Armenia and Cambodia, debt service refers to external public debt only. For the Philippines, income and exports of goods and services are used as the denominator. For Bangladesh, the ratio presents debt service payments on medium- and long-term loans as a percentage of exports of goods, nonfactor services, and overseas worker remittances.

Table A1 Growth Rate of GDP, % per year

	2019	2020	2021	2022	2023	2024	2025
Developing Asia	4.9	−0.6	7.4	4.3	5.0	4.9	4.9
Developing Asia excluding the PRC	4.0	−3.2	6.4	5.5	4.8	5.0	5.3
Caucasus and Central Asia	4.8	−1.9	5.8	5.2	5.3	4.3	5.0
Armenia	7.6	−7.2	5.8	12.6	8.7	5.7	6.0
Azerbaijan	2.3	−4.3	5.6	4.6	1.1	1.2	1.6
Georgia	5.0	−6.8	10.5	10.4	7.0	5.0	5.5
Kazakhstan	4.5	−2.5	4.3	3.2	5.1	3.8	5.3
Kyrgyz Republic	4.6	−7.1	5.5	9.0	6.2	5.0	4.5
Tajikistan	7.5	4.5	9.2	8.0	8.3	6.5	6.5
Turkmenistan	...	...	5.0	6.2	6.3	6.5	6.0
Uzbekistan	6.0	2.0	7.4	5.7	6.0	5.5	5.6
East Asia	5.4	1.9	8.0	2.9	4.7	4.5	4.2
Hong Kong, China	−1.7	−6.5	6.5	−3.7	3.2	2.8	3.0
Mongolia	5.6	−4.6	1.6	5.0	7.0	4.1	6.0
People's Republic of China	6.0	2.2	8.4	3.0	5.2	4.8	4.5
Republic of Korea	2.2	−0.7	4.3	2.6	1.4	2.2	2.3
Taipei,China	3.1	3.4	6.6	2.6	1.3	3.0	2.7
South Asia	4.0	−4.4	8.8	6.6	6.4	6.3	6.6
Afghanistan	3.9	−2.4	−2.1	−20.7	−6.2	...	...
Bangladesh	7.9	3.4	6.9	7.1	5.8	6.1	6.6
Bhutan	5.8	−10.2	4.4	5.2	4.0	4.4	7.0
India	3.9	−5.8	9.7	7.0	7.6	7.0	7.2
Maldives	7.3	−32.9	37.7	13.9	4.4	5.4	6.0
Nepal	6.7	−2.4	4.8	5.6	1.9	3.6	4.8
Pakistan	3.1	−0.9	5.8	6.2	−0.2	1.9	2.8
Sri Lanka	−0.2	−4.6	4.2	−7.3	−2.3	1.9	2.5
Southeast Asia	4.7	−3.2	3.6	5.7	4.1	4.6	4.7
Brunei Darussalam	3.9	1.1	−1.6	−1.6	1.4	3.7	2.8
Cambodia	7.1	−3.1	3.0	5.2	5.0	5.8	6.0
Indonesia	5.0	−2.1	3.7	5.3	5.0	5.0	5.0
Lao People's Democratic Republic	4.7	−0.5	2.3	2.5	3.7	4.0	4.0
Malaysia	4.4	−5.5	3.3	8.7	3.7	4.5	4.6
Myanmar	6.8	3.2	−5.9	2.4	0.8	1.2	2.2
Philippines	6.1	−9.5	5.7	7.6	5.6	6.0	6.2
Singapore	1.3	−3.9	9.7	3.8	1.1	2.4	2.6
Thailand	2.1	−6.1	1.6	2.5	1.9	2.6	3.0
Timor-Leste	2.0	−8.3	2.9	4.0	1.9	3.4	4.1
Viet Nam	7.4	2.9	2.6	8.0	5.0	6.0	6.2
The Pacific	3.2	−6.2	−1.9	7.9	3.5	3.3	4.0
Cook Islands	12.6	−15.7	−25.5	10.5	13.3	9.1	5.2
Federated States of Micronesia	2.4	−3.1	−1.4	−0.6	2.6	3.1	2.8
Fiji	−0.6	−17.0	−4.9	20.0	7.8	3.0	2.7
Kiribati	−2.1	−1.4	8.5	3.9	4.2	5.3	3.5
Marshall Islands	10.4	−2.8	1.1	−0.7	2.5	2.7	1.7
Nauru	9.1	4.1	7.2	2.8	1.6	1.8	2.0
Niue	−1.7	−4.7	−6.2	...	...	...	...
Palau	1.3	−6.7	−13.0	−1.7	−0.2	6.5	8.0
Papua New Guinea	4.5	−3.2	−0.8	5.2	2.0	3.3	4.6
Samoa	4.5	−3.1	−7.1	−5.3	8.0	4.2	4.0
Solomon Islands	1.7	−3.4	−0.6	−4.2	2.5	2.2	2.2
Tonga	0.7	0.4	−2.7	−2.2	2.8	2.6	2.3
Tuvalu	13.8	−4.3	1.8	0.7	3.9	3.5	2.4
Vanuatu	3.2	−5.0	−1.6	2.0	1.0	3.1	3.6

... = not available, GDP = gross domestic product, PRC = People's Republic of China.

Table A2 Growth Rate of Per Capita GDP, % per year

	2019	2020	2021	2022	2023	2024	2025	Per capita GNI, $, 2022
Developing Asia	**4.2**	**−1.1**	**7.0**	**3.8**	**4.0**	**4.2**	**4.1**	
Caucasus and Central Asia	**3.3**	**−3.1**	**4.4**	**3.2**	**3.9**	**2.8**	**3.5**	
Armenia	7.9	−7.0	5.7	12.7	8.2	5.2	6.0	5,960
Azerbaijan	1.4	−5.1	4.7	4.0	1.7	0.4	0.8	5,660
Georgia	5.2	−6.6	10.1	11.6	5.6	5.0	5.5	5,600
Kazakhstan	3.2	−3.9	3.0	0.0	3.4	2.0	3.4	9,620
Kyrgyz Republic	−3.7	−9.0	3.5	7.1	...	...	...	1,440
Tajikistan	3.1	4.5	7.1	5.9	7.3	4.5	4.9	1,210
Turkmenistan	...	...	3.5	4.8	4.9	5.2	4.8	...
Uzbekistan	4.2	0.2	5.6	3.9	4.2	3.5	3.8	2,190
East Asia	**5.0**	**1.7**	**8.0**	**2.9**	**4.7**	**4.5**	**4.2**	
Hong Kong, China	−2.4	−6.2	7.4	−2.8	0.6	2.9	2.6	54,370
Mongolia	3.7	−6.2	0.0	4.4	6.1	2.5	4.7	4,260
People's Republic of China	5.6	2.0	8.4	3.0	5.3	4.9	4.5	12,850
Republic of Korea	1.9	−0.8	4.4	2.8	1.3	2.1	2.4	36,190
Taipei,China	3.0	3.6	7.5	3.1	0.6	3.0	2.9	...
South Asia	**2.9**	**−5.6**	**7.7**	**5.4**	**−0.4**	**2.6**	**3.0**	
Afghanistan	1.5	−4.8	...	−30.0	−0.5	...	...	...
Bangladesh	6.6	2.3	5.8	5.9	5.2	5.7	5.5	2,820
Bhutan	4.7	−11.1	3.4	4.2	3.0	3.4	6.0	...
India	2.8	−6.8	8.6	5.9	−	−	−	2,390
Maldives	3.0	−37.3	33.4	9.6	0.1	1.1	1.7	10,880
Nepal	5.7	−3.3	3.9	4.6	0.9	2.6	3.8	1,340
Pakistan	1.1	−3.8	3.7	4.1	−5.2	−0.1	0.8	1,560
Sri Lanka	−0.8	−5.1	3.1	−7.5	−1.7	2.2	2.4	3,610
Southeast Asia	**3.7**	**−3.9**	**3.2**	**4.6**	**2.8**	**3.8**	**3.9**	
Brunei Darussalam	0.6	3.2	−1.3	−2.7	3.0	3.7	2.8	31,410
Cambodia	5.6	−4.4	1.7	2.8	3.4	4.2	4.3	1,690
Indonesia	3.9	−3.3	2.9	4.3	4.1	4.1	4.1	4,580
Lao People's Democratic Republic	3.1	−1.9	0.7	0.9	2.3	2.8	2.6	2,310
Malaysia	4.0	−5.3	2.9	8.2	1.6	3.8	3.8	11,830
Myanmar	6.1	2.4	−6.6	1.8	−0.1	0.5	1.5	1,270
Philippines	4.6	−10.8	4.3	6.2	4.3	4.8	5.1	3,950
Singapore	0.2	−3.6	14.4	0.5	−3.7	2.0	2.2	67,200
Thailand	1.8	−6.3	1.3	2.1	1.5	2.3	2.7	7,230
Timor–Leste	0.0	−10.1	2.8	2.3	0.2	1.6	2.3	1,980
Viet Nam	5.4	1.7	1.6	7.0	4.3	5.6	5.1	4,010
The Pacific	**0.9**	**−8.3**	**−14.7**	**5.6**	**1.2**	**1.0**	**1.7**	
Cook Islands	13.2	−15.3	−25.1	11.5	13.9	9.7	5.7	...
Federated States of Micronesia	2.3	−3.3	−1.6	...	...	...	...	4,140
Fiji	−1.1	−17.5	−5.4	19.3	7.2	2.5	2.1	5,390
Kiribati	−3.3	−4.6	6.7	2.2	2.5	3.6	2.3	2,810
Marshall Islands	13.2	−2.5	6.1	1.6	4.8	5.0	4.0	7,270
Nauru	8.1	2.5	5.9	2.0	0.8	1.0	1.3	17,800
Niue	−1.7	−4.7	−6.2	...	...	...	...	...
Palau	1.6	−6.4	−10.3	−3.7	−1.3	5.3	7.9	...
Papua New Guinea	1.3	−6.1	−19.3	2.0	−1.1	0.2	1.4	2,700
Samoa	3.6	−3.9	−7.8	−6.1	7.1	3.4	3.2	3,660
Solomon Islands	−1.1	−3.9	−2.5	−6.0	0.6	0.2	0.3	2,210
Tonga	0.8	0.5	−2.6	−2.1	2.9	2.7	2.4	...
Tuvalu	14.2	−14.0	0.9	−0.2	3.0	2.6	1.5	7,160
Vanuatu	1.0	−6.2	−3.7	−0.2	−1.2	1.0	3.6	3,650

... = not available, GDP = gross domestic product, GNI = gross national income.

Table A3 Growth Rate of Value Added in Agriculture, % per year

	2019	2020	2021	2022	2023	Sector share, 2022, %
Caucasus and Central Asia						
Armenia	−5.8	−3.7	−0.8	−0.7	0.2	11.4
Azerbaijan	7.3	1.9	3.3	3.4	3.0	5.1
Georgia	0.8	7.6	1.4	0.5	0.8	6.9
Kazakhstan	−0.1	5.9	−2.2	9.1	−7.7	5.6
Kyrgyz Republic	2.5	0.9	−4.5	7.3	0.6	12.8
Tajikistan	7.1	8.8	6.6	8.0	11.6	27.1
Turkmenistan	...	...	...	...	...	...
Uzbekistan	3.1	2.9	4.0	3.6	4.0	25.0
East Asia						
Hong Kong, China	−0.8	3.8	−2.5	−15.8	−2.7	0.1
Mongolia	5.2	5.8	−5.5	12.0	−8.9	14.6
People's Republic of China	3.1	3.1	7.1	4.2	4.2	7.7
Republic of Korea	3.9	−5.8	5.2	−1.0	−2.4	1.8
Taipei,China	−0.9	−1.5	−4.5	−5.0	0.9	1.4
South Asia						
Afghanistan	17.5	5.9	4.4	−9.8	−6.6	27.5
Bangladesh	3.3	3.4	3.2	3.1	3.4	11.7
Bhutan	1.7	4.0	1.4	−1.1	1.3	15.0
India	6.2	4.0	4.6	4.7	0.7	18.2
Maldives	−8.1	6.6	−0.7	3.1	3.1	5.6
Nepal	5.2	2.4	2.8	2.2	2.7	23.9
Pakistan	0.9	3.9	3.5	4.3	2.3	23.5
Sri Lanka	0.5	−0.9	1.0	−4.2	2.6	8.9
Southeast Asia						
Brunei Darussalam	−1.4	14.4	16.9	−3.3	−9.0	1.1
Cambodia	−0.5	0.6	1.2	0.3	1.1	23.7
Indonesia	3.6	1.8	1.9	2.3	1.3	13.0
Lao People's Democratic Republic	1.0	1.9	2.3	1.3	1.4	16.6
Malaysia	1.9	−2.4	−0.1	0.1	0.7	9.0
Myanmar	1.6	1.6	1.0	−2.5	−1.8	22.6
Philippines	1.2	−0.2	−0.3	0.5	1.2	9.5
Singapore	6.9	−4.2	11.3	−7.6	2.6	0.0
Thailand	−1.0	−3.2	2.2	2.5	1.9	8.7
Timor−Leste	2.5	0.6	5.5	5.4	3.0	19.1
Viet Nam	2.7	3.0	3.3	3.9	3.8	13.1
The Pacific						
Cook Islands	−1.8	−8.7	−7.3	3.9	−3.9	4.0
Federated States of Micronesia	6.6	−8.2	−3.6	...	...	...
Fiji	4.5	3.1	0.8	4.1	0.7	11.3
Kiribati	2.5	−1.8	5.0	...	...	...
Marshall Islands	54.5	−6.3	11.5	−15.4	...	20.7
Nauru	...	...	...	...	...	...
Niue	...	...	...	...	...	...
Palau	−5.6	−10.1	−3.8	0.4	...	3.6
Papua New Guinea	2.3	1.9	1.1	3.1	2.0	17.6
Samoa	−6.1	−1.4	0.9	−9.4	0.8	10.9
Solomon Islands	0.1	−3.8	−1.2	−10.0	3.3	33.1
Tonga	3.6	3.2	0.1	...	...	...
Tuvalu	13.9	...	...	...	...	...
Vanuatu	6.2	−2.7	2.7	1.2	−4.4	24.7

... = not available.

Table A4 Growth Rate of Value Added in Industry, % per year

	2019	2020	2021	2022	2023	Sector share, 2022, %
Caucasus and Central Asia						
Armenia	10.5	−2.5	2.6	9.2	5.5	27.7
Azerbaijan	1.0	−5.7	2.8	0.3	−0.1	60.4
Georgia	2.3	−6.6	3.2	15.2	3.4	24.6
Kazakhstan	5.5	1.5	4.4	2.7	5.6	37.7
Kyrgyz Republic	8.0	−9.5	2.5	11.1	4.9	28.1
Tajikistan	13.6	9.7	22.0	15.4	...	27.3
Turkmenistan	...	...	...	...	...	...
Uzbekistan	5.0	0.9	8.8	5.2	6.0	33.5
East Asia						
Hong Kong, China	−6.6	−11.4	1.2	5.1	4.3	6.4
Mongolia	3.1	−4.4	−3.7	−4.6	14.5	39.5
People's Republic of China	4.9	2.5	8.7	2.6	4.7	37.8
Republic of Korea	0.8	−0.7	5.5	1.4	0.8	34.7
Taipei,China	1.4	7.1	13.8	1.8	−6.1	37.6
South Asia						
Afghanistan	4.8	−4.6	−5.6	−12.8	−5.7	30.7
Bangladesh	11.6	3.6	10.3	9.9	8.4	35.3
Bhutan	−1.3	−14.4	3.9	5.6	−4.4	32.6
India	−1.4	−0.4	12.2	2.1	9.0	27.6
Maldives	2.6	−34.1	−4.6	25.2	8.6	11.6
Nepal	7.4	−4.0	6.9	10.8	0.6	14.3
Pakistan	0.2	−5.7	8.2	6.9	−3.8	21.5
Sri Lanka	−4.1	−5.3	5.7	−16.0	−9.2	31.3
Southeast Asia						
Brunei Darussalam	4.2	2.9	−4.2	−4.9	−1.4	66.9
Cambodia	11.3	−1.4	9.4	8.9	−0.2	40.3
Indonesia	3.8	−2.8	3.4	4.1	5.0	43.3
Lao People's Democratic Republic	3.7	1.4	4.6	4.3	2.4	36.8
Malaysia	2.3	−6.4	6.0	6.7	1.3	37.1
Myanmar	8.4	3.8	−9.6	5.0	2.2	35.3
Philippines	5.5	−13.1	8.5	6.5	3.6	29.2
Singapore	−1.0	−0.2	15.5	2.9	−2.9	28.0
Thailand	0.0	−5.2	3.7	−0.1	−2.3	35.2
Timor−Leste	4.8	−22.9	−11.2	−5.5	3.2	11.3
Viet Nam	8.2	4.4	3.6	7.5	3.7	41.7
The Pacific						
Cook Islands	29.2	−30.0	20.5	−37.8	−98.0	9.8
Federated States of Micronesia	19.4	−15.6	−0.9	...	...	...
Fiji	−0.9	−10.2	−6.7	5.7	1.9	19.5
Kiribati	−9.4	−2.8	21.1	...	...	...
Marshall Islands	14.6	−5.3	−6.3	10.2	...	10.4
Nauru	...	...	...	...	...	...
Niue	...	...	...	...	...	...
Palau	28.4	−4.4	0.7	−19.6	...	12.9
Papua New Guinea	7.5	−7.5	−7.9	6.6	−0.7	41.9
Samoa	10.3	−9.6	−9.6	−0.2	−1.9	12.4
Solomon Islands	3.5	−3.8	2.5	−6.8	5.2	18.8
Tonga	4.6	−3.5	1.2	...	...	...
Tuvalu	−5.6	...	...	...	...	...
Vanuatu	−8.3	4.0	−1.3	−3.7	11.5	8.8

... = not available.

Table A5 Growth Rate of Value Added in Services, % per year

	2019	2020	2021	2022	2023	Sector share, 2022, %
Caucasus and Central Asia						
Armenia	9.8	–8.7	7.6	17.8	12.1	60.9
Azerbaijan	3.8	–3.9	7.8	9.7	1.8	34.4
Georgia	6.4	–8.1	15.0	9.7	8.8	68.6
Kazakhstan	4.4	–5.3	4.4	2.5	5.7	56.7
Kyrgyz Republic	3.2	–7.9	6.9	6.8	6.2	59.2
Tajikistan	2.9	–2.6	7.9	16.0	13.6	45.6
Turkmenistan	...	...	...	...	...	...
Uzbekistan	6.7	1.1	9.5	8.5	6.8	41.6
East Asia						
Hong Kong, China	–0.6	–6.7	5.9	–3.3	3.7	93.5
Mongolia	6.4	–6.5	4.9	6.9	8.2	45.9
People's Republic of China	7.2	1.9	8.5	3.0	5.8	54.5
Republic of Korea	3.4	–0.8	3.8	4.2	2.1	63.5
Taipei,China	3.6	1.2	2.7	2.3	4.2	61.0
South Asia						
Afghanistan	–1.4	–5.9	–4.6	–30.1	–6.5	41.8
Bangladesh	6.9	3.9	5.7	6.3	5.4	53.1
Bhutan	15.1	–9.5	4.4	21.8	9.5	52.4
India	6.4	–8.3	9.1	10.0	7.5	54.2
Maldives	9.5	–31.7	43.4	14.7	5.0	82.8
Nepal	6.8	–4.5	4.7	5.3	2.3	61.8
Pakistan	5.0	–1.2	5.9	6.7	0.1	55.0
Sri Lanka	2.9	–1.9	3.4	–2.6	–0.2	59.8
Southeast Asia						
Brunei Darussalam	3.4	–2.1	2.5	3.8	5.9	32.0
Cambodia	6.2	–6.3	–2.7	3.4	12.0	36.0
Indonesia	6.4	–1.5	3.5	6.5	6.1	43.7
Lao People's Democratic Republic	7.2	–5.5	5.5	1.0	5.6	46.6
Malaysia	6.2	–5.4	2.3	10.9	5.3	53.9
Myanmar	8.3	3.4	–6.3	3.0	1.0	42.1
Philippines	7.2	–9.1	5.4	9.2	7.2	61.2
Singapore	2.1	–4.1	7.6	4.8	2.3	72.2
Thailand	3.9	–6.9	0.3	4.1	4.5	56.1
Timor–Leste	0.3	–7.3	6.4	4.8	1.4	69.5
Viet Nam	8.1	2.0	1.6	10.3	6.8	45.2
The Pacific						
Cook Islands	12.7	–14.8	–29.1	16.0	20.9	86.3
Federated States of Micronesia	0.4	–0.6	–1.8	...	...	...
Fiji	0.0	–16.9	–3.1	21.1	5.4	69.2
Kiribati	3.1	–0.5	1.4	...	...	...
Marshall Islands	–0.1	–0.4	–1.2	2.0	...	68.9
Nauru	...	...	...	...	...	...
Niue	...	...	...	...	...	...
Palau	–1.8	–6.9	–15.6	0.8	...	83.6
Papua New Guinea	2.5	–0.2	4.5	6.3	3.2	40.5
Samoa	4.5	–1.2	–6.8	–5.5	6.6	76.7
Solomon Islands	2.0	–3.0	–1.0	–0.3	1.6	48.1
Tonga	0.8	–0.3	–7.6	...	...	...
Tuvalu	77.0	...	...	...	...	...
Vanuatu	6.1	–6.7	0.4	2.0	1.1	66.5

... = not available.

Table A6 Inflation, % per year

	2019	2020	2021	2022	2023	2024	2025
Developing Asia	**3.2**	**3.2**	**2.6**	**4.4**	**3.3**	**3.2**	**3.0**
Developing Asia excluding the PRC	**3.5**	**3.9**	**4.2**	**6.8**	**6.3**	**5.1**	**4.4**
Caucasus and Central Asia	**6.8**	**7.4**	**9.6**	**12.9**	**10.5**	**7.9**	**7.0**
Armenia	1.4	1.2	7.2	8.6	2.0	3.0	3.5
Azerbaijan	2.6	2.8	6.7	13.9	8.8	5.5	6.5
Georgia	4.9	5.2	9.6	11.9	2.5	3.5	4.0
Kazakhstan	5.3	6.8	8.0	15.0	14.5	8.7	6.3
Kyrgyz Republic	1.1	6.3	11.9	13.9	10.8	7.0	6.5
Tajikistan	8.0	9.4	8.0	4.2	3.8	5.5	6.5
Turkmenistan	5.1	6.1	19.3	11.2	5.9	8.0	8.0
Uzbekistan	14.6	12.9	10.7	11.4	10.0	10.0	9.5
East Asia	**2.6**	**2.2**	**1.1**	**2.3**	**0.6**	**1.3**	**1.6**
Hong Kong, China	2.9	0.3	1.6	1.9	2.1	2.3	2.3
Mongolia	7.3	3.7	7.3	15.2	10.4	7.0	6.8
People's Republic of China	2.9	2.5	0.9	2.0	0.2	1.1	1.5
Republic of Korea	0.4	0.5	2.5	5.1	3.6	2.5	2.0
Taipei,China	0.6	−0.2	2.0	2.9	2.5	2.3	2.0
South Asia	**5.0**	**6.5**	**5.8**	**8.0**	**8.4**	**7.0**	**5.8**
Afghanistan	2.3	5.6	5.8	7.8	10.8	...	...
Bangladesh	5.5	5.7	5.6	6.2	9.0	8.4	7.0
Bhutan	2.7	5.6	7.3	5.6	4.2	4.5	4.2
India	4.8	6.2	5.5	6.7	5.5	4.6	4.5
Maldives	0.2	−1.4	0.5	2.3	2.9	3.2	2.5
Nepal	4.6	6.2	3.6	6.3	7.7	6.5	6.0
Pakistan	6.8	10.7	8.9	12.2	29.2	25.0	15.0
Sri Lanka	4.3	4.6	6.0	46.4	17.4	7.5	5.5
Southeast Asia	**2.2**	**1.5**	**2.0**	**5.3**	**4.1**	**3.2**	**3.0**
Brunei Darussalam	−0.4	1.9	1.7	3.7	0.4	1.1	1.0
Cambodia	1.9	2.9	2.9	5.3	2.1	2.0	2.0
Indonesia	2.8	2.0	1.6	4.1	3.7	2.8	2.8
Lao People's Democratic Republic	3.3	5.1	3.8	23.0	31.2	20.0	7.0
Malaysia	0.7	−1.1	2.5	3.4	2.5	2.6	2.6
Myanmar	8.6	5.7	3.7	27.2	22.0	15.5	10.2
Philippines	2.4	2.4	3.9	5.8	6.0	3.8	3.4
Singapore	0.6	−0.2	2.3	6.1	4.8	3.0	2.2
Thailand	0.7	−0.8	1.2	6.1	1.2	1.0	1.5
Timor−Leste	0.9	0.5	3.8	7.0	8.4	3.5	2.9
Viet Nam	2.8	3.2	1.8	3.2	3.3	4.0	4.0
The Pacific	**2.9**	**2.9**	**3.2**	**5.2**	**3.0**	**4.3**	**4.1**
Cook Islands	0.0	0.7	1.8	3.6	13.2	2.3	2.3
Federated States of Micronesia	1.3	−0.3	5.4	5.0	5.3	4.1	3.5
Fiji	1.8	−2.6	0.2	4.3	2.4	3.7	2.6
Kiribati	−1.9	2.5	2.1	5.3	9.7	4.0	3.0
Marshall Islands	−0.1	−0.7	2.2	3.2	6.5	5.5	3.7
Nauru	4.1	0.7	1.7	1.5	5.2	10.3	3.5
Niue	2.4	2.3	3.4	3.1	8.6	...	...
Palau	0.4	0.7	−0.5	13.2	12.4	5.5	1.0
Papua New Guinea	3.6	4.9	4.5	5.3	2.3	4.5	4.8
Samoa	2.2	1.5	−3.0	8.8	12.0	4.5	4.3
Solomon Islands	1.8	2.7	0.8	5.4	4.6	3.2	2.7
Tonga	0.5	0.2	2.3	8.2	9.7	4.5	4.2
Tuvalu	3.5	1.6	6.7	12.2	7.2	3.0	3.0
Vanuatu	2.8	5.3	2.3	6.7	13.5	4.8	2.9

... = not available, PRC = People's Republic of China.

Table A7 Change in Money Supply, % per year

	2019	2020	2021	2022	2023
Caucasus and Central Asia					
Armenia	11.2	9.0	13.1	16.1	17.4
Azerbaijan	20.0	1.1	18.7	23.6	5.3
Georgia	16.7	23.3	11.3	11.6	14.5
Kazakhstan	2.4	16.9	20.8	13.9	11.7
Kyrgyz Republic	12.8	23.9	19.1	30.6	15.0
Tajikistan	16.9	18.0	8.6	40.4	−0.8
Turkmenistan	12.9	11.8	18.1	19.9	...
Uzbekistan	16.2	17.7	29.7	30.2	12.2
East Asia					
Hong Kong, China	2.7	5.8	4.3	1.6	4.0
Mongolia	7.0	16.3	15.0	6.5	26.8
People's Republic of China	8.7	10.1	9.0	11.8	9.7
Republic of Korea	7.9	9.8	12.9	4.0	3.9
Taipei,China	4.5	9.4	7.3	6.7	5.6
South Asia					
Afghanistan	5.7	12.1	10.2	7.6	3.8
Bangladesh	9.9	12.6	13.6	9.4	10.5
Bhutan	13.1	27.7	13.1	9.2	3.2
India	8.7	12.3	8.7	9.0	12.8
Maldives	9.5	14.2	26.2	6.0	6.9
Nepal	15.8	18.1	21.8	7.6	11.2
Pakistan	11.3	17.5	16.2	13.6	14.2
Sri Lanka	7.0	23.4	13.2	15.4	7.3
Southeast Asia					
Brunei Darussalam	4.3	−0.4	2.7	1.3	...
Cambodia	18.2	15.3	16.4	8.3	12.5
Indonesia	6.5	12.5	14.0	8.4	3.5
Lao People's Democratic Republic	18.9	16.3	24.0	36.9	33.3
Malaysia	3.5	4.0	6.4	4.3	6.0
Myanmar	15.4	15.0	11.4	12.7	10.5
Philippines	11.5	9.6	7.9	6.9	6.2
Singapore	5.5	12.7	7.2	8.6	4.7
Thailand	3.6	10.2	4.8	3.9	2.0
Timor–Leste	−7.1	10.2	28.7	8.6	2.7
Viet Nam	14.8	14.5	10.7	6.2	10.3
The Pacific					
Cook Islands	7.3	14.8	−6.6	14.6	...
Federated States of Micronesia	...	...	...	...	...
Fiji	2.5	0.9	11.9	3.8	11.9
Kiribati	...	...	...	...	...
Marshall Islands	...	...	...	...	...
Nauru	...	...	...	...	...
Niue	...	...	...	...	...
Palau	...	...	...	...	...
Papua New Guinea	4.7	7.0	11.7	14.8	...
Samoa	9.9	−0.9	8.1	2.2	16.3
Solomon Islands	−3.1	6.6	1.9	5.3	5.9
Tonga	−33.0	6.2	10.1	70.8	...
Tuvalu	...	...	...	...	...
Vanuatu	7.0	−0.7	8.9	7.3	4.1

... = not available.

Table A8 Central Government Revenues, % of GDP

	2019	2020	2021	2022	2023
Caucasus and Central Asia					
Armenia	23.9	25.2	24.1	24.3	24.8
Azerbaijan	29.5	34.1	28.3	22.9	28.9
Georgia	26.2	25.2	25.4	26.8	27.7
Kazakhstan	18.3	20.6	18.9	19.5	20.9
Kyrgyz Republic	25.6	23.8	26.8	29.5	31.9
Tajikistan	26.8	24.8	27.6	27.8	31.0
Turkmenistan	11.2	11.4	10.7	12.0	10.8
Uzbekistan	27.7	25.6	26.0	31.0	33.0
East Asia					
Hong Kong, China	20.8	21.1	24.2	22.1	18.5
Mongolia	31.5	27.8	32.7	34.5	35.3
People's Republic of China	19.3	18.0	17.6	16.9	17.2
Republic of Korea	19.4	19.2	22.1	23.4	...
Taipei,China	11.0	10.9	11.0	12.0	12.3
South Asia					
Afghanistan	26.9	25.7	25.7	...	...
Bangladesh	8.5	8.4	9.3	8.4	8.2
Bhutan	22.8	29.1	30.9	25.1	25.7
India	8.7	8.5	9.4	9.1	9.2
Maldives	26.4	26.7	26.4	30.6	30.5
Nepal	22.4	22.2	23.3	20.5	16.9
Pakistan	11.2	13.2	12.4	12.1	11.5
Sri Lanka	11.9	8.8	8.3	8.4	10.2
Southeast Asia					
Brunei Darussalam	26.5	11.2	28.8	33.3	14.0
Cambodia	26.8	23.9	21.6	23.9	21.3
Indonesia	12.4	10.7	11.8	13.5	13.5
Lao People's Democratic Republic	15.8	13.4	14.7	14.8	14.6
Malaysia	17.5	15.9	15.1	16.4	16.2
Myanmar	18.2	20.5	14.3	12.5	11.7
Philippines	16.1	15.9	15.5	16.1	15.7
Singapore	17.8	17.8	17.6	16.3	18.9
Thailand	17.0	17.1	16.5	16.5	16.8
Timor-Leste	52.2	57.5	58.8	57.4	48.8
Viet Nam	20.2	18.7	18.8	19.0	15.9
The Pacific					
Cook Islands	40.2	41.7	52.5	50.9	38.8
Federated States of Micronesia	85.0	74.8	70.7	66.1	65.0
Fiji	27.1	25.4	23.4	21.3	22.1
Kiribati	122.7	131.9	115.4	112.7	128.5
Marshall Islands	64.0	70.6	70.3	67.0	61.6
Nauru	140.8	156.0	137.4	158.3	135.3
Niue	80.6	62.6	90.0	92.5	111.0
Palau	42.4	45.3	57.5	56.9	44.2
Papua New Guinea	16.3	14.7	15.1	16.7	18.3
Samoa	36.9	43.5	44.7	45.9	45.5
Solomon Islands	27.4	30.1	26.1	27.2	24.7
Tonga	41.7	44.2	48.3	48.7	48.5
Tuvalu	111.9	129.3	102.6	119.7	110.5
Vanuatu	41.8	38.1	40.4	33.6	36.4

... = not available, GDP = gross domestic product.

Table A9 Central Government Expenditures, % of GDP

	2019	2020	2021	2022	2023
Caucasus and Central Asia					
Armenia	24.9	30.6	28.7	26.4	26.8
Azerbaijan	29.8	36.5	29.4	23.9	29.6
Georgia	28.3	34.5	31.5	29.4	30.1
Kazakhstan	20.2	24.5	21.9	21.6	23.2
Kyrgyz Republic	25.7	26.9	27.0	30.5	30.9
Tajikistan	28.9	29.1	28.3	29.2	31.6
Turkmenistan	11.6	11.6	10.3	9.6	9.9
Uzbekistan	31.4	30.0	32.2	34.9	38.5
East Asia					
Hong Kong, China	21.4	30.5	24.2	28.9	24.3
Mongolia	30.2	37.3	35.8	33.8	32.6
People's Republic of China	24.2	24.2	21.4	21.6	21.8
Republic of Korea	23.7	26.7	27.3	30.2	...
Taipei,China	10.9	12.3	11.7	11.7	13.3
South Asia					
Afghanistan	28.0	27.9	27.9	...	...
Bangladesh	13.3	13.3	13.0	13.0	12.6
Bhutan	23.9	30.9	36.6	32.1	32.4
India	13.4	17.7	16.1	15.5	15.9
Maldives	32.9	50.4	40.7	42.2	44.3
Nepal	27.3	27.6	27.2	23.7	23.0
Pakistan	19.1	20.3	18.5	20.0	19.2
Sri Lanka	19.4	21.0	20.0	18.6	19.0
Southeast Asia					
Brunei Darussalam	32.1	28.8	34.9	31.8	25.7
Cambodia	23.8	27.3	28.6	23.8	24.3
Indonesia	14.6	16.8	16.4	15.8	15.4
Lao People's Democratic Republic	19.1	18.9	16.0	15.0	16.6
Malaysia	20.9	19.4	19.0	20.3	17.1
Myanmar	22.3	26.8	22.4	19.0	17.7
Philippines	19.5	23.5	24.1	23.4	22.0
Singapore	17.6	28.5	17.4	16.9	19.9
Thailand	20.9	28.8	33.2	27.2	26.5
Timor–Leste	83.0	83.3	104.1	115.5	89.8
Viet Nam	19.8	22.2	20.1	22.6	19.9
The Pacific					
Cook Islands	35.5	47.6	81.0	59.7	39.5
Federated States of Micronesia	65.3	68.7	66.4	57.5	62.0
Fiji	30.6	31.3	34.8	33.2	28.2
Kiribati	106.5	127.1	126.4	115.4	130.8
Marshall Islands	65.8	68.1	70.1	66.3	61.5
Nauru	112.6	123.3	93.0	133.5	116.2
Niue	81.8	55.7	98.9	108.9	137.3
Palau	42.7	58.3	64.8	60.0	44.6
Papua New Guinea	21.3	23.5	22.0	21.9	22.8
Samoa	29.1	35.6	42.6	39.5	41.7
Solomon Islands	29.0	32.6	29.6	31.3	31.2
Tonga	38.5	38.8	49.3	49.5	43.0
Tuvalu	113.0	121.2	116.4	111.0	109.3
Vanuatu	39.0	41.0	41.9	39.4	34.9

... = not available, GDP = gross domestic product.

Table A10 Fiscal Balance of Central Government, % of GDP

	2019	2020	2021	2022	2023
Caucasus and Central Asia					
Armenia	−1.0	−5.4	−4.6	−2.1	−2.0
Azerbaijan	−0.3	−2.4	−1.1	−1.0	−0.7
Georgia	−2.1	−9.3	−6.1	−2.6	−2.4
Kazakhstan	−1.8	−4.0	−3.0	−2.1	−2.3
Kyrgyz Republic	−0.1	−3.1	−0.2	−1.0	1.0
Tajikistan	−2.1	−4.3	−0.7	−1.4	−0.6
Turkmenistan	−0.3	−0.1	0.4	2.4	0.9
Uzbekistan	−3.8	−4.4	−6.2	−3.9	−5.5
East Asia					
Hong Kong, China	−0.6	−9.4	0.0	−6.7	−3.4
Mongolia	1.3	−9.5	−3.1	0.8	2.7
People's Republic of China	−4.9	−6.2	−3.8	−4.7	−4.6
Republic of Korea	−4.2	−7.5	−5.2	−6.8	...
Taipei,China	0.1	−1.4	−0.7	0.3	−1.0
South Asia					
Afghanistan	−1.1	−2.2	−2.2	...	...
Bangladesh	−4.7	−4.9	−3.7	−4.6	−4.4
Bhutan	−1.1	−1.8	−5.8	−7.0	−6.7
India	−4.6	−9.2	−6.7	−6.4	−6.6
Maldives	−6.5	−23.7	−14.2	−11.6	−13.8
Nepal	−5.0	−5.4	−4.0	−3.2	−6.1
Pakistan	−7.9	−7.1	−6.1	−7.9	−7.8
Sri Lanka	−7.5	−12.2	−11.7	−10.2	−8.8
Southeast Asia					
Brunei Darussalam	−5.6	−17.6	−6.1	1.6	−11.7
Cambodia	3.0	−3.4	−7.1	0.2	−3.1
Indonesia	−2.2	−6.1	−4.6	−2.4	−1.9
Lao People's Democratic Republic	−3.3	−5.5	−1.3	−0.2	−2.0
Malaysia	−3.4	−3.5	−3.9	−3.8	−0.9
Myanmar	−4.1	−6.2	−8.1	−6.5	−6.0
Philippines	−3.4	−7.6	−8.6	−7.3	−6.2
Singapore	0.2	−10.7	0.2	−0.6	−1.0
Thailand	−3.9	−11.7	−16.7	−10.7	−9.7
Timor−Leste	−30.7	−25.8	−45.3	−58.1	−41.0
Viet Nam	0.3	−3.5	−1.4	−3.6	−4.1
The Pacific					
Cook Islands	4.7	−5.9	−28.5	−8.8	−0.6
Federated States of Micronesia	19.7	6.1	3.0	8.6	3.0
Fiji	−3.6	−5.9	−11.4	−11.9	−6.2
Kiribati	16.3	4.8	−11.0	−2.7	−2.3
Marshall Islands	−1.8	2.5	0.2	0.7	0.1
Nauru	28.2	32.7	44.5	24.7	19.1
Niue	−1.2	6.8	−9.0	−16.4	−26.3
Palau	−0.4	−13.0	−7.3	−3.0	−0.5
Papua New Guinea	−5.0	−8.9	−6.8	−5.3	−4.4
Samoa	7.9	7.9	2.1	6.4	3.8
Solomon Islands	−1.5	−2.4	−3.5	−4.0	−6.5
Tonga	3.2	5.3	−1.0	−0.9	5.6
Tuvalu	−1.1	8.1	−13.9	8.7	1.2
Vanuatu	2.8	−2.9	−1.5	−5.8	1.5

... = not available, GDP = gross domestic product.

Table A11 Growth Rate of Merchandise Exports, % per year

	2019	2020	2021	2022	2023
Developing Asia	**−2.3**	**−1.1**	**30.8**	**8.5**	**−5.9**
Caucasus and Central Asia	**7.2**	**−19.6**	**40.1**	**32.9**	**3.8**
Armenia	23.3	−19.1	20.5	74.5	40.8
Azerbaijan	−4.5	−36.6	72.3	88.4	...
Georgia	12.2	−12.4	27.4	35.8	12.8
Kazakhstan	0.9	−26.0	49.3	30.1	−6.6
Kyrgyz Republic	6.6	−1.3	37.9	−19.4	...
Tajikistan	9.3	19.8	52.8	−0.4	15.0
Turkmenistan	8.1	...	...	...	...
Uzbekistan	22.1	−7.7	10.2	12.4	13.0
East Asia	**−2.3**	**3.4**	**28.1**	**4.2**	**−5.4**
Hong Kong, China	−4.4	−0.3	24.5	−8.8	−6.5
Mongolia	9.6	−2.7	16.4	21.1	41.0
People's Republic of China	−1.3	5.2	28.1	4.1	−5.0
Republic of Korea	−11.1	−7.0	25.4	6.9	−7.1
Taipei,China	−4.3	−8.3	33.5	5.7	−10.3
South Asia	**−3.2**	**−8.6**	**37.9**	**11.0**	**−6.0**
Afghanistan	−1.3	−10.1	−12.6	10.0	116.1
Bangladesh	9.1	−17.1	12.4	33.4	6.3
Bhutan	13.1	−5.4	20.0	−6.9	−11.5
India	−5.0	−7.5	44.8	6.3	−6.1
Maldives	6.3	−28.6	10.8	40.1	10.1
Nepal	12.6	−7.0	30.0	43.9	−19.9
Pakistan	−2.1	−7.1	13.8	26.7	−14.2
Sri Lanka	0.4	−15.9	24.4	4.9	−9.1
Southeast Asia	**−2.5**	**−3.2**	**28.8**	**16.1**	**−8.6**
Brunei Darussalam	11.4	−9.4	68.3	28.4	2.2
Cambodia	15.6	23.6	5.4	18.7	1.7
Indonesia	−6.8	−3.0	42.5	25.6	−11.3
Lao People's Democratic Republic	2.9	8.1	24.8	21.3	0.3
Malaysia	−4.1	−5.9	30.7	15.9	−18.0
Myanmar	−6.8	−4.1	−2.6	2.1	−14.0
Philippines	2.9	−9.8	12.5	6.4	−4.1
Singapore	−4.2	−5.2	22.5	15.1	−7.4
Thailand	−3.3	−6.5	19.2	5.4	−1.7
Timor–Leste	3.8	23.3	303.1	22.7	−26.5
Viet Nam	8.4	7.0	18.9	10.6	−4.6
The Pacific	**8.1**	**−16.2**	**18.3**	**23.1**	**−3.1**
Cook Islands	−56.3	110.6	−12.3	−40.5	38.5
Federated States of Micronesia	26.4	−12.6	−1.0	...	...
Fiji	2.2	−20.3	8.5	18.5	2.7
Kiribati	46.9	1.3	10.4	−11.6	13.1
Marshall Islands	−0.3	11.6	51.8	−2.8	...
Nauru	17.0	−61.5	126.4	156.8	−26.2
Niue	...	...	...	...	...
Palau	−20.8	−60.5	−75.3	96.9	57.3
Papua New Guinea	11.5	−17.1	24.3	27.2	−7.5
Samoa	38.0	−9.5	−23.1	−8.6	37.0
Solomon Islands	−14.0	−17.7	−2.1	−8.1	32.3
Tonga	9.9	14.3	−9.8	−6.4	−29.0
Tuvalu	132.7	−65.9	201.4	−64.6	8.4
Vanuatu	−26.1	−1.2	17.4	36.6	−25.7

... = not available.

Table A12 Growth Rate of Merchandise Imports, % per year

	2019	2020	2021	2022	2023
Developing Asia	**–3.6**	**–6.8**	**35.8**	**9.8**	**–5.9**
Caucasus and Central Asia	**12.1**	**–9.9**	**14.6**	**27.4**	**21.8**
Armenia	13.3	–19.3	16.6	58.5	38.8
Azerbaijan	3.5	–11.1	3.4	29.7	...
Georgia	1.8	–13.5	24.2	35.3	13.5
Kazakhstan	17.5	–7.5	9.2	21.8	20.1
Kyrgyz Republic	–5.7	–26.0	50.4	76.4	...
Tajikistan	6.3	–5.9	33.6	22.8	15.0
Turkmenistan	1.6	...	...	...	...
Uzbekistan	16.1	–10.1	21.0	24.1	25.0
East Asia	**–2.7**	**–1.3**	**32.7**	**2.8**	**–5.2**
Hong Kong, China	–7.0	–2.1	22.7	–7.6	–4.7
Mongolia	2.4	–13.1	29.2	27.4	10.5
People's Republic of China	–2.1	0.3	32.7	0.9	–4.0
Republic of Korea	–7.6	–8.3	31.2	18.3	–10.0
Taipei,China	–1.9	–16.6	39.0	13.4	–20.0
South Asia	**–6.7**	**–15.9**	**47.8**	**19.3**	**–8.3**
Afghanistan	–7.0	–4.6	0.1	–16.8	44.6
Bangladesh	1.8	–8.6	19.7	35.9	–15.8
Bhutan	–4.6	–12.7	35.4	29.3	–13.1
India	–7.6	–16.6	55.3	16.6	–4.8
Maldives	–0.8	–37.7	40.0	38.7	1.9
Nepal	5.2	–18.3	25.7	21.9	–22.0
Pakistan	–6.8	–15.9	24.4	31.8	–27.5
Sri Lanka	–10.3	–19.5	28.5	–11.4	–8.1
Southeast Asia	**–4.5**	**–12.2**	**31.6**	**17.3**	**–7.7**
Brunei Darussalam	21.8	3.5	60.8	7.9	4.5
Cambodia	18.3	–5.3	45.9	4.2	–17.0
Indonesia	–8.8	–18.1	39.9	21.6	–7.3
Lao People's Democratic Republic	–0.8	–10.8	13.6	20.1	7.4
Malaysia	–5.7	–8.5	30.7	19.6	–15.6
Myanmar	–13.8	5.9	–22.8	18.4	–5.5
Philippines	–0.2	–20.2	30.5	19.0	–5.0
Singapore	–3.3	–8.8	24.1	12.5	–10.9
Thailand	–5.6	–13.6	27.7	14.0	–3.1
Timor–Leste	–3.4	7.9	7.9	36.3	–5.4
Viet Nam	7.0	3.7	26.7	7.2	–9.2
The Pacific	**–0.7**	**–14.5**	**31.6**	**17.0**	**–0.3**
Cook Islands	–4.7	–5.3	–12.4	19.7	–8.6
Federated States of Micronesia	5.1	–10.2	7.4	...	...
Fiji	–13.6	–26.1	14.9	59.1	5.7
Kiribati	5.9	0.6	1.2	6.2	0.9
Marshall Islands	59.3	–37.0	11.4	–3.0	...
Nauru	0.7	4.8	24.8	8.4	–11.5
Niue	...	...	...	...	...
Palau	–0.1	1.5	–16.8	24.3	–18.0
Papua New Guinea	3.7	–11.4	40.6	3.1	–4.9
Samoa	6.2	–9.5	0.9	7.9	28.2
Solomon Islands	–6.2	–18.6	15.8	16.7	13.1
Tonga	2.2	–5.5	2.2	0.9	34.1
Tuvalu	98.7	–14.4	19.3	–25.3	46.7
Vanuatu	–10.5	–6.5	16.8	18.4	27.3

... = not available.

Table A13 Trade Balance, $ million

	2019	2020	2021	2022	2023
Developing Asia	425,367	692,804	675,710	641,269	646,319
Caucasus and Central Asia	14,614	–6,898	14,863	29,976	17,676
Armenia	–1,722	–1,382	–1,505	–1,859	–2,470
Azerbaijan	8,533	2,512	11,274	27,359	...
Georgia	–5,721	–4,709	–5,858	–7,964	–9,348
Kazakhstan	18,421	6,009	24,228	34,984	19,145
Kyrgyz Republic	–2,626	–1,440	–2,420	–6,919	...
Tajikistan	–2,165	–1,671	–1,953	–2,914	–3,351
Turkmenistan	7,186	...	...	...	...
Uzbekistan	–7,291	–6,216	–8,904	–12,711	13,700
East Asia	516,072	663,408	730,944	748,556	725,938
Hong Kong, China	–15,382	–5,328	3,174	–5,167	–16,382
Mongolia	1,158	1,756	1,370	1,233	4,369
People's Republic of China	392,993	511,103	562,706	668,633	608,000
Republic of Korea	79,812	80,605	75,731	15,620	34,092
Taipei,China	57,491	75,273	87,963	68,238	95,859
South Asia	–228,313	–163,081	–269,145	–364,683	–324,860
Afghanistan	–5,294	–5,101	–5,128	–4,444	–6,217
Bangladesh	–15,835	–17,858	–23,778	–33,250	–17,155
Bhutan	–304	–216	–392	–788	–672
India	–157,506	–102,152	–189,459	–265,291	–258,321
Maldives	–2,382	–1,450	–2,105	–2,916	–2,938
Nepal	–11,382	–9,186	–11,510	–13,759	–10,701
Pakistan	–27,612	–21,109	–28,634	–39,050	–23,955
Sri Lanka	–7,997	–6,008	–8,139	–5,185	–4,901
Southeast Asia	118,605	195,916	195,116	221,506	222,765
Brunei Darussalam	2,211	1,359	2,679	5,153	5,053
Cambodia	–7,255	–2,544	–11,205	–8,826	–2,986
Indonesia	3,508	28,301	43,806	62,672	46,347
Lao People's Democratic Republic	–1,408	–146	542	742	112
Malaysia	30,112	32,708	42,873	42,269	29,138
Myanmar	–2,978	–4,204	–1,216	–3,405	–4,029
Philippines	–49,312	–33,775	–52,806	–69,701	–65,788
Singapore	96,347	103,714	121,738	150,513	154,807
Thailand	26,725	40,402	32,354	13,543	16,972
Timor–Leste	–566	–607	–620	–853	–824
Viet Nam	21,221	30,708	16,971	29,400	43,963
The Pacific	4,389	3,459	3,932	5,913	4,799
Cook Islands	–121	–102	–90	–119	–103
Federated States of Micronesia	–125	–114	–127	...	...
Fiji	–958	–649	–798	–1,629	–1,753
Kiribati	–94	–95	–95	–103	–102
Marshall Islands	–139	–56	–34	–33	...
Nauru	–53	–68	–77	–59	–58
Niue	...	...	...	...	...
Palau	–141	–150	–127	–157	–127
Papua New Guinea	6,816	5,415	6,132	9,033	8,213
Samoa	–299	–271	–284	–313	–398
Solomon Islands	–36	–26	–97	–206	–167
Tonga	–206	–191	–198	–201	–279
Tuvalu	–31	–27	–32	–24	–35
Vanuatu	–224	–207	–242	–276	–391

... = not available.

Table A14 Current Account Balance, % of GDP

	2019	2020	2021	2022	2023
Developing Asia	**0.8**	**2.0**	**1.5**	**1.2**	**1.3**
Caucasus and Central Asia	**–2.9**	**–4.8**	**–0.3**	**4.1**	**–2.0**
Armenia	–7.1	–4.0	–3.5	0.8	–1.7
Azerbaijan	9.1	–0.5	15.1	29.8	...
Georgia	–5.5	–12.4	–10.4	–4.5	–4.1
Kazakhstan	–3.9	–6.4	–1.4	3.1	–3.8
Kyrgyz Republic	–12.1	4.5	–8.0	–44.5	...
Tajikistan	–2.2	4.1	8.4	3.3	–1.0
Turkmenistan	...	...	6.5	7.1	5.9
Uzbekistan	–5.6	–5.0	–7.0	–0.6	–1.5
East Asia	**1.5**	**2.6**	**2.9**	**2.8**	**2.2**
Hong Kong, China	5.9	7.0	11.8	10.2	9.3
Mongolia	–15.2	–5.1	–13.8	–13.4	0.7
People's Republic of China	0.7	1.7	2.0	2.2	1.5
Republic of Korea	3.6	4.6	4.7	1.5	2.1
Taipei,China	11.0	14.5	15.3	13.3	13.9
South Asia	**–1.3**	**0.4**	**–1.3**	**–2.6**	**–1.1**
Afghanistan	11.7	11.2	...	...	...
Bangladesh	–1.3	–1.3	–1.1	–4.1	–0.7
Bhutan	–12.9	–13.0	–20.1	–31.2	–25.2
India	–0.9	0.9	–1.2	–2.0	–1.2
Maldives	–25.9	–35.8	–8.7	–16.3	–22.4
Nepal	–6.9	–1.0	–7.7	–12.7	–1.4
Pakistan	–4.2	–1.5	–0.8	–4.7	–0.7
Sri Lanka	–2.1	–1.4	–3.7	–2.0	1.4
Southeast Asia	**1.7**	**2.8**	**0.9**	**0.8**	**1.9**
Brunei Darussalam	6.6	4.3	11.2	9.0	8.3
Cambodia	–10.9	–3.4	–40.4	–25.8	1.7
Indonesia	–2.7	–0.4	0.3	1.0	–0.1
Lao People's Democratic Republic	–12.2	–6.2	–2.3	–1.5	–4.6
Malaysia	3.5	4.2	3.9	3.1	1.2
Myanmar	0.4	–2.5	–1.3	–3.4	–5.5
Philippines	–0.8	3.2	–1.5	–4.5	–2.6
Singapore	16.0	16.6	19.8	18.0	19.8
Thailand	7.0	4.2	–2.0	–3.2	1.3
Timor–Leste	7.9	–17.7	9.7	16.3	–20.0
Viet Nam	3.6	4.3	–2.0	0.3	5.9
The Pacific	**8.7**	**6.5**	**5.8**	**6.1**	**10.6**
Cook Islands	31.7	9.6	–16.1	–7.0	5.1
Federated States of Micronesia	17.6	3.6	0.7	...	...
Fiji	–4.9	–13.6	–12.4	–17.2	–9.5
Kiribati	49.5	20.0	28.4	31.9	33.3
Marshall Islands	–31.3	15.0	22.5	17.5	...
Nauru	4.6	2.5	3.1	–0.6	3.5
Niue	...	...	...	...	...
Palau	–30.6	–43.9	–41.0	–48.8	–41.2
Papua New Guinea	14.8	14.1	13.2	16.6	19.7
Samoa	3.1	0.6	–17.7	–13.5	–4.9
Solomon Islands	–9.5	–1.6	–4.8	–13.5	–11.4
Tonga	–4.0	–7.5	–6.2	–6.2	8.4
Tuvalu	–22.2	16.3	24.1	4.6	2.2
Vanuatu	18.3	2.3	0.8	–13.0	–6.1

... = not available, GDP = gross domestic product.

Table A15 Exchange Rates to the United States Dollar, annual average

	Currency	Symbol	2019	2020	2021	2022	2023
Caucasus and Central Asia							
Armenia	Dram	AMD	480.45	489.01	503.77	435.67	392.48
Azerbaijan	Azerbaijan new manat	AZN	1.70	1.70	1.70	1.70	1.70
Georgia	Lari	GEL	2.82	3.11	3.22	2.92	2.63
Kazakhstan	Tenge	T	382.75	412.95	425.91	460.10	456.18
Kyrgyz Republic	Som	Som	69.79	77.35	84.64	84.12	87.86
Tajikistan	Somoni	TJS	9.53	10.32	11.31	11.00	10.80
Turkmenistan	Turkmen manat	TMM	3.50	3.50	3.50	3.50	3.50
Uzbekistan	Sum	SUM	8,837.00	10,065.00	10,623.00	11,050.15	13,000.00
East Asia							
Hong Kong, China	Hong Kong dollar	HK$	7.84	7.76	7.77	7.83	7.83
Mongolia	Togrog	MNT	2,663.70	2,813.20	2,849.25	3,141.40	3,467.40
People's Republic of China	Yuan	CNY	6.90	6.90	6.45	6.73	7.05
Republic of Korea	Won	W	1,165.65	1,179.60	1,144.54	1,291.88	1,306.14
Taipei,China	NT dollar	NT$	30.90	29.45	27.93	29.80	31.15
South Asia							
Afghanistan	Afghani	AF	78.40	76.80	76.90	83.55	88.50
Bangladesh	Taka	Tk	84.03	84.78	84.81	86.30	99.46
Bhutan	Ngultrum	Nu	70.42	74.11	73.94	78.60	82.60
India	Indian rupee/s	Re/Rs	70.90	74.22	74.50	80.36	82.94
Maldives	Rufiyaa	Rf	15.38	15.41	15.39	15.40	15.40
Nepal	Nepalese rupee/s	NRe/NRs	112.88	116.31	117.87	120.84	130.75
Pakistan	Pakistan rupee/s	PRe/PRs	136.10	158.00	160.02	178.01	248.00
Sri Lanka	Sri Lanka rupee/s	SLRe/SLRs	178.78	185.52	198.88	324.55	327.53
Southeast Asia							
Brunei Darussalam	Brunei dollar	B$	1.36	1.38	1.34	1.38	1.34
Cambodia	Riel	KR	4,070.00	4,078.00	4,095.00	4,115.00	4,065.00
Indonesia	Rupiah	Rp	14,147.75	14,581.92	14,310.00	14,849.92	15,236.83
Lao People's Democratic Rep.	Kip	KN	8,679.85	9,049.00	9,737.25	14,035.00	18,337.34
Malaysia	Ringgit	RM	4.14	4.20	4.14	4.40	4.56
Myanmar	Kyat	MK	1,525.82	1,429.05	1,490.40	2,100.00	3,050.00
Philippines	Peso	P	51.80	49.62	49.26	54.48	55.63
Singapore	Singapore dollar	S$	1.36	1.38	1.34	1.38	1.34
Thailand	Baht	B	31.05	31.30	31.98	35.07	34.81
Timor–Leste	US dollar	US$	1.00	1.00	1.00	1.00	1.00
Viet Nam	Dong	D	23,050.47	23,208.82	23,159.72	23,271.48	23,794.63
The Pacific							
Cook Islands	New Zealand dollar	NZ$	1.49	1.57	1.44	1.47	1.62
Federated States of Micronesia	US dollar	US$	1.00	1.00	1.00	1.00	1.00
Fiji	Fiji dollar	F$	2.16	2.17	2.07	2.20	2.25
Kiribati	Australian dollar	A$	1.44	1.45	1.33	1.44	1.51
Marshall Islands	US dollar	US$	1.00	1.00	1.00	1.00	1.00
Nauru	Australian dollar	A$	1.44	1.45	1.33	1.44	1.51
Niue	New Zealand dollar	NZ$	1.49	1.57	1.44	1.47	1.62
Palau	US dollar	US$	1.00	1.00	1.00	1.00	1.00
Papua New Guinea	Kina	K	3.39	3.46	3.51	3.52	3.58
Samoa	Tala	ST	2.62	2.70	2.57	2.61	2.73
Solomon Islands	Sol. Islands dollar	SI$	8.17	8.21	8.03	8.16	8.38
Tonga	Pa'anga	T$	2.27	2.31	2.28	2.28	2.28
Tuvalu	Australian dollar	A$	1.44	1.45	1.33	1.44	1.51
Vanuatu	Vatu	Vt	114.73	115.38	109.45	115.35	119.72

... = not available.

Table A16 Gross International Reserve, $ million

	2019	2020	2021	2022	2023
Caucasus and Central Asia					
Armenia	2,850	2,616	3,230	4,112	3,602
Azerbaijan	6,258	6,369	7,075	8,996	11,613
Georgia	3,500	3,900	4,300	4,900	5,000
Kazakhstan	28,958	35,638	34,378	35,076	35,965
Kyrgyz Republic	2,424	2,808	2,978	2,798	3,236
Tajikistan	1,385	2,238	2,498	3,322	...
Turkmenistan	...	...	...	...	...
Uzbekistan	29,172	34,904	35,139	35,768	35,600
East Asia					
Hong Kong, China	441,350	491,775	496,867	424,029	425,554
Mongolia	4,349	4,534	4,366	3,400	4,921
People's Republic of China	3,222,933	3,356,529	3,426,908	3,306,529	...
Republic of Korea	408,816	443,098	463,118	423,164	420,148
Taipei,China	478,126	529,911	548,408	554,932	570,595
South Asia					
Afghanistan	8,573	9,763	9,763	...	...
Bangladesh	32,717	36,037	46,391	41,827	31,203
Bhutan	1,214	1,454	970	767	533
India	477,807	576,984	607,309	578,449	626,163
Maldives	754	985	806	832	589
Nepal	9,500	11,646	11,753	9,535	8,169
Pakistan	7,285	12,132	17,299	9,815	4,445
Sri Lanka	7,642	5,664	3,139	1,898	4,392
Southeast Asia					
Brunei Darussalam	4,273	3,997	4,982	5,035	...
Cambodia	18,763	21,334	20,265	17,805	20,000
Indonesia	129,183	135,897	144,905	137,233	146,384
Lao People's Democratic Republic	997	1,821	1,737	1,480	1,782
Malaysia	102,376	102,861	117,503	114,365	113,478
Myanmar	5,668	6,772	7,800	...	...
Philippines	87,840	110,117	108,794	96,149	103,753
Singapore	279,450	362,305	417,904	289,484	351,031
Thailand	217,632	247,579	256,812	213,442	220,059
Timor–Leste	18,337	19,647	20,667	18,212	18,331
Viet Nam	78,517	95,149	109,439	86,694	92,302
The Pacific					
Cook Islands	...	...	...	...	...
Federated States of Micronesia	...	...	...	...	...
Fiji	1,027	1,011	1,546	1,558	1,494
Kiribati	102	173	139	116	...
Marshall Islands	...	...	...	...	...
Nauru	...	...	...	...	...
Niue	...	...	...	...	...
Palau	...	...	...	...	...
Papua New Guinea	2,313	2,686	2,878	4,026	3,583
Samoa	187	220	282	279	266
Solomon Islands	576	647	700	665	660
Tonga	213	235	314	382	...
Tuvalu	88	98	126	114	119
Vanuatu	510	572	678	647	703

... = not available.

Table A17 External Debt Outstanding, $ million

	2019	2020	2021	2022	2023
Caucasus and Central Asia					
Armenia	5,785	6,059	6,648	6,445	6,501
Azerbaijan	9,091	8,822	9,400	8,136	6,461
Georgia	15,324	17,043	18,358	18,731	20,467
Kazakhstan	159,544	163,980	164,133	160,609	...
Kyrgyz Republic	7,008	7,367	7,667	7,813	...
Tajikistan	2,922	3,247	3,015	3,228	...
Turkmenistan	...	...	...	...	...
Uzbekistan	26,331	36,295	43,400	49,000	45,449
East Asia					
Hong Kong, China	1,667,263	1,789,612	1,873,329	1,776,208	1,838,076
Mongolia	30,702	32,362	33,806	33,345	34,570
People's Republic of China	2,070,810	2,400,807	2,746,559	2,452,765	...
Republic of Korea	470,736	550,628	630,694	665,237	663,631
Taipei,China	184,659	189,873	213,592	202,146	206,499
South Asia					
Afghanistan	1,147	1,482	1,482	...	...
Bangladesh	38,475	44,095	50,880	55,602	59,214
Bhutan	2,741	2,990	3,012	3,023	3,049
India	558,372	573,663	619,076	624,192	648,031
Maldives	1,432	1,620	2,068	2,149	2,427
Nepal	5,366	6,745	7,828	8,026	8,316
Pakistan	106,348	113,014	122,294	130,196	126,141
Sri Lanka	54,811	49,041	51,775	49,678	...
Southeast Asia					
Brunei Darussalam	...	...	...	...	...
Cambodia	7,597	8,810	9,505	9,971	11,185
Indonesia	403,563	416,935	413,972	396,529	408,127
Lao People's Democratic Republic	16,572	17,431	17,188	...	...
Malaysia	231,506	238,844	258,706	259,384	270,616
Myanmar	11,100	12,900	13,000	13,900	...
Philippines	83,618	98,488	106,428	111,268	118,833
Singapore	1,560,182	1,689,455	1,833,976	1,799,818	1,858,890
Thailand	172,650	190,125	196,215	200,289	190,055
Timor-Leste	193	218	237	254	259
Viet Nam	117,338	125,065	136,213	...	...
The Pacific					
Cook Islands	62	55	115	148	139
Federated States of Micronesia	77	65	61	50	48
Fiji	674	788	1,170	1,528	1,590
Kiribati	37	37	39	34	33
Marshall Islands	73	68	66	63	60
Nauru	88	88	4	17	25
Niue	...	...	...	...	...
Palau	86	150	190	222	248
Papua New Guinea	4,228	5,185	6,531	7,429	8,032
Samoa	399	372	389	363	312
Solomon Islands	99	133	152	151	193
Tonga	186	181	193	192	188
Tuvalu	5	4	4	4	4
Vanuatu	360	357	378	355	342

... = not available.

Table A18 Debt Service Ratio, % of exports of goods and services

	2019	2020	2021	2022	2023
Caucasus and Central Asia					
Armenia	6.1	10.6	7.9	3.9	4.1
Azerbaijan	4.5	8.1	5.7	...	...
Georgia	19.3	27.8	24.2	23.1	...
Kazakhstan	55.0	69.2	44.6	45.2	...
Kyrgyz Republic	36.6	44.4	26.7	44.6	...
Tajikistan	13.9	15.9	15.4	...	...
Turkmenistan	...	...	...	...	...
Uzbekistan	15.7	23.3	17.1	18.1	18.1
East Asia					
Hong Kong, China	...	...	...	...	...
Mongolia	34.8	44.3	35.9	29.1	27.7
People's Republic of China	6.7	6.5	5.9	10.5	...
Republic of Korea	...	...	...	...	...
Taipei,China	4.8	2.6	2.3	2.3	2.6
South Asia					
Afghanistan	...	...	...	...	...
Bangladesh	3.4	4.4	4.3	3.4	2.3
Bhutan	9.0	5.9	11.7	15.1	15.1
India	6.5	8.2	5.2	5.3	6.8
Maldives	2.7	4.9	7.2	5.2	4.2
Nepal	8.2	10.9	4.6	3.4	11.6
Pakistan	38.3	52.1	42.5	38.1	58.7
Sri Lanka	29.7	35.2	30.7	15.3	...
Southeast Asia					
Brunei Darussalam	...	...	...	...	...
Cambodia	1.5	1.8	1.9	1.8	1.9
Indonesia	26.9	27.7	22.1	16.6	17.1
Lao People's Democratic Republic	11.5	10.3	8.6	...	...
Malaysia	12.8	14.5	10.7	11.4	13.0
Myanmar	4.2	5.4	5.3	6.6	6.4
Philippines	6.7	6.7	7.5	6.3	10.2
Singapore	...	...	...	...	...
Thailand	6.7	7.5	6.2	7.0	...
Timor–Leste	6.1	13.3	9.9	17.1	18.4
Viet Nam	5.8	5.6	5.9	...	...
The Pacific					
Cook Islands	4.5	6.6	9.8	–15.5	–1.9
Federated States of Micronesia	6.3	9.3	8.0	...	...
Fiji	1.9	4.3	19.7	1.5	3.1
Kiribati	4.5	6.0	7.7	8.1	7.6
Marshall Islands	8.9	7.8	5.6	5.9	...
Nauru	1.0	1.1	0.8	0.7	4.1
Niue	...	...	...	...	...
Palau	7.5	14.8	58.8	31.5	31.9
Papua New Guinea	1.3	1.5	0.8	0.8	1.6
Samoa	8.4	11.3	25.6	23.7	12.8
Solomon Islands	1.1	1.5	1.6	0.4	0.8
Tonga	8.2	13.0	19.1	19.7	104.5
Tuvalu	...	...	...	...	...
Vanuatu	7.7	18.6	38.3	23.5	9.9

... = not available.

9 789292 706579